Proceedings
Comparative Literature Symposium
Texas Tech University
Volume IX

ETHNIC LITERATURES SINCE 1776:
THE MANY VOICES OF AMERICA

Part 2

Edited by
Wolodymyr T. Zyla
Wendell M. Aycock

D1520516

Texas Tech Press
Lubbock, Texas
1978

INTERDEPARTMENTAL COMMITTEE ON COMPARATIVE LITERATURE
TEXAS TECH UNIVERSITY

Editorial Board for Volume IX

Roberto Bravo-Villarroel
Vivian I. Davis
Carl Hammer, Jr.

Proceedings of the Comparative Literature Symposium result from annual symposia organized by Texas Tech University's Interdepartmental Committee on Comparative Literature. *Ethnic Literatures Since 1776: The Many Voices of America* is the proceedings of a symposium held on 27 to 31 January 1976 in commemoration of our nation's bicentennial. Copies of the Proceedings may be obtained on an exchange basis from, or purchased through, the Exchange Librarian, Texas Tech University Library, Lubbock, Texas 79409.

ISSN: 0084-9103
ISBN: 0-89672-060-8
Library of Congress Catalog Card Number: 78-52073
Texas Tech Press
Texas Tech University, Lubbock, Texas 79409
Printed in the United States of America

Table of Contents

Part 2

Worlds Made of Dawn: Characteristic Image and Incident in Native American Imaginative Literature

Lester A. Standiford

ABSTRACT

Until very recently, American Indian or Native American imaginative literature existed only in an oral form. And while translations of those traditional songs and stories have been collected over the past 100 years, it was not until N. Scott Momaday published his novel *House Made of Dawn* and won the 1969 Pulitzer Prize that a contemporary imaginative literature of the Indian American was unshakably founded. Based on the interaction between traditional native cultures and Anglo-American culture, this contemporary work must be considered critically as a hybrid form, requiring a knowledge of both traditions for its full appreciation. Because many Native Americans view the notion of "Manifest Destiny" as a form of genocide that still threatens them today; because they share an Oriental view of man as a creature of equal spirit stature with all other things in the world, striving to maintain harmonious balance; because they hold fast to the traditional belief in the very real power of the word; and because they build on the influence of the oral literary tradition, with its symbolic density and intricate patterns of repetition, contemporary poetry and fiction by Indian Americans distinguishes itself from the so-called "mainstream." Critics unaware of these distinctions have made serious errors in discussing such works as Momaday's *House Made of Dawn* and James Welch's *Winter in the Blood*. On the other hand, Native Americans composing in English must be aware of the demands of that language, and remain particularly cautious of allowing political or philosophic contingency to overwhelm considerations of craft. Because the reservation continues to exist as tangible and spiritual heartland for the Indian American, the character and vitality of his literature seem likely to survive and even flourish. (LAS)

In any culture, myth, legend, and folklore serve to explain the unexplainable, to promote cultural continuity and survival, and also to entertain. In this regard, Native American oral literature is no different. The Oklahoma Cherokee storyteller Asudi explains the function of his art in this way: "That's the way you heard things, and if you didn't pay atten-

328

tion, you wouldn't know anything. If you had paid attention, you would know."[1]

And if contemporary Indian imaginative writers have taken on a non-traditional language and a more complex mode of expression, it is only because they must adapt the basic techniques of their essential function to a changing world. The voice of Wah' Kon-tah, the great spirit which moves through all being, must be passed on, whether we term its vehicle myth or art. Furthermore, if we of this cacaphonous age are to hear that voice, we must learn how to pay the all-important attention. Asudi's alternatives are unmistakable.

In one regard, ours is a particularly rewarding time to inquire into the literature of the Indian Americans, for it is a period of great publishing activity of the part of the Native American authors themselves. While there have been previous bursts of interest in ethnological transcriptions of oral literatures and flurries of anthologized translations of primitive poetry over the past 100 years, including A. Grove Day's *The Sky Clears*, William Brandon's *The Magic World*, and Jerome Rothenberg's *Shaking the Pumpkin*, it was not until 1968 that a written imaginative literature of the contemporary Indian American was unshakably founded. In that year, N. Scott Momaday, a Kiowa writer, published *House Made of Dawn*, a novel which won the Pulitzer Prize for 1969.

Momaday's work appeared simultaneously with a rebirth of political and social consciousness on the part of Indian Americans in the late 60's, most forcefully verbalized by Vine Deloria, Jr. in his 1969 manifesto, *Custer Died For Your Sins*. Since that time, expression on the part of Indian imaginative writers has grown synergistically along with the burgeoning interest in the social and political affairs of their people. In 1974 James Welch, a Blackfeet—GrosVentre writer, saw his first prose work, *Winter in the Blood*, termed "A nearly flawless novel about human life," by Reynolds Price in the *New York Times Book Review*.[2] Welch and Momaday have also written well received collections of poetry, and other young poets and fiction writers, among them, Grey Cohoe, Durango Mendoza, Simon Oritz, Gerald Vizenor, Phil George, Emerson Blackhorse Mitchell, Marnie Walsh, Patty Harjo, Leslie Silko, Alonzo Lopez, Ray A. Young Bear, Bruce Ignacio, Duane Niatum, and Harold Littlebird, have placed their work in our most respected magazines and in anthologies of national distribution.

In other words, we are witnessing the birth of a contemporary Indian American Literature unfolding in the 1970's, an imaginative literature that resembles the oral literatures of the Native American tribal cultures in some ways, yet which speaks through the contemporary American literary medium as a distinct and viable force. It is only natural that we seek a greater understanding and appreciation of that literature.

It was during one of those earlier periods of interest in primitive Indian literature—better termed as traditional Indian literature, for our purposes —that Louis Untermeyer reviewed a collection of translations from Indian oral poetries, calling it a document valuable chiefly for its ethnological interest which proved to him that "the harsh aborigine can commit poetry as trite and banal as many an overcivilized paleface."[3] He concluded his review by noting that "as a collection for the mere man of letters it is a rather forbidding pile—a crude and top-heavy monument with a few lovely and even lively decorations" (p. 241). Untermeyer's review brought a quick response from Mary Austin, a long-time student of Indian oral literatures, who made this provocative statement: "Mr. Untermeyer describes himself as a 'mere man of letters,' . . . but it begins to be a question in America whether a man is entitled to describe himself as a man of letters at all who so complacently confesses his ignorance of and inability to enter into the vast body of aboriginal literature of his country."[4]

Fifty years later, Vine Deloria, Jr. added a postscript to the matter of outside inquiry into the nature of things Indian. Writing in *Custer Died For Your Sins*, he in effect imposed a check on all researchers: "Perhaps we should suspect the real motives of the academic community. . . . Their concern is not the ultimate policy that will affect the Indian people, but merely the creation of new slogans and doctrines by which they can climb the university totem pole."[5]

It is between these poles that our inquiry is best directed, when we attempt to learn and enjoy without enforcing old assumptions on those new aspects of a literature that draws from sources outside the Anglo-American heritage. It is a very recent and still tenuous change in Anglo attitude that allows for an objective view of any so-called "emergent" or "minorities" literature as a literature of equal value to the familiar. But it is a healthy change, and one that forces a new perspective, as we see in this bit of Indian humor that Deloria describes in *Custer*: Two Indians are viewed hidden in the forest, watching the arrival of the Pilgrims at Plymouth. One has turned to the other with a look of great sadness, saying, "Well, there goes the neighborhood" (p. 148).

Before going further, I would like to make it clear that I am not interested in segregating literature into any permanent, exclusive categories. On the other hand, I am very much interested in bringing as much of the exciting contemporary creative work of this world into the widest possible fold of recognition. I believe that many readers either feel unnecessarily distanced from works identified as Indian-American, or they become indefensibly patronizing toward them—in either case, the reader loses out. While my remarks on the background and make-up of contemporary Indian American imaginative literature may appear to be aimed at enhancing its "emergence," I hope that they also serve to delineate the shape of imaginative literature in general, as well as to illuminate the particular strengths of a group of writings that any reader or writer might gain from. A greater understanding of the origins and characteristic image and incident patterns of any literature brings a reader close. This integral understanding should also work against the patronizing of the work by accepting it more for its sociology than for its status as imaginative art.

For those who would object at the outset that a so-called "minority" literature should be granted a completely distinct set of artistic criteria based on political contingency, let me quote from Gary Snyder's discussion "The Yogin and the Philosopher" in *Alcheringa: Ethnopoetics—A First Magazine of the World's Tribal Poetries*, where he distinguishes between the philosopher, who speaks "the language of reason and public discourse," and the poet/yogin, "who marries word and song together."[6] Snyder goes on to draw all poets together, saying: "The long 'pagan' battle of western poetry against state and church, the survival of the Muse down to modern times, shows that in a sense poetry has been a long and not particularly successful defending action. Defending 'the groves'—sacred to the Goddess—and logged, so to speak, under orders from Exodus 34:13, 'you shall destroy their images and cut down their groves' " (p. 3). Poetry is involved in a battle, all right, but not on behalf of anyone's politics—the battle is against politics itself.

In this view, poetry becomes a voice apart form the rhetoric of church and state. Poetry *is* its images and its groves, speaking not in service of church or state, but in service of itself. I will be speaking of contemporary Indian American poetry and fiction according to this archetypal conception of the poet as shaman who "speaks for wild animals, the spirits of plants, the spirits of mountains, of water sheds" (Snyder, p. 3). If you must have a notion of the wordly function of the poet, base it on this example from Snyder's remarks: "The elaborate, yearly, cyclical production of grand ritual dramas in the societies of Pueblo Indians . . . can be seen as a process by which the whole society consults the non-human powers and allows some individuals to step totally out of their human roles to put on the mask, costume, and *mind* of Bison, Bear, Squash, Corn, or Pleiades; to re-enter the human circle in that form and by song, mime, and dance, convey a greeting from the other realm. Thus a speech on the floor of congress from a whale" (p. 3).

Another way to explain the distinction is to point out that a poet who is lured away from the images and the groves to speak as a philosopher on the floor of congress will weaken and wither as does any magician who leaves off contact with the touchstone. On the other hand, poetry that speaks with the voice of the whale resounds the true power of Indian American imaginative literature. It is the power referred to by William

Carlos Williams when he characterized poetry as capturing the universal in the local.

A related controversy regarding the access of the "outsider" to Indian American literature might be dealt with at this point. It has been argued by some contemporary "minority" writers that their work is not intended for "outsiders," particularly Anglos, and in fact is unintelligible for the reader who has not experienced life in the way of the intended audience. In his introduction to *Shaking the Pumpkin: Traditional Poetry of the Indian North Americans*, Jerome Rothenberg responds: " . . . it has become fashionable today to deny the possibility of crossing the boundaries that separate people of different races & cultures: to insist instead that black is the concern of black, red of red, and white of white. Yet the idea of translation has always been that such boundary crossing is not only possible but desirable . . . . The question for the translator is not whether but how far we can translate one another. Like the poet who is his brother, he attempts to restore what has been torn apart."[7]

Of course, a short-sighted view of the application of minorities literature would exclude even those members of a group whose place might be validated by blood heritage, but whose life experience lies largely outside the normal experience of the group: i.e., should the Anglo farmer be permitted to read *Moby Dick*? In addition, the experience of the modern Indian has moved away from the traditional tribal ways toward the experience of many Americans, even in cases in which the Indian is most insulated from the "mainstream." William Kittredge makes this point as he reviews a number of modern translations from the oral literatures of the tribes: "The other day I talked with a friend raised in the Pipe Region on the Pine Ridge Reservation in South Dakota, close to the site of Wounded Knee, and asked if he thought the young people could ever go back to the old ways. He told me no, that nobody could ever be Indian again in that sense. Too many things have been lost."[8]

And if the experience of the modern Indian is similar in some respects to that of many others who live in the United States, when a literary work is composed originally in English there is an integral amalgam of tribal experience and American experience and thus an entree for any English-speaking reader from the start. As G. W. Haslam puts it in *Forgotten Pages of American Literature*, "language, unlike clay or pigment, is not a neutral medium; it imposes its own unique perceptual pattern and rhythm of expression. As a consequence, many literary forms are simply not transferable to English."[9] Thus a haiku written in, or translated into, English is no longer a haiku—the form is integrally bound to the dense suggestive power of the Japanese language in the same way that traditional oral poetries of the Indian American are bound to their original languages.

Haslam has described the native languages as "essentially polysyn-thetic . . . composed of word-like bursts of sound each of which reflects meaning approximating that conveyed by an entire English sentence" (p. 15). What results in English may be a pleasureable success, but the work is undeniably a hybrid—in the case of the haiku, it becomes an *Ameriku*; the Native American poem becomes Indian-American. Furthermore, the hybrid is likely to be most successful when it draws its influence from the original, but does not futilely attempt to copy it. While the following Chippewa war song, when accompanied by its original music and coming in the context of other, more explicit, war preparation lyrics, would have fully conjured the sense of stoic bravery to its tribal audience, it well may need explaining as such to the modern Anglo-American audience:

> in the coming heat
> of the day
> I stood there.[10]

Still, a modern Indian American writer can integrate such a simple natural image into a slightly longer context to reverberate similar unspoken meanings to any reader. Consider this portion of Ray A. Young Bear's "One Chip of Human Bone":

> One chip of human bone.
>
> it is almost fitting
> to die on the railroad tracks
> . . . .
>
> there is something about
> trains, drinking, and being
> an indian with nothing to lose.[11]

Because of the well-meaning liberal's desire to "give the downtrodden a break," and in some cases, his drive to expiate his own sense of guilt, it may seem difficult at first to understand that the only standard by which to judge an Indian-American work composed in English is that same artistic standard of unity of subject, style, and perceived intention that is generally applied to a work by Ernest Hemingway or Joyce Carol Oates. The only new knowledge necessary is an understanding of the cultural influences operating behind themes and styles of the Indian-American works. With this goal in mind, let us turn then to the question of a common Indian experience and its manifestation across the current poetic voices.

N. Scott Momaday, when asked to describe the Indian voice in contem-porary literature, gave this deceptively simple answer: "The phrase 'Ameri-can Indian Writer' I understand to indicate an American Indian who writes. It does not indicate anything more than that to me."[12] But it should be remembered that the term "Indian" is itself misleading, a white man's term that for many Native Americans operates to usurp distinct tribal identities in much the same way that slave names are viewed by many blacks. When Christopher Columbus arrived in the "New World," he believed that he had reached India, and accordingly labelled the inhabitants he met. It is estimated that at that time there were more than 2,000 independent tribes in the present United States, bearing 50 distinct language families; and while more than 300 tribes and some 250 dialects remain,[13] the label of "Indian" remains the common generic and conceptual term among non-Native Americans. Yet, as Harold Fey and D'Arcy McNickle explain in *Indians and Other Americans*, "To be an aboriginal of the Americas is to be Sioux, or Cree, or Mohawk, or Navajo—a tribesman. Among those who live most intimately with tradition, to talk about 'Indian issues' or 'Indian aspirations' is to talk a dangerous kind of nonsense. One might offend someone by seeming to speak for him."[14]

Nonetheless, a rising political awareness has led to the recognition of a common set of socio-economic problems that extant tribes share, so that a certain pan-tribal feeling exists regardless of the difficulty of defining that elusive term. Such groups as the National Indian Youth Council, founded by young Native Americans who found their tribal elders too accomodating to the whites, and the Indians of All Nations, the militant group that occupied Alcatraz in 1969, are representative of the move toward a new "Indian" consciousness.

Thomas Sanders and Walter Peek, editors of the comprehensive *Literature of the American Indian*, liken the process of defining a Native American to that of defining a Jew—it becomes largely a self-identification process. As the Jew knows he is a Jew because he recognizes himself as a part of an identifiable socio-historical heritage, so does the Indian know he is Indian because of his ties to the land, the remaining fragments of his oral literature, and his lingering awareness of heroic forbears.[15] Sanders and Peek cite La Donna Harris' reply to a group of University of South Florida students who asked her the difficult question during a 1972 campus lecture: "I can't define the Indian for you anymore than you can define what you are. Different governmental agencies define him by amount of blood. I had a Comanche mother and an Irish father. But I am Comanche. I'm not Irish. And I'm not Indian *first*. I'm Comanche first, Indian second. When the Comanche took in someone, he became Comanche. He wasn't part this, part that. He was *all* Comanche or he wasn't Comanche at all. Blood runs the heart. The *heart* knows what it is" (Sanders and Peek, p. 11).

Perhaps the most popular conception of Indian identity for all Americans springs from the tragic political history of nearly all the tribes. Archeological theory agrees that settlement of the North American continent began at least as early as 10,000 B.C. by tribesmen who crossed the

Bering Straits and moved southward. The movement is generally agreed to have ended with the arrival of the Eskimo approximately 2,000 years ago.[16] Thus, while the claim of some Indian writers that civilization actually began on the continent may be romantic speculation, the fact that the Indians were the original settlers on the land, maintaining advanced systems of government and cultural institutions, has been established beyond a doubt. Benjamin Franklin used the smoothly functioning Iriquois Confederacy as a model in attempts to end bickering among delegates to the Albany Conference (Sanders and Peek, p. 6), while Maya literature had developed by the sixteenth century to include "history, science, lives of great men, astronomy, astrology, prophecy, theology, ritual, legends, fables, medicine, grammar, 'certain songs in meter,' and 'comedies for the pleasure of the public,' "[17] all of which the good Bishop Landa of Yucatan burned as part of the Church's conversion efforts.

Despite these achievements on the part of the Native Americans, the arriving white man tended to classify Indians as either romantic simpletons or bloodthirsty savages, depending on political expediency. The familiar "vanishing American" concept has its roots in the white man's refusal to recognize the Indian's claim to his territory or his right to life. Because most Indian tribes recognized only "use" or territory rights to lands which remained under the ownership of the Great Spirit, they were unable to understand the white man's conception of land as a salable commodity. Fey and McNickle describe the ensuing battles as clashes between an agressive, acquisitive material society and a society which put the safety and welfare of the group above individual ambition. As the arriving Europeans valued a man for the amount of property he owned, the Indian with the most standing in his community was the man who gave the most to others (*Indians and Other Americans*, pp. 19-20). In accordance with General Philip Sheridan's observation that "The only good Indians I ever saw were dead,"[18] the population of Native Americans within the U.S. had dropped from an estimated 900,000 in 1492 to 250,000 by 1900 (Fey and McNickle, p. 10).

The series of wars termed "Indian Campaigns" or "White Man's Wars," depending on one's point of view have been recently recounted in terms sympathetic to the tribes by such writers as Fey and McNickle, Dee Brown in *Bury My Heart at Wounded Knee*, and by William Brandon in *The American Heritage Book of Indians*. While some critics have objected particularly to Brown's clear preference for the Indian's side of the story, there is no argument among Indians themselves who feel that the book is long overdue in the face of hundreds of years of Anglo-dominated interpretations of battles with "heathen," "brutish," "depraved savages," a one-sided saga that culminated in the twentieth-century Hollywood stereotype. David F. Beer's illuminating survey of the Indian image in early American literature charges that from the beginning, Euro-Americans wrote of the Native Americans only for the allied purposes of religious conversion and political exploitation.[19] Beer cites the remarks of Captain John Smith as the model of literary inaccuracy that predominated into the twentieth century: "They are inconstant in everything, but what fear constraineth them to keep. Crafty, timorous, quick of apprehension and very ingenious, some are of disposition fearful, some bold, most cautious, all savage . . . they are soon moved to anger, and so malicious that they seldom forget an injury" (p. 208). Beer summarizes the progression of the early Euro-American literary view by saying, "From the initial poorly-informed reports on the Red Man emerged the bigoted and ethnocentric literary attitudes of the pious but land-hungry Puritans. Soon to follow were the commercial and greatly fictional captivity narratives, and the turn of the century 'histories' of the Indian wars (never the 'White,' or 'Settlers' or 'Colonists' wars)" (p. 216).

In return for their lands, native tribes were shunted onto reservations often comprised of marginal land,[20] which were in turn reduced in size, until today, the per capita land base of the Sisseton Sioux has been valued at $19.12.[21] Nonetheless, reservation land remains the center of existence for most Native Americans, for it is estimated that 400,000 or 80% of the identifiable Indians in the U.S. live on reservations or similar tribal settlements (Fey and McNickle, pp. 10-12). This land, along with its allied political organization, is the means by which the tribes' existence is formalized; and as Fey and McNickle put it, Indians "are no more prepared to legislate themselves out of existence . . . than is any other group of people sharing a common history, a common language, and a system of commonly accepted goals in life" (p. 13). The peremptory action alluded to in this statement of allegiance to reservation land is the intermittent policy of "termination" employed by the U.S. government through its Bureau of Indian Affairs. Termination has its origins in the Federal Allotment Act of 1887, which attempted to turn Indians into "good American settlers"; the Act gave individual Indians title to small areas of land, anywhere from 10 to 640 acres, with all remaining acreage declared surplus land which the Department of the Interior was free to sell for white development. In this fashion, some 90 million of the 140 million acres designated as reservation in 1887 were lost to the Indian by 1934, when the Indian Reorganization Act stopped the practice of allowing reservation land to pass out of the hands of individual tribe members.

Yet, once again, in the 1950's the BIA moved toward termination of reservation holdings in an attempt to force the Indians away from their tribal ways and into the "mainstream" of American life. During this time, the lands of the Menominees of Wisconsin and the rich timber holdings of the Klamaths of southern Oregon were in fact broken into individual holdings, which then were acquired by white business interests in most cases.[22]

Since such a history of political oppression exists, it should come as no surprise to find political reaction a common theme in modern Indian literature, oratorical and imaginative alike. Leaving aside traditional instruments of war, today's most combative Native Americans have turned to the word. Vine Deloria, Jr., with such books as *Custer Died For Your Sins*, *You Talk—We Listen*, *God is Red*, and *Behind the Trail of Broken Treaties*, has emerged as the most eloquent of the modern orators, following in the footsteps of such illustrious native speakers as the Shawnee Tecumseh (whose people, he said, have vanished before the onslaught of the white man "as snow before a summer sun"), and Chief Joseph of the Nez Perce, author of the famous "I will fight no more forever" surrender speech. Representative samples of the growing body of contemporary Indian oratory can be found in Stan Steiner's *The New Indians* and an anthology compiled by Steiner and Shirley Hill Witt entitled *The Way*.

These problems relating to relocation, termination, and the reaction to genocide are perhaps the first themes that younger imaginative writers come to, with somewhat predictable results. Often, a native writer is overcome with the urgency of his message and forsakes all concerns of craft in the effort to make his point, as in these examples:

> It was the land of the free,
> and of the first Americans.
> Where has it all gone?

> Look around and you will see
> bare eroded lands, damned rivers,
> discarded hungry people . . .[23]

> In my own country I'm in a far off land
> I'm strong but have no force or power
> I win yet remain a loser . . . .[24]

> I've often wondered why it is said
> that the Indian Spirit is broken and dead—
> why such balderdash fills the air
> when in their midst like a grizzly bear
> is the sleeping red-skinned giant now on the prowl
> an answer to a lone Kiowa's vengeful howl.[25]

Given some background to the problems referred to in these works, any reader would be sympathetic to the sentiments expressed, but most readers looking for artful use of the language are likely to be put off by the prosaic stridency. Such Black writers as Albert Lee Murray and Ralph Ellison have seen their works criticized by some militants who seek more visible anger in the writing. But as Murray, in his *Omni-Americans*, and Ellison, in *Shadow and Act*, have made clear, forever reacting in rage to accusations only suggests the truth of the charges, and at any rate prevents positive action along a course of self-determination: the poet's most important initial task is to develop his own voice. G. W. Haslam has called for the day "when Indian writers as a group forsake blatant protest and employ more imaginative—and probably more persuasive—forms; the pressure of their plight has tended to force Indian writers into desperate excoriations of conditions. Like Afro-Americans who have found that subtlety is often a more effective social weapon than shrill anger, native American artists are beginning to discover their own most moving modes of expression" (*Forgotten Pages*, p. 24). Examples of poems that do operate according to such principles of subtlety and yet maintain their social force are found today in the work of James Welch, Simon Ortiz, and Anita Endrezze-Probst, among others.

In this section of Endrezze-Probst's poem "The Week-End Indian," we find understatement and suggestion working despite the deceptive prosaic quality and the highly charged subject matter:

> In red wool jacket and earflaps
> you circle your camp three times
> before you realize you're lost.
> You deny it, squinting at moss
> growing on the north of trees,
> and thumb through your new copy
> of "Indian Lore and Camp Book."
> The pages are blank.
>
> Your compass, with its glowing digits,
> whirs spastically toward your feet.
> Fur-lined and waterproofed, your boots
> are, in case of emergencies, edible.
> Your fishing line has become knotted,
> clumped in a thick-leafed bush,
> like a small bird's nest.
> The redwoods gather above you,
> waiting like many-winged vultures
> . . . .
>
> Lost, on the night of your first day,
> you huddle against a deep cliff
> whispering into your palms,
> cupping them against your ears.
> They answer you in slow echoes.[26]

And clearly, we see restraint working hand in hand with the same theme of loss and dispossession in this segment of Simon Ortiz's "Relocation," included in *The Way* (pp. 84-85):

> i see me walking in sleep
> down streets down streets grey with cement
> and glaring glass and oily wind
> armed with a pint of wine.

But Ortiz himself is prone to the occasional shift to more direct statement, as in this excerpt from the same poem:

> the deadened glares
> tear my heart
> and close my mind
>
> who questions my pain
> the tight knot of anger
> in my breast.[27]

However, it is in the works of James Welch that we find perhaps the most balanced and most convincing blend of suggestion, dense image, and socio-political theme. Consider this excerpt from "The Man From Washington":

> The end came easy for most of us
> . . . .
> we didn't expect much more
> than firewood and buffalo robes
> . . . The man came down,
> a slouching dwarf with rainwater eyes
> . . . He promised that life would go on as usual
> that treaties would be signed, and everyone—
> man, woman and child—would be inoculated
> against a world in which we had no part,
> a world of wealth, promise and fabulous disease.[28]

Similarly, this quote is from "The Only Bar In Dixon":

> These Indians once imitated life.
> Whatever made them warm
> they called wine, song or sleep,
> a lucky number on the tribal roll.
>
> Now the stores have gone the gray
> of this November sky. Cars
> whistle by, chrome wind, knowing
> something lethal in the dust.[29]

Welch's approach is even more understated in "Dancing Man," where the poem works equally well as lament for a boy's loss of innocence and lament for the loss of the lyric cultural heritage of an entire people:

> He swung gracefully into midnight
> that man on the plains.
> The stories he told were true enough
> and we were young
> to understand his beetle eye.

> It wasn't till later
> the dream broke
> and we spun solid as a rock
> back to the cold cactus ground,
> winehappy and stubborn.[30]

While such social and political concerns are easily enough discerned in Native American poetry, there is a more complex related theme underlying many works, one of a spiritual attachment to the land and man's inter-relationship with all things, organic and inorganic alike. While specific rituals differ from tribe to tribe, most commentators agree that traditional Indian religions stress a spiritual equality of all things: fish, trees, men, rocks, and rivers. Herbert Blatchford, one of the founders of the National Indian Youth Council and Director of the Gallup Indian Community Center, explains the thinking that girds many traditional myths and legends, and which applies to modern works as well: "To fully understand these stories, which to my mind are designed to teach moral behavior, a person has to think in terms of Universal Life Continuity; that is, that there is a related continuity of life and well-being between all living matter, and that this life and well-being are dependent upon all organic and inorganic matter."[31]

Blatchford asserts further that, due to the Indian's concern with main-taining harmony and thus disrupting the natural course of events as little as possible, the traditionally oriented Indian does not tend to project his goals far into the future ("Religion of the People," p. 176). Because the Indian believes there is a strength to be gained from maintaining this balance, his homeland and all its natural accouterments become an integral part of his life, with the cliffs and grasses as important to him as his neighbors and himself. N. Scott Momaday makes the concept clear in this passage from *House Made of Dawn*, where the grandfather takes his sons out upon the land for their first important lesson:

> He made them stand just there, above the point of the low white rock, facing east. They could see the black mesa looming on the first light, and he told them there was the house of the sun. They must learn the whole contour of the black mesa. They must know it as they knew the shape of their hands, always and by heart. . . . They must know the long journey of the sun on the black mesa, how it rode in the seasons and the years, and they must live according to the sun appearing, for only then could they reckon where they were, where all things were, in time.[32]

According to this view, life-time is no longer a linear journey—the quality of existence is measured in terms of lateral expansion, not attentuation.

A similar attitude toward an integrated life force is seen in this untitled poem by Vance Iron Good, where he describes the coming of spring, when the rains

> . . . awaken the earth
> as one would wake a dreamer
> or love a young girl
> gently at first.[33]

And in this segment from Momaday's poem, "Angle of Geese," we find also the sense of eternity in the moment, an emblem of the non-linear conception of time:

> And one November
> It was longer in the watch,
> As if forever
> Of the huge ancestral goose.
>
> So much symmetry!
> Like the pale angle of time
> And eternity.
> The great shape labored and fell.
>
> Quit of hope and hurt
> It held the motionless gaze,
> Wide of time, alert,
> On the dark distant flurry.[34]

Without a knowledge of this necessary oneness with the land and its attendant convictions, readers might completely misunderstand a story such as Grey Cohoe's "The Promised Visit."[35] In this work, a young Navajo leaves his home on the reservation to journey to the tribal council headquarters for a scholarship interview. The boy has decided to leave his family and the reservation to study "art," a decision which will also remove him from an atmosphere of primitive superstition he professes to disdain. At this point, most Anglo readers would applaud the boy's thinking as forward-looking and properly goal-oriented. However, as a result of a mystical encounter with a beautiful spirit girl who seems to embody many of the traditional aspects of "Navajo-ness," the boy begins to question his earlier resolve and finally suggests that he will turn down the scholarship and stay on with the land and the tilling and his people. By this time, the Anglo reader might fault the boy's final indecision as whimsical, irresponsible, and based hopelessly in superstitious fear. That judgement would constitute a misreading of the story, however, in light of the preceeding discussion. The key line exhibiting the Navajo point of view is this summary statement from the protagonist: "From that day I had proven to myself the truth of the Navajo superstitions" (p. 171). Through his fortuitous encounter with the strong spirit of his people, the boy has realized something of the absurdity of a Navajo's total renunciation of his own heritage in order to learn "art" in the white man's school.

In Durango Mendoza's story, "Summer Water and Shirley,"[36] there exists the possibility of another kind of misunderstanding on the part of the Anglo reader. The narrator is a twelve-year-old whose younger sister Shirley comes down with a sudden fever after taunting a *stiginee*, or witch/shaman, near the dry stream bed on their Oklahoma reservation. After the futile application of all traditional remedies for possession by evil water spirits and the equally useless visits from a white doctor, Shirley's mother and the rest of the community abandon hope. Everything possible has been done; the elders are resigned that the girl will die before the fourth sun rises.

The boy, however, is not content to sit by while his sister dies, and so he steals into the darkened room where she has been prepared for her passing. After a long night's vigil during which the boy directly confronts his fear of the dark unknown and prays for his sister's recovery, the dawn brings with it his sister's miraculous stirrings of recovery. This series of events could possibly confuse the reader unfamiliar with yet another pillar of the Indian-American cosmos. After all, not only has the white man's medicine failed, but so has that of the native. Thus the story might remain murky, a tale describing a miracle, perhaps signifying the efficacy of pious prayer to some, unless one were to consider more carefully the passage detailing the boy's most fervent efforts to take back his sister's life from the spirits of the dark: "And then he spoke softly, saying what they had done, and how they would do again what they had done because he had not given up, for he was alive, and she was alive, and they had lived and would *still* live. And so he prayed to his will and forced his will out through his thoughts and spoke softly his words and was not afraid to look out through the window into the darkness through which came the coolness of the summer night" (p. 504).

Here the key to understanding is the Native American conception of the great and inherent power of the *word*. Because the boy can force his will out through his thoughts and into words, he succeeds in his task. This sense of the power of the word derives from the thousands of years of the Native American oral literary tradition. From its labyrinthine and tenuous history the word arrives in the present with inestimable force. As Scott Momaday points out in his essay, "The Man Made of Words," the oral form exists always just one generation from extinction and is all the more precious on that account.[37] And this sense of care engendered for the songs and stories and their words naturally leads to an appreciation of the power of the word itself.

Properly cared for, preserved intact, a story has the power to sustain an entire culture as it literally did in the case of the Kiowa. Momaday recounts the beginnings of such a process at the conclusion of his retelling of the Kiowa myths in *The Way to Rainy Mountain*. Shortly after midnight on 13 November 1833, a spectacular meteor shower lit up the heavens above the Oklahoma camp of the Kiowa. Terrified, the people ran out upon the night, certain that the world was coming to an end. And in fact, it was only four years later that the Kiowa were forced to sign their first treaty with the government of the United States, an action which literally signalled the ensuing decline of one of the proudest tribes of the plains culture.[38]

Momaday first heard of that fateful night from Ko-Sahn, a venerable Kiowa woman who had not seen the event but who spoke of it in such detail that she surely had lived it in her mind's eye. Further, Momaday explains, seeing the shower as an omen of disaster gave the Kiowa the strength to bear what befell them thereafter—thus, his ancestors had imagined meaning and order into the event and it sustained them through chaos, as it in turn sustained Ko-Sahn (*Way to Rainy Mountain*, p. 105). For Momaday, man's very being is a function of his idea of himself, and the richest, most enduring expression of that being is to be found in its timeless expression in literature—from this, his conception of man *made* of words.

This appreciation of the word's power to create and shape is also to account for the repetition found in much traditional Indian poetry, as we see in this excerpt from the Navajo "Voice of the Bluebird," a song to bring the rain and raise the corn:

> The corn grows up. The waters of the
>   dark clouds drop, drop.
> The rain descends. The waters from the
>   corn leaves drop, drop.
> The rain descends. The waters from the
>   plants drop, drop.
> The corn grows up. The waters of the
>   dark mists drop, drop.[39]

And this appreciation of the word's power in turn explains those portions of modern Native-American poetry that might seem unnecessarily repetitive to the Anglo reader. While it is difficult to conjure the rhythm of an entire poem in an excerpt, this portion of Janet Campbell's "Nespelim Man" exemplifies the attempt to call the needed ancestor into the barren present via incantation. In the same fashion, his transitory nature and inevitable departure is underscored by the purposive echoes of the poet's grief:

> From the land of Nespelim he comes.
> His mother is the sky.
> His father is the earth.
> He is Nespelim Man.
> Oh, joy, he is Nespelim Man.
> Ya-che-ma, Nespelim Man.

To Many Lakes he has come.
Let our fields be fruitful.
Let our game be plentiful.
Ya-che-ma, he goes,
Ya-che-ma, he goes.

Over the mountains he goes
Across the waters he goes.
I weep, I weep, for he is gone.
Ya-che-ma, he is gone—
          He is dead![40]

Herbert J. Spinden, in his introduction to *Songs of the Tewa*, identifies such a device as "repetition with an increment,"[41] terming it the "outstanding feature of American Indian verse." Spinden, whose research turned up no evidence of the use of rhyme in traditional Indian poetry, proposes that this use of repetition was the Indian's counterpart to rhyme, giving the effect "not of rhyming sounds but of rhyming thoughts" (p. 58). And G. W. Haslam adds that, "Just as repetition may, despite all its variations, sound redundant and limited to Euro-Americans, the metrical and rhyming patterns of Euro-American poetry have the same effect on Amerindians. Each individual recognizes and enjoys the forms his culture trains him to favor; no poetic pattern is inherently superior to another."[42]

As a device in modern written poetry, of course, repetition must be muted and controlled, for the incantory effect which is necessary in the transitory oral presentation can become overwhelming in the printed context. Nonetheless, the modern reader familiar with the Hebrew Psalms can appreciate the similarity to Indian poetry in the repetition, free rhythmed cadences, and resultant loose stanzaic construction, an equation made by Mabel Major and T. M. Pearce.[43] William Brandon, in the preface to his collection of traditional poetry, *The Magic World*, describes the guidelines he employed in preparing his own translations of ceremonial works: "In the buffalo songs, for instance, it would not only be wearisome to follow faithfully all the magic numbers, but we might also, who knows, materialize a buffalo. We don't really want the buffalo. We only want the feeling of the earnest repetition, the feeling of the hypnosis, of the marvelous emerging, the feeling of the magic. All that we want from any of it is the feeling of its poetry."[44]

One final stylistic character of contemporary Native American literature to consider has been touched on before and is another that derives from the oral tradition. Because it was necessary to keep the literature intact and easily transmittable, the traditional poems and stories were constructed efficiently, with each word chosen to perform yeoman duty. The dense holophrasistic nature of the language where we see one word standing for an entire English phrase such as "fear-living-in-place-shakes-continually"[45] and the close-knit nature of the tribal cultures contributed to the compact character of the literature. In turn, the character of the languages and cultures were intensified by the inherited literature. Writing in the *English Journal*, G. W. Haslam calls attention to the resultant "cryptic" nature of later traditional poems such as this Chippewa "Song of the Trees":

> The wind
> Only
> I am afraid of.[46]

Yet, as Haslam points out, if one realizes that here the wind is representative of devine power and so the tree of man, we apprehend a more complex metaphorical statement than would at first be apparent (p. 711). Even without an intricate knowledge of the Chippewa cosmos, the realization that practically no Indian poem was without its ultimate application to man and his relationship to other *spirit*-ed things should provide entree to such compressed lyrics. One only needs to be attuned to this embedding technique.

Mary Austin once claimed that "No Indian ever says all his thought,"[47] and proceeded to share the remarks of Kern River Jim who told her bluntly that white men's songs talk too much. "You see Piuty man singin' sometime and cryin' when he sing, [but] it ain't what he singin' make him cry. It's what he thinking about when he sing make him cry" (cited in *American Rhythm*, pp. 60-61). Austin developed the notion of the native poem as a "shorthand note to the emotions,"[48] with the poem's "inside song" as its most important component. She included in her remarks that prefaced George Cronyn's collection of songs and chants the observation that the native poems made the then-current Imagist movement seem primitive, adding that "the first free movement of poetic originality in America finds us just about where the last Medicine Man left off" (*The Path On the Rainbow*, p. xvi).

In *American Rhythm*, Austin provides a direct example of this imagistic construction. One of her correspondents, Washoe Charlie, had given his girl a grass green ribbon upon her departure for Indian Boarding School. A few days later, still deeply mourning his loss, he caught a brief glimpse of another girl wearing the same kind of ribbon. According to Austin, Charlie expressed the incident perfectly in this compressed fashion: "The green ribbon when I saw a girl wearing it, my girl existed inside me" (*American Rhythm*, pp. 52-53).

Washoe Charlie's technique, so obviously similar to suggestive elements in Imagism, Deep Imagism, and Symbolism need not be explained further. The reader familiar with those aspects of Euro-American poetry is simply required to apprehend Native American use of those techniques in the same way he approaches those of William Carlos Williams. He may consider, for instance, the reverberation of peace, personal loss, and cosmic regeneration in Joseph Concha's short poem that speaks of the snow, which

> . . . comes last
> for it quiets down everything.[49]

Or, in Nancy Boney's "What This Poem Can Do," compression operates to kindle a wealth of social implications without the need for a traditional transition:

> Run through the woods like a deer eating
> sweet grass . . .
> . . . .
> Not caring about the thunder and the sound
>   of the whispering
> wind that blows through the trees and shakes
>   the autumn
> leaves that line the old gravel road or in a
>   back alley
> beat up and drunk.[50]

Because of an inability of unwillingness to understand such basic distinctions of Indian Literature as we have discussed, some otherwise able critics have done readers a grave disservice. Ignorance can result in a too hasty dismissal, as we see in the case of William James Smith's review of *House Made of Dawn*. "Something broken backed about that title to begin with,"[51] went Smith's introduction, immediately revealing his ignorance of a metaphor which suggests the central unity of nature, man, and life spirit, the very understanding that the protagonist Abel must finally accept. Smith goes on to say that Momaday's style "makes you itch for a blue pencil to knock out all the interstitial words that maintain the soporific flow. It is a style that gets in the way of content" (p. 636). Here again Smith misunderstands the concept of the power of the word and the use of repetition to suggest a ritual taking place, as in this passage describing Abel's symbolic reintegration with the Great Spirit: "The soft and sudden sound of their going, swift and breaking away all at once, startled him, and he began to run after them. He was running, and his body cracked upon with pain, and he was running on. He was running and there was no reason to run but the running itself and the land and the dawn appearing" (*House Made of Dawn*, p. 211). Of course, one could trim that passage down to something like "The rest of them started to run before Abel did, so he hurried to catch up and felt the true meaning of life as he did," but it is obvious that the passage depends upon, actually requires, the repetition to make the reader *feel* the change taking place.

In a final complaint Smith says that the characters in the novel remain "bemisted," and that the protagonist Abel "does not come through at all" (p. 636). But Smith, it would seem, is asking for a hero in the existential mode, a man who stands alone, chin thrust against the natural and man-made forces that assail him, a man apart, alone. Yet Abel's redemption in this novel lies in an opposite mode of being—he must become *a part of* his ancient and abiding world once again, or he will surely die, teeth kicked out, drunk, dead-drunk, in some Los Angeles back alley. As Carole Oleson, writing in the *South Dakota Review*, puts it: "*House Made of Dawn* is not a short novel about Abel, but a long prose poem about the earth, about the people who have long known how to love it, and who can survive as a people if they will cling to that knowledge."[52]

Critics of modern Indian-American imaginative works should heed this advice from John Bierhorst in his foreward to *Four Masterworks of American Indian Literature*. While he refers to traditional works, the principles remain operative: "(1) that Indian literature, if symbolic, is far from chaotic—each verbal element has a contributory meaning and each element has its proper place—and (2) that this literature, owing to its "geometrical" bias, cannot be read for style in the usual sense of the term; the ideas and images are there, but generally unwrapped (and spread out) rather than neatly packaged."[53] In *House Made of Dawn*, events and memories are chosen to suggest character and theme more than lay it out explicitly, while the language and phrasing, in like manner, suggest the meaning of the events themselves, a welcome subtlety. The sense of irrevocable loss is implicit in Ben Benally's utterance, "Look! Look! There are blue and purple horses . . . a house made of dawn . . . " (p. 114), and again in Abel when he struggles to express the remembered beauty of geese rising into the moon above a river of his childhood (pp. 118-19). The reader is not told exactly what emotion, or precisely what importance the visions have for the characters, but the vividness, the breathlessness of their telling, the focus on the recreation of the events rather than on their explanation—this non-directive approach—allows a reader the feeling and the meaning of the experience in his own turn.

In the progression of the novel as a whole, Momaday's approach sug-gests actuality. Events important to the protagonist are reported in the order that they recur in memory, outside strict chronology. Where blocks of time have passed without meaningful incident, they have fallen out of the novel in the way they naturally fade from the mind. Momaday's is obviously a purposeful method, one tied to the Indian-Oriental view of all experience as a continually flowing river where chronological time loses significance, where events leap out of context to recur and grow "in the mind's eye," where the seeming concrete quality of history proves illusory, relative to each perceiver. Here, event freed from analysis and stasis easily carries supernatural significance and cosmic reverberation, even becomes mythic in the way of the tradition which Momaday draws upon.

While critics such as Reynolds Price and Roger Sale gave James Welch's *Winter in the Blood* generally thoughtful consideration, both men mentioned a "flaw" in the book's construction which actually does not exist. Shortly after the protagonist, who is a modern reservation farming Blackfeet, discovers that his lineage is actually a proud one, untainted with white blood, the novel ends, with this unnamed narrator deciding to once again try and bring home his indifferent love, "a Cree from Havre, scorned by the reservation [Blackfeet] people."[54] The two critics seem troubled by this apparently impractical decision, as if agreeing with the agency doctors that it would be wiser for the narrator to go to the white man's hospital for a lengthy knee reconstruction. The central events of the novel, Sale contends, "leads the hero only to the sense that his own life hasn't been good since his father and brother died."[55] The narrator's discovery of his grandfather's true identity "opens no vista on the past" (p. 22). And while the book is "unnervingly beautiful" for Sale, he concludes that just what it means to be an Indian is "never once offered us for summary or conclusion" (p. 20). Price is not quite so troubled by the conclusion, and he remarks that, while the true light in the novel comes when the narrator learns his heritage, still the novel does not forecast total triumph, and suggests that our protagonist remains essentially "frozen" at the book's end.

However, both critics have overlooked the information that comes concurrently as the narrator learns of his true background: his grandmother, who had become an outcast among her own people, the Blackfeet, was saved by the humane care and constancy that the man Yellow Calf rendered her in secret. Eventually they became lovers, and the narrator's mother was born. Without that care and constancy, his grandmother would not have lived past her first long winter and he would not exist.

As he returns home, mulling this lesson, the narrator encounters a maverick cow stuck in a slough and has this initial reaction: "I wanted to ignore her. I wanted to go away to let her drown in her own stupidity, attended only by clouds and the coming rain. . . . She had earned this fate by being stupid, and now no one could help her. Who would want to?" (p. 166). And yet try to help her he does, all alone, with an aged horse, a bad leg, and no chance in hell. At the end of this heroic struggle, the narrator, still down in the mire himself, looks up into a rainstorm that has drifted upon him and says, "Some people . . . will never know how pleasant it is to be distant in a clear rain, the driving rain of a summer storm. It's not like you'd expect, nothing like you'd expect" (p. 172).

Yellow Calf's actions and the narrator's gradual realization of their meaning, of the essential relationship and ensuing responsibility between men and all other things is likewise to account for the narrator's decision to go after that scorned Cree from Havre once again. He remembers well an earlier encounter where, "In her black eyes I could see the reason I had brought her home that time before. They held the promise of warm things, of a spirit that went beyond her miserable life of drinking and screwing and men like me" (p. 113).

In this light, the narrator's final decision suggests he has opened a great vista upon his past—and it could be argued that his triumph is as total as a human could expect. Shall we have overhauled knees or humanly functioning hearts?

It should be clear now that a certain reorientation can make a great deal of difference in appreciating a work fully. It is the purpose of all my remarks to *begin* the process of that reorientation; the paper does not intend to be exhaustive *or* constricting. While the comments describing the literature which I have passed on are largely those of Indian Americans, those same commentators would caution that no definitive limits should be enforced upon a developing literature. We all await tomorrow's news. Likewise, no Indian American writer would argue that any single discussion could completely explain or conjure up the "total Indian experience." We are left with the individual works to speak for themselves, ultimately. There is no substitute for a careful reading where one trusts the work itself and not a body of preordained criticism. If these remarks help a reader to divest himself of certain inapplicable preconceptions, they serve as intended. But in every instance, attend first to the voice of the poet.

At this point, having considered the past and the present of Indian-American literature, we might well speculate as to its future developments. As I mentioned at the outset, contemporary written imaginative work by Indian Americans is a relatively new phenomenon, and thus is sure to foster many more tribally oriented writers. The names I have mentioned include a number of young writers who have yet to publish book-length works, but who surely will. Projects such as the Department of Creative Writing within the Institute of American Indian Arts suggests that there will be a steady flow of young writers who understand both their own native heritage and the artful use of poetic language. A wide ranging survey of the program's results is to be found in *Arrows Four*, edited by Terry Allen, director of the writing program, and published by Pocket Books (1974). Such respected journals as *Alcheringa: Ethnopoetics, A First Magazine of the World's Tribal Poetries*, edited by Dennis Tedlock and Jerome Rothenberg, and *Angwamas Minosewag Anishinabeg* (Time of the Indian) edited by James L. White, provide ready outlets for the writers.

Moreover, the chances for survival of the Native American voice as a distinct force in American letters enjoy a special, if tenuous, advantage. So long as the policy of termination lies dormant, the center of the tribal cultural world will remain intact. Destroy the reservation and its attendant interlocking cultural network, and the voice of the Native American will likely lose its singularity and fade into an echo of things past. A. Grove Day, in discussing the representation of tribes in his collection of traditional songs and poems, *The Sky Clears*, suggests what termination would mean: "It is probable, for example, that the Algonkian tribes of the eastern regions had poetry no less rich than that preserved among the Pueblo groups; but as few of the eastern specimens have survived the long period of decline and decay resulting from the intrusion of white settlers, we can only guess what this 'lost' literature might have been."[56]

It seems a remarkable achievement that a written tradition so new as that of the Native American could produce a Pulitzer Prize winner and another book deserving the front page of the *New York Times Book Review* within its first decade of flowering. Such accomplishments promise even greater contributions during the next ten years. Meantime, Indian writers have already expanded the vision of American readers and writers alike who seek an alternative to the predominant Puritan heritage of the United States. Reynolds Price titled his review of *Winter in the Blood*, "When is an Indian Novel Not an Indian Novel," and went on to explain that while the subject matter is tied to the land and reservation characters, its story "has as much to say of the bone-deep disaffection and bafflement, the famous and apparently incurable psychic paralysis of several million Americans now in their twenties and early thirties, as of any smaller group."[57]

Randall Ackley, who teaches writing on the Navajo reservation in Arizona recently spoke of a distinction to be understood between poets who continue to speak out of and through the tribal voice and those opportunists of the stripe that Vine Deloria, Jr. describes in *Custer Died For Your Sins*, who come looking to jump on an ethnic bandwagon with a suddenly discovered Indian grandmother in the family tree.[58] Still, one cannot manufacture the voice of the great spirit that moves all things, just as it is true that not everyone can hear it. I hope that these remarks will help in that regard, but as Sanders and Peek put it: "To listen for the voice out of Wah'kon-tah that drifts through the English phrasings is to hear language enriched beyond its spiritual bounds. Unfortunately, the ear that cannot hear it in the Indian's line cannot hear it in Hemingway's or Lawrence's either" (*Literature of the American Indian*, pp. 449-50).

To reverberate that voice once more before closing then, let me quote from this Incan/Ayacucho "Dance Song":

Wake up . . .
Rise up . . .
In the middle of the street
A dog howls.

May the death arrive,
May the dance arrive,

Comes the dance,
You must dance,
Comes the death
You can't help it!

Ah! what a chill
Ah! what a wind . . . .[59]

University of Texas at El Paso

NOTES

[1] "Storytellers on Storytelling," *Friends of Thunder: Folk Tales of the Oklahoma Cherokees*, eds. Jack S. Kilpatrick and Anna G. Kilpatrick (Dallas: Southern Methodist Univ., 1964), p. 5.

[2] Reynolds Price, rev. of *Winter in the Blood*, by James Welch, *New York Times Book Review*, 10 Nov. 1974, p. 1.

[3] "The Indian as Poet," *The Dial*, 8 March 1919, p. 240.

[4] "Correspondence," *The Dial,* 31 May 1919, p. 569.

[5] Vine Deloria, Jr., *Custer Died For Your Sins* (New York: McMillan, 1969), p. 94.

[6] Gary Snyder, "The Yogin and the Philosopher," in *Alcheringa: Ethnopoetics—A First Magazine of the World's Tribal Poetries*, 1, No. 2 (1975), 2-3.

[7] Jerome Rothenberg, *Shaking the Pumpkin: Traditional Poetry of the Indian North Americans* (New York: Doubleday, 1972), p. xix.

[8] "The Snow Never Falls Forever," *Harper's* (Nov. 1972), p. 120.

[9] G. W. Haslam, *Forgotten Pages of American Literature*, (Boston: Houghton Mifflin, 1970), p. 84.

[10] Francis Densmore, *Chippewa Music*, Nos. 45-53 (Washington: Bureau of American Ethnology, 1910-1913), rpt. in Jerome Rothenberg, *Shaking the Pumpkin*, p. 203.

[11] "One Chip of Human Bone," *Voices from Wah'Kon-Tah*, eds. Robert K. Dodge and Joseph B. McCullough (New York: International Publishers, 1974), p. 133.

[12] In a letter to the author from N. Scott Momaday, Standford Univ., 1 Dec. 1975.

[13] A. Grove Day, *The Sky Clears* (Lincoln: Univ. of Nebraska, 1970), pp. ix-x.

[14] Harold Fey and D'Arcy McNickle, *Indians and Other Americans*, rev. ed. (New York: Harper & Row, 1970), p. 239.

[15] Thomas Sanders and Walter Peek, eds., *Literature of the American Indian* (Beverly Hills: Glencoe Press, 1973), p. 10.

[16] See Fey and McNickle, pp. 14-15; and Sanders and Peek, pp. 3-5 for summaries of the basic archaeological theory.

[17] William Brandon, *The Magic World* (New York: Morrow, 1971), p. xi.

[18] Dee Brown, *Bury My Heart at Wounded Knee* (New York: Holt, Rinehart, and Winston, 1970), p. 170.

[19] "Anti-Indian Sentiment in Early Colonial Literature," *The American Indian Reader: Literature*, ed. Jeanette Henry (San Francisco: Indian Historian Press, 1973), p. 207.

[20] For a first-hand look at such governmental manipulation, see the records of the Republic of Texas' dealings with the Cherokee tribe, in *The Indian Papers of Texas and the Southwest*, eds. Dorman H. Winfrey and James M. Day (Austin: Pemberton Press, 1966), II, passim.

[21] William Brandon, *The American Heritage Book of Indians* (New York: Dell, 1964), p. 373.

[22] See *The American Heritage Book of Indians*, pp. 360-74; and Fey and McNickle, pp. 105-24 and 155-65, for accounts of the policy of termination and related matters.

[23] Edmund Hendricks, "It was Beautiful," *American Indian Reader*, p. 27.

[24] David Reeves, "Loser," *The Way*, eds. Shirley Hill Witt and Stan Steiner (New York: Vintage, 1972), p. 149.

[25] Kenneth Kale, "Sorry About That," *The Way*, p. 144.

[26] Anita Endrezze-Probst, "The Week-End Indian," *Voices of the Rainbow: Contemporary Poetry by American Indians*, ed. Kenneth Rosen (New York: Viking, 1975), pp. 110 and 112.

[27] Simon Ortiz, "Relocation," *The Way*, pp. 84-85.

[28] James Welch, "The Man From Washington," *The Way*, p. 139.

[29] Welch, "The Only Bar in Dixon," *Riding the Earthboy 40* (New York: Harper and Row, 1976), p. 39.

[30] Welch, "Dancing Man," *Earthboy 40*, p. 49.

[31] "Religion of the People," *The Way*, p. 176.

[32] N. Scott Momaday, *House Made of Dawn* (New York: Harper and Row, 1968), p. 197.

[33] *The Way*, p. 138.

[34] N. Scott Momaday, "Angle of Geese," *Forgotten Pages of American Literature*, pp. 59-60.

[35] Grey Cohoe, "The Promised Visit," *Myths and Motifs in Literature*, ed. David J. Burrows et al. (New York: Free Press, 1973), pp. 162-71.

[36] Durango Mendoza, "Summer Water and Shirley," Sanders and Peek, pp. 498-505.

[37] N. Scott Momaday, "The Man Made of Words," *Literature of the American Indian*, ed. Abraham Chapman (New York: Meridian, 1975), p. 108.

[38] Momaday, *The Way to Rainy Mountain* (Albuquerque: Univ. of New Mexico Press, 1969), pp. 85-86.

[39] "Voice of the Bluebird," *American Indian Reader*, p. 4.

[40] Janet Campbell, "Nespelim Man," *Voices from Wah'Kon-Tah*, p. 36.

[41] *Songs of the Tewa* (New York: Exposition of Indian Tribal Arts, 1933), p. 58.

[42] *Forgotten Pages of American Literature*, p. 19.

[43] Mabel Major and T. M. Pearce, *Southwest Heritage: A Literary History With Bibliography* (Albuquerque: Univ. of New Mexico Press, 1972), p. 16.

[44] *The Magic World*, p. xiv.

[45] Mary Austin, *The American Rhythm* (Boston: Houghton Mifflin, 1930), p. 60.

[46] Francis Densmore, *Chippewa Music*, No. 48, rpt. in G. W. Haslam, "American Oral Literature: Our Forgotten Heritage," *English Journal*, 60 (1971), 711.

[47] Austin, *The American Rhythm*, p. 60.

[48] Mary Austin, "Introduction," *The Path of the Rainbow: An Anthology of Songs and Chants from the Indians of North America*, rev. ed., ed. George Cronyn (New York: Liveright, 1934), p. XXV.

[49] *The Way*, p. 136.

[50] Brian Blacksetter, from "What This Poem Can Do," *Angwamas Minosewag Anishinabeg* (Time of the Indian [Winter 1974]), n.p.

[51] William James Smith, rev. of *House Made of Dawn*, by N. Scott Momaday, *Commonweal* 88 (1968), 636.

[52] Carole Oleson, "The Remembered Earth: Momaday's *House Made of Dawn*," *South Dakota Review*, 11, No. 1 (1963), 160.

[53] John Bierhorst, ed., *Four Masterworks of American Indian Literature*, (New York: Farrar, Straus, and Giroux, 1974), p. xvi.

[54] James Welch, *Winter in the Blood* (New York: Harper and Row, 1974), p. 6.

[55] "Winters Tales," *New York Review of Books*, 12 Dec. 1974, p. 22.

[56] *The Sky Clears*, p. xii.

[57] Reynolds Price, rev. of *Winter in the Blood*, p. 1.

[58] Randall Ackley, Address before the Western Americana Folklore Symposium, Rocky Mountain Modern Language Association, Denver, 17 Oct. 1975.

[59] "Dance Song," *American Indian Prose and Poetry*, ed. Margot Astov (New York: Capricorn, 1962), p. 344. This book was originally printed in 1948 under the title *The Winged Serpent*.

The Netherlandic Muse in the Forests, on the Plains, and in the Cities of America from 1850 to 1975

Walter Lagerwey

ABSTRACT

There are two Dutch speaking ethnic groups embraced in this study, the Dutch who came from the Netherlands and the Flemish who came from Belgium. Despite differences in their origins as well as in dialects, they have a common language, Netherlandic, which is the language of their literature. Necessarily excluded from consideration are Frisian literature and literature in the English language by writers of Dutch and Flemish origin though a great deal of significant literature has been written. Literature is here broadly defined to include memoirs and reminiscences, editorials and essays, sketches and sermons, dramas and short stories, hymns and poetry. This survey of Netherlandic ethnic literature includes writings in Yankee-Dutch, a dialect of Dutch and English which developed in the settlements of the Midwest, and also folk tales in Jersey-Dutch, an older dialect which was spoken in Upper New York, New Jersey, and Long Island among descendants of immigrants who trace their origins to the days of the Revolution. Much of the poetry written in the Dutch and Flemish settlements is religious whether written by clergymen or laymen. In the period after World War II there is a new immigration which embraces a wider spectrum of people. Among the postwar writers there is at least one important novelist and one very important poet. (WL)

The choice of the term Netherlandic in the title is deliberate to emphasize that our subject concerns the language and literature of two Dutch speaking groups who emigrated to America in the nineteenth century, the Flemish who came from Belgium and the Dutch who came from the Netherlands. The Flemish came from northern Belgium and their language is a dialect variation of Dutch. The Dutch came from many provinces of the Netherlands and they spoke many different dialects of Dutch. Nevertheless, the language of the educated Fleming and Dutchman is the same, generally speaking, and that common language we shall designate as Netherlandic. This Netherlandic language, with only minor variations, is the

353

language of the literature employed in the newspapers, journals, and literary publications of both ethnic groups regardless of the land of origin. Thus we are speaking of two ethnic groups with a common language, Netherlandic, but with quite different histories and cultural traditions ever since the northern and southern Netherlands were permanently separated in 1585 during the Eighty Years War (1568-1648).

While we include the Dutch and the Flemish in our overview, we exclude the literary contributions of the Frisians.[1] Although Friesland is a province of the Netherlands, the Frisian language is not a dialect of Dutch but a separate Germanic language. The Netherlandic contributions of Frisians will, of course, be included in our study.

One of the principal differences between the Flemish and Dutch immigrants was their religion. The Dutch immigrants were, in the main, Protestants, and orthodox Calvinists at that, whereas the Flemish were, generally speaking, Roman Catholics. Interestingly, both Dutch and Flemish immigrants formed communities around their churches. The principal Flemish settlements were in Detroit, Michigan; Moline, Illinois; and Delhi, Ontario. The story of Flemish emigration to America is recounted in *Vlaanderen in de Wereld* by Arthur Verthé in collaboration with Bernard Henry[2] and in *Belgians in America* by Philemon D. Sabbe and Leon Buyse.[3] The Dutch settlements originally were located principally in Michigan, Iowa, and Wisconsin (where a Dutch Catholic community was founded on the Fox River) and gradually expanded to many other states. The history of these settlements has received intensive study by several scholars. The standard scholarly study in the Dutch language is *Nederlanders in Amerika* by J. van Hinte.[4] This study is particularly fascinating because of the foreign, Dutch perspective of the author and because it was made at a time (1928) when the Dutch ethnic community had reached the peak of its cultural contribution in the Dutch language. By then the knowledge of Dutch was rapidly declining among second and third generation immigrants. In the English language we are fortunate to have the monumental study of Henry S. Lucas: *Netherlanders in America: Dutch Immigration to the United States and Canada, 1789-1950.*[5] We are also indebted to Lucas for two volumes of valuable source documents in the original Dutch and in English translations: *Dutch Immigrant Memoirs and Related Writings.*[6] Several studies deal with Dutch immigration from the early beginnings in the seventeenth century to modern times. A very readable account is that of Bertus Harry Wabeke, *Dutch Emigration to North America, 1624-1860.*[7] Gerald F. De Jong in *The Dutch in America, 1609-1974* takes a chronological approach and brings the history of the Dutch in America up to date.[8] Arnold Mulder also deals with the history of the Dutch from Colonial times to modern in *Americans from Holland.*[9] In a most delightful prose style, he presents a perceptive perspective on significant aspects of the Dutch ethnic communities in America.

All of these books discuss, in greater or less detail, the reasons for the Dutch emigration to America. There are two main reasons: one is economic, the other is religious. For the main body of nineteenth-century Dutch immigrants the principal reason was to gain religious freedom. Many of the Dutch immigrants were orthodox Calvinists who had seceded from the Netherlands Reformed Church when their attempts to restore orthodoxy in the pulpits failed. They encountered hostility in church and society and in some instances suffered for their religious convictions. Though initially they wavered between going to South Africa or to America, their choice fell upon America, where religious freedom was guaranteed, where they could establish orthodox Christian communities, and where there were good opportunities for making a living. When one considers the literature produced within these Dutch communities, this orthodox Calvinist background must be taken into account. For instance it is interesting that the Calvinist communities in America which developed around the Christian Reformed Church maintained ties with the orthodox Calvinists in the Netherlands, and that these ties existed when what is sometimes known as Neo-Calvinism developed there under the dynamic leadership of the theologian and statesman Abraham Kuyper. Thus the Free Reformed University, established under Kuyper in 1880, was the school of higher learning attended by many American Reformed scholars well into the twentieth century. The ideas of Kuyper had a profound influence among the orthodox Calvinists in America during this century.

When we turn to the subject of Netherlandic literature in America, we discover first of all that this is virgin terrain. There is no history of that literature and little in the way of bibliographical information. There is but one collection of Netherlandic poetry, *Anthology of New Netherland*, and that covers only the brief period of Dutch domination in New York.[10] The historians Van Hinte and Lucas give only brief introductions to the literature which was produced within the Dutch ethnic community.[11] When one takes into account that much of the literary material is to be found in old Dutch newspapers and periodicals, with runs of fifty years and more, the large scope of the task becomes evident. In this paper we can make only a selective beginning of an enquiry into Netherlandic literature in America. In the course of making this study I have gathered materials for an anthology of representative authors and types of literature, but that is only a beginning.

As we begin this somewhat hazardous undertaking of surveying the literature of the Dutch and Flemish in America, we have two scholarly guideposts, one by Henry S. Lucas and the other by Adrian J. Barnouw.

Lucas observes: "Certainly not much of this poetry is of the highest excellence. But from the standpoint of the Dutch immigrant's cultural history it serves well to illustrate the Hollander's thoughts and hopes."[12] And in one of his fascinating newsletters, Barnouw reviews Lucas' book and gives him a scholarly rebuke for including so much "trite poetry" by "obscure immigrants" while ignoring more significant cultural contributions to American civilization.[13] I must state at the outset that I found much that was significant and interesting in the Dutch immigrant literature, which includes memoirs, essays, sermons, hymns, patriotic verse, editorials, poetry, dramas, short stories, sketches and poetry in Yankee-Dutch, a dialect mingling of Dutch and English, and even a collection of folk tales in the so-called "Jersey-Dutch" dialect spoken in upper New York until the middle of the twentieth century. There are also two novels (one of which is presently a best seller in the Netherlands), a drama written by a young seminarian, and plays written and performed within the Flemish community of Detroit. Finally, there is poetry written by a new generation of Dutch immigrants, who came to America after World War II, including at least one naturalized citizen who is acknowledged to be one of the greatest living writers in the Dutch language.

The limitations of time and space did not permit the inclusion of literature produced in the English language by members of the Dutch ethnic community. That is another important and fascinating area in which significant contributions have been made. Under the heading "American Hollanders as Seen by Recent Writers," Lucas gives a brief survey of this literature up to 1955.[14] Lucas' list of writers now needs to be expanded to include such names as Pierre van Paassen, Peter De Vries, Jan de Hartog and others. A study of literature in the English language written by Dutch-Americans would be most rewarding. However, these works in English, like the Dutch literature translated into English by Americans, and the literature in Frisian, necessarily lie beyond the scope of this paper which, therefore, is limited to the Netherlandic Muse in America from 1850 to 1975.

From the outset, the Netherlandic language press played a vital role in the life of the Dutch and Flemish communities. Much of the literature was published in newspapers, religious weeklies, and some even in a church yearbook. The literary publications include memoirs and meditations, editorials and essays, serials and sketches, and poetry by clergymen as well as laymen. All of these writings reflect the life, the ideals, and the struggles of the immigrant community in the New World.

The Flemish immigrants were served especially by two newspapers: *De Gazette van Moline*, published at Moline, Illinois from 1908 to 1941, when it merged with the *Gazette van Detroit*, a weekly newspaper which is still appearing. The Dutch community was served by a much more extensive press. The principal religious weeklies were *De Hope* (The Hope) which served members of the Reformed Church of America from 1865 to 1933 and *De Wachter* (The Watchman) which has served members of the Christian Reformed Church continuously since 1868.[15] Among the more important religious journals are: *De Gereformeerde Amerikaan* (The Reformed American, 1897-1916) and *Onze Toekomst* (Our Future), which began in 1893 and continued into the 1920's. There were many newspapers, for the most part weeklies. The Dutch historian Van Hinte calls them *Nieuws- en advertentiebladen*, that is, news and advertising papers.[16] He was obviously surprised by the many pages of advertisements in the newspapers. The publisher was, after all, in the business to make a profit, and at times an outstanding editor like the Rev. B. D. Dijkstra, editor of *De Volksvriend* (The Friend of the People) of Orange City, Iowa between 1930 and 1933, would have conflicts with both the publishers and readers. Van Hinte also notes that almost all the Dutch newspapers have a very religious, indeed a strict orthodox character.[17] He speaks of the sensational reporting in some newspapers and of the high quality of editorials in others. Van Hinte also observed the gradual decline of the Dutch language in the press and in 1928 stated that "it is becoming increasingly a caricature."[18] Another researcher, Harry Boonstra, in a Masters dissertation for the University of Chicago entitled "Dutch American Newspapers and Periodicals in Michigan, 1850-1925," also comments on the decline of the Dutch language:

> As was suggested in the discussion on advertising, Dutch may have been precious and beautiful, but the use of it was far from pure. One factor contributing to a corruption of the language was the use of many dialects in the homes, the other was the anglicizing of Dutch idioms. The resulting Yankee-Dutch was often lamented in the press, but without much avail. It would seem that this corruption of the language was an unavoidable intermediate stage between the use of the two languages.[19]

Boonstra also comments on the religious character of the secular press: "It is often striking that those papers which intended to be primarily newspapers, nevertheless included church news and doctrinal issues in great detail."[20] Both of these observations will be pertinent to the discussion of Dutch immigrant literature which follows. We shall begin with immigrant memoirs in the Dutch language.

The principal source on immigrant memoirs, as we have already noted, is the two volume collection of Lucas. Many of these memoirs, however, are fragmentary in character, and Lucas was not concerned with arranging them on the basis of literary merit. One of the well written accounts of the early settlement is *De Pelgrim Vaders van het Westen* by Dingman Versteeg, published in 1886.[21] The account is charming because of its anecdotal

358

character. One chapter of this book is entitled "Onder de Amerikanen" (Among the Americans) and relates, among others, some very amusing situations that developed because the Dutch immigrants understood neither the language nor the culture of their American neighbors. There is, for example, the story of the Dutchman who walked from Saugatuck to Holland (nearly 15 miles) and worked alone in the shop on the Fourth of July quite unaware of the American holiday!

Another interesting autobiographical narrative is that of Bastiaan Broere: *Korte Beschrijving van het Leven en de Wonderbare Leidingen Gods met Bastiaan Broere in Nederland en in Amerika* (Short Description of the Life and Wondrous Leading of God with Bastiaan Broere in the Netherlands and in America).[22] The tale of Bastiaan Broere, a known supporter of the Union Cause during the Civil War, who suddenly finds his home within the Confederate lines, is an almost unbelievable adventure. He risks his life repeatedly as he first escapes north through the Confederate lines, later returns to pick up his family, flees with them in a rowboat to sea, narrowly escaping capture by a Confederate gunboat, and finally, after a safe arrival in Union territory, is for a time suspected of being a spy![23]

But in addition to such lively prose accounts there are many more in verse. The fortieth anniversary of the founding of the city of Zeeland, Michigan became an official occasion to celebrate and to recall the past. The Rev. Henry E. Dosker celebrated the occasion in verse, "Het veertigjarig Gedenkfeest te Zeeland, 31 aug., 1887."[24] The three sections of this occasional poem are entitled: "De Wildernis" (The Wilderness), "De Kamp" (The Struggle), and "Heden" (The Present). Another such poem by the Rev. A. Zwemer bears the title "Afscheidsgroet" (A Farewell Greeting), and recalls the departure of the colonists from their homeland in the province of Zeeland, Netherlands.[25] These are moving poems which express well the emotions of the immigrants, their struggles and successes, but also their gratitude to God for His goodness to them. The sixtieth anniverary of the founding of *De Kolonie* (The Colony), a name given to the settlements which developed around the nucleus of Holland, Michigan, was a major event in the life of the immigrants in the year 1907.[26] In addition to the many speeches in Dutch and English there were also recitations of Dutch poetry written for the occasion. Thus J. A. De Spelder wrote "Op 't zestigjarig feest" (On the Sixtieth Anniversary Celebration).[27] These anniversary celebrations, fortunately, provided the stimulus for the writing of memoirs and reminiscences, many of which were subsequently collected and published by G. van Schelven in *De Grondwet* (The Constitution), a newspaper which was published in Holland, Michigan from 1860 to 1938. Many of these memoirs were republished by Lucas in his two volume collection. Given this propensity for writing occasional verse, and bearing in mind that many of these Dutch Calvinists had seceded from the Netherlands Reformed Church in 1834, we are not altogether surprised that a Rev. A. Guikema should celebrate the 100th anniversary of that Secession in a long poem which is entitled "De Afscheiding" (The Secession) and which appeared in *De Wachter* in 1934.[28]

Another clergyman, the Rev. T. Van der Ark, wrote much autobiographical and occasional verse. One long poem tells the story of his life in several parts: in Friesland, in Gronongen, and in America. His poems are preserved in a typescript at Calvin College.[29] Even more interesting than the above poems are his rhymed accounts of his experiences as a clergyman on the Western prairies. From time to time the Rev. Van der Ark had to make long trips to preach for other congregations or to attend a classis meeting of several churches. Such trips could be filled with adventure, especially during the winter. The author tells of times when his train was delayed so long by snowstorms that he arrived too late to hold services: there was no congregation! Another poem tells the story of being lost with a parishioner in a raging snowstorm and finally finding shelter providentially. On his long journeys, which were often quite tedious, the Rev. Van der Ark recorded in verse, which is little more than rhymed prose, his adventures and impressions of the churches and congregations to which he ministered so faithfully.[30]

One also finds memoirs in the *Jaarboekje voor de Hollandsch Christel. Geref. Kerk in Noord Amerika* (Yearbook for the Holland Christian Reformed Church). The primary purpose of this booklet was to provide the denomination with information about the several churches. In the years between 1881 and 1918 the yearbook also has a section called *Mengelwerk* (Miscellany) in which there are necrologies (mostly of the clergy), memoirs, stories, proverbs, poetry and even a calendar with times of the rising and setting of the sun. In the *Jaarboekje* for 1891, for example, there is the interesting autobiography of Jan Gelock, an immigrant who had been born in the province of Zeeland. The narrative tells of his life and conversion in Zeeland, his joining the Seceders and coming to America where he joined the Holland Christian Reformed Church and became an elder and treasurer of the seminary.[31] The same *Jaarboekje* has several travel tales by G. D. De Jong, one of which concerns an adventuresome trip in which the intrepid Rev. Albertus C. van Raalte, the able leader of the Holland settlement, has to accompany a couple of thieves who must be brought to the sheriff in the neighboring town of Grand Haven. With Van Raalte at the helm and two unwilling oarsmen, the mission is accomplished in the small boat despite bad weather which compels them to spend a night on shore.[32]

Within the Flemish community there are also several notable examples of memoirs and reminiscences. One such narrative which bears the title "Milwaukie, 24 Februarius 1845" was written by Charles Louis Desmedt. It may be found in *Vlaanderen in de Wereld*, where it is described as the most fascinating account uncovered by the authors.[33]

Another Flemish immigrant, Philemon D. Sabbe, wrote two volumes of autobiographical reminiscences: *Beelden uit mijn Kinderjaren* (Pictures from my Childhood Years).[34] These reminiscences tell of events humorous ("Eerste Communie") and sad ("Marceltje"). Sabbe writes excellent Dutch prose with occasional Flemish phrases and dialogues. "Marceltje" is the moving tale of a neighbor boy who dies after a lingering illness.[35] These tales, as well as the poetry of Sabbe, first appeared in the Flemish newspaper *Gazette van Detroit*.

Articles which appeared in the monthly journal *De Gereformeerde Amerikaan* are also interesting. Thus the Rev. H. van Hoogen discusses the home and family life of the Dutch in America. After lauding the special virtues of family life among the Dutch, the clergyman defends smoking (the practice of smoking had been attacked by Methodistic Americans). Smoking, he says, citing an authority on the subject, creates *gezellige sfeer* (a cozy atmosphere) in the home. Of course, smoking is only for men.[36]

More important are several essays by the prominent clergyman and writer Dr. Henry Beets. In an article "De Nederlandsche Stam en Taal in Noord Amerika" (The Netherlandic Race and Language in North America), Dr. Beets extolls the Dutch language and the poets of New Netherland and pays tribute to American-Dutch poets like the Rev. Henry Dosker and the Rev. A. Zwemer.[37] The learned clergyman is rhetorically eloquent in his lament about the decline of the Dutch language in America in an article entitled: "Een stervende Taal" (A dying Language).[38] This defense is especially surprising when one considers that Dr. Beets was the first minister to use the English language exclusively in worship services. While he loved the Dutch language and wished to preserve it, he was a very patriotic American who wrote a book in Dutch on the life and times of Abraham Lincoln.[39] Yet he realized that the younger generation, which no longer was familiar with the language of the fathers, needed to be ministered to in the English language. This remarkable Dutch-American clergyman created a controversy in the churches, but he led the way to an inevitable Americanization.

Turning now to popular writers of sketches which deal with the Dutch immigrant community, we consider first Jacob H. Hoekstra, who wrote under the pseudonym Hans Hansen. He regularly published a column, usually humorous, in the weeklies *Het Oosten* and *Onze Toekomst*. One example, "The Prayer Meeting" (*Het biduur*), will illustrate his style.[40]

The author tells of taking to a midweek prayer meeting (the Calvinists did not hold such meetings) two upper class ladies who, after nice and proper prayers, interspersed with speeches, rush off to a fancy luncheon when the clock strikes twelve. But what is really offensive, to a real Dutchmen, is that they powder and paint their faces! Hansen is often critical of the theologians in Grand Rapids, seat of the seminaries of two competing Reformed Churches. He caustically attacks views which he opposes—for example, the doctrine of Common Grace which loomed large in a doctrinal controversy between several Reformed Churches in America. Hansen always writes in rhyme though his column is never printed as poetry. The result is a column that looks and reads like prose, but, as you read, you repeatedly stumble over the unexpected rhyme! Sometimes Hans Hansen writes in Yankee-Dutch, that bastard mixture of Dutch and English that developed as the immigrants gradually lost mastery of their mother tongue while learning English. A good example occurs in the humorous poem: "My First Auto Trip."[41] The author relates what happened after he bought his first automobile and drove it, presumably without any training. The humorous articles of Hans Hansen were collected and published in book form, but unfortunately I have been unable to locate a copy.

Another writer of sketches about the Dutch is Dirk Nieland. His sketches first appeared in *The Christian Journal* and were published as *Yankee-Dutch* in 1918.[42] Nieland tells delightfully humorous stories about the poor Dutch who are not familiar with either the language or the customs of their American neighbors. He lampoons the little conceits of his fellow countrymen. In one sketch entitled "Beroepskeuze" (Choosing a Profession), he describes the Nagelboom family which lives on a farm in Muddy Center, a very orthodox community.[43] The oldest son of Mr. and Mrs. Nagelboom must choose his life's work. Mother Nagelboom would like nothing more than to see her dear son in the pulpit, but father Nagelboom needs his son on the farm. The young man is not interested in higher learning, he would rather be a farmer. Mother gets her way, and in the fall father and son proceed in horse and wagon to the city to enroll their son in the academy of higher learning. En route they stop at a shop where they meet another man who impersonates a preacher. The father, who is tremendously impressed by the formal pulpit rhetoric of the clergy, thinks that he is actually speaking with a minister. While father Nagelboom engages in friendly conversation with the "preacher," his dear son attaches a cow's tail to the coat of the supposed clergyman. When this is exposed, the father begins to catch on, and he realizes that his son is really not a suitable candidate for the ministry. Thus Nieland exposes both the conceit of the clergy who use *preektaal* (pulpit language) outside the pulpit and the exaggerated respect for that language among the parishioners.

The subtitle of Yankee-Dutch states that the humoristic sketches, some in rhyme and some not in rhyme, are suited for declamation. Public recitations were a common and favorite activity in the Dutch immigrant community when it met for social occasions, whether for a Sunday School Picnic, an anniversary celebration, or a wedding. It is interesting to note that the Dutch scholar Van Hinte was surprised at the stress on public speaking in the American schools. The Dutch immigrants apparently readily adopted that feature of the American way. Another volume of declamatory verse was compiled by William B. Eerdmans and published as *Mijn Recitatieboek: Ernst en Luim* (My Recitation Book: Serious and Humorous Selections).[44] Some of the poems in this volume are borrowed from Dutch sources (Piet Paaltjes, E. Larillard, Helene Swarth, E. Halbertsma), but the Rev. G. K. Hemkes, a popular writer of prose and poetry, contributed eight poems, some humorous and others serious. The titles speak for themselves: "Waar is de Baby?" (Where is the Baby?), "Schijn bedriegt" (Appearances are Deceiving), "Het Ongeval van Boer Klaas" (The Accident of Farmer Klaas), "Zorgen der Grijsheid" (Cares of Old Age).

Another volume of sketches in Yankee-Dutch by Dirk Nieland is entitled: *'n fonnie bisnis*.[45] These delightfully humorous sketches about the immigrant painter Lou Verlak are without doubt the finest example of Yankee-Dutch writing. Some idea of the Yankee-Dutch dialect may be gained from the Table of Contents: "'n Bik Jaap" (A Big Job), "Henkie Moet 'n Treed Leeren" (Hank Must Learn a Trade), "'n Durdie Trik" (A Dirty Trick), "Sonnieschoel Pikkenik" (Sunday School Picnic), "Vijf-en Twintig Jaar Gemerried" (Married Twenty-Five Years), "Ons Dominie Heeft 'n Kol Deklaind" (Our Minister Has Declined a Call), "Ik Heb voor Dieken Gerund" (I ran for Deacon). In his very excellent introduction to this book Frederick Ten Hoor says:

> Now it is true that these sketches were meant to amuse you; and it would be folly to invest them with a grave purpose or to impute to them a serious intention. But Mr. Nieland, in drawing something approaching a caricature, has weighted it with other qualities than the power to cause uproarious laughter. He has drawn a character, who, as well as being a somebody in his own right, is also representative of a group. In Lou Verlak you will find not only the absurd idiosyncracies of speech which characterized certain of the Holland immigrants of an earlier day, but also their attitude, their ideology and, to a great extent, their philosophy of life impregnated as it was with their religious convictions.[46]

Another writer of Yankee-Dutch is John Lieuwen. His first volume of verse is entitled *Troebel en Fon*.[47] Here, as in *Sweat en Tears*, we have a charming multi-lingual versification of the simple, ordinary events in the life of the Dutch immigrant. Illustrations of Lieuwen's style and content may be found in such homespun poems as: "Manners teachen" and "10 below."[48]

Apparently there was also an oral literature tradition in the Eastern United States as late as the early twentieth century. In response to an advertisement for manuscript materials, I received from Dr. L. G. van Loon of Somerset, Pennsylvania, a typescript of a collection of folk tales which he had gathered in Upper New York from older members of the descendents of the early colonists and produced in the dialect which he himself had learned in his childhood.[49] This dialect, known as "Jersey Dutch" was once used extensively in New York, New Jersey, and a great part of Long Island, according to Dr. Van Loon. There is considerable variety in the collection of folk tales. For example, "Voor een Dronkeman te verbeetere" (To Reform a Drunkard) is a simple story which tells about the trials of a man who had to overcome his drinking habit.[50] Several tales seem to have an Indian origin. Thus the narrative "Twee Valle Saome, oft hoe een plaats achter de Maquas Rivier hetzun naom kreeg" (Two Fall Together, or How a Place Behind the Mohawk River Got Its Name) tells of an Indian tribe which has repeatedly suffered defeat in wars with other tribes and is threatened with extinction.[51] The tribe is saved, however, when an Indian maiden volunteers to fight and she drowns the evil monster (who represents the sinister forces of destruction) in a river though it costs her her own life. The place in the river where the maiden and the monster go to their death is called "Twee Valle Saome," and that is the imaginative tale of how a place on the Mohawk River got its name. I should add that Dr. Van Loon has also supplied me with a manuscript which contains his personal memoirs and reminiscences in the same Jersey-Dutch dialect. We are greatly indebted to Dr. Van Loon for making available these writings in the Jersey-Dutch dialect so that they may be preserved for posterity.

Although the literature we have discussed so far is very commonplace, it does give some indication of the importance of the *word*, both written and spoken, among the Dutch and Flemish immigrants who had settled in the forests, on the plains, and in the cities of America. The historian Lucas makes a very pertinent observation about the immigrants and their love of reading and especially of verse:

> The Dutch immigrant deeply enjoyed reading. He was fond of theological works, even though these required concentrated thought and some familiarity with Scripture. Among his favorite writers in this field ... were such substantial thinkers as Smytegeld, Brakel, Hellenbroek, and Comrie. Almost every Netherlander who came to America during the 1840's and 1850's carried with him some work by one of these writers, in addition to the inevitable Psalter, which also contained the Heidelberg Catechism, and the Bible. Next to writings on theology and the life of the spirit, the Dutch immigrant loved poetry. Most of the Dutch newspapers carried poetry fairly regularly. It was usually didactic or patriotic, or else devoted to topics of local interest. An anthology of the Dutch poetry written here would accurately reflect the life and problems of the Dutch immigrant. Such a collection would reveal that the authors

were influenced by Netherlands writers like Willem Bilderdijk, Izaac Da Costa, and Hendrik F. Tollens, as well as by the Dutch version of the Psalms.[52]

We shall find the rhetorical style of the nineteenth-century Netherlands poets reflected in that of their American literary descendents. That includes, among others, poetic diction, emphasis on meter and rhyme, and also on the expression of emotions in poetry. In his study of Dutch-American newspapers and periodicals in Michigan, Boonstra also comments on common features of Dutch immigrant poetry:

> Poetry was published in great quantity. Ministers and laymen alike contributed liberally. Most of the poems were of a devotional nature; others celebrated the wonders of both Holland and America, or commented on significant events, for example, the Boer War, or the death of a president, or a coming election. Much of the poetry was little more than rhymed prose, but an occasional poem displayed quality and strength.[53]

Let us consider first poetry dealing with America, for that is especially appropriate as we celebrate the bicentennial anniversary of our country.

The amount and range of patriotic verse are really surprising. There are Dutch translations of American national anthems and poems which celebrate American holidays. Philemon Sabbe published in *Gazette van Detroit* many patriotic poems: "Memorial Day,"[54] "Flag Day, June 14th,"[55] "July 4th,"[56] "Wapenstilstand" (Armistice Day),[57] "In Memoriam Franklin Delano Roosevelt,"[58] and "Dankdag" (Thanksgiving Day).[59] Sabbe also wrote poems for the Christian holidays like "De Paaschklokke" (The Easter Bell)[60] and "Kerstdag" (Christmas Day),[61] but these are much more Flemish and religious.

A clergyman, the Rev. B. D. Dijkstra, who was doubtless one of the more gifted of Dutch American poets, translated several of our national anthems. His translations "Het Schoone Amerika" (America the Beautiful)[62] and "Amerika" (My Country 't is of Thee)[63] appear in a volume of hymns which Dijkstra translated from English to Dutch and which was published as *Stichtelijke Liederen* (Hymns for Edification). Dijkstra also published a poem "Waffen Nieder" (Lay Down Arms) for Armistice Day 1932.[64]

Still another clergyman, the Rev. A. Zwemer, wrote two independence day poems; one celebrates the first independence day, the other is a tribute to America.[65] He also translated Whittier's Centennial Hymn "God of our Fathers" in 1876.[66]

A poet who came to America from Friesland, Wybe J. Van Der Meer, wrote a sad melancholy poem "Amerika."[67] The same somberly sad, reflectively melancholy tone appears in other of his poems, such as "Terugkeer in 't Vaderland" (Return to the Fatherland),[68] "Winternacht" (Winter Night)[69] and also in "Najaar" (Autumn).[70] But, in the poem "Winternacht op de Prairie in N.-America" (Winter Night on the Prairie of North

America),[71] the poet finds in the quiet and beauty of nature a symbol for inner rest and peace. Van Der Meer also wrote poems in Frisian which grow out of his immigrant experience—for example, Lânforhuzer (Immigrant)[72] and "Oan it Michigan Lake" (On Lake Michigan).[73]

A number of other clergymen published poetry, some of which has merit. There is first of all B. D. Dijkstra whose *Korte Gedichten* (Short Poems) were typeset by his own son Ivan (now Chairman of the Department of Philosophy at Hope College), and printed on a press in the author's home.[74] Most of Dijkstra's poems first appeared in the newspaper *De Volksvriend*, of which he was for several years the versatile and able editor. The range of Dijkstra's subject matter is wide; it reaches from "Dent de leon,"[75] a poem inspired by the beauty of a humble dandelion, to "De Profundis" (Out of the Depths),[76] a poem in which the poet responds to the tragic drowning of five young girls from the community of Orange City. The depth of Dijkstra's involvement in this tragic loss contrasts, in my judgment, with that of another clergyman, B. A. Hendriksen, whose poem "Troost voor 't Ouder Hart" (Consolation for the Heart of the Parent) seeks rather typically to console the grieving parents with Bible texts and theological affirmations expressed in verse form. Thus the loss of the children is compared to the cutting of a rose in a beautiful flower garden by the Lord of the garden, and to the disappointment of the garden keeper (the parents). Such a loss, however, is to the greater Glory of God.[77]

The Reverend Dijkstra was a scholar and linguist who had mastered many languages. Above each poem which appeared in *De Volksvriend*, there is always a title in a foreign language with the translation given in a footnote. Each poem also has its supporting Bible text. As editor of *De Volksvriend*, Dijkstra also regularly contributed a column for the farmer; this column appeared under the Latin heading *Agricola!* A farmer reading this column could get a liberal education from the learned editor, whether the subject was The New Deal (which he loathed) or a philosophy of the Christian farmer. Many of the articles in this column are literary gems, and are still a pleasure to read. Dijkstra also wrote fine editorials on many subjects, always enlightening the farm community, whether he was advocating higher education, arguing for the independence of the farmer, or promoting the arts. Whenever he could, he sought to promote pacificism. Scholar that he was, Dijkstra belonged to the land, to the farm on which he had grown up as a boy in Friesland, and he wrote with eloquence about the ideal of working the land and tilling the earth, a paradise-ordained task and calling for men.

The Rev. B. A. Hendriksen, as we have noted, was a much more traditional clergyman and poet. He was a prolific writer of verse which appeared very regularly in *De Wachter*, the denominational weekly of the Christian Reformed Church, and in *De Hollandsche Amerikaan*, a newspaper published in Kalamazoo, Michigan. One volume of his poetry was *Uit Het Hart Tot Het Hart* (From Heart to Heart).[78] Some of his shorter poems are sharp and pointed, they are didactic and sometimes militant. In several poems the clergyman is obviously displeased with the parishioners, who do not appreciate sufficiently the minister whose work is never done. In the poem "Preeklezen" (Reading the Sermon), Hendriksen chides people who stay away from the services because the sermon is being read by an elder in the absence of the minister.[79]

The list of clergymen is long, and we shall have to limit our discussion to a few who are exceptional in one respect or another. The Rev. H. Van Der Werp wrote poetry, hymns, and stories. Ten hymns for which he also wrote the music appear in a collection entitled *De Kroon* (The Crown).[80] Like the Rev. Dijkstra, the Rev. Van Der Werp also translated American hymns into Dutch. Van Der Werp states in the preface to *Cardiphonia*, a collection of hymns, that he wrote and translated hymns in order to preserve the mother tongue, Dutch.[81] The young people liked American gospel hymns, and to preserve the Dutch language it was necessary to provide translations of selected hymns. Van Der Werp states that the purpose of the hymns is to sing praises to God, to edify, to admonish, and to console believers. He had a clear idea about the importance of song and music in the life of the congregation, and as a poet-pastor he sought to minister to the special needs of his immigrant flock. On a popular level, he wrote a collection of simple tales and poems,[82] translated from English the story about a newspaper boy,[83] and published a volume of poetry suitable for reading and recitation.[84] But one of his most interesting publications is a volume of poems and prayers for children, *De Kleine Samuel.*[85]

Another clergyman who deserves at least passing mention is the Rev. H. Van Hoogen, for he is the author of a most unusual poem: a New Year's sermon in verse! The sermon in rhyme is complete with text, introduction, three points, and an application, all the marks of the typical Calvinist sermon![86]

The clergy sought to inspire and lead in many areas. One of these was missions, at home and abroad. One periodical, the name of which changes over the years, is *De Heidenwereld.* Many poems are written by clergymen for this periodical. There are contributions by A. Zwemer, B. J. Bennink, and H. Beets, to mention only a few.[87]

One young Reformed clergyman was so bold as to write and publish a drama in verse: *Dominee Kouwenaar of Zedelijk Dualisme* (Rev. Kouwenaar or Moral Dualism).[88] The dramatic plot involves an orthodox minister who impregnates his sweetheart and then deserts her in order to marry another girl. He leaves the maiden he has seduced, and who will not betray him, the minister, to bear the shame and ignomy of becoming an illegitimate mother! The play ends on a tragic note, for the minister does not repent; thus, Christianity and the clergy do not come off very well in this drama. It must have been a shocker to a Christian community which revered the office of the ministry as the highest calling. Nor is it surprising that the Rev. H. Hoeksema decided to withdraw his youthful literary effort from the market once he was established in his own pulpit. There is no evidence that the Rev. Hoeksema ever again wrote verse, but he was one of the greatest orators the Reformed community produced, a preacher who could hold a large audience spellbound on most difficult theological subjects.

In contrast to the Dutch Reformed community, there was considerable emphasis in the Flemish community upon drama. In the *Gazette van Detroit* there are numerous advertisements for plays which are to be presented by the Belgian literary clubs of Detroit. The Flemish communities in Detroit and Moline were characterized by what is described as *verenigingsdrang*, the desire to meet socially in clubs. There apparently even were Flemish bars in Detroit as well as drama and music clubs.

The drama club *Moedertaal en Volksvermaak* (Mother Tongue and Popular Entertainment), formed in 1901, put on three plays a year in the Dutch language. In 1910, a second drama club, *'t Roosje bloeit in 't Wilde* (The Little Rose Blossoms in the Wild), was formed to stage plays. The first chairman, Henry Van Slembrouck, was himself the author of a number of plays: "De Sheriff," "De Bedrogen Grootmoeder" (The Fooled Grandmother), "De Laatste Oproep" (The Last Call), "De Bedelaar" (The Beggar), "Naarden, het Slachtoffer voor 't Vaderland" (Naarden, the Victim for the Fatherland), "Gestorven voor Vlaanderen" (Died for Flanders), and "De Straf Gods" (The Punishment of God).[89] In 1923 a record number of 1600 people attended one of these performances. Unfortunately, my efforts to secure copies of the Van Slembrouck plays have not been successful. According to my informant Father Charles Denys (pastor of Our Lady of Sorrows Church in Detroit, and present editor of the *Gazette van Detroit*), these plays are buried in a garret, of known origin, and it is hoped that they will be preserved. I am greatly indebted to Father Denys for providing me with information and materials on the Flemish speaking communities.

We must now return to and conclude our discussion of poetry by the clergy. The Rev. Geerhardus Vos, who taught theology at Princeton University, published several volumes of verse: *Spiegel der Genade* (Mirror of Grace),[90] *Spiegel der Natuur* (Mirror of Nature),[91] *Spiegel des doods* (Mirror of Death),[92] and *Zeis en Garve* (Scythe and Sheaf).[93] These poems, dealing with the broad themes of grace, nature, and death are among the finest poetic expressions of deeply experienced joy and sorrow, joy in sorrow, and sorrow in joy. The poem which appears on the frontis-piece of *Charis*, a volume of English poetry by Vos, may well set the tone for his Dutch poetry as well:

> There is no song that travelleth
> The highway between Life and Death
> But stops twixt night-fall and to-morrow
> At the old inns of Joy and Sorrow.[94]

The reader of the poems of G. Vos may be guided by still another poem, "Godspeed":

> Go, little book, whose leaves to me are glowing
> With light caught from uncharted sea and land;
> I could not let thee go except for knowing
> Thou goest from mine into a friendly hand,
> Which, sensitive, will touch and turn thy pages,
> Aware of pulses to its own akin;
> Grateful to music where it pain assuages,
> In love with music for the pain therein.[95]

One may also read a poem, "Praeludium" which appears in *Spiegel der Natuur*, and is written in Dutch:

> Schoon simpel hun gemoed, 't zijn toch mijn eigen zangen;
> Een lied is als een kind gezien door moederoog,
> Getroeteld in een droom van dat het werd ontvangen,
> En, trots de smartgeboort, een voorwerp van verlangen,
> Gesierd met eenigst schoon, wat feil het hebben moog.
> Ik had u even lief, zoet maatgespeel van klanken,
> Bleeft gij bij mij tehuis, gespeend aan prijs of praal;
> 'K hoef voor mijn zingensvreugd de waereld niet te danken;
> Muziek is mij uw stem, al spreekt gij kindertaal.[96]

Vos is a gifted writer whose poetry is suited to his subject. In four poems in which he probes the different characters of the prophets Amos, Hosea, Isaiah, and Jeremiah, Vos uses different poetic lines to suit the content of each poem.[97] There are many more poems from the pre-World War II period that might be cited, but the above works give a selection of some of the more prominent authors.

After World War II many Dutch emigrants left their native land for the United States and Canada, hoping to establish a new life after the agony of five years of war and occupation. The spectrum of people who came to America is now much broader; though it continues to include many persons of Reformed persuasion, there are also many others who are Roman Catholic, some agnostic, and a few of the remnant of Jews who lived through the holocaust of genocide.

The Dutch immigrants again soon had weekly papers in which they could keep contact with each other and with events in the homeland. *Calvinist Contact* and *The Windmill Herald*, both published in Canada, in the Dutch language, serve that need for many. In *Calvinist Contact* as well as in *De Wachter*, poems in the Dutch language continue to appear with some regularity. In *Calvinist Contact* I was struck by sensitive poems by E. Van Duyvendijk and Tini Van Ameyde. Cor Barendrecht and Cornelius Lambregtse are also contributors, the latter with some regularity. Two of Lambregtse's poems impressed me especially: "Ikabod" and "Terugblik" (Looking Back).[98] In them one finds again the old Reformed faith as the well spring of a life which is meaningful despite sorrow and tragedy. For Lambregtse that tragedy involves suffering not only from illness, but also from the loss of an infant son who has died. And of that he has written a novel *In Zijn Arm De Lammeren.*[99] The setting of the novel is the province of Zeeland, where the author grew up. The work concerns the life of a typical Zeeland family, of the rigorous orthodox Calvinist type, whose youngest son, a promising lad and gifted, becomes ill and dies but with complete assurance that he is saved (and elect) and that he is going to meet Jesus in Heaven. This book has become a best seller in the Netherlands, I presume within the religious community. One wonders how literary critics will in the future regard the novel. Another novel by Lambregtse, *Het Scharlaken Koord* (The Scarlet Cord), is about to come off the presses.

One can scarcely imagine a greater contrast with this novel, rooted in the faith of the fathers, than one finds in the writings of two Dutch Jewish authors who have made America their home: Margot H. de Hartog and Leo Vroman. The poetry of Margot H. de Hartog, one slender volume which was made available to me in typescript, reflects all the loss of a generation and a people who lost nearly everything during the war, and who live in a world in which there is no longer any God, or any hope of restitution; it is a world of the lonely self seeking to understand itself, and to make the most of life, which is such a baffling mystery. This sense of loss is poignantly expressed in a poem like "Moeder" (Mother), which recalls the death of her mother in the gas chamber. The feeling of loss and sorrow are also expressed in "De Kiem" (The Seed), but especially in "Er is een leed" (There is a Sorrow).[100] Seven of her poems were published in *Hollands Maandblad.*[101]

This same world forms the background for much of Leo Vroman's poetry and prose. Vroman senses deeply the ambiguities of life and death because he is both a scientist and a poet. As a biologist who works in a laboratory, he daily deals with the analysis of chemical reactions in the body so that the question repeatedly rises: what is man, and what is thinking and feeling really? Vroman is preoccupied with the problems of time and space, the relationship of past and present, of here and there, and the dynamic flux of change that marks all of life. His collected poetry was most recently published as *Leo Vroman: 262 Gedichten.*[102] One can hardly say that his post-war poetry primarily reflects the American experience, though that is true of isolated poems and of his prose works *Brieven uit Brooklyn*[103] and *Het Carnarium.*[104] Vroman repeatedly poses such questions as Who am I? What of the Past is Me? How do I relate to the world of things and people *about* me, or perhaps we should say, *in* me? Vroman's poetry reflects a very complex reality in which languages (Dutch and English) and images are distinct and yet strangely merged, and in which even the chance encounter with persons is at the same time perceived to be complex cellular and psychological states with known and unknown antecedents. Leo Vroman is without doubt the most complex and gifted Dutch American poet today. He possesses an extraordinary wit and often one has the uncomfortable feeling that he is playing games with the reader, whom he confronts so directly in his poetry. I refer the interested reader to such poems as: "Indian Summer," "Inleiding tot een leegte" (Introduction to a Void), "Amerika," "Hoe moet ik schrijven" (How must I write), "Een vers zonder titel" (A poem without a title), "Zelf-portret 1954" (Self-Portrait 1954), and "Hulp gevraagd" (Help Wanted). Perhaps it is appropriate to conclude with that poem:

> Een ding weet ik zeker:
> ik heb een grote neus,
> want als ik een nauwe beker
> wil leegdrinken moet ik heus
> helemaal achterover hellen.
>
> Maar of ik een engel ben, een genie,
> of een schurkje, of wel alle drie,
> dat zal jij me moeten vertellen.[105]

Freely translated, the poem might read:

> One thing I know for sure:
> I have a big nose,
> because when I want to empty
> a narrow glass I really have
> to lean way over backward.
>
> But whether I am an angel, a genius,
> or a little rogue, or possibly all three,
> that you will have to tell me.

I suspect that Vroman does combine something of the angel, the genius, and the rogue. And so our survey of the Netherlandic muse in the forests and plains of America ends in the biggest city with the greatest poet.

Calvin College

NOTES

[1] A valuable source of information on the Frisians in America is *Frisian News Items*, a bulletin issued by the Frisian Information Bureau, at Grand Rapids, Michigan since 1944, of which Dr. B. Fridsma is the editor. For information on literary contributions by Frisian Americans consult B. Fridsma, "De Literatuer fan Fryske Lânforhuzers yn Amearika," *De Tsjerne*, 5 (1950), 27-36. See also B. Fridsma, "Frysk Amerikaenske Skriuwers," *De Strikel*, 1 (October 1958), 134-35, on Meindert De Jong; (November 1958), pp. 150-51, on David De Jong; (December 1958), pp. 168-69, on Frederick F. Manfred; 3 (July 1960), 94-95, on Marten ten Hoor. For articles in the English language the reader is referred to B. Fridsma, "Frisian-American Writers," *Frisian News Items*, 14, (1958) on Henry Kay Pasma; 15 (January 1959), on David De Jong; 15 (February 1959), on Meindert De Jong; 15 (May 1959), on Frederick Feikema Manfred; 15 (June-July 1959), on Marten ten Hoor; 15 (November 1959), on Frederick ten Hoor; 16 (January 1960), on Henry Zylstra; 16 (March-April 1960), on Albert Hyma. Another article of interest is Marten ten Hoor, "Frisians in the United States," *Michigan Alumnus Quarterly Review*, 58, No. 10 (December 1951), 50-56.

[2] Arthur Verthé and Bernard Henry, *Vlaanderen in de Wereld* (Brussel: D.A.P. Reinaert Uitgaven, 1971-1972).

[3] Philemon D. Sabbe and Leon Buyse, *Belgians in America* (Tielt, Belgium and The Hague, Holland: Lannoo, n.d.).

[4] J. van Hinte, *Nederlanders in Amerika: een studie over landverhuizers en volkplanters in de 19e en 20ste eeuw in de Vereenigde Staten van Amerika*, 2 vols. (Groningen: P. Noordhoff, 1928).

[5] Henry S. Lucas, *Netherlanders in America: Dutch Immigration to the United States and Canada, 1789-1950* (Ann Arbor: The University of Michigan Press and Geoffrey Cumberledge, Oxford Univ. Press, London, 1955).

[6] Henry S. Lucas, *Dutch Immigrant Memoirs and Related Writings*, 2 vols. (Assen, Netherlands: Van Gorcum & Co., 1955).

[7] Bertus Harry Wabeke, *Dutch Emigration to North America, 1624-1860* (New York: The Netherlands Information Bureau, 1944).

[8] Gerald F. De Jong, *The Dutch in America, 1609-1974* (Boston: Twayne Publishers, 1975).

[9] Arnold Mulder, *Americans from Holland* (Philadelphia and New York: J. B. Lippincott, 1947).

[10] Henry C. Murphy, *Anthology of New Netherland or Translations from the Early Dutch Poets of New York with Memoirs of Their Lives* (New York: Bradford Club Series, No. 4, 1865). For an excellent discussion of the culture and poetry of New Netherland see Ellis L. Raesly, "The New Netherland Muse, in *Portrait of New Netherland* (New York: Columbia Univ. Press, 1945).

[11] Van Hinte, *Nederlanders in Amerika*, II, 497-510. See also Lucas, *Netherlanders in America*, pp. 606-14.

[12] Lucas, *Netherlanders in America*, p. 614.

[13] A. J. Barnouw, *The N. A. F. Letter*, No. 6 ([November 1955], New York: The Netherland-America Foundation).

[14] Lucas, *Netherlanders in America*, pp. 625-35.

[15] Henry Geerlings, "The Reformed Church Press," *Flowering Wilderness. Containing Twenty Articles by Various Authors in Commemoration of the Centennial Celebration of Reformed Churches in the West*, ed. Seth Vander Werf, et al. (Chicago: Synod of Chicago Reformed Church of America, 1947).

372

¹⁶ Lucas, "The Dutch-American Press," in *Netherlanders in America*, pp. 529-41.

¹⁷ Van Hinte, "De Pers," in *Nederlanders in Amerika*, II, 472-96.

¹⁸ Ibid., p. 473.

¹⁹ Harry Boonstra, "Dutch-American Newspapers and Periodicals in Michigan, 1850-1925," Masters Diss. University of Chicago, 1967, p. 48.

²⁰ Ibid., p. 4.

²¹ Dingman Versteeg, *De Pelgrim-Vaders van het Westen, Een Geschiedenis van de Worstelingen der Hollandsche Nederzettingen in Michigan, Benevens eene Schets van de Stichting der Kolonie Pella in Iowa* (Grand Rapids, Michigan: C. M. Loomis & Co., 1886).

²² Bastiaan Broere, *Korte Beschrijving van het Leven en de Wonderbare Leidingen Gods met Bastiaan Broere in Nederland en in Amerika. Met een inleiding van J.J.A. Ploos van Amstel*, ed. H. De Vries (Amsterdam: J. A. Wormser, 1887).

²³ For the story of Broere's interesting spiritual development see Lucas *Netherlanders in America*, pp. 504-06. According to Lucas the novel *Ik Worstel en Ontkom* (I Struggle and Escape), published by the Dutch novelist P. J. Risseuw in 1951, also "in large part concerns the character and activities of Bastiaan Broere, an oyster fisher of West Sayville, on Long Island," p. 634.

²⁴ C. Van Loo, A. La Huis, H. C. Keppel ed., *Historical Souvenir of the Celebration of the Sixtieth Anniversary of Colonization of the Hollanders in Western Michigan, Held in Zeeland, Michigan August 21, 1907* ([Zeeland, Michigan], 1908), pp. 88-91.

²⁵ A. Zwemer, *Hartestemming en Leering* (Grand Rapids, Michigan: Van Dort & Hugenholtz, 1887), pp. 179-83. Also cited in *Historical Souvenir*, pp. 108-09.

²⁶ Marian M. Schoolland, *De Kolonie, The Church That God Transplanted* (Grand Rapids, Michigan: Board of Publications of the Christian Reformed Church, 1973-1974). This is a story about a small branch of the Church Universal called the Christian Reformed Denomination. Note the designation *De Kolonie* in this most recent popular, but well written narrative history of the colonization.

²⁷ *Historical Souvenir*, pp. 16-17.

²⁸ A. Guikema, "1834—Op Het Honderd-jarig Gedachtenisfeest Der Afscheding—1934," *De Wachter*, 17 October 1934, pp. 644-45.

²⁹ T. Van der Ark, "Iets over mijn leven in Friesland," "Iets over mijn leven in Groningen," "Iets over mijn leven in Amerika," TS, pp. 109-14. One copy of this typescript is in Heritage Hall, Calvin College, Grand Rapids, Michigan. The three above poems were published, probably in *De Wachter*.

³⁰ Ibid., "Een andere classisbeurt" (Another Classical Assignment), pp. 44-47; "Een dubbele classisbeurt gedeeltelijk vervuld" (A Double Classical Appointment Partially Fulfilled), pp. 48-50.

³¹ *Jaarboekje voor de Hollandsch Christel. Geref. Kerk in Noord Amerika voor het jaar 1891* (Holland, Michigan: De Grondwet Boekdrukkerij, 1890), pp. 49-66.

³² Ibid., pp. 73-76.

³³ Verthé, pp. 430-40.

³⁴ Philemon Sabbe, *Beelden uit mijn Kinderjaren*, 2 vols. (Detroit: Gazette van Detroit, 1944).

³⁵ Ibid., II, 35-37.

³⁶ H. van Hoogen, "Het Huisijk—en Familieleven der Hollanders in Amerika," *De Gereformeerde Amerikaan*, May 1898, pp. 145-51.

³⁷ Henry Beets, "De Nederlandsche Stam en Taal in Noord Amerika," *De Gereformeerde Amerikaan*, August 1905, pp. 369-76; September 1905, pp. 409-14.

[38] Henry Beets, "Een stervende Taal," *De Gereformeerde Amerikaan*, July 1900, pp. 269-73.

[39] Henry Beets, *Abraham Lincoln: zijn tijd en leven* (Grand Rapids, Michigan: J. B. Hulst and B. Sevensma, 1909).

[40] Jacob H. Hoekstra, "The Prayer Meeting" (*Het biduur*) *Het Oosten*, 17 May 1934, p. 7.

[41] Jacob H. Hoekstra, "My First Auto Trip," *Het Oosten*, 24 May 1934, p. 7.

[42] Dirk Nieland, *Yankee-Dutch: Humoristische Schetsen uit het Hollandsch-Amerikaansch Volksleven, Geschikt om voor te dragen, in rijm en onrijm* (Grand Rapids, Michigan: Eerdmans-Sevensma Co., 1919).

[43] Ibid., pp. 126-34.

[44] W. B. Eerdmans, comp. *Mijn Recitatieboek: Ernst en Luim* (Grand Rapids, Michigan: Eerdmans-Sevensma, n.d.).

[45] Dirk Nieland, *'n fonnie bisnis. With 14 Pen Drawings by D. Lam; Preface by Frederick Ten Hoor; Vocabulary by Anna Nieland-De Boer* (Grand Rapids, Michigan: Wm. B. Eerdmans Publishing Co., [1929]).

[46] Frederick Ten Hoor, Preface to *'n fonnie bisnis*, p. xi.

[47] John Lieuwen, *Troebel on Fon. With 24 Pen Drawings by the Author* (Corsica, S. D.: The Corsica Globe Publishers, [1938]).

[48] John Lieuwen, *Sweat en Tears* (Holland, Michigan: Schreur Printing Co., 1947), pp. 11-12 and pp. 16-18.

[49] L. G. Van Loon, *Folktales in the Jersey-Dutch Dialect*, T. S. in Heritage Hall at Calvin College, Grand Rapids, Michigan.

[50] Ibid., pp. 20-29.

[51] Ibid., pp. 39-47.

[52] Lucas, p. 606.

[53] Boonstra, pp. 17-18.

[54] Sabbe, *Gazette van Detroit*, 24 May 1946.

[55] Ibid., 15 June 1945.

[56] Ibid., 28 June 1946.

[57] Ibid., 12 November 1943.

[58] Ibid., 20 April 1945.

[59] Ibid., 22 November 1946.

[60] Ibid., 19 April 1946.

[61] Ibid., 20 December 1946.

[62] B. D. Dijkstra, *Stichtelijke Liederen* (Orange City, Iowa: B. D. Dijkstra & Zoons, n.d.), p. 26.

[63] Ibid., p. 8.

[64] *De Volksvriend*, Orange City, Iowa, 17 November 1932.

[65] A. Zwemer, "De Eerste Vierde Juli-Dag, 1776," pp. 62-65 and "*De Vierde Juli, 1876*," p. 66-68 in *Hartestemming en Leering*.

[66] Ibid., pp. 69-70.

[67] Wybe J. Van Der Meer, *Yn 'E Frjemdte* (Ljouwert, Friesland: W. A. Eisma, 1929), p. 67.

[68] Ibid., p. 64.

[69] Ibid., p. 55.

[70] Wybe J. Van Der Meer, *De Swalker* (Ljouwert: W. A. Eisma, 1925), p. 55.

[71] *Yn 'E Frjemdte*, p. 63.

[72] *De Swalker*, p. 7.

[73] Ibid., p. 12.

[74] B. D. Dijkstra, *Korte Gedichten* (Orange City, Iowa: B. D. Dijkstra en Zoons, 1935).

[75] B. D. Dijkstra, *De Volksvriend*, 25 May 1933.

[76] Ibid., 1 July 1934. See also *Korte Gedichten*, p. 16.

[77] B. A. Hendriksen, *De Volksvriend*, 2 August 1934.

[78] Bernardus Antonius Hendriksen, *Uit Het Hart Tot Het Hart* (Kalamazoo, Mich.: Gebr. Hendrikson, 1916).

[79] Ibid., pp. 143-44.

[80] Wm. F. Peters, ed., *De Kroon: Liederenbundel Christelijke Liederen voor Zondagschool, Christelijke School en Huisgezin Verzameld door Wm. F. Peters met een Tiental Oorspronkelijke Liederen door Ds. H. Vanderwerp* (Chicago: Paul W. Wezeman, n.d.).

[81] H. Van Der Werp, *Cardiphonia: Geestelijke Liederen voor Christelijke Gezinnen en Vereenigingen* (Holland, Mich.: De Grondwet Drukkerij, 1894), p. 6.

[82] H. Van Der Werp, *Boeiend en Leerzaam: Verhalen voor School en Huis* (Holland, Mich.: H. Holkeboer, 1897).

[83] H. Van Der Werp, *Hannes de krantenjongen: Zijn Levensgeschiedenis, door Hemzelven verteld. Uit het Amerikaansch* (Holland, Mich.: H. Holkeboer, 1897).

[84] H. Van Der Werp, *Lentebloemen voor de Huiskamer en het Reciteervertrek* (Kampen, Netherlands: G. Ph. Zalsman, 1896).

[85] H. Van Der Werp, *De Kleine Samuel: Bede, Dank en Lof uit Kindermonden, Een Boekje voor het Christelijk Huisgezin*, 3rd ed. (Grand Rapids, Mich.: B. Sevensma, 1908).

[86] H. Van Hoogen, *Nieuwjaars-Preek: Uitgesproken op Zondagavond 1 Januari, 1905 in de Gemeente Prospect Park, New Jersey* (Holland, Mich.: H. Holkeboer, [1905]).

[87] The missionary monthly appears in new format as *De Heidenwereld* (The Pagan World) in November 1896.

[88] Herman Hoeksema, *Dominee Kouwenaar of Zedelijk Dualisme* (Grand Rapids, Mich.: Eerdmans-Sevensma Co., 1919).

[89] Verthé and Henry, *Vlaanderen in de Wereld*, pp. 370-73.

[90] Geerhardus Vos, *Spiegel der Genade* (Grand Rapids, Mich.: Eerdmans-Sevensma, 1922).

[91] Geerhardus Vos, *Spiegel der Natuur* (Princeton, N. J.: n.p., 1927).

[92] Geerhardus Vos, *Spiegel des Doods* (Grand Rapids, Michigan: Wm. B. Eerdmans, [1932]).

[93] Geerhardus Vos, *Zeis en Garve* (Santa Ana, California: n.p., 1934).

[94] Geerhardus Vos, *Charis: English Verses* (Princeton, N.J.: Princeton Univ. Press, 1931), p. ii.

[95] Ibid., p. vi.

[96] *Spiegel der Natur*, p. 9.

[97] "Quatuor Prophetae," *Spiegel der Genade*, pp. 13-46.

[98] Lanbregtse's poems have appeared in *De Wachter*.

[99] Cornelius Lambregtse, *In Zijn Arm De Lammeren* (Franeker, Netherlands: T. Wever, 1971).

[100] Margot Helene de Hartog, *Oor aan het hart*, TS. Heritage Hall, Calvin College, Grand Rapids, Michigan, n.p.

[101] Margot H. de Hartog, "Zeven Gedichten," *Hollands Maandblad* (October 1973), pp. 19-22.

[102] Leo Vroman, *262 Gedichten* (Amsterdam: Em. Querido, 1974).

[103] Leo Vroman, *Brieven uit Brooklyn* (Amsterdam: Em. Querido, 1975).

[104] Leo Vroman, *Het Carnarium* (Amsterdam: Em. Querido, 1973).

[105] *262 Gedichten*, p. 590.

Pressed Flowers and Still-Running Brooks: Norwegian-American Literature

Gerald Thorson

ABSTRACT

Norwegian-American literature had its beginnings in the 1870's. By the 1890's an impressive literary activity flourished in the immigrant communities of the Upper Midwest. Reaching its height in the 1920's, Norwegian-American literature had all but disappeared by 1940. Over two hundred novels were published; added to that were collections of short stories, dramas, volumes of poetry, travelogues, autobiographies, histories—plus the innumerable works in newspapers and literary magazines. The bulk of this literature was nostalgic or didactic (chiefly to promote temperance or religion); yet there was also a conscious attempt to record and interpret the immigrant experience. A dominant concern was the conflict of cultures faced by the immigrant, and especially interesting have been the changing attitudes toward Norway and America found in the literature. Written almost entirely in the Norwegian language for and about the immigrants, but influenced by literary developments on both sides of the Atlantic, Norwegian-American literature provides insights into the Norwegian immigrant experience. (GT)

> Take me to Norway, oh, dreams, on your way,
> Norway, the land of the silvery bay,
> Nestling up north on her saga-lit shore,
> Haunting and calling my heart as before.[1]

These lines, the first stanza of a poem by John A. Hofstead, did not appear in print until 1951, but they capture an attitude ingrained in much of the literature of the Norwegian immigrant to give it its special characteristic. For, as the author of Norwegian America's most popular poem, set to music and sung repeatedly down through the years, recognized, he could never forget old Norway; that bastion of the north would always remain his native land:

> Kan du glemme gamle Norge?
> Aldrig jeg det glemme kan!

375

> Disse stolte klippeborge
> Er og blir mit fødeland.[2]

This nostalgia for a place and a life left behind resulted in fiction and poetry on Norway, tributes to Norway's heroes, and references to the Vikings or Old Norse mythological characters. One of the earliest immigrant novelists, Bernt Askevold, for example, set three of his four novels in Norway: *Hun Ragnhild* (1876, Ragnhild); *Familien paa Skovsaet* (1888, The Family at Skovsett); and *I den gamles sted* (1893, In the Old Man's Place). The poetry of Wilhelm Pettersen and Theodore Reimestad, professors at Augsburg Seminary in the late nineteenth century and two most gifted poets, contained such titles as "Til Norge" (To Norway), "Norges Skjønhed" (Norway's Beauty), "Ole Bull," and "Hjem til Norge" (Home to Norway).[3] This nostalgia pervades Norwegian-American literature in more subtle ways than references to Norway or its history, however, for its consequences in the life of the immigrant led to those distinguishing features which set Norwegian-American literature apart from Norwegian literature, which it resembled in language and literary influence, and American literature, to which it was often similar in subject matter, setting, and event. Even the American-born children of the immigrants were not immune to the influence of that land across the ocean. Peer Strømme, born of Norwegian immigrants in Wisconsin, once remarked: ". . . I am more than an ordinary American–I am a Norwegian American."[4]

At the same time, the conscious literary artists among the Norwegian immigrants found both their inspiration and their subject matter in the American experience, and it was this experience that they sought to record and interpret. In addition to numerous poems which described the American scene or expressed the attraction of the new land, there were those narratives that attempted to faithfully record the immigrant experience. Ole Buslett, the Wisconsin author, gave poetic expression to the writers' intentions in his novel, *Sagastolen* (The Saga-Chair):

> No one is morally just in his writing
> Unless he is sure what he states is said truly;
> No one has claim to the rake of inditing
> Who has not first on the harvest looked duly.
> Parts widely scattered we fashion in mystery
> Faithful in all to the Truth in its greatness.
> Art let it be, or if not it is history,
> Planting the footprints of life with sedateness.[5]

In its realistic concern and its creative intent, Norwegian-American literature grew out of the experience of the Norwegian immigrants in America and was written primarily for and about the immigrants in the Norwegian language.

Important in the development of this literature were the Norwegian newspapers and publishing houses. *Skandinaven* and the John Anderson Publishing Company in Chicago were the most influential in the early years. Later publishing ventures, especially in the Upper Midwest, supported the literary endeavors of the immigrants by printing their fiction, poetry, and literary discussions as well as Norwegian literature and translations of English and American authors. These efforts of the editors to keep alive the literary traditions of the homeland reminded the immigrants that there were other Norwegians in America and that they shared a common heritage. They also perpetuated the Norwegian language and encouraged the kind of intellectual ferment and cultural awareness without which Rølvaag's *Giants in the Earth* would have been impossible.

In a period of less than seventy years Norwegian-American literature flourished. No comprehensive history of this literature has been written; there is no definitive bibliography.[6] During that time over two hundred novels were published; added to that are volumes of short stories, collections of poetry, dramas, and sub-literary genres—not to mention those works that found publication in newspapers and periodicals. When Ludwig Lima published an anthology of Norwegian-American poetry in 1903, he included the poems of forty-five different authors. Although the Norwegians very early established their own theaters and dramatic organizations, they tended to rely on the performance of Scandinavian dramas—at least, few plays seem to have been written by the immigrants themselves. No brief overview can encompass all aspects of this literary development. The intention here, therefore, is simply to suggest the range of this literature, name some of those who wrote, and indicate the dominant thematic concerns that emerge.

Although ballads, travelogues, promotional treatises, and, especially, lyrics appeared shortly after the first Norwegians set sail for the United States in 1825, the real beginnings came during the rise of local color literature in America in the 1870's. The major writers were acquainted with literary movements on both sides of the Atlantic, and their works often reflected definite literary influences—especially of Bjørnson and Ibsen, but also of such American writers as Twain, Emerson, and Longfellow.

Much of the early literature, however, came out of the tradition of religious piety among the immigrants. The first collection of poetry by an immigrant was Rasmus O. Reine's *En liten samling af psalmer og religiøse digte* (A Little Collection of Psalms and Religious Poems), published in 1871. The first two novels also originated in this tradition: in 1874 *For Hjemmet* published two novels by Nicolai Severin Hassel as serials. "Alf

Brage, eller skolelaereren i Minnesota" (Alf Brage, or the Schoolteacher in Minnesota) and "Redselsdagene: et norsk billede fra indianerkrigen i Minnesota" (Days of Terror: A Norwegian Picture from the Indian War in Minnesota) are both didactic religious tracts with excessive moralizing and lengthy digressions.[7] For example, at one point in the latter novel Uncle Karl, surveying the destruction that was done in New Ulm during the Indian War, remarks to his nephew Alf, protagonist of both novels, that New Ulm was, after all, settled by German agnostics who built a gymnasium instead of a church. He observes that few Norwegians lost their lives in the bloodbath. The reason, he concludes, is that they were true to God's Word and Luther's teachings. Yet even in their exaggerated piety and loose construction the novels of Hassel are significant, and not only because they were the first to be written. In finding literary materials in the life of the Norwegian immigrants in America, the author was a pioneer, opening the way for a more serious attempt to clothe the life of the Norwegian immigrant in artistic form. Furthermore, Hassel's novels contained essential characteristics of later fiction: a Midwest setting, a focus on Norwegian settlers, real-life situations, excessive moralizing, and concern for the problems of the immigrant in the new land.

This concern for the problems of the immigrant is reflected even more strongly in the literature which grew out of the temperance movement. In fact, throughout the whole history of Norwegian-American literature, no other issue received so much attention. Almost every work seemed to contain a section on the saloon, and the works advocating temperance included those of some of the best writers. The novelist Simon Johnson once stated that the temperance issue was *the* inspiration for Norwegian-American authors.[8] Hans Anderson Foss explained it this way in his novel, *Den amerikanske saloon* (The American Saloon):

> Proud was our Norsemen's fame
> More fair than theirs no name,
> Did not so many sink
> Into the vice of drink.[9]

Kristofer Janson, for whom the drunkenness of the Norwegian was a frequent subject in his fiction, stated: "The difference between an American and a Norwegian when they are drunk is that the American shamefully sneaks home the back way; but the Norwegian goes right down the middle of the street, shouting and yelling."[10] One of the earliest and most prolific writers to come out of the temperance movement was Ulrikka Feldtman Bruun, whose life and work spanned the entire history of Norwegian-American literature. Coming to Chicago in 1874, she established Hope Mission, Bethany Home for Girls, and Harmony Hall, published the temperance magazine, *Det hvide baand* (The White Band), and wrote poems, song books, and fiction as aids in her fight for temperance.[11]

The writers' focus on the life of the immigrant also resulted in journalistic exposés and didactic tracts. The innumerable works of Lars Stenholt, the Minneapolis author who dealt in diatribes and trash and was purported to be the only Norwegian-American author able to make a living from his pen,[12] included such diverse titles as *Norge i Amerika: Skildringer af Nordmaenenes Liv i Amerika* (1898, Norway in America: Pictures of the Life of the Norwegians in America); *Chicago anarkisterne* (1888, The Chicago Anarchists); *Falk og jødinden* (1901, Falk and the Jewess), a work about the popular Lutheran pastor in Minneapolis; *Paul O. Stensland og hans hjaelpere, eller milliontyvene i Chicago* (1906, Paul O. Stensland and His Associates, or the Millionaire Thieves in Chicago), a fictionalized account of a Norwegian-American banker who absconded with the bank's funds in 1906; *Paven i Madison, eller Rasmus Kvelves merkvaerdige liv og haendelser* (1908, The Pope in Madison, or Rasmus Kvelve's Remarkable Life and Doings), an attack on the University of Wisconsin professor, Rasmus B. Anderson; and *Minnesota bibelen* (1901, The Minnesota Bible).

Some of the early authors wrote for purely literary reasons. They wanted to tell a good story, to record and to interpret the immigrant experience. One of the earliest of these was Tellef Grundysen, who published *Fra begge sider af havet* (From Both Sides of the Ocean) in 1877. His novel, set in southeastern Minnesota and developing a tale of intrigue and crime in a Norwegian settlement, went through at least five editions.

During the 1870's two men played a special role in the development of a Norwegian-American literature as they attempted to promote their own accomplishments by instilling in the immigrants a consciousness of themselves as Norwegians and a pride in their Norwegian background. Capitalizing on the popularity Scandinavian writers were enjoying among Americans, Rasmus B. Anderson and Hjalmar Hjorth Boyesen published their own works, carried on a correspondence with each other, and attempted to inform both Americans and Norwegian Americans about the literature and mythology of Norway. They also encouraged the immigrants to write. Both men published works in 1874: Boyesen's *Gunnar*, which William Dean Howells had printed as a serial in *The Atlantic Monthly* the year before, was issued in book form; and Anderson's *America Not Discovered by Columbus* was published by S. C. Griggs of Chicago. Boyesen, who arrived in the United States in 1869, went on to become an American author, critic, and professor of Germanic languages at Cornell and Columbia. Anderson, born in Wisconsin and educated at Luther College, later became professor of Scandinavian languages at the University of Wisconsin, United States Minister to Denmark, and a newspaper editor. In his writings for *Skandinaven* in the 1870's and later, Anderson supported those who attempted to write the story of the immigrant.[13] Thus many budding poets turned to him for help in getting their work published.

When Nils Kolkin wrote *Winona*, an epic poem based on Native American legends and imitative of Longfellow, he sent the manuscript to Anderson.[14] "I want to be a poet," Ole Buslett wrote to Anderson in 1884. Anderson encouraged him, and he went on to become one of Norwegian America's most dedicated authors.[15]

During the last two decades of the nineteenth century, the period which saw the largest number of Norwegians coming to the United States, several immigrants began writing and publishing their reactions to the New World. Most popular were a novel that captured the immigrant's dream of success in his American adventure and a slapstick comedy of a Wisconsin immigrant woman's trip to Chicago. Hans Anderson Foss's *Husmandsgutten* (The Cotter's Son), first published as a serial in *Decorah-Posten* in 1884-1885, went through at least ten editions and was translated into *Nynorsk* as late as 1950. In the novel Foss brought a poor but intelligent Norwegian cotter boy to America to seek the fortune that would allow him to return to Norway to win the hand of the landowner's daughter. In Illinois and Wisconsin Ole Haugen acquires wealth by working on a farm and speculating in land. Later, in Chicago, he finds the means to an even larger fortune: warned by a friend of the impending closing of the bank in which he has deposited his money, Ole withdraws his money, invests in real estate, then "Clipper" stock, and builds what eventually becomes the "leading drygoods and grocery store" in Chicago. A short time later Ole sells his store and returns to Norway "with the best of wishes, a great deal of money, and a trunkful of American curios . . . ." In Norway everyone acknowledges that "he looked more like a well-to-do merchant than the cotter's son that they used to know." He arrives in time to claim the girl of his dreams so that he can live happily ever after in a large white house on the Norwegian mountain side.[16]

In *Farmerkonen Marit Kjølseths erfaringer i Chicago* (1887, Farmer Wife Marit Kjølseth's Adventures in Chicago), Alan Saetre brought Marit from the farm in Wisconsin to Chicago, where she had a number of ludicrous encounters with strange city life before returning to the farm in Wisconsin, apparently none the worse and none the better for her experience. What Saetre captured in the novel, if its twenty-four editions are any indication, is the bewilderment and the discomfort which the immigrant felt in the new world. Neither of these popular works is great literature, but each manages to capture familiar experiences and dreams, and to this the immigrant responded.

The life of the immigrant fared better, however, in the writings of five persons who began publishing in this period. Three of them—Hans Anderson Foss, Ole Amundson Buslett, and Peer Strømme—continued writing in the twentieth century. The other two, Kristofer Janson and his wife

Drude, returned to Norway in 1893. All five were primarily writers of fiction, though Buslett, Janson, and Strømme also published poetry and Buslett tried his hand at drama. All, to some degree, produced works of social protest, aiming their satire at the immigrant and American society.

Foss, who edited various newspapers in North Dakota and Minnesota before becoming a grain inspector for the state of Minnesota, used his fiction as platforms for his two main interests: prohibition and the Populist party. Among his novels, in addition to his early success, *Husmandsgutten*, were *Livet i Vesterheimen* (1885, Life in the Western Home), *Kristine* (1886), *Den amerikanske saloon* (1889, The American Saloon), *Hvide slaver* (1892, White Slaves), and *Valborg* (1927). All, marred as they are by Foss's didacticism and manipulation of event, suffer as works of literature; but they nevertheless manage in their awkwardness to detail several features of the life and mind of the Norwegian immigrant.

A more gifted writer was Ole Buslett, who arrived in Wisconsin in 1868 at the age of thirteen. At one time postmaster, justice of the peace, and town clerk in Waupaca County, he edited various newspapers and served one year in the state legislature. A prolific but never very popular writer, Butlett aimed to free the immigrant from his inferiority complex, his "cotter's spirit." Faulting the immigrant for his narrow-mindedness, his materialism, and his desire to masquerade as an American rather than as a Norwegian, Buslett wanted his poetry and fiction to awaken the immigrants to the beauty of the spirit and to a promising future. Although he wrote realistic narratives, his most interesting works were his dream sagas and fables, in which he made extensive use of symbol and allegory. *Sagastolen* (1908, The Saga-Chair), *Glans-om-Sol og hans folks historie* (1912, The Gold King and the Story of His People), *Veien til Golden Gate* (1915, The Way to the Golden Gate), *Fra min ungdoms nabolag* (1918, From My Childhood's Neighborhood), and *Benediktus og Jacobus* (1920, Benedict and Jacob) remain his most significant works.

Kristofer Janson, one of the leading authors in Norway in the 1870's (along with Ibsen, Bjørnson, and Lie, he had received a stipend from the government in 1876), arrived in Minneapolis in 1881 to establish Unitarian congregations among the Scandinavians. In Minneapolis he continued his writing, chiefly fiction dealing with the rural immigrants in the Upper Midwest. Imbued with a strong humanistic philosophy, Janson's optimistic and idealistic view of life prompted him to use his fiction as a platform for his ideas and social criticism. In *Praeriens saga* (1885, The Saga of the Prairie), *Et arbeidsdyr* (1889, A Beast of Burden), and *Fra begge sider havet* (1890, From Both Sides of the Ocean), he attacked the narrow-mindedness of the immigrants, their drunkenness, and the servile position they gave to women; he also criticized the intolerance of the Lutheran clergy, which he found responsible for both the drunkenness of the immigrant and the condition of the immigrant woman. A more complimentary picture of the immigrant is found in *Femtende Wisconsin* (1887, The Fifteenth Wisconsin), a fictional account of the Norwegian-American volunteer regiment in the Civil War, and *Vildrose* (1887, Wild Rose), which recounted the experiences of Norwegian immigrants in the uprising of the Native Americans in southwestern Minnesota in 1862.

In his last two novels, reflecting his growing disenchantment with American life, Janson broadened his scope to attack American society, especially for its treatment of workers, women, and immigrants. *Bag gardinet* (1889, Behind the Curtain), set in Minneapolis in the 1880's, satirizes American culture and attempts to disclose the evils "which are concealed under the disguise of the newly-rich."[17] The *nouveaux riches* in *Bag gardinet* are the Plummers, whose home on South Seventh Street is over-elaborate and gaudy, with cheap, always large, copies of famous paintings on the walls. Attending an exhibit of foreign art in the city, the Plummers are dismayed: " 'They perhaps don't realize that in America we can get larger paintings for five dollars,' " says Mrs. Plummer. " 'But then industry has a much higher position here' " (p. 156). " 'We old-fashioned Yankees aren't too much occupied with culture,' " says Mr. Plummer. " 'What do we want with culture here in the West? That's merely for show and nonsense and a waste of money and only makes life bitter and tiresome for others' " (pp. 56-57).

The most cultured person in the Plummer household is Agnes Pryts, the Norwegian servant girl, who has had a good education in Norway and has become a talented musician. During the course of the novel she becomes known in the community as a musician and is constantly sought after by Americans who want her to give piano lessons to their children. This allows her to leave her position in the Plummer household, but she has been there long enough for young Frank Plummer to be attracted to her and to seek her hand in marriage. It is in this episode that Janson most delightfully presents one of his issues, the place of the Scandinavian immigrant in Minneapolis in the 1880's.

Mrs. Plummer opposes her son's wishes to marry Agnes, and when he asks her if Scandinavians aren't as good as other people, she replies: " 'Do you think so? Don't we see them coming to town in boxcars and crowding the depots so honest people can hardly get in? Their clothes smell as if they have been kept in their food chests, and they always have dirty children hanging on them. They're the ones who clean the streets, work in the sewers, and do all the common labor; they're the ones who fill the saloons and houses of prostitution. And such people you want to drag into the Plummer house?' " (p. 97).

Mrs. Plummer then goes over to see Mrs. Pryts, Agnes' mother, to make sure that Agnes will not marry her son. On the wall of the Pryts living room Mrs. Plummer sees a picture of Raphael's Madonna.

> "Is that one of your relatives, Mrs. Pryts?"
> Mrs. Pryts couldn't keep from smiling a little as she answered,
> "No, that is, of course, the Madonna."
> "Madonna—Mrs. Madonna? Does she live in Minneapolis?"
> "No, that is the Virgin Mary with the Christ Child."
> "Well, she ought to have put some clothes on him. Do you think
> it is based on reality, Mrs. Pryts?"
> "No, that is the artist's own imagination," Mrs. Pryts answered,
> barely able to keep from laughing. (pp. 98-99)

Mrs. Plummer then says that the Prytses have it very comfortable in their home, that they probably weren't used to such comfort in Norway. Mrs. Pryts disagrees.

> "Well, but I seem to remember that people in your part of the
> world lived in small sod huts, isn't that so?"
> "People tell so many lies about foreigners, Mrs. Plummer."
> "Then you have real glass in your windows and regular houses?
> I had always pictured Norway as a horrible country, full of ice
> and mountains and bears," said Mrs. Plummer. (p. 99)

Mrs. Plummer then brings up the subject of Frank and Agnes. She doesn't want a misalliance, she says.

> "I am entirely in agreement with you, Mrs. Plummer," answered Mrs. Pryts
> quietly, "and I believe you can have confidence in Agnes. Her education has
> made her superior to your son both in knowledge and in culture, and I do not
> believe marriages are happy when the wife is superior."
> Mrs. Plummer sat very much amazed. That was just the opposite of what
> she had meant. (p. 100)

Janson also satirizes American hypocrisy. At one point in the novel young Frank Plummer escorts what is assumed to be an authentic French count around the city (it is actually the real count's valet):

> The count and Frank walked over to Washington Avenue. The lights in the
> splendid shops had long since been extinguished. Only a single flame was lit, so
> the patrolman could see if anyone was inside who wanted to lay his hands on
> his neighbor's property. The streets were almost empty; it wasn't like Paris,
> where the rumble of carriages and throngs of people plague a person at night
> as much as in the day; where happy young people sit with their coffee or ice
> cream or glass of wine outside the cafes; and where you can hear laughter and
> music and the shouting of waiters at a time when all honorable Yankees have
> long since pulled their nightcaps over their ears and are dreaming about grain
> speculations and the stock market, while their better halves still see before
> their half-closed eyes the beautiful new set of jewels displayed that day at
> Eliot's.
> Minneapolis gives the impression of being a respectable city, a Puritan city,
> even at night. No fluttering women assailing you with their questions; no

chattering young men on the sidewalks discussing the theater or politics; at the most only a couple of sluts, who can pass by you on a dark street, throw a sandbag at your head, and rob you of your watch and money—if you have any.

But the respectability is still not so great as it appears to be. There is something which is called "behind the curtains"—and there is much in Minneapolis that goes on behind the curtains. The newspapers report that such and such an evil is stamped out, but it really has only been moved—behind the curtains. And the city lifts high its pretty, moral face for all to see, just as moral as an American Sunday—but no one talks about what goes on—behind the curtains. (p. 65)

Janson's final novel, *Sara* (1891), attacks both the Norwegian community and the American society for intolerance, an interest in profits rather than in human lives, and a concept of values that relegates women to an inferior position. Running away from her clergyman husband in Wisconsin to Chicago, the heroine discovers that a penniless immigrant woman is easy prey for the capitalists. Only two avenues are open to her: to become a work animal or a prostitute. Sara experiences the former but is spared any consideration of the latter when she is rescued by a wealthy American woman. In this American home she is allowed to educate herself, largely through her reading of contemporary Scandinavian literature and her contacts with contemporary Norwegian artists, and to discover meaning and purpose in her life. Her later attempt to return to the Wisconsin immigrant community to educate the Norwegians is a failure, however. " 'The Norwegian people choose to sleep—so let them sleep soundly,' " she concludes.[18] The disillusionment is also Janson's. Two years after this novel appeared he left Minneapolis for a "temporary absence in Norway."[19] He did not return. In his American fiction, though, Janson responded with vigor to the American scene, revealing a sensitive concern for individuals and a singular grasp of the American condition.

Janson's wife, Drude, also wrote fiction while in Minneapolis. *En saloonkeepers datter* (1887, A Saloonkeeper's Daughter), takes young Astrid Holm from Oslo to Cedar Avenue in Minneapolis, where her father runs a saloon. The ruling passion in Astrid's life is to become an actress. From early childhood, when she sees a famous Swedish actress on the stage and learns that her mother, too, had been an actress, until the day she becomes a Unitarian preacher in the Midwest—a type of actress—Astrid dreams of nothing else. Around this conflict in Astrid's life—that between the dream and reality, the stage and the saloon—the strands of her life experiences are woven. Interestingly enough, escape from her life as a saloonkeeper's daughter in the United States comes through the real presence of all that modern Europe stands for in the memory of Drude Krog Janson—the stimulating, refreshing involvement in the world of ideas embodied in Bjørnstjerne Bjørnson, whom Astrid meets in Minneapolis when

Bjørnson is on his lecture tour of the Midwest in 1880-1881. It is he who advises her to become a liberal preacher. Every woman, he says, has a double duty in life: " 'to raise her own position and then to help the thousands of other women to arise.' "[20] Mrs. Janson's second novel, *Ensomhed* (1888, Loneliness), inferior to her first novel, detailed the life of an immigrant woman in rural Minnesota. Her final work, published in 1897 after her separation from her husband and her return to Europe, was a fictional autobiography called *Mira*.

Least polemical of all the immigrants who began writing in the nineteenth century was Peer Strømme. Born of Norwegian parents in Wisconsin in 1856 and educated at Luther College and Concordia Theological Seminary, he went on to become one of Norwegian America's best known personalities. As a clergyman, editor, campaign speaker for the Democratic party, world traveler, and humorist, Strømme traveled in both Norwegian and American circles. He published poetry, short stories, novels, and essays, and he translated innumerable works from Norwegian into English or English and German into Norwegian. His best-known novel, *Hvorledes Halvor blev prest* (1893, How Halvor Became a Minister), is a largely autobiographical account of growing up in a Norwegian community in Wisconsin and life at Luther College. *Unge Helgeson* (1906, Young Helgeson) continues the adventures of Halvor as a pastor among the Norwegians in the Red River Valley. While *Halvor* is limited almost entirely to the Norwegian-American community, *Unge Helgeson* shows more of the encroaching American influences in the life of the Norwegian pioneer. There are several American characters in the novel, and we get more of the Norwegian settler's entrance into American life, especially his participation in politics. For satirical comment Strømme singles out a newspaper editor, politicians, and a student pastor from Augsburg Seminary in Minneapolis. In the final chapter of the novel, Pastor Helgeson visits Norway, where people are constantly amazed that he can speak Norwegian. He explains that in America there is also a Norway, with good Norwegian schools and Norwegian teachers from Norway. There are even many people born in America, he says, who use no speech but their parents' Norwegian dialect. But "that this could be true, people in Norway seemed to have difficulty in believing."[21]

In his final novel, *Den vonde ivold* (1910, In the Clutches of the Devil), Strømme drew upon his experiences as an editor in Chicago and his familiarity with the novel of decadence in Norway. Strømme takes his protagonist, Halvdan Moe, and Nils Holmsen, two dissolute students in Oslo, to Chicago, where they proceed on an ever downward trek as they find odd jobs translating for a Norwegian publishing house and reporting for Norwegian and English newspapers and become addicted to poker and alcohol.

Three years later (1896) Nils has committed suicide and Halvdan writes his memoirs while awaiting death in the sanitarium at Dunning. Interesting both for its psychological realism and its depiction of life at the fringes of society *Den vonde ivold* is an unusual literary achievement.[22]

By the time Strømme's novel was published the number of second-generation Norwegians had already surpassed the number of foreign-born immigrants, and new inroads were being made into the Norwegian-American communities. The need for maintaining a Norwegian culture dominated the literature that followed. Then came World War I and its aftermath, which stirred up antagonisms toward foreign-speaking immigrants. On the one hand were those immigrants who saw their future in America apart from the Norwegian-American community; on the other hand were those who worked for the retention of immigrant culture and traditions in the United States. The latter group's response was not simply a negation of the American melting-pot hysteria. Earlier in the century positive forces were already at work in Norway and in the United States which fostered a renewed Norwegian patriotism among the immigrants. In 1905 Norway received complete independence from Sweden and selected its own king, a prince from the royal family of Denmark. In 1914 Norway celebrated the one hundredth anniversary of its independence from Denmark. Both events were heralded in the Norwegian-American press and brought numerous immigrants back to Norway to share in the festivities. A new relationship developed between the immigrant and his homeland. National societies, such as the Norwegian Society of America, formed in 1903, promoted the preservation of the language, history, and traditions of Norway. Literary magazines were established, such as *Symra, Vor Tid*, and *Eidsvold*. All tended to stimulate thought and discussion of Norway and the retention of Norwegian culture in the United States. The twentieth century also witnessed a new development in the literature of the immigrant which, with a marked display of literary power, culminated in some of its most significant works in the 1920's, a decade that saw a renewed interest in American regional literature.

Among the several authors who are prominent in the twentieth century, mention can be made of only a few. One of the most prolific was Waldemar Ager, novelist, short story writer, poet, editor, and temperance speaker from Eau Claire, Wisconsin. Arriving in Chicago in 1885 at the age of sixteen, Ager learned the printer's trade before moving on to Eau Claire, where in 1903 he became editor of *Reform*, a temperance newspaper. A humorist, often sentimental in his fiction, Ager developed realistic yet satiric narratives of the immigrant. In such works as *Fortaellinger for Eyvind* (1906, Stories for Eyvind), *Kristus for Pilatus* (1910, Christ before Pilate), *Paa veien til smeltepotten* (1917, On the Way to the Melting Pot),

Gamlelandets sønner (1926, Sons of the Old Country) and *Hundeøine* (1929, Dog Eyes), he displayed distinct artistic talent.

Julius Baumann, who worked as a lumberjack when he first arrived in the United States in 1891, published some of the finest immigrant poetry. In *Digte* (1909, Poems) and *Fra vidderne* (1915, From the Wide Open Spaces), he gave full lyrical expression to his deeply felt emotions, for as Waldemar Ager has noted, Baumann "knows how to select word and image to express precisely what he himself feels."[23] Agnes Wergeland, related to Norway's famous poet Henrik Wergeland and the first Norwegian woman to receive a Ph.D., was also a poet of talent, though she was little read by the immigrants in her day. For several years a professor of history at the University of Wyoming, Miss Wergeland did not publish her first book, *Amerika og andre digte* (America and Other Poems), until two years before her death in 1914. A second volume was published posthumously.

Simon Johnson, who arrived in the Dakota territory in 1882 at the age of eight, was associated in his lifetime with two newspapers: *Normanden* in Grand Forks and *Decorah-Posten* in Iowa. A spokesman for prohibition and Norwegian culture, he used his fiction on the lives of the Dakota settlers to promote both causes. Johnson revealed his interest in individualists in *Et geni* (1907, A Genius), and *Lonea* (1909). A better novel, *I et nyt rige* (1914, In a New Kingdom), is essentially a lamentation for the passing of the frontier community on the stark and lonely Dakota prairies. In 1922 Johnson related the downfall of a wealthy Norwegian farmer in *Fallitten paa Braastad* (The Braastad Bankruptcy). *Frihetens hjem* (1925, The Home of the Free), showed the devastating effects of World War I upon that same family.

Another editor who wrote novels was Johannes B. Wist, editor of *Decorah-Posten* from 1901 until his death in 1923. In a humorous trilogy he brought the young Norwegian immigrant from the streets of Minneapolis to western Minnesota, where he founded his own town. In *Nykommerbilleder* (1920, Immigrant Scenes), *Hjemmet paa praerien* (1921, Home on the Prairie) and *Jonasville* (1922), he satirized the immigrant's attempts at Americanization and presented a devastating account of small-town life in the Red River Valley.

Most evasive of all the Norwegian-American writers was the farmer-poet Jon Norstog, who on the prairies of North Dakota wrote lyrics, epics, dramas, and novels—over twenty volumes in all. Norstog wrote his work in his native Telemark dialect. Few people bothered, or were able, to read his work. Most of his titles bore Biblical names, such as *Moses*, *Israel*, *Exodus*. *Moses*, a five-act drama, was 531 pages long, and *Israel*, a twelve-act drama, ran to 885 pages. In addition, Norstog's verse was obscure, for he worked primarily in symbol and allegory. He solved the need to interest a publisher in his works by doing his own typesetting, printing, and binding. A puzzle on the prairie, he may also have been a literary genius. Reflecting the neo-romanticism of Norwegian literature in the 1890's, Norstog developed such themes as the search for a father and the conflict of the artist and society as he probed the universal themes related to the immigrant experience.

Best known of all Norwegian-American writers beyond the Norwegian-American community was Ole Rølvaag, who arrived in South Dakota in 1896 at the age of twenty. Graduating from St. Olaf College in 1905, he spent a year in graduate study at the University of Oslo before joining the St. Olaf faculty in the department of Norwegian. In his twenty-five years there he published eight novels, poetry, short stories, essays, and textbooks for his classes in Norwegian and carried on a voluminous correspondence to promote the college and the retention of Norwegian culture among the immigrants. He played an influential role in the Norwegian Society of America and, in 1925, in the establishment of the Norwegian-American Historical Association. This interest in Norwegian culture permeates all his fiction, including *Giants in the Earth*, and allows him to detail the depth and the complexity of the immigrant experience. From *Amerika-breve* (1912, America-Letters), to *Den signede dag* (1931, That Blessed Day; translated into English as *Their Fathers' God*), Rølvaag, with the touch of the artist, depicted the central paradox inherent in immigrant life. In his tragic vision he

> . . . saw the drama of the soul compressed
> To finite spheres, forgotten on the path
> Toward new beginnings, yet another birth.[24]

It is precisely this concern, the retention of Norwegian culture in America, that unites all these writers of the twentieth century. Ole Buslett put it in the form of an allegory in *Veien til Golden Gate*, where all Americans are recast in the Yankee Swamp as they journey from Castle Garden to the Golden Gate. The quickest route to the new Utopia, that through the Yankee Swamp, the American wasteland, also proves to be the most destructive. Those who instead build on the edge of the swamp are able to retain their native traditions, the sole possession they can bring with them to the Golden Gate. American culture, Buslett suggests, will be achieved not through a melting-pot destruction of all foreign cultures but through the preservation and gradual assimilation of all cultures. By continuing their own traditions, the Norwegian immigrants will be able to effect a deeper, more significant, culture in America.[25]

Simon Johnson argued for the same thing on a more realistic level in *Fallitten paa Braastad* and *Frihetens hjem*. These novels about the downfall of a wealthy Norwegian farmer on the Dakota prairies show the effects of World War I on the family and the results of neglect of their heritage. They built their fortresses without the resources of Norwegian culture; they forgot what is most needed: "A little good old Norwegian Viking spirit." Johnson argues that the law that allows the English immigrants to draw on their heritage must also allow all immigrants to maintain their own traditions.[26]

Waldemar Ager wanted a "fencing in" period, where both Norwegian and American influences would be shut out and a peculiarly Norwegian-American culture would be created. This culture would find its expression, he said, in the Norwegian language and would have its own literature, music, and fine arts. It would then be able to bequeath a valuable legacy to the future of the United States.[27]

This concern is perhaps most concisely stated in the words of the pastor in Rølvaag's *Den signede dag:* " '*A people that has lost its traditions is doomed!*' "He tells Peder Holm: " '. . . we must nor forget that all through the nineteenth century we have followed the crowd; we were not the leaders; it wasn't our people that blazed the trail. . . . we are ashamed of the age-old speech of our forefathers. And we find it embarrassing to admit our Norwegian ancestry. Such an attitude can never, I tell you, *never* build a nation. Like dead timber we go into the building. We may harm, but we cannot be of much help.' "[28]

Rølvaag's insistence on the retention of language and culture gives focus to his tragic vision of the immigrant life. He gave expression to it in his very first novel, *Amerika-breve.* There the young immigrant writes a letter home to his brother in Norway, relating a Fourth of July speech he had just heard:

> "When we severed our ties with our Fatherland, we became not only strangers among strangers, but we were cut off from our own nation and became strangers to our own people. Our pulse no longer throbs in rhythm with the hearts of our own kindred. We have become strangers; strangers to those we left, and strangers to those we came to. The Fatherland to which we had centuries of inherited rights, we have given away, and we of the first generation can never get another. Let me repeat: We have become outsiders to the people we left, and we are also outsiders among the people to whom we came. . . . In short, we have become rootless. . . . We are alienated. . . . Herein lies the tragedy of emigration. If you give up your Fatherland for good, it can never be regained; neither can you get another in its place, no matter what you do."[29]

It is this view of life, so poignantly expressed by Rølvaag, that informs and characterizes the whole body of Norwegian-American literature, written as it is against the backdrop of cultural and spiritual loss. Various writers responded to this loss in various ways. Yet behind all their expressions stands that terrible chasm that the immigrant crossed when he sought to build his new home, his new Utopia, in the promising gardens of the

New World. The dominant image, capturing so clearly the early immigrant's hopes, in the two early immigrant success stories of Buslett and Foss has changed.[30] No longer is it the large house high on the mountain side of Norway to which the immigrant returns to live out his life. Those twentieth-century works depicting success find that goal in the United States, and, as in M. Falk Gjertsen's *Harold Hegg* (1914), it is often found in political office and attained in large part by a second-generation protagonist who has not neglected the values of his Norwegian heritage.[31] On the other hand, as one surveys the images that remain in the numerous narratives that the immigrant wrote about the first-generation immigrant, he finds them invariably depicting loss.

There is the clenched fist of the immigrant farmer's wife rising from the scum of the pond in southwestern Minnesota, where she has just drowned herself.[32] There is the frozen corpse of Daniel Nielsen dangling by a rope on the front porch of the wealthy American in south Minneapolis.[33] There is the solitary immigrant writing his memoirs in the death cell in the sanitarium, a victim of the Chicago labyrinth.[34] There is Lars, the immigrant who wants to be a respected businessman, sitting on his front steps, reading the *Decorah-Posten* with the *Daily Chronicle* outside of it so that passers-by would think he was reading an American newspaper.[35] There is Christian Pederson, sitting alone in his small shack on the wind-swept plains of North Dakota and writing his memoirs of the fiasco he made of life in Chicago.[36] There is Jonas Olson, who went from common laborer in south Minneapolis to grocer to town matador in a town in the Red River Valley that bore his name, sitting alone, his children gone, realizing that "though a person was duty bound to be an American, he still did not actually have permission to be one"—shunned by the very people and culture he spent his life emulating, forever an outsider.[37] And then there is Nils Vaag, Rølvaag's lost soul in *The Boat of Longing*, standing on the busiest corner of a nameless town, "searching, like a lone gull perched watchful on some bold headland round which the ocean current runs swift"—adrift in the New World.[38]

These are the overpowering images of this literature. There were individual victories, certainly, just as there were losses. But the lives depicted were inevitably lived in the midst of conflict and change. And yet there is another image, and in its ambivalence, in the central paradox that is there, lies the key to this literature. For there is that final scene in Rølvaag's *Giants in the Earth* when the body of Per Hansa is discovered by the haystack: ". . . His face was ashen and drawn. His eyes were set toward the west."[39] There is death, certainly, but there is also an indication of hope. And this coincides with the basic irony in the discovery of death in spring. The ambiguities of the immigrant experience, the romance and the tragedy of a transplanted life, the loss and the future promise—these are, after all, at the essence of life. This the Norwegian immigrant author recognized.

Norwegian-American literature, both an aspect and an instrument of Norwegian-American culture, recorded and interpreted the immigrant experience. Since both the community in which these works found their existence and the language in which they were written were constantly being eroded, Norwegian-American literature frequently reflected a sense of urgency, almost desperation, in its unfolding drama. "No one knows what a magnificent cultural achievement Norwegian-American literature is," wrote Sigurd Folkestad, "until he has himself lived on the Western prairies and felt the language imperceptibly withering away in a new natural setting, a new social environment, under the pressure of a strange cultural and linguistic world, and without a constant cultural interchange with Norway."[40] Sigrid Undset, the Norwegian novelist, recognized this. After her visits to Norwegian-American communities in the Midwest in the early 1940's, she wrote: "The attempts to keep up Norwegian customs in America resulted in something reminiscent of pressed flowers in an album. Recent arrivals from Norway are frequently reminded in a strange way of the world of their grandparents when they attend social functions among Norwegian Americans or read American newspapers in the Norwegian language."[41]

A reading of Norwegian-American literature produces the same response: it is as though we are looking through an album of pressed flowers. And yet there are also those works that run deeper, arresting for us those still-running brooks that flowed through the years on the prairies of the Dakotas or in the streets of Chicago and Minneapolis. They reveal a group unique—a part of, yet apart from, the American society in which they found their homes. And the reason for that can be underscored by quoting the final stanza of Franklin Petersen's poem "Leif Erikson":

> Oh, we Norsemen are proud that today we can stand
> On Leif Erikson's shores and be free,
> With a song on our lips and a flag in our hand
> Sending memories over the sea
> Because we are reminded of sagas of old
> And are proud of the land we forsook.
> Can it be that the blood of the Vikings has flowed
> In our veins like a still-running brook?[42]

In 1900 Waldemar Ager wrote to his fellow novelist, Ole Buslett, that people waited to write letters only about what was wrong with their books, and all they found to comment on, he said, were the anglicisms present. "Still there is a field for us," he continued. If in the future the Norwegian population would be swallowed up by the rest of the country, he wrote, then their literary attempts would be the best witness to the culture of the Norwegian Americans. When people start to look for the culture of the Norwegian Americans, he said, "the literature will become the measuring stick because it is art and history at the same time."[43] In that evaluation, as this brief study attempts to indicate, both pressed flowers and still-running brooks can yield their special insights into the immigrant experience.

St. Olaf College

NOTES

[1] John A. Hofstead, "Take Me to Norway," *Nordmanns forbundet*, 44 (1951), 137.

[2] See " 'Kan du glemme?': Gjennom det siste aarhundre er det skrevet flere 'norsk-amerikanske nasjonalsanger,' " *Nordmanns forbundet*, 64 (1971), 251-52.

[3] See *Norsk-amerikanske digte i udvalg*, ed. Ludvig Lima (Minneapolis: Ungdommens Ven Pub. Co., 1903), pp. 263-89.

[4] Unpublished letter, Waldemar Ager to Sigurd Folkestad [c. 1922], in the Norwegian-American Historical Association.

[5] From Ole Buslett, *Sagastolen* (Chicago: John Anderson Publishing Co., 1908), p. 5. Translation mine.

[6] For brief studies, not always accurate, in English, see Arlow W. Andersen, "Literature in the Making: From Boyesen to Rølvaag," *The Norwegian-Americans* (Boston: Twayne Publishers, 1975), pp. 157-74; Richard Beck, "Norwegian-American Literature," *The History of the Scandinavian Literatures*, ed. Frederika Blankner (New York: Dial Press Inc., 1938), pp. 74-84; Aagot D. Hoidahl, "Norwegian-American Fiction, 1880-1928," Norwegian-American Historical Association, *Studies and Records*, 5 (1930), 61-83; Lawrence M. Larson, "Tellef Grundysen and the Beginnings of Norwegian-American Fiction," Norwegian-American Historical Association, *Studies and Records*, 8 (1934), 1-17; and Dorothy Burton Skaardal, "The Scandinavian Immigrant Writer in America," *Norwegian-American Studies*, 21 (1962), 14-53.

[7] "Alf Brage" ran from 15 Jan. to 15 June 1874; "Raedselsdagene" ran from 30 June to 15 Oct. 1874.

[8] This observation was made to the author in an interview with Simon Johnson in Decorah in 1952.

[9] H. A. Foss, *Tobias: A Story of the Northwest*, trans. J. J. Skørdalsvold (Minneapolis: H. Petersen and Co., 1899), p. 4. Foss's novel was first published as *Den amerikanske saloon* (Grand Forks: Forfatterens Forlag, 1889).

[10] *Amerikanske forholde: fem foredrag* (Kjøbenhavn: Gyldendalske Boghandels Forlag, 1881), p. 102. Translation mine.

[11] These works include *Fjendens faldgruber* (Chicago: C. Rasmussens Forlag, 1884) and *Sange, digte, og rim* (Chicago: Skandinavens bogtryk, [1920]).

[12] See Waldemar Ager, "Norsk-amerikansk skjønliteratur," *Norsk-amerikanernes festskrift*, ed. Johs. B. Wist (Decorah, Iowa: The Symra Company, 1914), p. 296.

[13] See Gerald H. Thorson, "First Sagas in a New World: A Study of the Beginnings of Norwegian-American Literature," Norwegian-American Historical Association, *Studies and Records*, 17 (1952), 108-29.

[14] Unpublished letters, Nils Kolkin to Rasmus B. Anderson, 22 Mar., 8 Sept., 6 Dec. 1878, in the Wisconsin Historical Society. *Winona* was published in 1878 by the John Anderson Publishing Co., Chicago.

[15] Unpublished letter, Ole Buslett to Rasmus B. Anderson, 29 Jan. 1884, in the Wisconsin Historical Society.

[16] H. A. Foss, *The Cotter's Son*, trans. Joel B. Winkjer (Alexandria, Minn.: Park Region Publishing Co., 1963), pp. 113, 116. When *Husmandsgutten* first appeared in *Decorah-Posten* (3 Dec. 1884 to 23 Apr. 1885), the subscriptions to the newspaper increased by six thousand new subscribers. See Olaf Norlie, *History of the Norwegian People in America* (Minneapolis: Augsburg Publishing House, 1925), p. 300.

[17] See *Saamanden*, 3 (1889), 29. *Bag gardinet* (Minneapolis: C. Rasmussens Bogtrykkeri, 1889). Translations mine. Other references from *Bag gardinet* are indicated by page numbers cited parenthetically in the text.

[18] *Sara* (Christiania og Kjøbenhavn: Alb. Cammermeyers Forlag, 1891), p. 383. Translation mine.

[19] *Saamanden*, 6 (1893), 252.

[20] *En saloonkeepers datter*, 3rd ed. (Minneapolis: C. Rasmussens Forlags Boghandel, 1891), p. 186. Translation mine.

[21] *Unge Helgeson* (Grand Forks: Normanden's Bogtrykkeri, 1911), pp. 151-52. Translation mine. All but the last chapter of this novel was printed in *Vor Tid* in 1906.

[22] For an account of Strømme's novels see Gerald Thorson, "The Novels of Peer Strømme," Norwegian-American Historical Association, *Studies and Records*, 18 (1954), 141-62; and Gerald Thorson, "Peer Strømme: Winchester's Native Son," *The Round Table*, 1 (Trinity 1975), 16-26.

[23] Waldemar Ager, "Norsk-amerikansk skjønliteratur," p. 302.

[24] From Ju Strand, "To Ole Rølvaag (1876-1931)," *Ole Rølvaag: Artist and Cultural Leader*, ed. Gerald Thorson (Northfield, Minn.: St. Olaf College Press, 1975), p. iv.

[25] Ole Buslett, *Veien til Golden Gate* (Northland, Wis.: n.p., [1915]).

[26] Simon Johnson, *Fallitten paa Braastad* (Minneapolis: Augsburg Publishing House, 1922); and *Frihetens hjem* (Minneapolis: Augsburg Publishing House, 1925).

[27] See Waldemar Ager, "Vore kulturelle muligheder," *Kvartalskrift*, 1 (April 1905), 2-10; and Waldemar Ager "Norskhetsbevaegelsen i Amerika," *Nordmandsforbundet*, 18 (1925), 211-19.

[28] *Their Fathers' God*, trans. Trygve M. Ager (New York: Harper & Brothers Publishers, 1931), pp. 207, 208. Rølvaag's italics.

[29] *The Third Life of Per Smevik*, trans. Ella Valborg Tweet and Solveig Zempel (Minneapolis: Dillon Press, Inc., 1971), pp. 126-27.

[30] See O. A. Buslett, *Fram!* (Chicago: John Anderson Publishing Co., 1882); and H. A. Foss, *Husmandsgutten* (Decorah, Iowa: Decorah-Posten Bogtrykkeri, 1885).

[31] Melchior Falk Gjertsen, *Harald Hegg: billeder fra praerien med skildringer af norsk-amerikansk folkeliv* (Minneapolis: Augsburg Publishing House, 1914).

[32] See Kristofer Janson, *Praeriens saga* (Chicago: Skandinavens Boktrykkeri, 1885).

[33] See Janson, *Bag gardinet*.

[34] See Halvdan Moe [Peer Strømme], *Den vonde ivold* (Grand Forks: Normandens Bogtrykkeri, 1910).

[35] See Waldemar Ager, *Paa veien til smeltepotten* (Eau Claire, Wis.: Fremad Publishing Co., 1917).

[36] See Waldemar Ager, *Hundeøine* (Oslo: H. Aschehoug & Co., 1929).

[37] See Arnljot [Johs. B. Wist], *Jonasville: (et kulturbillede)* (Decorah, Iowa: The Anundsen Pub. Co., 1920).

[38] See O. E. Rølvaag, *The Boat of Longing*, trans. Nora O. Solum (New York: Harper & Brothers Publishers, 1933).

[39] See O. E. Rølvaag, *Giants in the Earth*, trans. Lincoln Colcord and O. E. Rølvaag (New York: Harper and Brothers Publishers, 1927), p. 465.

[40] Sigurd Folkestad, "Den norsk-amerikanske skjønliteratur," *Nordmandsforbundet*, 18 (1925), 219-20; trans. Einar Haugen, *The Norwegian Language in America: A Study in Bilingual Behavior* (Philadelphia: Univ. of Pennsylvania Press, 1953), I, 124.

[41] Sigrid Undset, "Norway and Norwegian Americans," *Common Ground*, 2 (Spring 1942), 74-75.

[42] From "Leif Erikson," *Norsk-amerikanske digte i udvalg*, p. 257. Translation mine.

[43] Unpublished letter, Waldemar Ager to Ole Buslett, 19 Aug. 1900, in the Norwegian-American Historical Association. Translation mine.

The Polish American Experience: An Anthropological View of Ruth Tabrah's *Pulaski Place* and Millard Lampell's *The Hero*

Paul Wrobel

ABSTRACT

After a review of the available sources, I have concluded that works written *about* Polish Americans far outnumber those written *by* members of this ethnic group. After suggesting some reasons for this conclusion, I examine Ruth Tabrah's *Pulaski Place* and Millard Lampell's *The Hero*, and show how these novels portray Polish American community life. I also discuss some of the problems that sons and daughters of immigrants face when they encounter the larger society. For many immigrants, growing up in America is a cross-cultural experience, an experience filled with discontinuities between ethnic community life and dominant American culture. (PW)

Since my field is anthropology rather than literature, I began preparing for this paper on Polish American literature by talking with people who were more likely to be familiar with fiction written (in the English language) by Polish Americans. All of the individuals I spoke with were Polish Americans; most were associated with universities or libraries; all were in the humanities rather than the social sciences.

One of the first questions I asked my friends was the following: who are the three best-known Polish American authors? Without exception, my colleagues were embarrassingly silent. At first I thought they were embarrassed because they didn't know the leading writers. But later I discovered the real reason: they felt there were few, if any, widely known Polish American authors. Indeed, one colleague suggested that, while novels by Polish Americans have been published, it would be a mistake to say that there is a body of works we can refer to collectively as "Polish American literature."

Frankly, I was perplexed. For I had looked forward to doing the research: reading novels and analyzing them from an anthropological point of view. But now I wasn't so sure. There were too many questions in my mind, questions I didn't think I'd have to deal with. And the first one was: were my friends correct?

In an attempt to answer this question I first examined *Ethnic Writers in America*, a book by Myron Simon.[1] This work is a collection of writings which illustrates America's ethnic pluralism and the "functional stages through which modern American ethnic literature has evolved and is still evolving."[2] But most of the authors in this anthology are Jewish or Black. Not one is a Polish American.

Next I turned to an annotated bibliography entitled *The Image of Pluralism in American Literature*.[3] This study of the literature of European immigrant groups lists forty-nine entries which deal with the Polish American experience. But only eight of the forty-one authors included in this section of the bibliography seem to be Polish Americans.[4] And I am not certain that all of those eight are indeed Polish Americans.

Richard Bankowsky, for example, is the author of *The Glass Rose* (1958), *After Pentecost* (1961), *On a Dark Night* (1964), and *The Pale Criminal* (1967). Since I was not sure of Bankowsky's ethnic background I called him on the phone. "Well," he said, "I've never considered myself an ethnic writer. I'm just a writer who writes about Polish Americans. But my mother is Polish and my father is Russian." So what does that make Richard Bankowsky? I am not sure, but I do know that we have a serious problem when we attempt to determine a writer's ethnic background by analyzing his or her last name.

For if this method is misleading with regard to names that *seem* Polish, what about all those Poles who changed their names in this country, or those who write under a pseudonym? A search through various publications which provide autobiographical information on American writers often reveals that their ethnic background is completely neglected.

However, *Polish American History and Culture*, a recent classified bibliography by Joseph Zurawski (1975), includes sections on novels and short stories. In the former chapter there are ninety-seven entries, ten of which are written by five different Polish Americans.[5] Richard Bankowsky, who might *possibly* be called a Polish American, accounts for three of the ten works. In the chapter on short stories there are thirty-six entries, only two of which are written by Polish Americans.[6]

On the basis of this admittedly brief review of the existing sources, I am prepared to say that it seems as if my friends were right. I wish my findings were different, and with this in mind I encourage those with additional information—or those who disagree—to write and share their knowledge with me. But, for now, I must conclude that works written *about* Polish Americans far outnumber those written by Polish Americans.[7]

In light of these findings I have altered my plans for this paper. Instead of looking at novels written by Polish Americans, I intend to describe and analyze two works of fiction—by non-Polish Americans—which tell us about the Polish American experience.

But before doing so I want to offer an explanation for why there is so little fiction by Polish Americans. Doubtless this is a complex problem with many dimensions. But perhaps my efforts will encourage further discussion by those more knowledgeable and qualified than I.[8] Let me begin with a personal experience.

I was looking forward to being in Detroit again. And I was excited about my plans to do an anthropological study of a Polish American neighborhood. But soon after I returned to my hometown—after a ten-year absence—it became clear that others did not share my enthusiasm.

Indeed, when I told one old friend what I intended to do he only laughed and said "Why do you want to study those narrow-minded bigots?" Others reacted in similar fashion:

You mean you really want to live in the "old neighborhood?"

So you're moving into Archie Bunker land, eh? And after all those years in graduate school. What a pity.

"What a pity." I want to repeat this phrase, for it sums up how a large number of third-generation Polish Americans felt about one who was planning to live with and study their own parents and grandparents—the people who live in the "old neighborhood." Why did they react this way?

Very simply, young people who are ashamed of being Polish American cannot quite understand why someone of their generation would choose not to be ashamed. They, who are trying to forget, do not understand one who wants to remember. So they have pity.

What a tragedy! For those who reject their ethnic background and feel ashamed of their parents and grandparents are in fact rejecting themselves. Indeed, they are ashamed of themselves—for being Polish American.

Yet these feelings are a rational response to living in a society that has encouraged homogeneity rather than cultural diversity. Such a point of view is symbolized by the notion of the melting pot, first described by Israel Zangwill in his play of 1908:

America is God's crucible, the great melting pot where all the races of Europe are melting and reforming! Here you stand, good folk, think I, when I see them at Ellis Island, here you stand in your fifty groups, with your fifty languages and histories, and your fifty blood hatreds and rivalries. But you won't be long like that, brothers, for these are the fires of God you've come to—these are the fires of God. A fig for your feuds and vendettas! Germans and Frenchmen, Irishmen and Jews and Russians—into the crucible with you all! God is making the American.[9]

But the melting pot theory is not quite valid. There are many Americans, and in many ways they are more dissimilar than they are alike. In Detroit alone there are over fifty identifiable ethnic groups, each with a distinctive life style and set of values. Still, it has never been advantageous to be "ethnic" in America. To be sure, there are Polish American lawyers and doctors, as well as a large number of successful engineers and other professionals. But often that success comes with a price: the loss of cultural heritage.

Thus my parents did not teach me Polish, because they wanted me to be an American, and they knew that Americans who spoke with an accent had a more difficult time getting ahead.[10] My parents were not alone; many third-generation Polish Americans don't speak the language. Nor are they aware of many of the customs and traditions so loved by their grandparents. While it is a fact that the resurgence of ethnic consciousness has done a great deal to change the situation, it is also true that a significant number of Polish Americans prefer to forget rather than remember their heritage.

Is it any wonder, then, that we lack a body of literature we can call Polish American? Certainly not. Indeed, it is to be expected considering our society's assimilationist orientation, for Polish Americans and other groups have been discouraged from writing about themselves and their own communities. And, according to Simon, that is how ethnic writers began to write: ". . . by serving as the loyal interpreters of their people to the nation."[11] Thus the melting pot ideal has resulted in both a lack of fiction from our ethnic groups, and an inaccurate picture of American society. For when people don't write about the life style, patterns of behavior, and values of their own groups, we fail to learn about the nature and extent of cultural diversity within our society.

In the next section of this paper I would like to focus on two novels which deal with the Polish American experience. The first is *Pulaski Place* (1950), by Ruth Tabrah, and the second is *The Hero* (1949), by Millard Lampell.[12] My purpose is anthropological in nature: to describe and analyze what happens when an individual from one culture encounters a different way of life. More specifically, I am interested in Polish Americans and their cross-cultural experiences with the larger society.

The novel *Pulaski Place* draws its title from the name of a street located in the heart of an urban Polish American neighborhood. That neighborhood is a section of a city called Milltown, a name obviously chosen to reflect the fact that a large number of Polish Americans have indeed settled in so-called "milltowns."

The first thing we learn about the Polish American neighborhood described in this novel is that it is more than a row of houses and a series of streets. It is a community: a group of people who interact more with one another than with outsiders, a geographic and social entity with an identity and a sense of togetherness. This community is based on the Polish parish located in its midst.[13] Families who live in the neighborhood are linked together through participation in the social and religious life of the parish. And the people who live on Pulaski Place and other streets in the area are both neighbors and fellow parishioners.

They are also Polish Americans. And that, in part, is why they have chosen to live together. They are more comfortable living in an environment where Polish is spoken, where Polish customs and traditions are maintained, where everyone understands everyone else. But they also live together for quite another reason: the fact that other Milltown residents are cool if not outright hostile to Polish Americans. Thus, forming a community is in a sense a refuge from the larger society, as well as a matter of choice.

Should a young second-generation Polish American choose to leave this community and be different from his parents? Or should he remain, living very much like his parents did, and working—like his father—in the local factory? These are the questions which constitute the main focus of Tabrah's story. A young man is faced with a dilemma: if he decides to leave is he rejecting his parents and his cultural heritage? If he decides to stay will he be happy? These are the questions facing Steve Kowalski, the main character in this novel. They are posed in the following excerpt from the first section of the novel:

> Steve had spent all but four of his twenty-six years on this street. His father, Anton Kowalski, had been born in this house before him, only a year after Grandfather Kowalski brought his family over from Poland. It must have looked much the same when his father was a boy, Steve reflected. The Bolt Works had been new then, and maybe not so free with its soot and grease belching through the parish. Our Lady church had been newly built then too, the darkened spire shiny and the bricks clean red. Steve's earliest memory was sitting on the front porch in his mother's lap, looking from one to the other of these two landmarks, the tall dark spire of Our Lady on one horizon and the black stacks of the Bolt Works on the other, and feeling as if they fenced him in—cut him off from something big and important. It had been the hardest thing Steve ever had to do to come back to Pulaski Place after four years away in the army. But there was his old job at the plant waiting for him, and no surety of what he would find if he went anywhere else. There was Irene's deep attachment to this neighborhood in which she too had grown up. And there was, finally, the pull which was home, and which was a deep, warming part of him in spite of his ambition away from it. All these things had weighed heavily against the urge to escape before the treadmill of life in Our Lady's parish caught him, erased all the restlessness and ambition of his youth and pushed him into a stolid, dull, dead end of living as it had his father, and his father's father, living as if the wide, exciting different country outside the parish did

not exist. Steve moved restlessly on the hot boards of the porch. Were it not for one glimmering chance, one opportunity that might change everything for him soon, he would take Irene today and leave Milltown, strike out for anywhere as long as it was far enough away from Our Lady's spire and the Bolt Works' stacks and the noisy Polish stem of Foundry Street and Pulaski Place.[14]

The opportunity that Steve refers to is the chance to join Milltown's police force. It so happens that Milltown's police chief was one of Steve's commanding officers in the army; based on Steve's performance overseas, he was highly respected by the new police chief, who had asked him to take an exam to qualify for the force. For Steve the police force represented the larger society, a society that was less than willing to accept foreigners, especially Polish Americans. For example, some police officers expressed their prejudice at Steve's wedding at the local hall:

The guests began crowding in the door behind Steve and Irene [sic] the line buzzed with mild jokes and polite repetitions. "May God bless you with many children . . . ." "May you always be so happy. . . . May life smile on you . . . ." Papa Walecki grew more and more pleased, Julie more flushed, and the groom more nervous as the evening wore on.

The festivity in Dom Polski Hall was in full, noisy swing two hours later when the Milltown police patrol car cruised by. It slowed almost to a stop. Officer Larson, at the wheel, stuck his head out the window. He spoke with a flat unpleasant accent. "Another one of them Polack weddings!"

"All that excitement just to settle down and have seventeen kids." Schmidt shook his head. "I was married in August. I tell you anybody's nuts to get married when it's this hot."

"Look at 'em in there, will you?" asked Larson, "Like a bunch of sandflies, that's what they look like. And listen to 'em jabber. That's what gets me, that there Polack jabber!"

"You better get your ears turned up then," advised Schmidt. "This guy that was Chief Goodman's top sergeant when he was overseas is getting on the force next appointment, I heard. He's a Polack from somewhere down here."

"A Polack!" snorted Larson.

"Yeah. His name is Kowalski."

"A Polack on the force. By God, I don't believe it! I'll quit before I'll work with one of them bastards! What's got into Goodman? He must be just talking . . ."

"I'm only telling you what I heard."

"Well, by God, when it comes right down to it I don't think Goodman'd dare put a Polack on the force! The people wouldn't stand for it, that's what!

What's this town coming to? Next my kids will be wanting to marry a goddam Polack! I'll break her [sic] head if she so much as looks at one, I will!" Larson's eyes fixed on Dom Polski Hall, his face was gloomy with suspicion. "We'll keep an eye on that party in there. Out of three hundred of the bastards we're bound to get some trouble."

"Listen to 'em once," marveled Schmidt. "I'd give a fiver to go to one of them things."

"Aaah!" snorted Larson contemptuously. "A Polack on the police force! That I should like to see. Kow-what-did-you-say?

"Kowalski," said Schmidt. "Steve Kowalski."[15]

But despite how these and other policemen felt, Steve passed the test and became a police officer. The Polish community was proud, but they were also unrealistic. They expected Steve to "go easy" on individuals from the community who committed crimes. But Steve didn't feel this way. He ticketed his own brother for a parking violation and arrested another member of the community—a next door neighbor—for a more serious crime: stabbing a police officer while in a rage about his daughter's attempted suicide. These actions gained respect for Steve in the eyes of his fellow officers, but not among those in the Polish community. His brother accused him of being ashamed of his Polishness, and his father and mother also reacted strongly, especially after Steve announced he had rented a home in another section of town—far from Pulaski Place.

"... It's true! It's true!" Marya Kowalski [his mother] began to weep in her apron. "That talk around us, Steve. Your father can't have no peace! He can't hold up his head! When I go to the store the women all stop talking like I was a stranger to them!"

"For my sake, I ask you to stay here," begged his father. "Stay until they forget what you do to Mike Pachek. It looks like what they think is true—that you don't care about your people—about your family . . . ."[16]

Steve's decision to leave the community is hastened by the fact that people believe his pregnant wife to be hexed, because she viewed an attempted suicide. At any rate, Steve does leave the community and is disowned by his father.

But, finally, Steve is brought back home to his family and community when a tragedy occurs: his younger brother is killed in an automobile accident. And when Steve arrives home he realizes that being away was not all that pleasant. He and his father are reconciled, and Steve talks about the need to retain his ties to the family and community—to live his own life, yes, but not to forget

the warmth, the pulsing mixture of good times and sad ones woven inextricably together, of a pattern of living that, he realized now, he had missed acutely in the past weeks.[17]

Tabrah's novel may be melodramatic, but she is very accurate in describing the realities of day-to-day life in one urban Polish American community of a generation ago. Moreover, she has skillfully illustrated what we might call the assimilation dilemma. Steve Kowalski asked, "who am I and where do I belong?" These questions are inevitable for second and third-generation Polish Americans when they encounter the larger society. Yet, as I suggested earlier, they are not always answered so easily as they are in *Pulaski Place.*

The Hero is a somewhat similar novel, though it is more clearly focused on the assimilation dilemma. Steve Novak is a second-generation Polish American who lives in a New Jersey milltown called White Falls. After a sensational career as a high school football player, Steve is awarded a four-year athletic scholarship to Jackson College, a small school in Virginia not unlike the prestigious ivy-league universities of the East.

Through various experiences at Jackson College, Steve becomes aware of his ethnic background and realizes that he is "different" from his fellow students, primarily WASP's who come from wealthy families. One such experience was Steve's first encounter with the most important fraternity on campus. His teammate and friend, Whittier, had suggested that he visit the fraternity house during Rush Week in order to be considered as a possible pledge. Whittier stops at Steve's room to take him to the Beta house:

"Set?" He looked at Steve and for the briefest moment his eyes clouded with annoyance.

"What's wrong?"

"Nothing, let's go."

Steve knew instantly what it was. The suit, the tweed suit he and Poppa had chosen. From the first he had sensed that it was wrong; he had seen no others like it. He ran his fingers along the jacket as though he wished by some sleight of hand to change the fabric.

Whittier said, "Haven't you got anything else?"

"No, just old things."

"Old things are fine."

"Not mine," Steve walked toward the bureau and stared at himself in the mirror. "The tie isn't right either."

Whittier's voice was kindly: "Where did you ever get it?"

Whittier took his arm, "Come on, I'll let you have some things." He said it without condescension or implied judgement. Steve went with him down the hall, and Whittier brought out a pair of grey flannels, a brown tweed jacket, and some socks. The jacket was the softest Steve had ever felt, a beautiful cashmere.

"Here, I'll get you a tie." Whittier got a black knitted one. He said apologetically: "You ought to get one of these. Go with anything. Handy."

Steve put on the clothes. He knew that they were perfect, that he could never have chosen them himself. He wondered how it was that Whittier's clothes were exactly right, and that his were wrong. Who determined which clothes were right? He decided that he would ask Whittier to help him choose clothes. He half started to ask it then, but something about Whittier—the graceful, handsome silhouette, the curly reddish hair, the fine brow—something in Whittier's pose as he leaned against the window deterred Steve, and he merely nodded his readiness and they left.[18]

But the perfect clothes didn't work, for Steve was Catholic, and once the Beta boys realized this they lost interest in him. When Steve became aware of their feelings ". . . he was suddenly aware of the clothes he was wearing, Whittier's soft jacket. He felt that it did not fit, that he must look very foolish in it. He turned quickly and walked through the library and out of the house."[19]

While there were many similar experiences at the college, Steve really began to learn about himself—and the society in which he lived—when he returned home for the holidays:

At Christmas Steve returned to White Falls, Poppa sat in his dusty green chair next to the fireplace, his face dark and scowling.

"How goes the college?"

"The food is good?"

"Yes."

Poppa's face had a ghost of a smile. "But no pot roast, eh?"

"No, I missed the pot roast."

"And the classes, you work hard?"

"I'm doing okay. It's tough, but not as tough as I thought, I think I could have made the honor list, only football takes it out of you, it's not so easy to practice all afternoon and then study. And I had to miss Saturday-morning classes when we played away from home. But I'll make it up this spring."

"Nice," Poppa said. "You look nice." He patted the arm of the chair. "Come sit by me."

Steve sat beside Poppa, thinking, it's all different. Or maybe this is the way it always was. Maybe I'm really seeing for the first time. This is really Poppa—

this stooped man with the old-country face. This is really the house—these dark rooms with the wallpaper beginning to peel, the cheap furniture, the cracked plaster in the bathroom, the damp smell of cooking and plumbing, I never realized it smelled.

It was a busy Christmas. Steve went to Mass with Poppa and Joey, and spent the first days seeking out the boys he'd played with at high school, and the evenings with Poppa in Manuel's. White Falls seemed shabby and unexciting.

Steve found himself taking the bus to New York to seek out places he had heard mentioned at Jackson, the college haunts, Madden's Steak House, and the German-American Rathskeller. They were filled with fresh-faced Yale and Dartmouth boys and their laughing, well-groomed girls. It pleased Steve to sit among them, to be dressed like them, to strike up a conversation at the bar and admit that he was at Jackson, and that, yes, he played some ball. . . . They drank beer and sang—Steve had the premonition of a magnificent experience about to happen—but somehow it never did. The evening ended and the other boys piled into their cars; Steve found himself alone on the jolting bus back to White Falls, tired and faintly frustrated.[20]

What Steve learned, then, was that he didn't know himself; he didn't know who he was. There were discontinuities between life at home and life at school. In other words, they were two different worlds, two different cultures, if you will. And now Steve knew that he didn't belong to either.

This is the assimilation dilemma. It is based on the fact that, for many, growing up in America is a cross-cultural experience. What makes that experience so difficult for the sons and daughters of immigrants is that some cultures are more valued than others. More specifically, it is the dominant WASP culture that people aspire to, and their own that they try to forget.

But, like Steve Kowalski, Steve Novak realized what he was doing, and he too attempted to come to terms with the problem. First he rejected the dominant culture:

Steve knew, suddenly, that he was not one of them, that he would never be one of them. His mind brought back, in a flood, a hundred incidents when he had felt isolated, excluded, different. That time at the Beta house. He felt a sense of revulsion and hatred, as though he had been mocked, as though he had been cast out. He knew that he would never again feel easy in this place.[21]

Then, upon returning home, he looked towards the future. He felt

a sense of peace, and of belonging. A feeling of growth and creativity. To deny nothing, to admit the world as it was and then build from there. To begin with himself, with this shabby town with its mingled acrid smells, with the fumbling and foolishly gruff man who now lay dead in the living room at home. To accept it all, saying these are the roots, this is what brought me forth. To begin with this, then—to go where? He was not sure. . . . But . . . For the first time in as long as he could remember, he felt that he was not running away from anything.[22]

Perhaps not running is the solution. And yet, today, as we celebrate America's two-hundredth birthday, people are still running away from their own cultures. Let us hope that, soon, they will no longer feel the need.

Both of these novels dealt adequately with the Polish American experience. As I have attempted to show, they focus on what we might call the push and pull of both a Polish American community and the larger society, and they illustrate the problem of growing up in one culture and attempting to fit into another. Thus both *Pulaski Place* and *The Hero* are more than interesting fiction; they are historical and sociological documents on both Polish Americans and American society. Indeed, I strongly recommend that they be added to reading lists of courses dealing with the history and sociology of this nation's ethnic groups.

This point brings me to the final section of this paper. For some time now I've been thinking about the relationship between social science and the humanities. As I read through novels dealing with the Polish American experience I began to realize that scientific students of society and writers of fiction are both concerned with expressions of human nature, with describing ways of thinking and feeling, with understanding men, women and children, with understanding ourselves.

The anthropologist Robert Redfield recognized this fact when he discussed (over two decades ago) what he called the double-nature of social science:

> In the circle of learning, its place adjoins the natural sciences, on the one hand, and the humanities, on the other. . . . With half his being the social scientist approaches his subject matter with a detachment he shares with the physicist. With the other half he approaches it with a human sympathy he shares with the novelist.[23]

While Redfield advises social scientists to acquire the skills of the novelist, he realizes that they are difficult to learn. So he gives us some advice. What we need, says Redfield, is human sympathy. As he puts it,

> The exercise of this capacity is demanded in every study of a community. It is exacted in every consideration of an institution in which men with motives and desires like our own fulfill the roles and offices that make it up; it is required in every interview. One may be taught how to map a neighborhood, or how to tabulate and treat statistically the votes cast in an election; but to know how to do these things is not to be assured meaningful conclusions. Besides these skills, one needs also the ability to enter imaginatively, boldly, and, at the same time, self-critically into that little fraction of the human comedy with which one has become scientifically concerned.[24]

In short, what Redfield wants us to do is ". . . become a part of the human relations we study . . . use our own humanity to understand humanity."[25]

But we have not followed Redfield's advice. I realized this after reading *The Hero* and *Pulaski Place*. These novels provide a fairly accurate picture of the day-to-day life in two urban Polish American communities. They tell the reader what it is like to live in such communities. In short, they tell about Polish Americans as living and breathing human beings, as people who laugh and cry. In comparison, the social science literature on Polish Americans is primarily concerned with advancing this or that theory, with proving a hypothesis. Further, most studies of this ethnic group focus on the extent to which its members are becoming Americanized. In summary, then, social scientists have not looked at Polish Americans as objects of study in their own right. Novelists have, and we're all better for it.

So I think social scientists need to be more aware of what Redfield calls the "Art" of social science. This is especially true at the present time, when we are in the midst of the computer age. Thousands of questionnaires can be tabulated in a few moments in the quest for a methodologically elegant analysis, yet so often the results are superficial because they tell us little about "how men wrestle with the problem of being human."[26]

The Merrill-Palmer Institute

NOTES

[1] Myron Simon, ed., *Ethnic Writers in America* (New York: Harcourt Brace Jovanovich, Inc., 1972).

[2] Ibid., p. 5.

[3] Babette F. Inglehart and Anthony R. Mangione, eds., *The Image of Pluralism in American Literature* (New York: Institute on Pluralism and Group Identity of the American Jewish Committee, 1974).

[4] Those eight are John R. Abucewicz, *Fool's White* (New York: Carlton Press, 1969); Richard Bankowsky, *The Glass Rose* (New York: Random House, 1958), *After Pentecost* (New York: Random House, 1961), *On a Dark Night* (New York: Random House, 1964), and *The Pale Criminal* (New York: Random House, 1967); Antoni Gronowicz, *Bolek* (New York: Thomas Nelson and Sons, 1942) and *An Orange Full of Dreams* (New York: Dodd, Mead and Company, 1971); Victoria Janda, *Star Hunger* (Minneapolis: Polanie Press, 1942), *Walls of Space* (Minneapolis: Polanie Press, 1945) and *Singing Furrows* (Minneapolis: Polanie Press, 1953); Monica Krawczyk, *If the Branch Blossoms and Other Stories* (Minneapolis: Polanie Press, 1950); Wanda Kubiak, *Polonaise Nevermore* (New York: Vintage Press, 1962); Lois Lenski, *We Live in the North* (Philadelphia: J. V. Lippincott, 1966); and Stella Rybacki, *Thrills, Chills and Sorrow* (New York: Exposition Press, 1954). Janda's works are collections of her poetry, and Lenski's book is for young children.

[5] Most of the works cited by Joseph Zurawski's *Polish American History and Culture* (Chicago: Polish Museum of America, 1975) are mentioned in the Inglehart and Mangione bibliography.

[6] Polish Americans who have written short stories include E. Falkowski, "Our Fathers and We," in *Polish Authors of Today and Yesterday*, ed. Irene Morska (New York: S. F. Vanni, 1947) and Peter Mankowski, "The Holy Basket," *Woman's Day*, April, 1943. Also listed in this section is a translation of work by a Pole, Henry Sienkiewicz, *Western Septet: Seven Stories of the American West*, trans. Marion Moore Coleman (Chesire, Connecticut: Cherry Hill Books, 1973).

[7] Towards the end of my research for this paper I discovered three novels by Maia Wojciechowska: *The Hollywood Kid* (New York: Harper and Row, 1966), *A Single Light* (New York: Harper and Row, 1968), and *The Rotten Years* (Garden City, New York: Doubleday and Company, 1971). None of these is included in the bibliographies consulted earlier.

[8] The Polish Institute of Arts and Sciences in America and the Kosciuszko Foundation should encourage and support a concerted effort to study this problem.

[9] As quoted in Milton Gordon, "Assimilation in America: Theory and Reality," in *Race, Creed, Color, or National Origin: A Reader on Racial and Ethnic Identities in American Society*, ed., Robert K. Yin (Itasca, Illinois: F. E. Peacock, n.d.), p. 120.

[10] For a fuller discussion of this point, see Paul Wrobel, "Becoming a Polish American: A Personal Point of View," in *White Ethnics: Their Life in Working-Class America*, ed. Joseph A. Ryan (New York: Prentice Hall, 1974), pp. 52-58.

[11] Simon, p. 4.

[12] Ruth Tabrah, *Pulaski Place* (New York: Harper and Brothers, 1950), and Millard Lampell, *The Hero* (New York: J. Nessner, Inc., 1949). See also John Petras, "Polish Americans in Sociology and Fiction," *Polish American Studies*, 21, No. 2 (1964), pp. 16-22, and Walter Zebrowski, "A Critical Appreciation of Ruth Tabrah's *Pulaski Place*," *Polish American Studies*, 16, No. 3-4 (1959), 120-28.

[13] The Polish parish continues to play an important role in the lives of working-class Polish Americans. For further discussion, see Paul Wrobel, "An Ethnographic Study of a Polish American Parish and Neighborhood," unpublished Ph.D. dissertation (Catholic University, Washington, D.C., 1975).

[14] Tabrah, p. 5.

[15] Ibid., pp. 12-13.

[16] Ibid., p. 238.

[17] Ibid., p. 280.

[18] Lampell, pp. 85-86.

[19] Ibid., p. 89.

[20] Ibid., pp. 95-97.

[21] Ibid., p. 232.

[22] Ibid., p. 296.

[23] Robert Redfield, "The Art of Social Science," *American Journal of Sociology*, 54, No. 3 (1948), p. 188.

[24] Ibid., p. 186.

[25] Ibid., p. 184.

[26] Miles Richardson, "Anthropologist—the Myth Teller," *American Ethnologist*, 2, No. 3 (1975), 530.

The Contribution by Americans of Portuguese Descent to the U.S. Literary Scene

Francis M. Rogers

ABSTRACT

The voice of Americans of Portuguese descent as published in book form consists of five volumes of verse in Portuguese and, in English, seven novels and two autobiographies. They appeared beginning in 1935, but two books of poems and two novels appeared only in 1975. This ethnic literature is balanced by American writings about the group and is greatly enlarged by the publications over five decades of John Roderigo Dos Passos, whose paternal grandfather was born in Ponta do Sol, Madeira, in 1812 and immigrated to Baltimore in 1830. Of the fourteen books of ethnic literature, only two novels treat true ethnic themes. Elvira Osorio Roll's *Hawaii's Kohala Breezes* (1964) focuses on prejudice concerning the Portuguese in Hawaii, and James A. Carvalho's *Haole, Come Back* (1975) points out the dangers of separatism inherent in ethnicity. The fact that these and two other novels come out of Hawaii, where current immigrants from Portugal do not choose to settle, suggests that ethnic literature, as distinguished from immigrant literature, is one of nonrevitalized maturity. The earlier wave of Portuguese immigrants did not create an ethnic literature. Rather, they assimilated, suppressing or neglecting their origin. Their literary voice was secondhand, expressed chiefly and often pejoratively by "American" members of the original Provincetown theater troupe and others in close contact with local Americans of Portuguese descent. On the West Coast, however, Jack London had earlier sung the praises of Azorean immigrants. In touch in middle life with the writers and Portuguese in Provincetown, Dos Passos exemplified the literary potentiality of the Portuguese ethnic group. Throughout his creative writings, correspondence, and oral reminiscing, he reflected his heritage and his many visits to Portuguese-speaking lands, including Madeira. (FMR)

In my preparation for this paper, I first outlined what I hoped to find: novels, short stories, plays, poems, and essays sincerely depicting with literary flair the personal experience over the past century and a half of Portuguese immigrants and their descendants *qua* identifiable members of an identifiable ethnic group and with few if any overtones of either inter-

409

national, domestic, or intragroup politics. Whether this creative belletristic literature was written in Portuguese or English, whether published in the United States or in a Portuguese-speaking land, was irrelevant. Being given the symposium's subtitle, "The Many Voices of America," however, I felt that the voices had to be heard and understood, and widely so, both within and outside the ethnic group, and that they had to be unfettered voices, free as America herself was free. I therefore decided that I should seek published literature issued in permanent book form, a form that could be catalogued in libraries, and, ideally, in the common interethnic English language.[1]

* * *

Within the Portuguese tradition, men and boys, including priests, write verse in voluminous quantities, although not all are poets of the caliber of a Luís de Camões, Antero de Quental, or Fernando Pessoa, or of a David Rafael Wang or a Tomás Rivera. It is thus natural that, within the American ethnic group, versifiers abound. Four men, all Portuguese-born, have produced five books, all in Portuguese; and I have heard of five more volumes of verse in Portuguese now in the making, by Heldo T. Braga, José Brites, Rosendo Evora Brito, Alfred Lewis, and José Reinaldo Matos. The verse is very uneven in quality. Some of it is so superpatriotically Portuguese as to tempt me to rule it out altogether as ethnic literature.

Guilherme Silveira Gloria, born on the island of Pico in the Azores in 1863, early studied for the priesthood. He migrated to California, was ordained, and switched to a family role. In Sacramento in 1900 he founded a Portuguese-language newspaper which later appeared in Oakland. He continued as its publisher for many years, and in 1935 its printing press issued his lengthy volume of collected verse entitled *Poesias*. The book is marred by a nationalistic and indeed Salazaristic foreword filled with references to "a Raça"—with a *c* cedilla and not a *z*—and guaranteed to dissuade any true American of whatever descent from penetrating farther.

The first part of the book (224 pages) brings together a miscellany of chiefly occasional verse. Thus, one poem, dated 20 March 1913, is dedicated to the memory of the poet Manuel Garcia Monteiro, a native of Horta, Fayal, Azores, who migrated to the United States, studied medicine, and for many years practiced in the Greater Boston area. Two Gloria poems, respectively of 8 July and 8 August 1924, recall the visit to California of the Portuguese aviators António Brito Pais and José Manuel Sarmento de Beires, who had shortly before completed a flight from Lisbon to Macao which I describe in some detail in *Precision Astrolabe*.[2] Although Gloria is greatly admired by many Portuguese in California, much of his verse has been succinctly and aptly characterized by one of my students as "very sweet and icky," to which I would add that many of the poems reflect an excessive attachment to representatives of the Government of Portugal.

The second part of the book (95 pages) consists of an epic poem about Juan Rodríguez Cabrillo, that is, João Rodrigues Cabrilho, the sixteenth-century Portuguese maritime explorer who, in the service of Spain, first entered San Diego Bay. This poem is dedicated to the author of the foreword and his spouse.

Arthur Vieira Ávila (1888-1962) was likewise born on Pico and also migrated to California. He became active in Portuguese-language journalism on the West Coast and, from 1930 until his death, ran a daily Portuguese radio program which rendered him beloved of a large following. His two volumes of Portuguese verses, *Desafio Radiofónico* and *Rimas de Um Imigrante* (*Versos para a Rádio*), both published in Oakland in 1961, reflect his radiobroadcasting activity, his sentimentality, and his Portuguese patriotism. A single example, "Portugal," from *Rimas de Um Imigrante* hardly needs translation:

> Portugal terra d'encantos,
> Terra de alegria e sol;
> Pátria de heróis e de santos,
> Da civ'lização farol.
>
> Bem longe, és nosso ideal,
> Pátria linda, idolatrada.
> Da nossa alma és fanal
> E dos nossos passos estrada.
>
> Salve, torrão meu, querido,
> Nação qu não tem rival.
> Nunca me sais do sentido,
> Meu amado Portugal.[3]

Father José Reinaldo Matos, born in the north of Continental Portugal in 1925, is a poet of quite different caliber from the two preceding versifiers. He was educated in his homeland and was ordained there in 1950. He visited the United States for several months in 1964. In 1967 he became an immigrant and in March 1975 an American citizen. He first served as a priest in the so-called "Portuguese national parish" in Cambridge and now ministers to Portuguese Catholics in the Lawrence-Methuen area of Massachusetts.

Father Matos's sonnets from America written over the years 1970-1974 are sophisticated and, as to be expected, heavily religious to the point of being beautiful prayers. Superbly printed, they are accompanied by excellent drawings from the pen of Samuel Emrys Evans of Hanover, Massachusetts. The sonnets are ethnic in the sense that life in America produced them, but their themes are in general universal: God, love, one's native land. The poem "Saudades da Minha Terra" (Longing for My Native Land), however, is typically Portuguese, *saudade* constituting a ubiquitous form of nostalgia or *Sehnsucht*:

> Minha Terra natal, qu'rida e saudosa aldeia,
> Presépio sempre em flor, tão longe e tão presente!
> Passeio-te de dia, à neve e ao sol ardente;
> Passeio-te de noite, à luz da lua cheia.
>
> A clara luz do dia, como se recreia
> Minh'alma que moldaste; e que feliz se sente,
> Compartilhando amor com toda essa gente,
> Assim tão boa e sã, que nos comove e enleia!
>
> Passeio-te de noite, àquela hora morta
> Em que pode haver cocas atrás duma porta,
> Lobisomens e bruxas nas encruzilhadas;
>
> Ou mais cedo um pouquinho, quando os serandeiros
> Dão a cheirar, à roda, em aidos e quinteiros,
> Maçãs e manjericos, pelas desfolhadas.[4]

Father Matos, who merits listing in the canon of Portuguese literature as a distinguished poet, tells me that some of the sonnets from America are now being set to music.

José Joaquim Baptista Brites was born in 1945 in a village in the center of Continental Portugal. He completed vocational high school, served three years in the Portuguese Air Force voluntarily as a jet mechanic (but in Europe, not in Africa), then worked three years in the same capacity for TAP (Transportes Aéreos Portugueses—The Airline of Portugal). He immigrated into the United States in 1970. He lives in Bethlehem, Pennsylvania, and is employed as a metal worker.

The title of Brites' *Poemas sem Poesia* (Poems Devoid of Poetry) is indeed a misnomer, for the book is filled with true poetry. Humanistic rather than orthodoxically religious, the poems open with the observation that humanity might be better off if the time lost in supplicating the gods were taken advantage of to make demands of men.

Although in general the poems are hardly ethnic, the first reflects the immigration of the poet. He began in the Old World and arrived at the New World. He goes around the world, and the world goes around him. The world goes around him as does the little wooden horse on the merry-go-round. In spite of another rotation, and another voyage, the picture on the background panel does not change. Always people, people, the masses of the people ("gente, gente, povo"). The poem concludes:

> E eu à volta do Mundo,
> o Mundo à volta de mim;
> —o Mundo é mesmo assim . . .[5]

In other words, there is interaction between the individual and society, an apt conclusion for a perspicacious and intelligent wanderer of the late-twentieth century. Understandably, this poem won first prize for poetry in the series of literary contests sponsored by Southeastern Massachusetts University in 1972 as part of the commemorations associated with the fourth centenary of the publication of *Os Lusiadas*, Portugal's national epic poem written by Luís de Camões. The judges were Professors Jorge de Sena, Ernesto Da Cal, and Anson C. Piper.

The other poems by José Brites are more universal, or at least more Portuguese than ethnic. They include the themes of emigration and of violent opposition to war. They reveal the anguish of a free-spirited Portuguese maturing within a national dictatorship at war in Portuguese Guinea, Angola, and Mozambique, and for a few hours in India. They do not paint a dreamland Portugal à la Gloria or Ávila devoid of all defects, a Portugal so perfect as to puzzle outside observers who see a stream of both emigrants and migrant workers constantly sallying forth. They depict reality, albeit poetically, and with considerable *poesia*. They sing of the plight of the black man. They do not hesitate to allude to the defects of this New World, this *televisamericanada*.

Brites knows his predecessors, including the Azorean Antero, who was born and committed suicide in Ponta Delgada, São Miguel. An allusion to Antero's famous sonnet "Palácio da Ventura" appears in a poem devoted to Liberty and to the end of War. This composition is entitled "Poema pra 27 de Janeiro," the allusion being to 27 January 1973, the day the Vietnamese War supposedly ended and a joyful one for the poet. A most powerful series of lines in this poem returns to the theme of begging men and not the gods:

> Ergui do Espírito as mãos e pedi
> (não aos santinhos e anjinhos,
> que de tanto se lhes pedinchar
> nunca estenderam as mãos pra dar)
> pedi aos Homens com Poderes sobre a Terra
> —que se amem por Amor dos Homens—
> e por especial favor
> não comecem algures outra Guerra!   ...[6]

Thus, a long poetic distance separates José Brites from William Gloria.

* * *

The literary contribution by Americans of Portuguese descent written in prose includes two parallel novels which appeared in 1951, both written by immigrants, both describing not the U.S. experience but life on Portuguese Atlantic islands. In the 1960's and 1970's five novels were published, four written by descendants of Portuguese who had settled in Hawaii. Of the seven novels in English I discuss six at this point, reserving Elvira Osorio Roll's *Hawaii's Kohala Breezes* for special consideration.

Fausto P. Lage was born in 1894 in the far northeast of Continental Portugal. He studied medicine at the University of Oporto. No sooner was he graduated than he was commissioned a lieutenant in the Portuguese Army's medical corps. In 1921 he was sent to the Cape Verde Islands on a mission to eradicate bubonic plague. In 1924 he was assigned to the island of Fogo as Health Delegate and Military Commandant, his real specialty being tropical diseases. In 1925 he immigrated into the United States.

Lage settled in Lowell, Massachusetts, practiced medicine, and wrote. He today resides in retirement in San Leandro, California. In 1948, his novelized life of Joan of Arc appeared in Portuguese. And in 1974 he left in Portugal the manuscript of "Uma Família Portuguesa na Nova Inglaterra" (A Portuguese Family in New England). This obviously valuable book has not yet appeared in print.

Fantastic Dilemma, of 1951, discusses a mixed American-British-French scientific mission to the Fogo of what was in 1951 the future, the 1970's. A long short story, it has nothing to do with the Portuguese ethnic group in the United States except that a highly sophisticated member wrote it, and the story's island setting is a source of many other members. The book is remarkable in presenting a most sympathetic view of the Cape Verde Islands from the pen of a Continental Portuguese settled in the United States. It is valuable in giving an authentic glimpse of the difficulties of life in that arid and volcanic archipelago off Mauritania and Senegal, difficulties of a type which the International Center for Arid and Semi-Arid Land Studies (ICASALS) of Texas Tech University has striven to alleviate in various parts of the world.

Alfred Lewis, of Los Banos, California, was born on the island of Flores in the Azores in 1902 of a whaling father who had emigrated to California and returned to his native island to marry. Young Alfred attended his village school and received supplementary private instruction from his teacher and also from the local priest. He early took to writing short stories and the inevitable poetry. At age nineteen he, too, migrated to California.

In America, Lewis continued to write in Portuguese, some of his productions being published in William Gloria's newspaper. Living in the United States, he concluded that he should try writing in English. He persevered, and in 1949, at age forty-seven, he attended the University of Colorado's writers' conference. Well-known Americans present encouraged him to continue writing both prose and poetry.

The Azorean Florentine's first novel, the highly autobiographical *Home is an Island*, was published by Random House two years after the writers' conference, was well received, and later appeared in braille. Its author continued to write in English. In recent years, ever more touched by *saudade*, he has reverted to verse in Portuguese and has put together a volume entitled "Aguarelas Florentinas" (Aquarelles of Flores) for which he is at present seeking a publisher.

The chief worth of *Home is an Island* is not its contribution to Portuguese ethnic literature in the United States but its detailed description, for the general English-reading world and also for the scholar and student, of Azorean living in the early-twentieth century, at the height of the first wave of mass Portuguese immigration. As might be expected from the title, however, it expresses the author's *saudade*, so much so that it begins with a Camões quotation in Portuguese, the opening ten lines of the famous poem based on the 136th/137th Psalm which Leonard Bacon has rendered thus at the end of his translation of *Os Lusiadas*:

> By the rivers of Babylon,
> I found me. And on that shore
> I sat me down and wept sore,
> Remembering all that was done
> In Sion long years before.
> And the river of tears flowed on,
> That from my eyes was fed,
> For, when all has been rightly read,
> Present evil is Babylon.
> Sion is time that is dead.[7]

Lewis via Luís identifies the United States with his present ills. He is careful, however, not to identify the mother country with all that was wonderful. Rather, he refers simply to past times. In other words, the Island-Portuguese immigrant suffers doubly. "Home" is isolated, devoid of amenities, and backward. Life in America is difficult at best, and many who essay it fail to achieve the hoped-for material success.

Reading *Home is an Island*, one sees, feels, and smells the island's fruits and vegetables (strawberries, apples, plums, figs, anise-greens, water cress, potatoes, squash, kale, pears, grapes), its seafood (squid, morays, limpets, bonito), and its corn porridge, cow's and goat's milk, and kale soup. One becomes acquainted with clothing (the women's dark shawls, the shoes only for Sunday best); the nature of a typical home (two rooms, with an addition built later for the child) and its furniture (some brought from America, some like the cradle made by the father himself); flowers (hydrangeas and roses); mutual dependence based upon friendship and not upon gain or *escudos*; superstitions (souls from the other world, witches, ghosts); corporal punishment in school; and, finally, the unimaginative Catholicism as practiced there in those days, the skepticism concerning it, the lack of comprehension of its Latin. The American traveler desirous of reading up on the Azores prior to a visit could do no better than read Alfred Lewis's novel.

Incidentally, there are works of Island-Portuguese literature, chiefly novels, which differ from those by Lage and Lewis only in having been written in the Portuguese language by natives of Portuguese Atlantic islands resident on their islands. These books invariably mention America and discuss the theme of emigration to that continent. An example from the Azores is *Pedras Negras* by Dias de Melo, a novel set on Pico and replete with details of Yankee whaling of old. Another, this one from the Cape Verde Islands, is Baltasar Lopes da Silva's novel *Chiquinho*, by a native of São Nicolau who has spent many years as a secondary school teacher on São Vicente. *Chiquinho* narrates the forced emigration—forced by the arid and semi-arid conditions—of a young man whose father had left for America because of the drought of 1915 and had lived at 102 South Second Street, New Bedford, Massachusetts. The book even tells of the arrival in the archipelago of the barks *Wanderer* and *Charles W. Morgan*—two famous names in New England maritime history—and the procedure for recruiting local boys as crewmen to serve during the rest of the whaling voyage.

Elvira Osorio Roll is the first author on my list of twelve who was born in the United States. The first of only two women, she is also the first to devote herself to peculiarly American problems. She has no desire to return to a distant Sion. Rather, she wishes to improve the quality of life here in Babylon by focussing on a serious problem crying for a solution: ethnic prejudice.

Mrs. Roll was born in Honolulu in 1888, in the days of the monarchy, that is, prior to the U.S. annexation of 1898. Her father, a well-educated businessman, had been born in eastern Continental Portugal. Her mother had come from a village on the south coast of Madeira a little west of the birthplace of John Dos Passos's paternal grandfather. (Be it remembered that, although Yankee whaleships with Portuguese crewmen stopped in the Hawaiian Islands throughout the nineteenth century, mass Portuguese immigration began only in 1878 with the arrival of the first shipload of contract laborers and their families from Madeira to work the sugar plantations.)

Mr. Osorio initially lived in Honolulu on Oahu. He then moved to the island of Hawaii, first to the Kohala district to the northwest and finally to Hilo on the eastern side. In all he had thirteen children, three sons and ten daughters. Elvira was preceded by one of the sons. In a typically Portuguese family this order of arrival causes problems and creates complexes in the daughters, especially talented girls, leading them to assert themselves dramatically, to make something of themselves. So with Elvira, who, in anticipation of Laurinda Andrade soon to be discussed, became a school-teacher. She taught for ten years in public schools. In 1911 she married Professor Albert T. Roll, who subsequently changed his profession from teacher to medical doctor.

Mrs. Roll has written two novels of life in Hawaii, both published in 1964 by the Exposition Press, then of New York City, now of Hicksville, Long Island, New York. I consider the first of the pair, *Hawaii's Kohala Breezes*, which is very little known, to be the single most important piece of United States-Portuguese ethnic literature—always excepting the works of John Dos Passos—and am pleased to be able to announce that the publisher, proud of his contribution to ethnic literature well before ethnic studies became a fad, is considering a reprinting. I shall discuss the novel more at length after I mention the remaining works on my list.

Elvira Osorio Roll's *Background: A Novel of Hawaii* only incidentally treats of the Portuguese ethnic group. It is a novel of social distinctions, the title referring to Mrs. Adams's disapproval of her daughter Bernice's boyfriend. Mrs. Adams, née Adele Rogers, charges that he has no culture, that he can boast of no background. At one point Bernice is being discussed by a group of haole ladies otherwise busy playing cards. Mrs. Lambert catches sight of another lady:

> "Ah, there is Mrs. Small. She's such a quiet little thing. Too bad. She must feel like a fish out of water in our crowd. So demure and then—she being—a foreigner—I mean—a Portuguese—not of our kind . . . ."[8]

Mrs. Lambert is not allowed to pass such a remark with impunity. Another lady retorts:

> "But, Mrs. Lambert, Mrs. Small is no more a foreigner than you or I. She's an American of Portuguese and Spanish ancestry. Their ancestors have been here longer than yours or mine, since 17-."
>
> "You don't say! But we are white, haoles, and Portuguese can't be classed as white."
>
> "Oh, yes they can. They belong to the Caucasian race, same as we do."
>
> "Oh! I knew it was something like that. Pshaw! Back home in England," explained Mrs. Jennings with an audible click of her false teeth, "we consider this bally American mixture just terrible, makes it a race of mongrels, mixed breeds. I can hardly get used to it."
>
> "You should go back to England, Mrs. Jennings, if America is too much for you to tolerate."[9]

The preceding conversation, multiplied by one hundred, constitutes the novel *Hawaii's Kohala Breezes*. Multiplied by one million, it constitutes the United States-ethnic experience of Americans of Portuguese descent and birth, the experience which should be the subject of more novels, from New England, New Jersey, and California as well as from Hawaii—and I should add from Bermuda.

Enough of the eternal longing after the abandoned homeland; to quote the lines of Gloria:

> Meu lindo Portugal, minha Pátria adorada,
> Para mim serás sempre um sacrário de amor;
> Não mais esquecerei teu sorriso de fada,
> Teu carinho de mãi, tua benção sagrada,
> Teu magnético olhar, teu rosto encantador.[10]

But we have had enough of the mutual admiration, enough of the conservative attention devoted to the morass of internal Portuguese politics, which is after all none of America's ethnics' business. United States ethnic literature by definition is concerned with American problems, on which articulate immigrants and their descendants could shed so much light if they so willed.

Oswald A. Bushnell, a distinguished microbiologist and writer, was born in the Hawaiian Islands in 1913. His paternal grandfather, named Busnalli, came from northern Italy. His paternal grandmother immigrated from Madeira.

Bushnell's *The Return of Lono* obviously has nothing to do with the Portuguese in the Hawaiian Islands. His *Ka'a'awa: A Novel About Hawaii in the 1850's*, which was published in 1972 by the University Press of Hawaii, has very little to do with them. Named for Kaaawa on the northeastern shore of Oahu, it only incidentally brings in "Pordagee" Joe, who labored for the Yankee hero, that is a haole, along with the kanakas and who lived in a cluster of shacks. The St. Anthony who is mentioned is not an ethnic reference but rather an allusion to him of the Desert, better spelled St. Antony.

James A. Carvalho is a prominent Honolulu radio announcer of Portuguese descent. Active in Portuguese-descent circles, he is the publisher-editor of a monthly *Portuguese Journal*. Both he and his parents before him were born on the Big Island (Hawaii), he in 1928. His grandparents came from Madeira and from the Azorean island of São Miguel (St. Michael's).

At the end of 1975 a paperback short novel appeared in Chicago, *Haole, Come Back*. The author presents himself as James Oaktree, apparently because he was unsure of Hawaiian reception of his creation. (A *carvalho* is an oaktree, as all devotees of Fátima and the apparitions there of the Virgin in 1917 are well aware.)

At first blush far-fetched and even naive, *Haole, Come Back* quickly reveals itself as a quite profound satire aimed at vociferous enthusiasts of ethnicity. Indeed, in a sense it is anti-ethnic, yet I joyfully list it as an item of Portuguese ethnic literature.

For over three years, various ethnic groups in Hawaii, Alaska, and the mainland United States have laid claim to all land in these states,

Hawaiians to Hawaii, Eskimos to Alaska, and Indians to the rest. The United States Supreme Court has just ruled in favor of the plaintiffs. The United States Attorney General is appealing to the World Court in The Hague for a reversal of the decision. Meanwhile, chaos has befallen the United States. Violence is breaking out. In Hawaii all non-Hawaiians are packing up and leaving. Two families on the island of Hawaii, however, decide to hide and ride out the storm. They suspect that the Hawaiians will not be able to operate their complex technical civilization without haole assistance. John Carter and Antonio de Costa with respective wives and children go into hiding together. Costa's parents "had come from Portugal in 1878 and had worked the land from scratch," and, in author Jimmy Carvalho's view at least, these Portuguese are haoles.

Television broadcasting closed down, then the telephone company, then the electric company. The prison was opened, the post office and schools closed. The two refugee families recognized that a Christian Reverend, descendant of those Yankee missionaries who first carried Christ to the islands in the early nineteenth century, was to blame for the whole mess because he had fought for and encouraged his Hawaiian people at the expense of the other inhabitants:

> . . . In fighting for his people, he had abandoned all others and in the process had unwittingly violated the very foundation of his church. He had divided man. In expressing love for the Hawaiians, he inferred and created hatred for the non-Hawaiians.[11]

The Carters and Costas held many discussions in their mountain retreat. They recalled that even the Hawaiians were ultimately outsiders. Mrs. Costa saw a lesson in that fact, "simply that all of us came from someplace originally and, if we were to go back far enough, we'd all end up again in the Garden of Eden."[12] It is highly significant that Mrs. Roll's thinking ran along parallel tracks, for in *Hawaii's Kohala Breezes* she has young Infelice exclaim:

> "Once you said we all came from the Garden of Eden, Mamae, and we were all brothers and sisters. And I want it that way, for I want to love the whole world."[13]

To make an interesting short story even shorter, the Hawaiians became aware of the impossibility of their new situation, the World Court over-ruled the Supreme Court, and a plea went out for the haoles to come back. Meanwhile, the Costa daughter has fallen in love with a Hawaiian. The phrase "Haole, come back" thus balances "Yankee, go home" within the history of American civilization.

It took Jimmy Carvalho of Honolulu to remind the distinguished and learned audience assembled in Lubbock that a great danger lurks behind ethnicity, ethnic studies, ethnic heritage programs, ethnic literature, and head counts. The shades of his ancestors and of mine shout "Cuidado! Beware! "

Carvalho, backed by Mrs. Roll, is not alone in his thinking. An editorial in the *Honolulu Star Bulletin* of 15 January 1976, concluded:

> The current resurgence of interest in Hawaiian culture and pride in Hawaiian identity is encouraging. However, in this multiracial society it is difficult at best for government to single out any group for special benefits, no matter how legitimate its grievances may be. The problem is compounded in the case of the Hawaiians by the predominance of intermarriage with other races, which has left Hawaiian identity as much a matter of ethnic consciousness as of race.[14]

On that same day, Martin Luther King Day, Lieutenant Governor Nelson K. Doi of Hawaii made a speech in which he called for an end to the "divisive element of separatism" in our society. He called for fair and equal treatment of all persons but said that goal will not be achieved "if members of a group hold themselves apart from the general community."[15]

Jack Martin was born near Lisbon. In 1961, twenty-three years old, he migrated to California. Residing in Stockton and the Bay area, he has carved out a local name for himself as a singer and entertainer. He has married an American girl of Portuguese descent from Tulare down the San Joaquin Valley where many persons from the Azorean island of Terceira have settled.

Martin's first novel has nothing whatsoever to do with Portuguese anywhere. A highly imaginative adventure story, *Hallucination of Death*, published in Reseda, California, by Mojave Books in 1975, may vaguely reflect Fernão Mendes Pinto at his worst. I mention the book only because its author is a relatively recent immigrant from Portugal who has become Americanized so fast that he reflects our violent drug- and abortion-riddled civilization and its slang ("broads" for girls) intertwined with a vaguely remembered Catholicism.

* * *

In order to be deemed creative literature, an autobiography must be exceptionally well written. The two on my list merit inclusion for their sincerity and their revelations of ethnicity as well as for the pleasing style devoid of excessive literary embellishments in which they are written.

Laurinda C. Andrade's autobiography, *The Open Door*, is the more elaborated and introspective of the pair. It has been widely consulted by young social scientists who are turning their attention to the Portuguese ethnic group.

Miss Andrade, who lives in well-deserved retirement in New Bedford, was born on Terceira in 1899. She had an older brother who, in accordance with the Portuguese family tradition which affected the Hawaiian Osorio family, received the lion's share of attention. But Laurinda was as capable as he, if not more so, and she was determined to demonstrate that fact to the world. She did. An early espouser of equal rights for women, she came to the United States one month after we entered World War I. She settled in New Bedford, worked hard, combatted illness, and worked harder. Throughout, her determination, backed by her strong religious faith, was to become a teacher. She entered New Bedford High School in 1924. In 1931, in her thirties, she received her A.B. from Brown University's Pembroke College, at the height of the Depression.

Unable to find a teaching position in New Bedford, she worked for a Portuguese-language newspaper in Newark and, eventually, in the Portuguese Legation (today Embassy) in Washington. By this time she was fired with the desire to introduce the teaching of the Portuguese language and literature into her own New Bedford High School. She perceived her opportunity with the advent of World War II and emerging importance of the Portuguese language in connection with—not Portugal, alas, or the strategically located Azores and Cape Verde Islands which so preoccupied the United States Government and its armed forces in the late spring and the summer of 1941—but with Brazil, the Good Neighbor Policy, and the airfields in Belém, Natal, and Recife.

In 1942 Miss Andrade began her new career, which she pursued for a quarter-century until retirement in 1966. She was instrumental in founding the Portuguese Educational Society of New Bedford in 1944. Years later she gained national prominence at a symposium on the teaching of Portuguese held at the University of Wisconsin in Madison. Her autobiography, published in 1968, represents a crowning achievement.

Lawrence Oliver's autobiography entitled *Never Backward*, of 1972, is the sincere record of a poor immigrant boy born on Pico in 1887 who, unschooled, immigrated into the United States in 1903. He subsequently acquired an education and became a most successful businessman and unstinting civic leader. Today he lives graciously and hospitably in a beautiful home out on Point Loma overlooking the Bay first revealed to Europe by Cabrillo.

Aged almost eighty-eight, in February 1975, Oliver personally drove Mrs. Rogers and me out to the tip of Point Loma to visit the magnificent Cabrillo National Monument in connection with which he has played a prominent role. The chapter in *Never Backward* entitled "The Case Of The Kidnapped Statue," one of the most interesting and certainly the most amusing, details this role. It is required reading for those in Southeastern New England who are importuning the Government of Portugal to furnish

Two views of the ethnic exhibit "Ethnic Literatures: Manuscripts, First Editions, and Photographs," displayed in The Museum of Texas Tech University. (Photographed by Kathy M. Hinson)

a statue of Miguel Corte-Real for the Commonwealth of Massachusetts's Dighton Rock State Park.

* * *

Mrs. Roll's first novel, *Hawaii's Kohala Breezes*, coincides with my personal ideas of what Portuguese ethnic literature should be about. It is my nominee for any list of recommended ethnic reading.

The Portuguese ethnic group goes back at least to 1820. It consists of the descendants of all Portuguese immigrants over the decades—including those of partial Portuguese descent like William Madison Wood, John Philip Sousa, John Randolph Dos Passos, Frank Leo Rogers, John Roderigo Dos Passos, and me—plus Portuguese-born immigrants whether naturalized American citizens or resident aliens. When the new immigrant arrives, he faces a double-melting problem: melting into United States society in general and melting into the pre-existing ethnic group. His Americanization consists of becoming acquainted with American history in general and with the history—and literature—of his ethnic group. So Americanized, he comes to realize that problems which he thinks peculiar to him and his age most often have been common to the entire group from the beginning. One of these is ethnic discrimination.

Mrs. Roll's novel, which treats this subject, is far from perfect. The first edition has a few typographical errors, what seem to be many howlers in Portuguese, and one glaring historical mistake, all of which the publisher promises to correct in his reprinting. And Americanists and Comparatists would probably not consider the book great literature, another *Manhattan Transfer*.

The simple plot involves the Damus family, Madeiran Portuguese, and the Walker family, Scotch-Irish. Hawaiian-born Infelice Damus and Hawaiian-born Jack Walker fall in love, marry, and at the novel's end conceive a child. The Damuses are "Poregees," the Walkers haoles. The Damuses are Catholic, the Walkers Protestant. The Damuses are proud Portuguese, and they are of excellent background. Father, mother, and older sister Athena immigrated in 1878 but paid their own fare; they were not contracted for. The Walkers, on the other hand, are not of such noble lineage. Jack's father was Scottish, his mother Scotch-Irish. After the birth of Jack and his younger sister, the mother died and her husband married a part-Hawaiian girl of loose morals.

The novel provides a quite complete description of life in Hawaii immediately following the beginning of mass Island-Portuguese immigration in 1878. The complex shared by Mrs. Roll and Miss Andrade vis-à-vis an older brother is here reflected in Infelice's attitude toward her brother Christopher. And Infelice, of course, attends normal school in Honolulu and becomes a teacher. The deleterious effects of excessively narrow

Catholic upbringing and convent schooling are adumbrated and remind the reader of Studs Lonigan's schooling. Infelice's final conclusion is forceful: "To hell with hell." Black John from the Cape Verde Islands reminds us of the presence of "Bravas" among the Portuguese in Hawaii. Infelice's use of pidgin English, and notably of the particle "stay" as in "Mr. Walker, you more better quick go. The boss, he stay mad if you stay go slow," combined with Jack's reply, "I stay go quick like hell! "[16] raises the question of possible Cape Verdean *Crioulo* influence on the Pacific islands and also the likelihood of the universality of creole phenomena.

The primary importance of the novel, its lesson for American society as today constituted, lies in the Damus family's insistence that Portuguese are white, are Caucasian. The Damuses refuse to be put down by haoles, whatever they are. The Damuses, like my late mother and like me, cringe at hearing the word "Poregee," or "Portygee" with a *y* as we spell it in New England, "Portugee" with a *u* as Fuselli uses the word in *Three Soldiers*.

If the Damuses were living today in Boston, Massachusetts, they would object vociferously, as I recently did, to the archdiocesan school system's classifying Portuguese students as "Hispanics" and as such distinct from Whites.[17] If they were living today in Newark, California, they would react with passion, as I react, to a classification of households which makes a separate category of Portuguese apart from "White, non-Spanish."[18]

An important character in *Hawaii's Kohala Breezes* is Mrs. Bess Carter of Skunk Hollow, Iowa. Obviously no relative of Mrs. John Carter in *Haole, Come Back*, Bess is the plantation gossip and personification of haole prejudice, as is illustrated by this conversation:

> The evening shadows were falling and still Mrs. Carter remained. There was nothing to do but ask her to dinner. Yes, she would be delighted to stay for dinner. Her maid, Mitsu, cooked such unpalatable dinners, she informed Infelice with a despairing gesture of her hands.
>
> "And I hear you Portuguese are such excellent cooks," she said significantly, with an acquired set of her head and eyebrows raised innocently. Infelice straightened. Ah, the cat was out! Soon would come the clawing. She had arranged the spring. Jack smoked on in a leisurely way, a smile on his face, quite unaware of claws and springs. Then Infelice spoke.
>
> "But you see, Mrs. Carter, we did not bring our Portuguese cook along, so I am afraid you are doomed to disappointment. If you do not object to potluck, I can furnish you with my plain American cooking."
>
> "Oh, how disappointing! I have always wanted to meet you for an express purpose, really, and I must confess my interest was a rather gluttonous one. I so wanted to eat a Portuguese dinner. I love garlic, only don't breathe it to a soul. How disappointing! " There was affected regret in her voice. "I see you have a guitar. I suppose you dance and sing Portuguese dances and songs? It must be rather quaint and amusing for Jack. So different for him. I believe you still have a little of the Portuguese accent. It is quaint, isn't it, Jackie? I can barely detect it, of course."[19]

Another example of a disgusting monologue is:

> Still the ungenerous tabby pursued the subject, and entirely ignored the warning signals given her by Mrs. Miller.
>
> "You should have married your own kind, Infelice. Jack would have been so much happier in his own element. As it is, he's really ostracized. I know he is awfully lonely. Marriage is such a serious thing. And then, when the children come, the trouble will begin," she went on, encouraged by Infelice's silence. Her enjoyment was intense. She had jumped on the cage. Now to get the bird and crunch its head until—until—"Maybe Jack doesn't intend to raise a family. He knows how it would be. That would be rather unfortunate for all concerned. The poor little ones would have so much with which to contend, especially among the haole children. You know what I mean. When they start to go to school, they would be half-whites. And half-breeds, my dear, in Mexico, where there is so much of that misfortune, they grow up to be neither one thing nor the other. Usually the result, for the youngster, is tragic. You see, they would forever be reminded of the fact—half-white—"[20]

At that point, Infelice threw Mrs. Carter from Skunk Hollow, Iowa, out of her house.

My mother, whose father was born in Horta on Fayal in the Azores and whose mother was born on Pico, spent her life span of eighty-six years in Massachusetts overhearing Mrs. Carters because, to quote a hallowed phrase, my mother did not "look Portuguese" and my father's family name betrayed no Portuguese origin. Indeed, Standard Oil tycoon Henry Huttleston Rogers had a home right across the Acushnet River in Fairhaven, and our Yankee neighbors could draw any conclusion their little hearts desired. My mother died exactly one year ago still rebelling against stupid ethnic prejudice involving Portygees, Micks, Wops, Polacks, and Canucks. She reflected and transmitted to me the Catholic and Portuguese heritage of stress on universality rather than on diversity.

* * *

I hazard two simple conclusions: (1) belletristic ethnic literature contributes much more extensively and profoundly to a real understanding of a United States ethnic group than limited social science studies, however technically perfect these studies may be; and (2) in order to attain to a complete understanding of a United States ethnic group it is essential to know the civilization, and above all the intimate language(s), of the group's land(s) of origin.

I draw an additional and major conclusion: true ethnic literature is a literature of maturity. Almost by definition, ethnic literature normally has to be written by immigrants resident here for many years and by descendants born here. The ethnic literature of Americans of Portuguese descent and birth forms part of American literature, not of Portuguese literature. It treats American problems, not Portuguese problems.

One is tempted to draw a distinction between ethnic literature and immigrant literature. The latter would include the volumes of poems and journalistic essays written in their native language by recent immigrants, writers who are, for the moment at least, transplanted Portuguese. Of considerably more formal schooling than the earlier immigrants, these new arrivals, often young ex-university or ex-seminary students, remain in close intellectual and even publishing contact with their fatherland. A portion of them tend to be highly critical of democratic America, which they have barely come to know. They are not really ethnics, and they are not really writing ethnic literature.

Perhaps it is nonrevitalized maturity which explains why a disproportionate amount of Portuguese ethnic literature has come out of Hawaii. Portuguese immigration there began early in the nineteenth century and even included Cape Verdeans. With 1878 and the arrival of the bark *Priscilla* came a great increase. Since the renewed post-quota Portuguese immigration which began with the Azorean Refugee Acts of 1958 and 1960, however, very few Portuguese have indicated an intention to settle in Hawaii, only two out of over eleven thousand, for example, in 1973-1974.

Hawaiians of Portuguese descent thus are possessed of a perspective on themselves undisturbed by a recent influx of relatives from the Old Country, and that perspective is mirrored in the novels by Elvira Osorio Roll and James A. Carvalho. It is also reflected in many other writings. An example is furnished by the short stories of Elma T. Cabral (née Elma Tranquada), several of which have been published in *Paradise of the Pacific*: "Grandpa was a Troubadour" (1946, about the original ukulele, introduced by the Portuguese), "Boas Festas: A Nostalgic Story of Christmas in Hawaii as Celebrated by a Family Newly Arrived from Portugal" (1947), "The Romance of Roza das Vacas" (1948), "The Bells Tolled with Passion" (1949), " 'Turn da Roun' Dahlia! ': A Story of Portuguese Immigrants in Hawaii" (1952), "Maezinha's Dilemma: A Story of Early Portuguese Immigrants in Hawaii" (1953), and "The Irresistible Henrique" (1954).

Another example is José Tavares de Teves' rollicking ballad reminiscent of "A Nao Catharineta" (even to the infinitive *pasmar* at the end of the second line). Entitled "Um Acontecimento," it was originally published in Portuguese in 1886 in the newspaper *O Luso Hawaiiano*. It was reprinted with English translation by Professor Edgar C. Knowlton, Jr., in Carvalho's *Portuguese Journal* in the April-May 1974 issue. Teves was born on São Miguel and arrived in Hawaii aboard the *Suffolk* on 25 August 1881, when about twenty-six, as a contract laborer. He married a woman who arrived with him on the same vessel, and they had eleven children. A poet, songwriter, and musician, José died at age sixty-four.

It is perhaps characteristic of the ethnic maturity of the Hawaiian Portuguese that, when they quote the Portuguese language, they make many linguistic errors. Indeed, what I have attributed to Mrs. Roll as howlers in Portuguese may in fact be faithful images of an ethnic dialect. The Portuguese language is rather far removed from Hawaii in both space and time, whereas that of the Northeasterners and the Californians is constantly reinforced by recent arrivals.[21]

* * *

When I embarked on this study I naively supposed that, after analyzing the little Portuguese ethnic literature with which I was acquainted, I would have time to answer the questions "Why so little? " and "Why so late? " I intended to call attention to the relative smallness of the Portuguese ethnic group; to the relative proximity of its members to the several homelands, especially the Azores; to the relative lack of education of the vast majority of Portuguese immigrants over the decades; and to their relative lack of familiarity with freedom of thought and of criticism. Most important of all, I wished to point out the deleterious effect on the Portuguese immigrants and their descendants of American racism, of a tendency of the past especially prevalent in New England to note that most Cape Verdeans were of mixed African-European origin or were black while yet of Portuguese nationality and to conclude that all Portuguese were nonwhite and ipso facto inferior. This noting was not merely oral but very often expressed in writing in works of American literature.

The effect of the tendency was to cause members of the Portuguese ethnic group to change their family names (or, as in the case of my paternal grandfather from Horta, to accept a change imposed upon them by nonlinguistically trained inspectors at the gate) and to melt completely. Such ethnics were clearly not disposed to compose ethnic literature, and they did not.

* * *

A list of works of American literature which discuss Portuguese characters or themes wholly or in part includes a Longfellow poem and a Frances Parkinson Keyes novel to call attention to the existence of the Portuguese Jews; an Irving Stone novel to call attention to the Madeira Protestants of Illinois; a Michener novel to remind us once again that the Portuguese presence is significant in Hawaii; a recent Carlos Heard Baker detective story to embrace Martha's Vineyard within the zone of Portuguese settlement; Jeremiah Digges' superbly written *In Great Waters* to cause us in Massachusetts to continue to couple Provincetown and Gloucester; and the beautiful little poèmes en prose by a Dabney—in English but entitled *Saudades*—to render homage to the generous and unprejudiced Dabney family which for three generations, from 1806 to 1891, contributed distinguished United States consuls to the Azores.

The remaining books on such a list reflect typical American ethnic prejudice and stereotypy. They range from Kipling's *Captains Courageous* with its "Portugoosey" Manuel and his "curly black hair" to Garside's *Cranberry Red* and its Cape Verdean Joe Gonsalves, "stooped monkey" with "bluish lips, like cuts of frozen veal."[22]

Harvard University

NOTES

[1] Originally, I had thought that I would claim John Roderigo Dos Passos (1896-1970) as one of my Portuguese ethnic writers for this paper. I had become seriously interested in Dos Passos' Portuguese heritage at the time (17 June 1961) when he received the Peter Francisco Award of the Portuguese Continental Union of the United States of America. It soon became apparent that time would not permit me to discuss in this paper the many direct references and indirect allusions to and passing reflections of his Madeiran paternal grandfather to be found throughout Dos Passos' writings. In a separate monograph entitled *The Portuguese Heritage of John Dos Passos* (Boston: Portuguese Continental Union, 1976), I discuss and quote from these books, include mention of O'Neill's *Mourning Becomes Electra* (New York: Horace Liveright, 1931) with its Portuguese fishing captain Joe Silva, and conclude by repeating a passage from Dos Passos' last work, *Century's Ebb: The Thirteenth Chronicle* (Boston: Gambit, 1975):

> Finally I said suppose we all slept on it, and started for home. Down in the entrance lobby I spied a phone booth. I went in and called Jay Pignatelli. His voice sounded friendly, another thing that reminded me of Rio. He wasn't any Brazilian but he was kind of like one in a way .... (p. 414)

The Portuguese Continental Union had my monograph printed so as to make it available to members of the Portuguese ethnic group and to others in order that they might realize that Dos Passos was indeed, in part, one of the many ethnic voices of America.

Furthermore, I have excluded works from the following categories:

(1) *Unpublished works.* For example, there are two short plays by Americans of Cape Verdean origin, "The Cape Verdean-American Tie" by John P. (Joli) Gonsalves and "Nita: Teatro" by Rosendo Évora Brito. The latter is also a poet. A native of the island of Santo Antão, he left home in 1962, settled first in Yonkers, New York, and now resides in East Providence, Rhode Island. An interview in the *Boston Sunday Globe*'s magazine of 7 December 1975, quotes an English version of one of his poems, "We Are Returning" (p. 64), typical of Cape Verdean-American sentiments:

> As migratory birds
> We shall return to sing in the valley
> And to hear the echo of our laughter
> Among the murmuring cliffs.
>
> Like migratory eels
> We shall return to dart in the waves.
> We shall climb over castles in the warm sand
> And tug on the nets of the fishermen.
>
> Like spawning salmon
> We shall once again cross the mad waters
> The day following the heavy rain
> When the dry river beds are choked with blond waters.

There we will dig in the belly of the earth
For the umbilical cord we left behind.
We shall unearth the relic of our forefathers
In the search for our beginning.

And then
We shall have found ourselves.
We shall defy droughts, hardships and famine
And defy everything that defied us.

(2) *Works in Portuguese-language newspapers.* I am forced to the conclusion that these newspapers as a whole represent a political and cultural projection of Portugal in the United States—or at least of a particular and very conservative brand of Portuguese thinking—which is quite a different thing from ethnicity. Although these newspapers on occasion publish creative literature of merit and also excellent scholarly studies, writings so disseminated do not receive the national projection which in my opinion qualifies them to fall under the classification of ethnic literature in the United States. Ethnic literature, to be a true voice, must reach the ears of others, and notably members of more dominant groups.

(3) *Folklore.* Although folk tales, folk medicine, and folk religion are widespread among Americans of Portuguese birth, especially recent immigrants, and although survivals extend to children and grandchildren born here, this folklore seems to me to be a Portuguese phenomenon and not an American or ethnic one. I regretfully omit consideration of it, in spite of the contributions by such scholars as Henry R. Lang, Elsie Eells, Elsie Clews Parsons, Anna H. Gayton, George Monteiro, Joanne B. Purcell, and Manuel da Costa Fontes. The folk medicine of Portuguese immigrants in Cambridge, Massachusetts, is today being studied seriously and competently by Robert Like, a student at the Harvard Medical School.

(4) *Visitor literature.* Books published in Portugal by visitors or temporary residents who return home and write up in Portuguese what they experienced in the United States are of great interest, for example Natália Correia's highly critical *Descobri que Era Europeia: Impressões duma Viagem à América* (1951), which even aims a barb at me. But they hardly constitute ethnic literature.

(5) *Transplanted Portuguese literature.* Such works have been written by distinguished Portuguese literary figures living in the United States like José Rodrigues Migueis, Jorge de Sena, and Galician-born Ernesto Guerra Da Cal, some of whom teach in our universities.

(6) *Scholarly studies.* The few published books dealing with the Portuguese ethnic group do not constitute literature and are left out of consideration. I also omit scholarly books on Portuguese subjects written by Americans of Portuguese descent. Methodological rigor, moreover, forces me to exclude a book recently published in Portugal and of which I received an advanced copy three weeks before the symposium began. By Onésimo Teotónio Almeida, a recent immigrant born on São Miguel in the Azores and now a graduate student in philosophy at Brown University, it is entitled *Da Vida Quotidiana na L USA lândia, Luso* being a Portuguese adjective meaning Portuguese. The book reprints articles or parts of articles published in a column of the *Portuguese Times* of New Bedford between January 1973 and April 1975. It could conceivably be viewed as a volume of literary essays, and it does contain many challenging sections, including a rather audacious criticism of the Portuguese program at Harvard University. Finally, I eliminate scholarly studies on non-ethnic subjects by Americans of Portuguese descent and birth, for instance, Richard A. Pimetel's *Invertebrate Identification Manual* (1967), George C. Avila's

The Pairpoint Glass Story (1968), George Arnold Salvador's *Paul Cuffe, The Black Yankee, 1759-1817* (1969), John R. Fonseca's *Handling Consumer Credit Cases* (1972, written in collaboration with Barkley Clark), and Earl J. Dias's *Henry Huttleston Rogers: Portrait of a "Capitalist"* (1974).

(7) *Creative literature.* This literature is written by members of the Portuguese ethnic group but has nothing to do with that group, for example, Fausto P. Lage's *Joana d'Arc: O Romance da Vida da Donzela de Orleans* (Lisbon: Editorial Minerva, 1948) and Oswald A. Bushnell's *The Return of Lono: A Novel of Captain Cook's Last Voyage* (Boston: Little, Brown, 1956).

My criteria unfortunately left me with a very slight literary contribution by Americans of Portuguese descent as an identifiable voice, excepting of course the work of John Dos Passos. It amounts to fourteen books. One volume of verse and two novels were published after I submitted the summary of this paper several weeks before the meeting.

The principal facts concerning the Portuguese ethnic group are (1) that the vast majority of Americans of Portuguese descent and birth reflect four quite distinct proveniences—Continental Portugal, Azores Islands, Madeira Islands, and Cape Verde Islands—the majority of the vast majority being from the Azores; (2) that Continentals, Azoreans, and Madeirans are, by and large, whites or "Caucasians" and Cape Verdeans are, by and large, of mixed European and African origin; and (3) that the Cape Verde Islands became independent on 5 July 1975, and that movements for greater autonomy, if not outright independence, are today active in the other two Atlantic archipelagoes. For information concerning Portuguese in America, see Francis M. Rogers and David T. Haberly, *Brazil, Portugal, and Other Portuguese-Speaking Lands: A List of Books Primarily in English* (Cambridge: Harvard Univ. Press, 1968), pp. 33-35; Francis M. Rogers, *Americans of Portuguese Descent: A Lesson in Differentiation* (Beverly Hills, Calif.: Sage Publications, 1974), Sage Paper No. 90-013 (contains "References" with 26 items and "Suggested Additional Reading" with 72 items); Francis M. Rogers, *Portuguese in North America* (Philadelphia: The Balch Institute, 1974), The Balch Institute Historical Reading Lists No. 6; and Manoel da Silveira Cardozo, *The Portuguese in America 590 B.C.-1974: A Chronology & Fact Book* (Dobbs Ferry, New York: Oceana Publications, 1976), Ethnic Chronology Series No. 22 (contains many additional references). A most useful bibliography has recently appeared—Leo Pap, *The Portuguese in the United States: A Bibliography* (Staten Island: Center for Migration Studies, 1976).

[2] Francis M. Rogers, *Precision Astrolabe: Portuguese Navigators and Transoceanic Aviation* (Lisbon: Academia Internacional da Cultura Portuguesa, 1971— distributed in the United States by Wm. S. Sullwold, Publishing, Taunton, Mass.).

[3] Arthur Vieira Ávila, "Portugal," in *Rimas de Um Imigrante* (Oakland, Calif.: The author, 1961), p. 79.

[4] José Reinaldo Matos, "Saudades da Minha Terra," in *Sonetos da América* (Braga, Portugal: Barbosa & Xavier, 1975), p. 60.

[5] José Brites, "O Mundo é mesmo assim," in *Poemas sem Poesia* (Bethlehem: The Author, 1975), p. 15.

[6] Brites, "Poema pra 27 de Janeiro," in *Poemas sem Poesia*, p. 45. The translation reads: "I raised my hands from the depths of my Spirit and I beseeched / (not little saints and little angels / who however much I might opportune them / never extended their hands to grant) / I beseeched Men with Power here on Earth / —that they love each other for the Love of Men— / and that as a special favor / they not begin anywhere another War." Translation mine.

[7] Leonard Bacon, tr., *The Lusiads of Luiz de Camoes* (New York: The Hispanic Society of America, 1950), p. 411. Alfred Lewis died on 10 January 1977.

[8] Elvira Osorio Roll, *Background: A Novel of Hawaii* (New York: Exposition Press, 1964), p. 170.

[9] Roll, *Background*, pp. 170-71.

[10] Guilherme Silveira Gloria, *Poesias* (Oakland, Calif.: Tipografia de "A Liberdade," 1935), p. 1.

[11] James A. Carvalho, *Haole, Come Back*, by James Oaktree [pseud.] (Chicago: Adams Press, 1975), p. 43.

[12] Carvalho, p. 55.

[13] Elvira Osorio Roll, *Hawaii's Kohala Breezes* (New York: Exposition Press, 1964), p. 21.

[14] *Honolulu Star Bulletin*, 15 January 1976.

[15] Ibid.

[16] Roll, *Hawaii's Kohala Breezes*, pp. 165 and 166.

[17] *The Pilot*, Boston 28 November 1975, p. 1.

[18] "Ethnic Character by Household, by Census Tract & Area, Newark, Ca. Sept. 1975," p. 16 of a report, a xerox of the page having been sent me by Mr. Joseph Milton Freitas of Fremont, California.

[19] Roll, *Hawaii's Kohala Breezes*, p. 183.

[20] Ibid., p. 230.

[21] This first portion of my paper has been in reality a collective research enterprise. For references to the Hawaiian materials, I am greatly indebted to my former student, Professor Edgar C. Knowlton, Jr., of the University of Hawaii. I also wish to express my gratitude to Mr. Alberto S. Lemos, Publisher-Editor of Oakland's *Jornal Português* for assistance with the California dimension; to Director James D. Hart of the Bancroft Library of the University of California at Berkeley for an additional attempt involving California; to Mr. Alonzo Smith, Director of Promotion & Sales, Exposition Press, Inc., for the generous loan of Mrs. Roll's *Hawaii's Kohala Breezes*; to Professor Manoel da Silveira Cardozo of The Catholic University of America for first calling my attention to the poetry of Guilherme Silveira Gloria and for other suggestions; to Mrs. Celeste Alice Santos Ávila for providing me with considerable information about her husband, Arthur Vieira Ávila; and to Miss Laurinda C. Andrade, Dr. Fausto P. Lage, Father José Reinaldo Matos, and MM. Onésimo Teotónio Almeida, Heldo T. Braga, José Joaquim Baptista Brites, James A. Carvalho, Alfred Lewis, and Lawrence Oliver for their biographies, photographs, and writings. Moreover, I am grateful to Rabbi Louis C. Gerstein of Congregation Shearith Israel in New York and to Professor Herman P. Salomon, Editor, *The American Sephardi*, for their aid in an attempt to find contributions by Americans of Portuguese Jewish descent. Lastly, for considerable assistance and many sensible suggestions, I thank my Harvard/Radcliffe students in Portuguese 101, "Language, Literature, and Lifestyle of the Portuguese in the United States" (Fall, 1975-1976) – Diana Clark, Timothy Freitas (from Hilo, Hawaii), Jaime da Silva, and John Tavares.

[22] All but three of these books I discussed in a paper entitled "The Portuguese Experience in the United States: Double Melt or Minority Group? " read at a symposium at Adelphi University on 2 December 1975, and published in *The Journal of the American Portuguese Society*, 10, No. 1 (Spring 1976), 1-16. Two of the books omitted at Adelphi, the relatively recent Cannon and Wolfson books, I include to complete the record, the first with its "Portygee" Joe Felipe, "dark-complected" and with "black hair," the second with its Vinnie Cabral, "like an ape," a "dirty

'Portugee,' " "swarthy as a Moor," with skin of "bronzed olive-darkness": LeGrand Cannon, Jr., *Look to the Mountain* (New York: Henry Holt, 1942), p. 5, and Victor Wolfson, *Cabral* (New York: Avon Books, 1972), pp. 8 and 9. The third book, *Mourning Becomes Electra*, is mentioned in note 1 above.

The *Jíbaro*: Symbol and Synthesis

María Teresa Babín

ABSTRACT

In Puerto Rican literature the *jíbaro* image embodies a diversity of modes and meanings. The persistence of its original mark has remained as the core of the artful elaborations derived from the analogy with a human and spiritual entity, a metaphor of flesh and soul evoking telluric and timeless mystery. From the early appearance of the *jíbaro* in prose and poetry, the image became the inspiration for an optimistic search of the essence of Puerto Rican culture. There are degrees of sophistication in the style of the authors, but they share the common intention of keeping alive the symbolism of the traditional folk hero while depicting the evils of modern times. To the romantic spirit of the mythical and telluric being created in the nineteenth century, the poets of the vanguard movements attributed an increased sensitivity to nonconformity. The urban *jíbaro* emerged, taking the place of the rustic peasant immortalized in poetry and fiction. The contemporary Puerto Rican authors on the Island and in the United States have remained faithful to the matrix of the primitive symbol. Its diffused and pervading presence is a substantive concept that permeates the whole structure of Puerto Rican life and creativity. (MTB)

Among the multiple offshoots loosened from the homogenous trunk of Puerto Rican literature, there stands out, because of its persistence through time, the image of the *jíbaro* or peasant, symbol and synthesis of a concept of art and life, a changing theme in a diverse variety of tones and meanings which finds its way into the style of the best poets and prose writers. The mark or original sign was coined in the heat of romantic realism on the forge of the nascent Americanist conscience which proclaimed intellectual independence, and this mark persisted in the nucleus of artistic creations and associations derived from the analogy with a human and spiritual entity, a metaphor of flesh and blood, a creature of the mind and imagination who evokes a timeless telluric mystery. Myth, legend, and rupestrian carving, and the voice and breath of tropical nature are involved in this stylized figure drawn in tapestries and artistic pictures next to the elements which comprise his worldly existence: the horse or hack, the "bohío" (peasant hut), the "batey" (esplanade), the rooster, the ox, or the dark-brown bull, the machete, the dagger or sickle-sword, the grey kingbird, the banana stain and other objects, animals, birds and plants which constitute a constellation whose center is the presence of his solitary existence in constant movement. While other literary symbols have been shaped as stereotypes fixed with their own proper names, such as Don Quixote, Don Juan, the Celestina, Martín Fierro, Hamlet or Moby Dick, the coherent form of the *jíbaro* symbol is more nearly a person than a character, although he may not be a replica of any known subject with realistically transferred characteristics nor have a proper name which identifies him. The *jíbaro* is the national seal of what is Puerto Rican, a substantive concept which permeates the whole structure of existence and creativity of the people. Research and interpretation of sources known to scholars interested in the *jíbaro* make the following points manifest.

(1) The concept and the term *jíbaro* is identified with a human being who inhabits the mountainous region of the island of Puerto Rico.

(2) The language spoken by the *jíbaro* and imitated by writers with spelling and phonetic adaptations is a living, archaic Spanish, full of coloration.

(3) The dominant traits of the *jíbaro* reflect ethical values and the ideal of romantic liberty of the nineteenth century: pride, dignity, resistance, perseverance.

(4) The transformation of the traditional *jíbaro* in works of fiction and lyric and dramatic poetry in the twentieth century manifests the profound traces that his history has left in the life and culture of Puerto Rico.

Although the historian Salvador Brau says that the term *jíbaro* was already in use in the eighteenth century, the essayist Antonio S. Pedreira affirms that the concept as such existing in our cultural atmosphere dates from the nineteenth century. Following the paths traced by these and other scholars, one can appreciate the fact that the term *jíbaro* is the most generalized and valid for Puerto Rican literature.[1] From the earliest image of the *jíbaro* till the final stage of romantic realism and naturalism, one may observe the gradual disappearance of the picturesque element while he searches for the essence of the symbol, as revealing the hardships of rural life. The interior voice remains faithful to the primary matrix, rescued from pages printed in newspapers, Christmas literary selections and almanacs of the first decades of the nineteenth century.[2] The twentieth century molds the image and gives it new forms under the modernist influences and the stylistic currents of the Vanguard "isms." With the accelerated passage of time, the free and romantic being of mythical and telluric roots, attached to the land and the surrounding countryside, begins to acquire overtones of tragedy and threats, making more acute his non-conformist sensitivity. The city *jíbaro* appears, displacing the rustic peasant immortalized in poems, vignettes, theatrical works and narrations of a past American idyll.

José Pablo Morales,[3] an illustrious journalist who used the nom de plume of "Un Campesino" (A Peasant), attempted an ingenious explanation of the origin of the name *jíbaro*, while other authors later perceived the gradual adaptation of the symbolic sign to the necessities of "a way of civilization quite different which marked for him new and different norms of life."[4] The modernists lament the loss of traditions with melancholy and lyrical recollections, with romantic tones, or they set out in defense of the most esteemed attributes of the *jíbaro* inherited from his forefathers. Virgilio Dávila and Lloréns Torres represent these modes of tones and sentiments in several poems. "Elegy of Kings," dedicated to the Three Wise Men by Virgilio Dávila, is a lament of the *jíbaro* who has seen disappear a whole world of traditions and feels the hard present reality as a sign of ill omens:

> Llora, llora, corazón
> que ves pasar al olvido
> lo que en nosotros ha sido
> encanto, dicha, ilusión.
> ¡Ya se fue la tradición
> que más nuestros nos hacía!
> ¡Ay, Madre Melancolía,
> que ya no somos nosotros!
> ¡Ahora es igual que los otros
> el que fue nuestro gran día![5]

Lloréns Torres exalts the *jíbaro*'s resistance to the temptations of the "pitiyanquis"* who strive to paint to him in attractive colors the new era of Americanization, while he affirms the indelible mark of the seal of his identity with pride and patriotic love. Let us examine the two learned "décimas" (ten line stanzas) in which the great poet honors the *décima jíbara* and the powers of his will to persist in the path of his choice:

I

> Llegó un jíbaro a San Juan
> y unos cuantos pitiyanquis
> lo atajaron en el parque
> queriéndolo conquistar:
> le hablaron del Tío Sam,
> de Wilson, de Mr. Root,
> de New York, de Sandy-hook,
> de la libertad, del voto,
> del dólar, del habeas corpus,
> y el jíbaro dijo: ¡nju. . . !

*Combination of the French *petit* (small) and the English "Yankee."

II

Mata de plátano, a ti,
a ti te debo la mancha
que ni el jabón ni la plancha
quitan de encima de mí.
Desque jíbaro nací,
al aire llevo el tesoro
de tu racimo de oro
y tu hoja verde y ancha,
llevaré siempre la mancha
per sécula, seculorum . . . ![6]

During the Vanguardist period the image of the *jíbaro* is fortified in literature. The fact that, in 1917, Puerto Ricans officially became citizens of the United States imparted to the symbol a greater luster as an image of faith and inspiration in the optimistic search for the essence of national culture. Writers went to the extreme of reflecting the existential drama of the *jíbaro*, both barefoot and dispossessed, and they thus reaffirmed the integrity of the surviving symbol. The spiritual anguish of a people against the ravages of political history were manifested in a virile prose and poetry, divested of the foliage covering the image lost in the dreamt paradise of past time. This literature traced with dexterous hand the foreshortening of the effigy in its tragic skeleton, in living flesh. Short story writers and essayists like Antonio S. Pedreira, Miguel Meléndez Muñoz, Emilio Belaval, and Enrique Laguerre began to penetrate the significance of the symbol, a synthesis of a national concept of life and culture. The 1930 generation and the successive waves of writers have manipulated the symbolism of the *jíbaro* with subtle gradations of style and esthetic intentions. The migration of many Puerto Ricans to the United States had carried the *jíbaro* image—a new Bayoán*— to multiform adventures of metaphor in which the unanimous intention of saving the folkloric element produces a Baroque contortion for protest and exaltation of the myth. If at the end of the nineteenth century the euphoria of the *costumbristas jíbaros*[7] had flowed into the naturalist vision of the sick world of rural life,[8] giving the symbol the heads or tails of its destiny in times of Spain, during the seventy-six years of the twentieth century, with the exodus of many families from the country to the city and from the small town to the gigantic metropolis in the United States, both learned literature and popular literature have taken over the significance of the *jíbaro* in his urban, cosmopolitan and universal perspective. Let us go back a bit to trace the steps of the *jíbaro* in the prose and poetry of yesteryear to that of today, marking the limits in each moment of what constitutes the weight and measure of its persistence and its future destiny.

*Bayoán is the Indian name to personify Puerto Rico in the Romantic novel *The Pilgrimage of Bayoán*, by Eugenio María de Hostos.

Satire, humor and picturesque description are repeated in the examples gleaned from newspapers and books during the first stage of native literature between 1814 and 1849. The pseudonym *El Gíbaro paciente* (The patient peasant)—notice the adjective *patient*—hides the personality of the man who signs an article published in number 41 of the newspaper *El Diario Económico* of 17 June 1814.

The anonymous composition, *Coplas del Jíbaro* (Peasant Couplets) is not long in appearing (1820). Miguel Cabrera, the author, is identified in another newspaper, *La Gaceta de Puerto Rico*, on 30 June 1820, in which he made clear his intention in writing these couplets. Hence, we are in the historical moment of the absolutism of Ferdinand VII, between 1808 and 1833, when the collective voice of the people in Puerto Rico is externalized under the guise of the anonymous patient *jíbaro*, singer of couplets to express his misfortunes. The precarious and unstable island society gives signs of being alert to the legal and political changes which affected its life when the writer from Arecibo, Miguel Cabrera, imitates rustic speech and offers the first poem of which we have notice, with words, spelling and attitudes revealing the feeling and thinking of a *jíbaro* from the beginnings of the nineteenth century:

Vamos Suidadanos
jasta ei pueblo oi,
poique tío Juan Congo*
tocará ei tamboi.

Mire prima Sica,
múdeme ej lichón
que yo voy a vei
la Costitución.

Isen la an tragío
en un gran papei,
de juro la a embiao
deje España, ei Rei.

Se viene poaquí
mi compai Cirilo
ígale se vaya
ai pueblo de jilo.

Que ha salío cierta
la Costitución
y van a jasei
una gran funsión.

Ella debe sei
según lo que suena
una ciscustancia
ea diablos, muy güena.

*The name indicates the African origin of this character.

El paire Vicario
que es muy entendío
está de gritai
con un gran gipío.

Jablando de lelles
¡qué güenas que son
las que a conducío
la Costitución!

Usté pué si quiere
cuando está enfadao
pegalle a su paire
una bofetá.

Y si usté a una mosa
la jecha a peidei
usté se va limpio
sin que le pleité.

Usté que se encuentre
una cridatura
y quiere casaise,
va de jilo ai Cura.

Ni paires ni maires,
ni tidos ni agüelos,
a nengunos pueden
cortarles los güelos.

Si cualquiera Jues
no le jabla bien
pué uste si quiere
gritalle también.

Yo por mí lo igo,
si ei Gobeinadoi
me falta ai respeto
de jilo le doi.

Me han asegurao
con gran sijilio
que no pagaremos
ya nengún susilio.

Ni paa la iglesia
se ha de dai un rial,
las pitimas toas
se van a cabai.

Que toos los presos
se echarán ajuera
y que ya ca uno
jará lo que quiera.

Agora que en cuanto
a sei uno gente,

ésta es juna cosa
que anda muy caliente.

Y que otro Cabildio
se pone deje hoi,
pudiendo cuaiquiera
ei sei rugidoi.

Y poi más que tenga
guaidia en su batei,
sabrá que yo soy
tan güeno como ei.

Pues jesta escribío
con letras de moide,
que no hay estensión
de ricos ni probes.

Jasta los casaos
puen tener su jembra
con la condición
que an de mantenella.

Poique son enrreos
estos matrimoños,
que ai fin y ai cabo
nos lleva el demonio.

Mañana en ei día
mato mi lichón
para celebrai
la Costitución.[9]

In parallel with this humorous flowering with malicious roguishness, one discovers the testimony of foreigners who begin to reach Puerto Rico early in the nineteenth century; their observations bring judgments and important details for understanding the reasons which caused the Puerto Rican writer to envisage the *jíbaro* as a symbol and synthesis of national identity. George Dawson Flinter, the author of a report published in London in 1834 that depicts the condition of the island, describes the life and customs of the peasant who then inhabited the mountainous region.[10] According to Flinter, this peasant enjoyed many comforts and good fortune, a fortunate view which coincides with the image projected in some poems and folkloric vignettes of famous authors of Romanticism and *costumbrismo* such as Manuel A. Alonso, the author of *El Gíbaro* (First Part, 1849), or the skit writer Manuel Méndez Quiñones, the author of several comic sketches, among which stand out *Los Jíbaros Progresistas* (The Progressive Peasants), in 1882. The emotion of Flinter, a regiment commander, upon describing a visit he made one rainy day to a peasant's house, expresses the esteem he feels for the humble, generous and hospitable folk who welcome him to their "bohío." Another foreigner, Charles

Walker,[11] relates in letters written from Puerto Rico between 1835 and 1837 the customs and the character of the inhabitants of Puerto Rico, and in his exact manner of selecting details he demonstrates a fine sensitivity for perceiving expressions of rural life in the Guayama zone, including a wake for a young child and a description of the town market.[12] In those same years that Flinter and Walker visited the island, learned Puerto Ricans were forging the self portrait of their Puerto Ricanism with the substance of speech, the traditional inheritance and the perception of the human qualities of the *jíbaro*. There is a gallery of characters and scenes in which we see the identification, already evident in *El Gíbaro* of Alonso, between being Puerto Rican and feeling in accord with the *jíbaro* essence of the symbol personified in the peasant. Santiago Vidarte sang to the idealized peasant girl surrounded by her treasures: the hut, palm tree, cocoanuts, lemons, mamey fruit and the blossoming rose bush. Pablo Sáez dedicated a poem to the criollo woman and Manuel Alonso devoted another to the man, in a flare of virtuosity for the physical and moral portrait of the true human being and of another dreamt of Puerto Rican, the prototype of striking *jíbaro* qualities:

> Color moreno, frente despejada,
> Mirar lánguido, altivo y penetrante,
> La barba negra, pálido el semblante,
> Rostro enjuto, nariz proporcionada,
>
> Mediana talla, marcha acompasada;
> El alma de ilusiones anhelante,
> Agudo ingenio, libre y arrogante,
> Pensar inquieto, mente acalorada,
>
> Humano, afable, justo, dadivoso,
> En empresas de amor siempre variable,
> Tras la gloria y placer siempre afanoso,
>
> Y en amor a su patria insuperable:
> Este es, a no dudarlo, fiel diseño
> Para copiar un buen puertorriqueño.[13]

A marked preference is manifested for certain strophic forms and meters in the learned poetry which derived from the anonymous popular poetry of the people, and there arise in the first anthologies between 1843 and 1869 the first battles between the native and foreign perspectives, in popular poetry as well as in prose. The "aguinaldo," so dear to the Christmas tradition, served to baptize the first bunch of verses and narrations with which begins the sequel of albums, song books and almanacs in which the diverse tones of Antillean literature of the period abound. Refined language and rustic speech are intertwined with Romantic and costumbrista tendencies in "letrillas," epigrams, ballads, "décimas" and couplets, where we see the transformation of the *jíbaro* symbol as the basis of

poetic creativity in language, thematics and versification. A defender of
"las vulgares coplas de Navidad" is an educated man, Francisco Vasallo,
who chooses the following from his repertory:

> Alabar a Dios
> Por ser lo primero
> Y después de alabao
> Me siento en el suelo.
>
> Naranjas y limas,
> Limas y limones,
> Más vale la Virgen
> Que todas las flores.
>
> Por la yerva vengo
> Pisando el rosido,
> Y traigo el estógamo
> Bastante aflejido.
>
> Naranjas y limas,
> Limas y limones,
> Más vale la Virgen
> Que todas las flores.
>
> Si nos dieran queso,
> Dén-noslo en tajadas,
> Porque en la otra casa
> Quiso haber trompadas.[14]

Extremely learned in its Spanish heritage, the "décima" is rooted in the
lands of the New World and it flowers in the island poetry of the Caribbean as an independent plant. There is an abundance of *jíbaro* poems in
the oral tradition of Puerto Rico. Overflowing with ancestral wisdom, the
poet peasant is accustomed to improvise to the rhythm of the bass guitar
or the treble guitar or the four-stringed guitar. The intimate philosophy of
the *jíbaro* has remained in these words, worthy of Jorge Manrique or
Calderón de la Barca, filled with the knowledge of salvation of Spanish
mysticism:

> En esta vida prestada
> que es de la creencia la llave,
> quien sabe salvarse, sabe,
> y el que nó, no sabe nada.
> ¿Qué se hicieron de Sansón
> las fuerzas que en sí mantuvo,
> o la belleza que tuvo
> aquel soberbio Absalón?
> ¿La creencia de Salomón
> no es de todos alabada?
> ¿Dónde está depositada?
> ¿Qué se hizo? Ya no parece;
> luego nada permanece
> en esta vida prestada.[15]

On other occasions the *jíbaro* poet thinks of his destiny and of that of his country:

I

Soy jíbaro borinqueño*
nacido en humilde cuna;
mi casa mi dicha encierra,
no envidio suerte ninguna.

II

Bajo tus verdes palmares
cuántos suspiros lancé,
Borinquen, cuánto lloré
la libertad de mi tierra.[16]

The poetry of the Modernist and post-Modernist period will reveal its attachment to these primary sources, the transcendental lyrical heritage for the elaboration of the learned "décima." What in the nineteenth century was folklore, *costumbrismo* and pure daily life has been transformed into one of the strongest forces to counterarrest the historical tribulations which culminated in the abolition of slavery and autonomy in the close of the final fruitful stage of that century. A vigorous naturalistic novel, *La Charca* (The Stagnant Pool), by Manuel Zeno Gandía, reflects the painful life of the *jíbaro* society in that traumatic end of the century.[17] In casting herself down a ravine towards the Río Grande of Arecibo, the female character, Silvina, is the decadent symbol of the image idealized by poets and prose writers before Zeno Gandía who had sung of the beauty of paradise, lost and abolished through destructive misery. The tragedy of *La Charca*, however, seems to be lessened with the magical nature of the river, "a living being, with a past hidden in the abrupt hills, with a non-conforming present . . . with an uncertain future."[18] Hence, there is a rebirth of the *jíbaro* symbol which is to manifest itself in urban literature and in the literature of exile throughout the twentieth century.

Many famous patriots survived the conflict of 1898 and devoted their efforts to literature and political questions in the first years of Puerto Rico's American experience under the flag of the United States. Inheritors of the *jíbaro* image, they followed faithfully his folkloric attributes, enriching them with the esthetic lines and colors of Modernism while removing from them the picturesque and the superficial glitter and exotism. The writer of Puerto Rico, in that grave moment of transition, had a concept of his obligation to his homeland's destiny; this is why he evaded the ivory tower and the ornamental, placing himself in a creative plane of beauty and harmony, but with protest and defensiveness in light of the question of an uncertain present and a hazy future filled with perplexities.[19] Neme-

Borinquen is the Indian name of the island of Puerto Rico.

sio Canales, Virgilio Dávila, José de Diego, Luis Lloréns Torres, among other essayists, poets and short story writers, kept alive the native fiber of indigenous culture within the stylistic orbit propagated in the writings of Martí, Rubén Darío, Amado Nervo, Gutiérrez Nájera, Herrera y Reissig, Lugones and other Modernists. Luis Muñoz Rivera, in counseling Canales and Lloréns to establish the magazine *Juan Bobo*, asked them to make it "clearly Puerto Rican, clearly 'jíbaro.' "[20] Luis Muñoz Rivera was often called the *jíbaro* of Puerto Rico, for having been born in Barranquitas, a town in the mountainous heart of the island, and for having identified fully with the *jíbaro* in his work and in his social and political activity, for he recognized the true prototype of the homeland in the symbolism of this image. *La Jibarita* of a little town of olden days and of the fragrance of the land is a vignette of the shadow that passes by the eyes of Virgilio Dávila:

> Simbólica figura de esta región tendida
> entre apacibles mares y cielo de zafir,
> allá va con su carga por la vereda angosta
> la jibarita anémica, la jibarita triste,
> como una flor escuálida de malogrado abril.[21]

Introspection goes deep in the poets and prose writers who were to surpass the decorations of refined language in order to lay bare, bravely, the painful splinters of the *jíbaro*'s existential drama, a synonym already of Puerto Rico's existential drama. Miguel Meléndez Muñoz said much the same thing in his short stories and essays, affirming that "the 'jíbaro's' reality is in ourselves."[22] Later Antonio Oliver Frau reaffirmed Muñoz's observation in his legends of the coffee plantation; Frau drew strength from weakness in order to relate skillfully the plot and to invoke, "That night in the mountain the 'jíbaro' asleep in my heart awoke."[23]

Luis Palés Matos, admired for his Negroid poetry and his love lyric, cultivated the learned *jíbaro* essence, as did Lloréns Torres, not merely in traditional form with vestiges of peasant language, but in the intimacy of some of his preferred allusions to the rooster, the he-goat, plants and beings of many of his poems. In his *Sonetos del Campo* (Sonnets of the Country) Palés offers a vignette of "a musty peasant" whom he defines as his alter ego, the inversion of his "I" in the defining sign of the Puerto Rican:

> Vamos sobre caballos que huelen a maleza
> rumbo al Carite dulce de don Antero Aponte.
> Yo escondo en el camino miradas de tristeza,
> *y el otro*, su aromada sinceridad de monte.
>
> *El otro*, un hombre magro cuyo genio benigno
> con nobles complacencias nuestra bondad escarba;
> *un jíbaro mohoso*, tan pálido y tan digno,
> que como un hongo oscuro desarrolla la barba.[24]

The "décimas" of Palés Matos follow the structure of the cantos of *Martín Fierro*, accentuating those musical instruments and other rhythmic accompaniments that concretize the image. The most delightful fiesta in Puerto Rican traditions, the day of the Three Wise Men, and all the elements of daily life appear in his verses (the "cuatro encoldao," the "seis chorreao," "correl los Reyes," the "chongo," "banastas," "freno," "la cualta de mascaúra," and the "barijero talante"*):

> El compae Fele es testigo.
> que si pongo sentimiento,
> parese que el estrumento
> se pone a lloral conmigo.
> Esto, señores, lo digo,
> sin ofensas ni temores. . . .
> lo saben los ruiseñores
> que imitan en su retiro
> el eco de mi sospiro
> y el llanto de mis dolores.[2][5]

Palés speaks with a *jíbaro* voice: "estoy como sosobrao/se me palte el corazón en camándulas de llanto."[2][6]

What has already been left behind is the gallant Donjuanism sung by Manuel Fernández Juncos in *La Serenata*, an echo of the peasants during the fiesta of Utuao and the peasant wedding that Alonso had set in the nineteenth-century scene. Such scenes involved a hubbub of revelry, dancing and cock fights, in a landscape undulating in green where some bird of ill omen or a slight passing cloud punctuated sporadically the serene fullness of the colony in its struggle to consolidate both its desired liberty and its dream of immortality. But the writers who begin to publish poetry, essays and narratives, theatrical works and articles around the decade of the 1930's gave indications that the symbol had reached the heart of creative consciousness. The identification with the authentic image without the slightest adulteration expressed the creative intellect of the Puerto Rican, an act of deliberate selection and a gesture of free will in which the authentic Rubric for the future is signed. At the same time the natural borders between town and country were erased, formerly separated farms were joined, and the journey to distant lands became accelerated. The creator struggling with the word to express his essence finds in the quarry of legendary clay a ductile material ready for the allure of fantasy and intelligence. Francisco Manrique Cabrera utters the cry of discovery in *Poemas de mi tierra, tierra*, beautiful poems which possess "per secula, seculorum" the stain of the banana that Lloréns Torres had proclaimed as

*"cuatro encoldao" (the tuned four-string guitar); "seis chorreao" (dance, typical of *jíbaro* music); "correl los Reyes" (to celebrate Epiphany, 6 January); "chongo" (the old horse, a hack); "banastas" (baskets); "freno" (horse's bridle); "la cualta de mascaúra" (chewing tobacco); "bariyero talante" (good-looking appearance).

the flag of national identity. The "güiro" (musical instrument) and the "batey" (esplanade in front of the hut) are for Cabrera the measure of his faith: "la voz jíbara terca, alma de la montaña"; "mi guícharo y yo auténticos jíbaros amigos."[27] Francisco Hernández Vargas will say it point-blank, "Yo soy lo jíbaro," proclaiming himself the spokesman of the mountain: "lo puro de mi tierra, por mí habla."[28] Juan Antonio Corretjer mixes the "décimas" of *Jíbaro Juan* with the sap of his own autobiography:

I.

Al truco de la poesía
pregunté en vano el secreto.
Lo encontré escrito en un seto,
Jíbaro Juan, otro día.
¡Qué poesía! , ¡qué alegría
la que acabó mi tristeza!
La señal no era riqueza.
Tampoco melancolía.
¡Era valor, patria mía!
¡Eran valor y fiereza!

II.

A mi libro silencioso
¡cuánto tu mano ha enseñado!
Al libro domesticado
¡cuánto enseña el monte hermoso!
Jíbaro Juan, ¡qué alborozo
mirarte el alma a través!
Que no hay quiebra en tu revés
hecho de hiel y de azada
¡ni es bilingüe tu quebrada
que al nunca dice después! [29]

The linguistic and ideological paradox of the Puerto Rican, stranded on a shoreless sea, with his spirit afire to orient himself in present day life, infuses the symbol of the *jíbaro* with an unaccustomed breath in images coined during the decade of the thirties.

If Emilio S. Belaval, in *Cuentos para fomentar el turismo* (Stories to foster tourism), utilizes the "esperpento" (deformation) and satire to caricature the suffering, sickness and depression that scare away tourism instead of attracting it, it is also certain that his intention as narrator is the same as in his essays: to affirm the salvation of man subject to the cruelest and most unjust conditions of life with a providentialist faith in the indestructible *jíbaro* roots of natural culture. And Antonio S. Pedreira seeks the "internal jíbaro essence" and utilizes the concepts of the "historical, modern" and "authentic" *jíbaro*.[30]

In the eve of the decade of the fifties, the first steps were taken towards the opening of creative art against the obstacle of the Vanguardist "isms" of nationalistic character in order to ally themselves with political ideologies and universal esthetics.[31] Would the *jíbaro* symbol disappear or would it form part of the paths chosen by the young generations of poets and prose writers? There does not exist the slightest doubt of the symbol's persistence and reincarnation in the anxieties expressed against one thing or another, the denunciation of prejudices, political colonialism and social and economic injustice, themes repeated in novels, short stories and plays of prominent writers like Pedro Juan Soto, René Marqués, Enrique Laguerre, José Luis González,[32] and poets who make strident rhythm and language to shout instead of sing, with a rending of language and a tortured spirit. Exile and migration of many Puerto Ricans who abandoned the island to take up residence in New York or other cities in the United States revived the human drama with a charge of subjective nuances which revealed the *jíbaro* origin subjected to the pressures of change. Pedreira had had a premonition of it since 1935: "Cuando ese jíbaro regresa a su conuco, como cuando regresó del Campamento las Casas, o cuando regresa de Brooklyn o de Nueva York, es un hombre diferente, transformado, que va a influir en los compañeros que no han salido tanto."[33]

The reverse side of the coin is the persistence of the *jíbaro*'s umbilical cord in the Puerto Rican who remains in the United States and maintains his faithful reserve of vital energy nurtured through recollections, nostalgia, language, beliefs and unrealizable dreams. The silk-cotton tree in the planter, the labyrinth and the crossroads, the conflicts of the beings ensnared in the infected slums of the city, crossing streets, airports, dark hallways, resounding in his intimacy the echo of another antivernacular tongue—all that is the terrible surrealistic and monstruous world that poets and prose writers have transformed into the testimony of exile. The theater of Manuel Méndez Ballester, René Marqués and Francisco Arriví, and the short stories of José Luis González and Pedro Juan Soto present psychological states and situations in which they make manifest the trauma of a people which feels and suffers as a *jíbaro* trapped in a violent circumstance with no possible exit. Ester Feliciano Mendoza tells a moving tale of a *jíbaro* peon transplanted to a farm in the United States. The cobwebs of times past in his homeland and the intent of erasing the stigma of the banana stain are revealed in his buying a camera, two-tone shoes, wrist watch, bright-colored handkerchiefs and shirts, hats. . . . Who is now going to say he's a *jíbaro* from Puerto Rico? On the island they follow his movements and they love to wait for his return, but they see him "made a good-looking Yankee and speaking a little Inglish." Attached to the recollection of the mother-island he keeps his secret talisman under his bright-colored clothing; the melody of a Christmas carol rises to the surface of his soul, thanks to the unerasable banana stain. The Puerto Rican Jesús Colón writes, in English, his "Puerto Rican in New York," vignettes and narrations inspired by the desire for social justice and the loving defense of the working class. The experience of exile in his own flesh is expressed with profound tenderness in *Grandma, please don't come*, with the emotional recourses of the good peasant rooted to the land of his childhood. Piri Thomas, who has a Puerto Rican mother, recalls in his novels the countryside, the rain, the little birds, the way of life and the lay of the land that the voice of his mother bequeathed to him in the Spanish tongue, contributing to Piri's mental bilingualism and his peasant-like attitudes in style, although he may write in English and is one of the effective North American writers of contemporary narrative.[34]

Puerto Rican poets in New York belong to different generations. Some came from the island a half century ago, others arrived as children and have grown up in Manhattan, Brooklyn, the Bronx or in any other part of New York and the other states. Those born here still call themselves Puerto Rican. Among them there are many differences of poetic language and style, as is to be expected from their ages, inclinations, sensitivity and the esthetic influences they have received. Juan Avilés[35] is one of the eldest. A traditionalist and classic on account of his metrical preferences, he maintains a balance between the tastes of Modernism and those of Vanguardism. Among his favorite themes is the coffee plantation of his youth in the town of San Sebastián del Pepino, and the learned language of his poems preserves the savor for the juiciest words of *jíbaro* origin. Pedro Carrasquillo brought to New York a legacy nurtured by rural reminiscences mixed with his hard life and his social credo of protest against inequality and injustice. Two books of his, *Requinto* (Small guitar) and *Quirindongo*,[36] amount to a personal manifesto in *jíbaro* language of the life and ideals of a worthy Puerto Rican, identified fully with the symbol of the *jíbaro*. The vernacular language of these poems is so multiplied in exile that it seems as though they are seeking to squeeze from Spanish the blood that gives them rest and consolation for the poetry in which they pour their dreams and restlessness. Víctor Hernández Cruz[37] reconstructs mental pictures in collage style and writes verse and prose in which the Latin neighborhood of the Puerto Ricans in New York and the vignettes of the island harmonize, interspersing in his English-Spanish words of *jíbaro* roots and sense. Like Avilés, César G. Torres,[38] is another poet from San Sebastián. For some forty years, Torres has had profound roots in New York, but he is nonetheless a constant and fervent lover of his homeland. In his work *Resolana*, he has dedicated a complete section entitled *Poemas Jíbaros*, amongst which we encounter emotional sweet verses that recall Modernism and have at the same time the naive sentiment of absence. He calls himself the "jíbaro culto" and has for the fruits of his land verses like "Guineítos niños," songs of youthful grace quite surprising in a man so far from Puerto Rico in distance and time. Examples like these are numerous.

Someone devoted to studies of language could gather a wealth of terms of the *jíbaro* and images and metaphors in Puerto Rican literature of exile. Such terms, images, and metaphors assure the survival of the symbol's roots in a foreign atmosphere, a stimulus for poetic creation and propagation of the authentic image of Puerto Rican culture.

In the last twenty years, the playwright who has written works for festivals sponsored by the Institute of Puerto Rican Culture (under the direction of Francisco Arriví) has maintained, among his themes, the *jíbaro* as key personnage of Puerto Rican essence. This personnage reappears in spite of the predominance of new stylistic currents that derive, as in the narrative of Puerto Rico from 1950 onward, from contemporary literature in the United States, France, England, Mexico and other intellectual centers of the present-day world. What then happens is that the metaphysical essence of the *jíbaro* symbol is transfused to the mind of those beings who people the scene, and one can see from within the gesticulating puppets, the language and the subjective plot that gives them reality on the stage, the ability of our artists to save the fiber of their own agonizing essence in the new style. Folklore, *costumbrismo*, history, sociology, economy, politics, psychology, and the infinite gamut of perturbing offshoots that have left in the literary creators the mark of their branding-iron are diluted in the esthetic whirlpool which destroys and creates with demoniac fury the future symbol of the *jíbaro*. The *jíbaro* thus transcends geography—mountain, city, island, continent—and is the man of today, sonambulant, adrift, with hooks of words that tie him to a sorrowful patriotic feeling.

While the romantic evocation of the *jíbaro* of yesteryear persists in Puerto Rico in the works of Abelardo Díaz Alfaro for radio shows in which the legendary image abounds, as he had already done with overtones of social and pedagogical ethics in his famous skit *Terrazo*, a masterpiece of learned *jíbaro* essence,[39] the authors in foreign lands who set the themes and characters of short stories, novels and plays, normally utilize the archaic language of the peasant, his favorite metaphors and the metamorphosis of the myth into legend. When oral expression is interspersed with Anglicisms or is altered with meanings adapted from industry and from urban experiences, the writer who wishes an unadulterated portrayal of the peculiar speech of the people must alter phonetic and spelling features of the language in order to accomplish significant acoustic and plastic effects. Silent reading, however, is difficult for those not accustomed to such speech patterns. The *jíbaro* matrix that from the past had given the pure Spanish language the color and accent so often reproduced with variants through a century and a half of literary history continues to be the mold of the language in new stylistic adventures. If the *jíbaro* image has been evolving its makeup through the journey from the mountain to the town, to the slums of the city, and from there to the cosmopolitan metropolis in the United States, language has passed through the same transformation: from country to town, and from there to another land, where, besides the environment's having been altered, the ear and sensitivity in contact with another tongue is changed. Spanish and English wage a battle to take over the humiliated being who becomes disturbed and confused but does not surrender. Rather, he seeks through all means—sign language, gestures, silences, cries—to live together and to communicate with his fellowman. His spiritual refuge will continue to be the vernacular tongue, his material defense will be the language learned, and his drama will be the source of inspiration for poets and prose writers. With the least possible rhetoric José Luis González has achieved the above in several narrations;[40] he is no doubt the narrator who is most preoccupied with brevity and synthesis, followed in this sense by Pedro Juan Soto,[41] the best interpreter of the reality lived by Puerto Ricans in New York. Soto, who lived nine years in New York, and who knows it well, has struggled as a creator conscious of the two languages. He is a living paradox, for his personality is both timid and violent. In the case of Soto, then, the autobiographical element is manifested in his own words in referring to his works.

Ardiente Suelo, Fría Estación (Burning Earth, Cold Season), a novel published in 1959, and the short story "Esa Antigua Fragancia" (That Old Fragrance) in 1960 are clearly related to the life of Pedro Juan Soto between the two poles of his life experience: Puerto Rico and New York. A curious historical reference is intertwined with the theme of death in the story:

> Ese cuento acerca de la dueña de una tienda de flores artificiales a quien da muerte una flor natural, ocurre en el próximo siglo, ¿no? Lo único que determina la época es una vajilla comprada durante el tricentenario de la Batalla de Bunker Hill. Por lo tanto la acción del cuento se libra después del año 2005.
>
> Pues sí. Me preocupa el futuro de los puertorriqueños. El libro de cuentos en que trabajo ahora, del cual formará parte "Esa antigua fragancia," dramatizará la vida que se avecina para nosotros. Ahí procuro extremar algunas de las circunstancias del presente hasta ver en qué condiciones de vida futura pueden transformarse.[42]

As he thinks of the future, Soto speaks of the present in commenting on *Ardiente Suelo*: "La crisis de identidad nacional y personal que le sobreviene al puertorriqueño en Nueva York, no se resuelve con dinero. El choque sufrido con un modo de vida basado en el anonimato, es algo más que lamentable. El puertorriqueño, ente colonial, viaja a Nueva York sin saber quién es, de qué pasado brota, hacia qué futuro se encamina."[43]

450

The background of these works and of others before, like *Spiks* in 1956, reveals the torturing nightmare of the learned creator who bears in his spirit the banana stain, who is at the same time author and protagonist of the *jíbaro* symbol disfigured by the violence of existential reality. The Spanish language in the style of Pedro Juan Soto is a moving document and is very important as a means of penetrating the mystery of the "Neo-Rican" and the Puerto-Rican. The esthetic synthesis of the conflicts with which Soto makes narrative and dramatic material, presents, furthermore, problems of mental bilingualism of alarming proportions.

La carreta[44] (The Oxcart) can be considered the apotheosis of the migration of the *jíbaro* symbol in the decade of the fifties. Besides being written with the spelling and phonetics imitating rural speech, it presents in three acts the ravages of moving and the flight of the Puerto Rican who abandons the country for the slums of San Juan and from there flies to the United States, where the last act takes place. The hope of returning to the place of origin is an optimistic end for the *jíbaro* family, with which it again renews the original roots of an ideal and a dream of possible happiness. At present the author has retired to live and write in a beautiful rural setting on his island, away from the din of the big city, as though he foresaw that the truth is in the land and nature, a Romantic sign of good *jíbaro* origin. For several years René Marqués directed the educational division of the community in the Department of Instruction of Puerto Rico, wrote several works on the peasants, and also prepared magnificent scripts for movies on the *jíbaro* theme. His activity in the short story, theater, essay and novel offer stimulating thoughts about the study of the language, style and, most important, themes of fiction till 1971. Among these themes appears that of *Juan Bobo*, the folkloric *jíbaro*-like hero who for Marqués is the incarnation not of the fool, but of the always shrewd, clever peasant.

The spiritual fiber and the burning word of the absent sun, plastically coined in verbal contorsions, tortured and denigrated without losing its unique sense, in daily Puerto Rican speech as well as in the prose and poetry of authors who continue writing in Spanish in the United States and those who while writing in English still feel the ties with their vernacular tongue, are pointed signs of the paths towards the future.[45]

City University of New York

NOTES

[1] Salvador Brau, *Historia de Puerto Rico* (New York: Appleton & Co., 1904), p. 181, note 18. Brau declares that "the term 'jíbaro' . . . which is applied for the first time to the peasants of Puerto Rico in official documents of the eighteenth century is of Indian origin." Antonio S. Pedreira, *El periodismo en Puerto Rico* (Havana: Impr.

Ucar, García y Cía, 1941). Pedreira offers data on the term *jíbaro*. See also Antonio
S. Pedreira, "La actualidad del jíbaro," *Boletín de la Universidad de Puerto Rico*, 6,
No. 1 (1955). This and all subsequent translations are mine.

[2] Ana Margarita Silva, *El Jíbaro en la literatura de Puerto Rico* (1945; rpt.
Mexico: n.p., 1957).

[3] José Pablo Morales, "El jíbaro," in *Miscelánea histórica* (San Juan: Tip. La
Correspondencia de Puerto Rico, 1924), p. 51. Published originally in the *Almanaque
de Aguinaldo*, 1876. The author offers this list, based on a classification of castes in
the *Leyes de Indias*:

Español con india, sale mestizo.
Mestizo con española, sale castizo.
Castizo con española, sale español.
Español con negra, sale mulato.
Mulato con española, sale morisco.
Morisco con española, sale salta-atrás.
Salta-atrás con india, sale chino.
Chino con mulata, sale lobo.
Lobo con mulata, sale jíbaro.
Jíbaro con india, sale albarrazado.
Albarrazado con negra, sale cambujo.
Cambujo con mulata, sale calpan-mulato.
Calpan-mulato con sambaigo, sale tente en el aire.
Tente en el aire con mulata, sale no te entiendo.
No te entiendo con india, sale ahí te estás.

[4] Miguel Meléndez Muñoz, "La Realidad del Jíbaro," *Puerto Rico Ilustrado*, No.
28, 5 June 1937, pp. 12, 72.

[5] Virgilio Dávila, *Obras completas* (San Juan: Instituto de Cultura Puertorriqueña, 1964), I, 34. *Aromas del Terruño* (1916) and *Pueblito de antes* (1917) are
two famous books by the poet.

[6] Luis Lloréns Torres, "Decimario," in *El Jíbaro de Puerto Rico*, ed. Enrique
Laguerre and E. Melón (Sharon, Conn.: Troutman Press, 1968), pp. 103-04. Torres,
besides utilizing the learned "décima," praised the "copla" (couplet): "The 'jíbaro'
couplet! The ancestral soul of the people sings it. It arises from the pure fount of
criollo spirituality." See the review *Bayoán*, 3 (San Juan, 1950), pp. 3-7.

[7] Ramón Méndez Quiñones wrote *Los Jíbaros progresistas* (1882). There are four
characters: Siña Chepa, Juaniya, Cleto and Antón. One can appreciate the author's
perspective in the stage description: "Muebles adecuados: sillas de cuero, banquillos
de madera, una mesa con avíos de planchar, otra, sobre la cual habrá platillos, tazas,
un jarro, y muñecos de barro; una hamaca de cuerdas, una barandilla con quesos, un
armarito de pino, banastas, aparejos, un machete y algunas mazorcas de maíz col-
gadas en varas del techo." See *El Jíbaro de Puerto Rico*, p. 212.

[8] See Manuel Zeno Gandía's trilogy *Crónicas de un mundo enfermo*, comprising
La Charca, *Garduña* and *El Negocio*, published by the Institute of Puerto Rican
Literature in 1955, the centenary of Zeno Gandía's birth.

[9] See Antonio S. Pedreira, *El periodismo en Puerto Rico*, I (Havana: n.p., 1941),
pp. 41-42. Reprinted in *El Jíbaro de Puerto Rico*, pp. 81-82. It is interesting to note
that during that time the term "jíbaro" was written with "g." It thus appears in the
title of *El Gíbaro* by Manuel A. Alonso, 1849.

[10] George Dawson Flinter, *An Account of the Present State of the Island of
Puerto Rico* (London: Longman Press, 1834). There is a commentary quoted by Kal

Wagenheim and Olga Jiménez de Wagenheim in *The Puerto Ricans: A Documentary History* (New York: Praeger Publishers, 1973). See Anchor Books Edition of the *Edinburgh Review*, 60 (1835). On page 53 of this publication quoted by Wagenheim one reads: "A few coffee-trees, and plantains, a machete, a cow and a horse, an acre of land in corn or sweet potatoes, constitute the property of what would be denominated a comfortable *Xivaro*—who mounted on his meager and hardworked horse, with his long sword protruding from his baskets, dressed in a broad-brimmed straw hat, cotton jacket, clean shirt, and check pantaloons, sallies forth from his cabin to mass, to a cockfight, or to a dance, thinking himself the most independent and happy being in existence."

[11] Charles Walker, *Letters from Puerto Rico: 1835-1837*, Introd. Kenneth Scott, Documents, *Caribbean Studies*, 5, No. 1. I wish to thank Kenneth Scott for sending the offprint with the six famous letters written in Puerto Rico by Charles Walker. In the Introduction Scott says that around 1840 Walker bought "La Concordia," a farm near Guayama. His niece, Susan Walker Morse, was the daughter of Samuel Morse, who visited her and established the first telegraph line in Puerto Rico between Arroyo and the farm where Susan lived ("La Enriqueta"). She was married to Charles Line.

[12] The allusions to which I refer concerning the child's wake and the market are in the letter dated 22 December 1835:

When I was going to the theatre one night I saw many lights in a house and persons going in and coming out. I went in and there on a table, on a bed of flowers, was a dead child laid out in a beautiful dress, and all the friends and relatives and strangers around laughing and talking. All were happy for such are angels, say they. The table was in the middle of a large room and a candle on each end. The babe, or rather boy of 18 months old, had gone pure to Heaven and all were satisfied, and on my return they were at supper and at cards in the same room and soon with martial music the little innocent was taken and deposited in the cathedral. . . . The town market is supplied by small farmers or gardeners, who bring every thing in on small pacing horses, in two large baskets, swung over their backs and the strength of these horses is very great. (p. 38).

The last commentary recalls the famous popular song of Rafael Hernández, *Lamento Boricano*, another of the *jíbaro* constants in the culture of Puerto Rico.

[13] Manuel A. Alonso, *El Gíbaro*, Centenary Edition (1849; rpt. Río Piedras, Puerto Rico: Colegio Hostos, 1949), p. 22. *El Gíbaro* (1849) was followed by a second part published in 1884. It is considered the first important work of Puerto Rican literature. See David Cruz López, *La lengua del jíbaro en la novela costumbrista puertorriqueña* (San Juan: Departamento de Estudios Hispánicos, Universidad de Puerto Rico, 1950); Modesto Rivera, *Concepto y expresión del costumbrismo en Manuel A. Alonso Pacheo (El Gíbaro)* (San Juan: Departamento de Estudios Hispánicos, 1952); Jorge Luis Porras Cruz, "Un costumbrista puertorriqueño del siglo XIX," *Asomante*, 11 (San Juan, 1945), 59.

[14] Francisco Vasallo, in *Aguinaldo Puertorriqueño*, with a Prologue by Francisco Matos Paoli, Centennial Edition (1843; rpt. San Juan: Editorial Universitaria, 1946), pp. 203-04.

[15] See "Décimas anónimas," in *El Jíbaro de Puerto Rico*, pp. 74-75.

[16] Ibid., p. 76.

[17] Manuel Zeno Gandía, *La Charca* (1894; rpt. Barcelona: Ediciones Puerto, 1973).

[18] See ibid., Chapter 11, pp. 218-20.

[19] Modernism has been widely studied. See Luis Hernández Aquino, *El Modernismo en Puerto Rico: Poesía y prosa* (San Juan: Editorial Universitaria, 1972), and Enrique Laguerre, *La poesía modernista en Puerto Rico* (San Juan: Departamento de Estudios Hispánicos, 1942).

[20] See C. Rosa Nieves, *Plumas estelares en las letras de Puerto Rico*, I, Siglo XIX (San Juan: Ediciones la Torre, 1967), p. 367. Luis Muñoz Rivera, poet, journalist, renowned politician, held the position of Resident Commissioner in Washington from 1910-1916. The Institute of Puerto Rican Culture has edited his *Obras completas*, 8 vols. (San Juan: Instituto de Cultura Puertorriqueña, 1968).

[21] Virgilio Dávila, "La Jibarita," in *Aromas del Terruño* (San Juan: Ed. Cordillera, 1963), p. 40.

[22] Meléndez Muñoz, "La Realidad del Jíbaro," p. 12.

[23] Miguel Meléndez Muñoz has been the precursor of contemporary narrators and essayists who have written on the *jíbaro*. His extensive writings have been collected by the Institute of Puerto Rican Culture in two volumes. See his *Obras completas* (San Juan: Instituto de Cultura Puertorriqueña, 1970). Antonio Oliver Frau, author of the book entitled *Leyendas del Cafetal* (1938), anticipated the literature of social consciousness and workers' problems which continue to be cultivated in the decade of the forties.

[24] Luis Palés Matos, *Poesía (1915-1956)*, preliminary study by Federico de Onís, Introducción (San Juan: Editorial Universitaria, 1971), p. 36.

[25] Ibid., p. 81.

[26] Ibid., p. 82.

[27] Francisco Manrique Cabrera, *Poemas de mi tierra, tierra* (San Juan: Puerto Rico Progress, 1936), p. 55.

[28] Francisco Hernández Vargas, "Yo soy lo jíbaro," in María Teresa Babín. *Panorama de la Cultura Puertorriqueña* (New York: Las Américas, 1958), p. 120.

[29] Juan Antonio Corretjer, *Jíbaro Juan*, in *Poesía nueva Puertorriqueña*, Antología (San Juan: Ed. Edil, 1971), p. 60.

[30] Antonio S. Pedreira, besides being the author of the best *Bibliografía Puertorriqueña (1493-1930)* till that date (Madrid: Ed. Hernando, 1932), has published *Insularismo* (Madrid: Tip. Artística, 1934) and exercised both in the university chair and in literature an enormous influence. On the *jíbaro*, he wrote the aforesaid *La Actualidad del Jíbaro* (1935). Emilio S. Belaval, essayist, short story writer, and playwright, also developed a work of profound impact during the generation of the thirties and forties.

[31] On the waves of poets between 1950 and 1969 there are several anthologies. I recommend that of Luis Antonio Rosario Quiles, *Poesía Nueva Puertorriqueña* (San Juan: Editorial Edil, Producciones Bondo, 1971).

[32] René Marqués, *Ensayos (1953-1966)* (San Juan: Editorial Antillana, 1966).

[33] Antonio S. Pedreira, "La Actualidad del Jíbaro," in *El Jíbaro de Puerto Rico*, ed. Enrique A. Laguerre and Esther M. Melón (Sharon, Conn.: Troutman Press, 1971), p. 7.

[34] References to other works of modern authors can be taken from diverse books. In the following anthologies, some selections can be read: Enrique A. Laguerre and Esther M. Melón, eds., *El Jíbaro de Puerto Rico* contains selections of seven essays, poetry by fifteen poets, seven narrations and one play. Esther Feliciano Mendoza's story, *The Stain of the Plantain*, is on pages 199-203. Some works in English of Puerto Rican writers are partially included in *Borinquen: An Anthology of Puerto Rican Literature*, ed. María Teresa Babín and Stan Steiner (New York: Alfred A. Knopf, 1974).

[35] Juan Avilés' *Penúltimo Canto* contains his lyrical work of fifty years (1921-1971), almost entirely written in New York, where he has resided from youth.

[36] Pedro Carrasquillo, *Requinto* (New York: Las Américas, 1958). His posthumous work *Quirindongo* has just appeared (New York: Colección Mensaje, 1975). The editor, Odón Betanzos Palacios, holds the opinion that "los estudiosos de esa realidad jíbara no podrán dar un paso en firme si no cuentan con la obra de Pedro Carrasquillo" (p. 9).

[37] Victor Hernández Cruz's works are *Snaps* (New York: Random House, 1969), and *19 Necromancers from Now*, ed. Ishmael Read (New York: Doubleday, 1970). Selections are found in *Borinquen: An Anthology of Puerto Rican Literature*.

[38] César A. Torres, *Resolana*, Antología poética, Prologue by Odón Betanzos Palacios, 2nd rev. ed. (New York: Unida Printing Corp., 1974).

[39] Abelardo Díaz Alfaro, *Terrazo* (San Juan: Ed. Yaurel, 1947). This work is a collection of stories and vignettes in which Díaz Alfaro uses the symbols of the "megass," "the sullen one," the fact that "he wasn't born for the yoke," the "gray king-bird," and the "gentlemen of beak and feathers" (metaphor of *pitirre*, a bird), in order to lend to the symbolism of the *jíbaro* greater meaning and lineage.

[40] José Luis González wrote *El Hombre en la Calle* (1948), *Paisa* (1950), and *La Galería* (1972). René Marqués says of him that he was the first short story writer to initiate the path of the "city dweller" theme. See René Marqués, "El cuento puertorriqueño en la promoción del cuarenta," in *Ensayos*, p. 88.

[41] An explanation of the themes and of the art of narration of Pedro Juan Soto is found in *A Solas con Pedro Juan Soto* (Río Piedras: Ediciones Puerto, 1971). These are self-interviews in which the author questions himself and answers the questions.

[42] Pedro Juan Soto, *A solas con Pedro Juan Soto* (Río Piedras, Puerto Rico: Ediciones Puerto, 1971), p. 95.

[43] Ibid., p. 86.

[44] When *La Carreta* was published in 1953, it was considered a turning point in Puerto Rican theater.

[45] Stan Steiner, *The Islands: The Worlds of the Puerto Ricans* (New York: Harper & Row, 1974). This author devotes Chapter 7 (pp. 87-101) of the work mentioned to the theme of the *jíbaro*. In the bibliographical section, "Sources," on page 504, he states: "The reaction to the *jíbaro* determined the intellectual's viewpoint" and "The uniqueness of the island's literature has remained uniquely its own."

Russian Literature, Literary Scholarship, and Publishing in the United States

Nikolai P. Poltoratzky

ABSTRACT

Russian immigration to the United States started a long time ago and passed through several stages. However, the Russian literary scene in this country has acquired sufficient significance and quality only since the 1940's and especially the 1950's, as a result of the events connected with World War II. Poetry and fiction are now well represented, while drama has been practically neglected. Literary criticism is often linked with literary scholarship, the latter being of much greater importance. Literary activities connected with periodicals and publishing undertakings are also noteworthy. On the whole, the contemporary Russian literary scene in the United States deserves close attention. (NPP)

The purpose of this paper is to present a survey of the Russian literary scene in the United States. In addition to poetry, fiction and drama, this survey will include literary scholarship, criticism, and memoirs, and literary periodicals and publishing houses engaged in the production of literary and literature-related books. Because of its proposed scope, this survey must necessarily be somewhat general. The subject of the Russian literary scene in America is still little explored. To my knowledge, there are no major works or even shorter studies that are specifically devoted to the all-embracing task which has been set forth for this paper. However, there are a few works which have been quite helpful—in various degrees—in the preparation of this survey.

Gleb Struve, the well known specialist on Soviet and Emigré literatures, devotes, unfortunately, only a few pages to American developments in his pioneering study of Russian emigré literature, *Russkaia literatura v emigratsii* (New York: Chekhov Publishing House, 1956). However, his book gives a general perspective which must be taken into account whenever studies of any "local" emigré literature are undertaken. Moreover, Struve discusses Russian writers in America in some of his English language essays, two of which include more recent developments.[1]

There is also a book by Ivan K. Okuntsov, *Russkaia emigratsiia v Severnoi i Iuzhnoi Amerike* (Buenos Aires: Seiatel', 1967), which attempts to present a large panorama of Russian immigration to and activities in the United States since the very beginnings. Its author, however, died on 19 April 1939, and the latest data he used does not transcend the mid-thirties. Moreover, he devotes only a few pages to the activities which are the subject of this paper, and he writes of them in a superficial non-scholarly way. The importance of Okuntsov's book for this paper is that it allows us to arrive at some definite negative conclusions.

Still another book to single out is an anthology of Russian poetry, *Sodruzhestvo: Iz sovremennoi poezii Russkogo Zarubezh'ia* (Washington: Victor Kamkin, Inc., 1966), edited by Tat'iana P. Fesenko. It includes poems by seventy-five Russian poets, living in various parts of the globe, and not just in the United States. And only poets who were still alive in the mid-sixties are included in the anthology. However, with these limitations, the anthology has a very important additional feature: it gives, in the second part, autobiographies of the participants, and thus indicates those poets who were living at that time in the United States.

An important bibliographical source is a two-volume reference work, compiled by Liudmila A. Foster, *Bibliografiia russkoi zarubezhnoi literatury, 1918-1968* (Boston, Mass.: G. K. Hall & Co., 1971). Though not always exact or complete, this work lists Russian authors with their books, poems, articles, and book reviews. However, by contrast with the often extensive bibliographical data, the biographical information is limited to only last name, first name, patronymic, and year of birth of the author (and pen name and year of death, where applicable), though in many instances possible biographical sources are also referred to. Like *Sodruzhestvo*, *Bibliografiia* lists Russian emigré authors from all over the globe, but unfortunately it does not mention the country of residence of the authors.

Finally, there is a collection of articles in Russian with English résumés by some thirty American, Canadian, and European authors, edited by Nikolai P. Poltoratzky, *Russkaia literatura v emigratsii* (Pittsburgh, Pa.: Department of Slavic Languages and Literatures, University of Pittsburgh, 1972). The essays and articles that are of more immediate concern to us here are those by Fabii Zverev, Leonid D. Rzhevskii, and Roman B. Gul', and, to a lesser extent, by Nikolai E. Andreev, Liudmila A. Foster, Iurii P. Ivask, C. Nicholas Lee, and Rostislav V. Pletnev.[2] However, this volume, too, deals with Russian literature and other literary activities, approaching the emigration as a whole—distinguishing, in some instances, between various "waves" of the emigration, but not grouping emigrés according to countries which they adopted as their "home away from home." Though more recent than the books mentioned previously, it too could not include information with regard to the last few years.

In view of these limitations, incompleteness or outdatedness of sources, I decided to at least partially add to my data by directly contacting those Russian poets, writers, and literary scholars in the United States, whose addresses I was able to obtain. Some fifty people received from me a questionnaire accompanied by a request to supplement their answers with any pertinent documents, such as curriculum vitae, copies of most accurate reviews of their books by others, their own writings on authors living in the United States, etc. The questionnaire was reduced to the following basic questions: (1) First name, patronymic, and last name, (2) Year and place of birth, (3) Year of arrival to the United States, (4) What was published by you during the years you lived in the United States, (5) Which of your works you consider to be the main ones (not only for the American period), (6) What are you working on now, (7) What do you consider to be your distinguishing traits as a poet, fiction writer, literary scholar, critic, editor, or publisher? [3]

Almost all of those contacted responded to the questionnaire and some sent supplementary materials. I take this opportunity to express my gratitude to those who took the time and made the effort to be of help in a task which I considered to be our common one, though I am afraid that only a small portion of the information received could be used immediately—because of space-limitations and the need for a certain uniformity in the presentation of the material.

Thus, the information which will be found on the following pages is based mainly on answers received from respective authors and supplemented with information from the sources referred to above. These sources became of primary importance with regard to authors who responded in a perfunctory way or to those that I was not able to contact.

On the basis of data collected, the Russian literary scene in the United States will be surveyed here under four major sections: poetry, prose, literary scholarship and criticism, and periodicals and publishing. Since the survey deals primarily with areas of literary and literature-related activities, the same author may be considered in more than one section. In such instances, the information with regard to place and year of birth and year of arrival to the United States are given only when the author is first introduced. Within each section authors are listed according to the Latin alphabet. Russian names (and titles of works) are given in transliteration, according to the Library of Congress transliteration system, without the diacritical marks. In some cases, when there is a significant difference between the transliterated and the "passport" form of the last name, the "passport" form is given in parentheses. Only authors who have published at least one book are treated separately. Those who did not collect their writings into special editions, but deserve to be mentioned, as well as those regarding whom the information is too incomplete, are grouped together at the end of each section.

But before we proceed to a specific discussion of areas of literary activities and their representatives, we must briefly consider the historical background of the Russian emigration. For a proper understanding of the Russian literary scene in the United States, it is important to bear in mind, in addition to information concerning individual authors, the following characterization of the Russian emigration in general and of the immigration to the United States in particular.

* * *

The post-revolutionary Russian emigration is usually divided into three categories: the first or "old," the second or "new," and the third or "newest" emigration. The first was caused by the Russian Revolution, the seizure of power by the Bolsheviks in 1917, and the ensuing Civil War. This emigration, which included numerous first-rate cultural elements, settled essentially in Europe, with Paris as its "capital" and Prague, Berlin (in the 1920's), Belgrade, and Riga as its main additional centers. The second emigration was the result of the German-Soviet War in 1941-1945. The older representatives of the intelligentsia of this emigration belonged mostly to the Soviet technical or military intelligentsia. By the late 1940's and early 1950's they were able to leave Germany and settle in other countries of the globe, especially in the United States. For a while the name "newest" emigrés was applied to those former Soviet citizens who defected from the Soviet side (in most instances, from the Soviet Armed Forces in Western Europe) in the late 1940's and in the 1950's. However, with the beginning of the mass emigration of Soviet citizens of Jewish or Russian-Jewish origin and the expulsion from the Soviet Union of a number of dissidents of various national origins in the 1970's, the name of third or "newest" Russian emigration is now more properly applied to this new wave of emigrés. Most of them go to Israel, but a significant number of people who were in the past engaged in literary activities came to the United States or live now in Western Europe.

This general characterization of the three main categories of Russian emigration must be supplemented by a brief characterization of the various waves of Russian emigration to the United States. With regard to the topic of this paper one could single out five main stages, periods or "waves" of Russian immigration to the United States: (1) before World War One, (2) from the 1917 Revolution and Civil War in Russia to the eve of World War Two (basically, however, in the 1920's), (3) the World War

Two years, (4) from the end of the 1940's to the middle of the 1950's, and (5) from the end of the 1960's to the present time.

The contribution to the Russian literary scene in the United States of these five "waves" of Russian emigrés is very uneven. Those who came before the first World War left Russia, more often than not, for economic reasons (with the exception of the Russian Jews who had also religious-political reasons) and were quite often uneducated people. Their contribution to Russian literature is, generally speaking, negligible. Those who came in the 1920's belonged to a higher cultural strata, but very few of them engaged later in literature-oriented activities. By contrast, those who immigrated during the Second World War—for the second time in their life: first fleeing from the Bolsheviks in Russia, and then the Nazis in Western Europe, mainly France—had been, in many instances, active writers in the past, and almost immediately they resumed their literary activities in the United States. The contribution of these "old" emigrés became quite significant, their main monument being the foundation of a "thick" literary-political journal in New York City, *Novyi zhurnal* (The New Review). However, the most extensive contribution to all fields of Russian literary life in the United States has turned out to be that of the fourth "wave" of emigrés—best known, summarily, as DP's (Displaced Persons)—who came here in the late 1940's and early 1950's. This "wave" consisted of both "new" emigrés, who until the beginning of the 1940's lived in the Soviet Union under Stalin's regime, and "old" emigrés, who left Russia as a result of the Civil War (some were born even later, outside of Russia) and for a quarter of a century lived in various countries of Central and Eastern Europe. A fraction of them remained in Europe for another decade or so (often being employed by such American organizations as, for example, Radio Liberty in Munich), and, having arrived in the United States, only strengthened the literary contribution of the major "wave" of the early 1950's. The general historical, social, and cultural backgrounds of the immigrants of the fifties and the sixties were identical. A totally different group were, however, the immigrants of the current, fifth, "wave"—Soviet citizens, who lived not under Stalin's, but under Khrushchev's and Brezhnev's regimes and were allowed to leave the country, or were expelled, in the late sixties and the seventies. Their contribution to the Russian literary scene is too recent to be fully and properly evaluated. It is clear, though, that for many of these "newest" immigrants—former Soviet writers, poets, critics, and literary scholars, often of Russian-Jewish origin—the Russian language will remain the main element of their creativity and that their contribution may eventually become significant. Some of them—like the poets Naum Korzhavin and Andrei Klenov, the critic and literary scholar Arkadii Belinkov, or the writer Iurii

Krotkov—were immediately noticed by the Russian reading public in the United States. This paper, however, is concerned primarily with the already definitive contribution of Russian immigrants of the third and fourth "waves."

* * *

In his article on the poetry of the "old" emigrés in the collection *Russkaia literatura v emigratsii*, Iurii Ivask singles out, among those who lived in the United States, Vladimir Nabokov and Igor Chinnov, mentions Georgii Golokhvastov, Boris Volkov, the brothers Iosif and Veniamin Levins, Aleksandr Bisk, Gisella Lakhman, Khristina Krotkova, Tatiana Ostroumova, Mikhail Chekhonin, Elena Rubisova, and Aleksandr Brailovskii, and refers briefly to Vladimir Dukel'skii, Vsevolod Pastukhov, Evgenii Raich, Nikolai Arsen'ev, and Gleb Struve. This list of poets representing the "old" emigration—some of whom arrived after 1939 or even 1949— could be somewhat longer, but not much longer. True, there were many people writing poetry who came from among the first "waves" of Russian immigrants, but the artistic quality of their poetry was, generally speaking, rather low. Genuine flourishing began only with the influx of new blood in the 1950's. A few among the newcomers belonged to the "old" emigration, while the majority were new emigrés. Fabii Zverev, in his article on the poetry of the "new" emigration in the collection *Russkaia literatura v emigratsii*, pays special attention to Gleb Glinka, Boris Filippov, Ol'ga Anstei, Ivan Elagin, Ivan Burkin, Vladimir Markov, Nikolai Morshen, Oleg Il'inskii, Aleksandr Rostovskii, and Aglaia Shishkova. He also mentions the work of Gennadii Panin, Rodion Berezov, A. Kasim (Al'tamentov), Sergei Maksimov, Mirtala Kardinalovskaia, Vladimir Iurasov, Vladislav Ellis, Tat'iana Fesenko, Anatolii Darov, and Elena Matveeva. These selective listings of poets representing the "old" and "new" emigrés could be supplemented with several other names, including the "newest" emigrés.

Surveying the Russian poetical scene in the United States, I should like to present here the following alphabetical list, by no means exhaustive, of poets, who live or lived in America and who have published at least one collection of poems.

Lidiia Alekseevna Alekseeva, born in Dvinsk in 1909, came to the United States in 1949. She has written four books of verse: *Lesnoe solntse* (1954), *V puti* (1959), *Prozrachnyi sled* (1964), and *Vremia razluk* (1971).[4] Nikolai Nikolaevich All (pen name of Dvorzhitskii) was born in St. Petersburg, and has been in the United States since 1923. He has written a collection of poems entitled *Ekten'ia* (1923). He is a member of the Circle of Russian Poets in America which published the collection *Chetyrnadtsat'* (1949). Amari (pen name of Mikhail Osipovich Tsetlin, 1882-1945), wrote *Prozrachnye teni* (1920) and *Krov' na snegu* (1939).

Ol'ga Nikolaevna Anstei (pen name), born in Kiev in 1912, came to the United States in 1950. She is the author of *Dver' v stene* (1949) and *Na iuru* (1976). She also translated into Russian Stephen Vincent Benet's *The Devil and Daniel Webster* (1960), as well as poetry from English and German. Her distinguishing traits are a religious perception of the world, a closeness to the sources of folk-speech, and a special aptitude for poetic translation.

Elena Anatol'evna Antonova-All, born on the train from Siberia to St. Petersburg in 1904, wrote the collection *Otrazheniia* (1944), and contributed to the collection *Chetyrnadtsat'* (1949). Nikolai Sergeevish Arsen'ev was born in Stockholm in 1888, and came to the United States in 1947. He has written the collections of poems *Bezbrezhnoe siianie* (1972) and *Otbleski* (1976). Nonna Sergeevna Belavina (Miklashevskaia), born in Evpatoriia in 1915, has lived in the United States since 1949. She is the author of three collections of poems: *Sinii mir* (1961), *Zemnoe shchast'e* (1966), and *Utverzhdenie* (1974). She is now working on a fourth volume.[5] Aleksandr Akimovich Bisk, born in Russia in 1883, is the author of translations from German, *Izbrannoe iz Rainer Maria Rilke* (1957), and of a collection of selected poems from the years 1903-1961, *Svoe i chuzhoe* (1962). Aleksandr Iakovlevich Brailovskii, born in Russia in 1884, has written a collection of poetic translations, *Iz klassikov* (1943), and *Dorogoiu Svobodnoi* (1955).

Iosif Aleksandrovich Brodskii, born in Leningrad in 1940, was expelled from the Soviet Union and came to the United States in 1972. He has written *Stikhotvoreniia i poemy* (1965), *Elegy to John Donne and Other Poems*, translated and introduced by Nicholas Bethell (1967), *Ostanovka v pustyne* (1970), *Selected Poems*, translated and introduced by George L. Kline, with a foreword by W. H. Auden (1973), and *The Funeral of Bobo*, translated by Richard Wilbur (1974). From the very beginning of his fame, critics have pointed out a certain metaphysical and surrealist quality of Brodskii's poetry that is developed against a background of everyday life, books, poets (such as the seventeenth-century English metaphysical poet John Donne), or nature. And he has been accepted as a talented, but difficult and uneven poet—completely different from other poets who grew up in the Soviet Union.[6]

Ivan Afanas'evich Burkin was born in Penza in 1919, and came to the United States in 1950. He has written two collections of poems, *Rukoi nebrezhnoi* (1972) and *Puteshestvie iz chernogo v beloe* (1972), and he is working on a third one.[7] David Davidovich Burliuk was born in the government of Khar'kov in 1882, and came to the United States in 1922; he died in New York in 1967. He was one of the first Russian Futurists and organizer of the group of Cubo-Futurists. Though engaged here primarily

462

in artistic activities, Burliuk published several booklets of poetry, including a collection of poems from the years 1898-1923, *Avtobiografiia i stikhi* (1924), and another collection, covering the years 1882-1932, *1/2 veka* (1932). David Burliuk, together with Mariia N. Burliuk, also published a magazine, *Color and Rhyme* (1961-1962).

Igor Vladimirovich Chinnov, born in Riga in 1909, came to the United States in 1962. He has written six collections of poems: *Monolog* (1950), *Linii* (1960), *Metafory* (1968), *Partitura* (1970), *Kompozitsiia* (1972), and *Pastorali* (1976). He is now working on a new collection, "Dissonansy." A book of English translations of his poetry by William Chalsma is ready for publication. Responding to the questionnaire, Igor Chinnov wrote that in his poetry he "strives for (1) melodiousness, (2) sonorous saturation and expressiveness, (3) wealthy new imagery (lately often grotesque), (4) transformation of poeticisms (dried by irony) and prosaisms (ennobled by musicality) into a single poetic whole, (5) reflection of that beauty that exists in life against a background of the tragic and even disgusting in it."[8]

Vladimir Aleksandrovich Dukel'skii (Vernon Duke) was born in Pskov in 1903, and died in the United States in 1968. A composer, he was also a poet, an author of four collections of poems, published in Munich: *Poslaniia* (1962), *Stradaniia nemolodogo Vertera* (1962), *Kartinnaia gelereia* (1965), and *Poezdka kuda-to* (1968). Ivan Venediktovich Elagin (pen name of Matveev) was born in Vladivostok, and came to this country in 1950. He has published six collections of poems: *Po doroge ottuda* (1947), *Ty, moe stoletie* (1948), *Po doroge ottuda* (1953), *Otsvety nochnye* (1963), *Kosoi polet* (1967), and *Drakon na kryshe* (1973). As Elagin sees it, his most important poems will be found in a new collection, *Pod sozvezdiem topora* (1976). Elagin also wrote a comedy-farce, *Portret madmuasel' Tarzhi* (1949), and a collection of humorous-satirical poems, *Politicheskie fel'etony v stikhakh* (1959). He translated into Russian some 12,000 lines of Stephen Vincent Benet's *John Brown's Body* and some 3,000 lines from a number of other American poets. Leonid D. Rzhevskii, a major interpreter of Elagin's poetry, considers that its main theme is "comprehension of reality in those catastrophic shifts, in which, in the poet's sensation, this reality was globally and fatally dislocated"—which leads to Elagin's lyrical voice acquiring burlesque flat, half-angry being combined with half-pain, half-sarcasm with half-compassion, and co-experiencing with opposition.[9]

Tat'iana Pavlovna Fesenko was born in Kiev in 1915, came to the United States in 1950, published a collection of poems, *Propusk v byloe* (1975), and compiled and edited the collection of poems by seventy-five contemporary Russian emigré poets, *Sodruzhestvo* (1966). Boris Andreevich Filippov (Filipoff) was born in Stavropol' in 1905, and came to the

United States in 1950. He wrote a number of books, including the collections of poems *Grad Nevidimyi* (1944), *Veter Skifii* (1959), *Nepogod'* (1960), *Bremia vremeni* (1961), *Rubezhi* (1962), *Stynushchaia vechnost'* (1964), and *Za tridtsat' let: Izbrannoe, 1941-1971* (1971). All of them, except the first one, were published in Washington.

Gleb Aleksandrovich Glinka, born in Moscow in 1903, had a long literary career in the USSR. He came to this country in 1951. He has published two collections of poetry, *V teni* (1968) and *Bylo zavtra* (1972). Some of the poems prepared for the third collection were published in *Novyi zhurnal*. As a poet and man of letters in general, Glinka, in his own words, appreciates most of all "the sharpness of original thought and the freshness of a verbal drawing" and considers that, in his second and projected third books, "everything is from oneself and expressed in one's way, in other words, is *otsebiatina*, in the direct meaning of this word," where, among other things, one will find "aphorisms pertaining to philosophy, poetics, and psychology of the creative act."[10]

Georgii Vladimirovich Golokhvastov (1882-1963) has written *Polusonety* (1931), a poem, *Gibel' Atlantidy* (1938), *Zhizn' i sny* (1944), and *Chetyre stikhotvoreniia* (1944). He also published a translation of *Slovo o polku Igoreve* (1951). Irina Iassen, who died in 1957, is author of *Zemnoi plen* (1944), *Dal'nii put'* (1946), *Lazurnoe nebo* (1950), *Pamiat' serdtsa* (1956), and *Poslednie stikhi* (1959). Oleg Pavlovich Il'inskii was born in Moscow in 1932, came here in 1949, published three collections of poetry under the title *Stikhi* (1960; 1966). He has translated German and American poetry into Russian.[11] Vladimir Ivanovich Iurasov, born in Sibiu, Rumania, in 1914, has been living in the United States since 1951. He wrote a book of soldiers' folklore, *Vasilii Terkin posle voiny* (1952). In the last twenty years he switched to prose.

Iurii (George) Pavlovich Ivask, born in Moscow in 1910 and residing in this country since 1949, published four collections of poems: *Severnyi bereg* (1938), *Tsarskaia osen'* (1953), *Khvala* (1967), and *Zolushka* (1970). In his opinion, his most important work is a set of poems "Igraiushchii chelovek," published in the review *Vozrozhdenie* (Paris, 1973, Nos. 240-242). Ivask defines the style of his poetry as Neo-Baroque, and acknowledges the influence of Derzhavin, O. Mandel'shtam, and the English metaphysical poets of the seventeenth century—Crashaw, Donne, and others.[12] Ivask is also the editor of one of the major anthologies of Russian emigré poetry, *Na zapade* (1953).

Mirtala Sergeevna Kardinalovskaia (Bentov) was born in Khar'kov. She came to the United States in 1947. A sculptor, she is also author of a collection of poems, *Stikhi*, prefaced by Roman Yacobson (1972). Vladimir L'vovich Korvin-Piotrovskii was born in Russia in 1891, and died in

California in 1966. Before the War, he published, under the name of Piotrovskii, six collections of poetry, including dramatical poems, *Beatriche* (1929). After the War, he published his collections *Vozdushnyi zmei* (1950), *Porazhenie* (1960), and a collection of poems and dramatical poems in two volumes *Pozdnii gost'* (1968). Khristina Pavlovna Krotkova, who died in 1965, published a collection of poems, *Belym po chernomy* (1951). Gizella Sigizmundovna Lakhman, born in Kiev in 1895, came to the United States in 1941; she died in 1969. She took part in the collection *Chetyrnadtsat'* (1949) and published two collections of her own poetry, *Plennye slova* (1952) and *Zerkala* (1965). Iraida Ivanovna Legkaia was born in Latvia in 1932 and came to the United States in 1949. She has written a collection of poems, *Poputnyi veter* (1968).

Iosif Mikhailovich Levin, born in Russia in 1894, published *Skazanie o vorone* (1945) and *Ulov* (1966). Veniamin Mikhailovich Levin (1892-1953) is author of *Pesn' o Pekine* (1927) and *Lik sokrovennyi* (1955). Dmitrii Antonovich Magula was born in St. Petersburg in 1880 and has resided in the United States since 1918. His work was included in two early collections of poems by several authors, *Iz Ameriki* (1925) and *Chetyrnadtsat'* (1949), and he has published three collections of his own poetry: *Svet vechernii* (1931), *Poslednie luchi* (1943), and *Fata Morgana* (1963). Vladimir Fedorovich Markov was born in Leningrad in 1920 and came to the United States in 1949. He has published two collections of poems, *Stikhi* (1947) and *Gurilevskie romansy* (1960). He compiled and edited the collection *Priglushennye golosa* (1952) and Velimir Khlebnikov's *Works* in four volumes (1968-1971). He received the 1968 P.E.N. Club award for the best English translation of the year for his anthology *Modern Russian Poetry* (1966).

Nikolai Nikolaevich Morshen (pen name of Marchenko) was born in Kiev in 1917, and has been in this country since 1950. He has written two collections of poems, *Tiulen'* (1959) and *Dvoetochie* (1967); at present he is working on a third collection. Saying that he is an enemy of all kinds of questionnaires (a man for whom only verses count) and that the rest of his autobiographical data was unimportant, Morshen conceded that what distinguishes him from some others is rejection of self-analysis—the latter being dangerous "for any creative activity, nourishing on the subconscious," especially the poetical activity (Questionnaire). Morshen, who wrote first on civic themes, later became a philosophical poet; he is rational and yet constantly experimenting with new forms of verse. In Leonid Rzhevskii's view, playing with ringing sounds is organic to Morshen's poetics and his finds in this field are "original and significant for their wealth and attempts to 'fuse' sound and meaning."[13]

Vladimir Vladimirovich Nabokov, born in St. Petersburg in 1899, came to the United States in 1940. Known primarily for his fiction in Russian and English, he also published a collection of poems in Russian, *Stikhot-vorenija* (1952). Boris Anatol'evich Nartsissov was born in the government of Saratov in 1906 and arrived in this country in 1953. He has written five collections of poetry: *Stikhi* (1958), *Golosa* (1961), *Pamiat'* (1965), *Pod'em* (1969) and *Shakhmaty* (1974). He sees his distinguishing traits in a "continuation of the general thrust of the Silver Age on a contemporary level, with the starting point located somewhere between Bunin and Blok" and with an emphasis on the "symbolism of the perceptions of color" (Questionnaire).[14]

Vsevolod Leonidovich Pastukhov (1896-1967), who came to the United States during the War, published a collection of poems, *Khrupkii polet* (1967). Evgenii Raich (pen name of Evgenii Isaakovich Rabinovich) was born in St. Petersburg; he came to the United States in 1938. He has written a collection of poems, *Sovremennik* (1963), and he has been working for several decades on a translation into Russian of Goethe's *Faust*. Aglaia Shishkova (pen name of Agniia Sergeevna Rzhevskaia) was born in Russia in 1923 and has been living in this country since 1963. She is the author of the collection *Chuzhedal'* (1953). Kira Markovna Slavina, who spent her childhood in Leningrad, has been living in the United States since 1928. Her work was included in the collections *Estafeta* (1948) and *Chetyrnadtsat'* (1949), and she has published two collections of her own poetry, *Bumazhnye kryl'ia* (1944) and *Pesochnye chasy* (1966). She has translated American poets into Russian and Russian fairy tales, folk songs, and poems by Russian poets into English.

Strannik (pen name of Archbishop John of San Francisco, be-fore ordination—Prince Dmitrii Alekseevich Shakhovskoi) was born in Moscow in 1902 and has been living in the United States since 1946. In the last fifteen years, he has published five collections of poems, among which he singles out *Izbrannaia lirika* (1974) and *Uprazdnenie mesiatsa* (1968). As a poet, he defines his distinguishing traits as follows: "Service to the Logos—in the transparency, purity, lightness, softness, clarity of the Russian poetic word, [and] contemplatedness [sic] (by way of pan-en-theism: 'Everything is in God'). My every poem can be, actually, devel-oped into a philosophic-contemplative chapter. My poems are a crystalliza-tion of the entire essence of terrestrial life, as the beginning of a New World—in God" (Questionnaire).

Gleb Petrovich Struve, born in St. Petersburg in 1898, came first to the United States from England in 1946, and the following year moved to this country for good. A distinguished scholar, he has also published a collec-tion of poems, *Utloe zhil'e: Izbrannye stikhi 1915-1949 gg.* (1965). Zinaida Sameevna Trotskaia, born in Vil'na in 1902, arrived in the United States in 1941. Her works appeared in the collection *Chetyrnadtsat'* (1949), and she has published three books of her own poems: *Bezgolosye pesni* (1928), *Otgoloski* (1944), and *Vpolgolosa* (1961). M. Vizi (pen name of Mariia Genrikhovna Turkova) was born in New York and has lived in San Francisco. She has written poetry in Russian and in English and translated into both languages. She is the author of two volumes of *Stikhotvoreniia* (1929; 1936).

Books of poetry have also been published by Vladimir Ant (*Moi tanki*, 1964; *Mal-kok-tut*, 1966), Viktoriia Babenko (*Grust'*, 1972), Rodion Berezov (pen name of Rodion Mikhailovich Akul'shin, whose numerous collections are devoted to religious themes), Mikhail Chekhonin (*Stikhi*, 1946), Vladislav Ellis (*Izbrannoe*, 1969), Iurii Gertsog (*Nachalo epopei*, 1968), the "newest" emigré Naum Korzhavin (*Vremena: Izbrannoe*, 1976), Galina Kuznetsova (*Olivkovyi sad*, 1937), Tatiana Timasheva (1891-1950; *Izbrannye stikhotvoreniia*, 1953), Boris Volkov (1894-1953; *V pyli chuzhikh dorog*, 1934), Nikolai Vorob'ev (*Kondratii Bulavin*, 1965), and others. Some authors of collections of poetry—like Sofiia Pregel', Leonid Strakhovskii, Elena Rubisova—have only temporarily been associated with the Russian literary scene in America.

There are also some other poets who have been, in various degrees, familiar to readers of Russian newspapers, reviews, and anthologies in the United States. Among them are Nina Berberova (who edited and published a collection of Vl. Khodasevich's poetry), Anatolii Darov, Richard Ianin, Viktoriia Iankovskaia, Vladimir Il'iashenko (who was the initiator of an early collection of poems by several Russian poets living in America, *Iz Ameriki*, published in New York in 1925, and later took part in the collection *Chetyrnadtsat'*), A. Kasim (pen name of Al'tamentov), Aleksandr Korona, Sergei Maksimov, Elena Matveeva, Gennadii Panin (who is both a student of history and a practitioner of acrostic), Tatiana Ostroumova, Aleksandr Rostovskii, Georgii Shirokov, Mariia Tolstaia, and others.

Concluding this survey of poetic activities, I also want to mention some anthologies whose compilers or editors were not referred to previously: *Zhemchuzhiny russkogo poeticheskogo tvorchestva*, comp. T. A. Bereznii (1964), *Russkaia lirika ot Zhukovskogo do Bunina*, comp. A. A. Bogolepov (1952), *Neopalimaia kupina: Evreiskie siuzhety v russkoi poezii*, comp. Alexander Donat (1973), and *Mnemozina i Kaissa*, comp. Emmanuil Shtein (1973).

Even such an unavoidably incomplete listing of poets and their books as this one testifies to the existence of an active poetic life among Russian immigrants in this country—especially intensified in the last twenty-five years, beginning with the mass immigration around the year 1950.[15]

The most popular Russian poets in the United States nowadays are, probably, Lidiia Alekseeva, Igor Chinnov, Ivan Elagin, Gleb Glinka, Oleg Il'inskii, Iurii Ivask, and Nikolai Morshen. They are very different from one another. And when one surveys the entire poetic scene this diversity becomes no less pronounced. Still, from time to time, attempts have been made to generalize, if not with regard to individual poets as such, at least with regard to their themes and general mood.

In the foreword to his anthology of Russian emigré poetry, *Na Zapade*, Iurii Ivask singles out three major interrelated themes: Russia, exile, and solitude. These themes result in a lyrical poetry, inseparable, however, from some publicistic elements. Acknowledging that exile is always misfortune, Ivask states that it is not always a failure, since creativeness and creative achievements are as possible in exile as they are in the homeland. His conclusion is that the very fact of emigration has enriched Russian poetry with a "new trembling"—and, consequently, misfortune has also been good fortune.[16]

Elsewhere Ivask also dealt with other aspects of the general tone of Russian emigré poetry. Between the two world wars the so-called "Parisian note" was dominant. Its inspirer, the critic and poet Georgii Adamovich, appealed to emigré poets to write simply, yet write about what is most important—suffering, death, solitude, God. But after World War II this toned-down and ascetic Parisian note became supplanted by what could be called an "American note," characterized by bold images (a new "imaginism"), ecstasy of words and sounds, experimentalism, a special feeling of spaciousness in poetry, a definite fervor and challenge to our mad century, and joyful amazement that in spite of the expected end of humanity, we still live, breath, and give thanks for the miracle of life.[17]

* * *

Among Russian prose-writers in the United States there are no outstanding names representing the "waves" of immigrants preceding the Russian revolution of 1917. After the Revolution, two authors who were already known in Russia, Georgii Grebenshchikov and Sergei Gusev-Orenburgskii, came to the United States, where they continued their literary activities until their deaths in the 1960's. The most famous among those who immigrated during the World War Two years is, of course, Vladimir Nabokov. Another famous writer, Mark Aldanov, returned later to France and thus could hardly be considered a Russian-American writer. On the whole, most of the prose-writers who form the contemporary Russian literary scene in the United States immigrated after the last war, in the 1950's and 1960's. The following is a listing—again unavoidably incomplete—of the better known Russian prose-writers and their major publications.

Vasilii Ivanovich Alekseev was born in Vladimir in 1906 and came to the United States in 1951. The New York-based Chekhov Publishing House published two of his tales, *Nevidimaia Rossiia* (1952) and *Rossiia soldatskaia* (1954). Gennadii Andreevich Andreev (Khomiakov), born in Tsaritsyn on Volga in 1906, first came to the United States in 1959 and has been living here permanently since 1967. He published a book of stories and feature-stories, *Gor'kie vody* (1954), feature-stories, *Solovetskie ostrova* (1950), and a book about a Soviet concentration camp and the flight from it, *Trudnye dorogi* (1959). At present he is working on feature-stories reflecting World War II and captivity, "Minomet-chiki," which began to appear in *Novyi zhurnal.* As a prose-writer, Andreev considers "truthfulness, to the limit of exactness, of what is depicted or described" to be of outmost importance, especially with regard to Soviet reality, in all its aspects and details; in the Soviet Union this reality "is invariably distorted, garbled—and the responsibility for its truthful depiction falls upon us" (Questionnaire).

Argus was the pen name of Mikhail Konstantinovich Eisenstadt (Zheleznov), who was born in the government of Minsk in 1900. He came to the United States in 1924 and settled in New York City in 1934, where he lived until his death in 1970. For some thirty-five years he was the topical satirist of the Russian newspaper *Novoe russkoe slovo.* He wrote two books in Russian, *Polushutia, poluser'ezno* (1959) and *Drugaia zhizn' i bereg dal'nii* (1969), and two books in English, *Moscow-on-the-Hudson* (1951) and *A Rogue with Ease* (1953). In addition, he edited two books of translations from English into Russian, *D'iavol i Daniel Webster and Other Stories* (1959) and an anthology of American humor, *Amerika smeetsia* (1962). The Russian literary critic Georgii Adamovich, in his introduction to Argus' book *Drugaia zhizn' i bereg dal'nii*, fully agreed with the judgment of Ivan Bunin that in Argus' prosaic and poetic writings one can find brilliant lines everywhere. Adamovich distinguishes between Argus' humorous stories, some of which are worthy of inclusion in a general anthology of Russian humor, and his poetry, in which he sees an irreconcilable struggle between lyricism and irony. Adamovich concludes that Argus, who gave himself up equally to lyricism and irony, was a most original phenomenon in Russian emigré literature.[18]

Rodion Mikhailovich Berezov (pen name of Akul'shin), born in Russia in 1896, was functioning as a writer long before leaving the Soviet Union during the last war. In the United States he published no less than twenty books, among them a book of stories and poems, *Chudo* (1961), the novel *Razluka* (1965), collections of stories *Dalekoe i blizkoe* (1952), *Russkoe serdtse* (1954), *Zolotaia raketa* (1956), *Zvezda* (1966), and others. Leonid Bogdanov (pen name of Bogdan Ivanovich Sagotov, 1918-1961) wrote a satirical tale *Telegramma iz Moskvy* (1957), a collection of humorous stories *Bez sotsialisticheskogo realisma* (1961), and a story *V storone ot bol'shoi dorogi* (1964).

Anatolii Andreevich Darov, born in Bui in the government of Iaroslavl'
in 1920, arrived in this country in 1961. Here he published a novel, *Blo-
kada* (first, in installments, in the newspaper *Novoe russkoe slovo* and then
as a book by Rausen in New York), sketches about contemporary and
eternal Athos *Bereg Net Cheloveka* (1966), and the novel "Na Zapad idti
ne legko" serialized in *Novoe russkoe slovo*. The same newspaper published some twenty chapters of another novel, "Glavnaia liubov'," and the
first chapters of a novel from postwar French life, "S poputnym vetrom."
In addition to the latter novel, Darov is working now on a novel about the
life of Russian immigrants in the United States, "Irratsional'nye." In his
opinion, what distinguishes him from other writers, is a commitment to
experimental prose and the use of the emotional feature-story or sketch
(Questionnaire).

Nina Fedorova (Antonina Fedorovna Riazanovskaia), born in Russia in
1895, is author of several novels: *Sem'ia* (1952), first published in English
as *The Family* (1940); *Deti* (1958), first in English as *The Children*
(1942); "Chetyre zhenshchiny v zhizni mistera Grema" (serialized in *Vozrozhdenie*, 1965-1966); *Zhizn'* vol. I (1964), vols. II and III (1966); and
Natashina liubov' (first in *Vozrozhdenie*, 1959-1960, then by Victor Kamkin, 1968). The poet and editor Tat'iana Pavlovna Fesenko is also author
of *Povest' krivykh let* (1963) and the travelogue *Glazami turista* (1966).

Boris Andreevich Filippov published, in addition to special collections
of poetry, many books of prose and of prose combined with poetry: the
stories *Kresty i perekrestki* (1957), a tale in four stories *Skvoz' tuchi*
(1960), the stories *Pyl'noe solntse* (1961), the stories *Polustanki* (1962),
the stories *Muzykal'naia shkatulka* (1963), the stories, sketches and poems
Tuskloe okontse (1967), poems and prose *Veter svezheet...* (1969), the
stories, legends and poems *Mimokhodom* (1970), the stories, legends and
poems *Predan'ia stariny glubokoi* (1971), the stories, sketches and poems
Mig, k kotoromu ia prikasaius' (1973), the stories *Pamiat' serdtsa* (1974),
and a revised version of a tale in thirteen stories, *Skvoz' tuchi* (1972). With
the exception of *Tuskloe okontse* all these books were published in Washington. Georgii Dmitrievich Grebenshchikov (pen name, Sibiriak), born in
the government of Tomsk in 1883, was an established Siberian writer and
journalist before the Revolution, and came to the United States after the
Civil War. He died in Florida in 1964. Grebenshchikov is best known for
his multi-volume épopee *Churaevy* (1922-1937).

Roman Borisovich Gul' was born in Russia in 1896, came to the United
States in 1950. As a writer he created a name for himself while still in
Europe. Here his main energies are devoted to the publication of the
review *Novyi zhurnal*. However, he has managed to rework, sometimes
significantly, several of his earlier books. In the last two years he repub-

lished his historical novel *Azef* (4th ed., 1974), his historical chronicle *Bakunin* (1974), and his autobiography *Kon' ryzhii* (1975). Critics singled out the picturesqueness of the author's style and language as well as his ability to choose from the wealth of historical evidence that which is most important and deserving of creative interpretation.[19] Sergei Ivanovich Gusev-Orenburgskii (pen name of Gusev) was born in Orenburg in 1867 and after the Russian Revolution lived in New York, where he died in 1964. Much older than Grebenshchikov, Gusev-Orenburgskii was well known as a writer in pre-revolutionary Russia. In this country, he published a novel, *Strana detei* (1928), and collections of stories *Goriashchaia t'ma* (1926), *Glukhoi prikhod* and other stories (1952), and emigré stories *Sviataia Rus'* (1957).

The poet Vladimir Ivanovich Iurasov also wrote two novels, *Vrag naroda* (1952) and *Parallax* (1966). The second novel, which first appeared in English, was later serialized in Russian in the newspaper *Novoe russkoe slovo* and published also in book form. Critics noted that Iurasov writes in the good old manner of Russian realist novel, paying special attention to plot and structure, revealing characters and ideological problems in dialogues, emphasizing details, and allowing the reader to not only hear, but also see what is happening.[20]

Alla Ktorova (pen name of Viktoriia Ivanovna Shando-Kochurova), born in Moscow in 1926, was able to leave the Soviet Union for the United States in 1959. Here she has published a book, *Litso Zhar-Ptitsy*, with the challenging subtitle "Scraps of an unfinished anti-novel" (1969), and another book, *Eksponat molchashchii i drugoe* (1974), in which she collected her best writings for the years 1960-1972. The Parisian critic Iu. Terapiano was one of the first to point out that, in her depiction of the miserable and tragic Soviet everyday life, Ktorova "has her own intonation, her own manner to conduct narration using brief, energetic sentences, her images are distinct, expressive, with a tone, now lyrically-sad, now protestingly-rebellious."[21]

Sergei Sergeevich Maksimov, born in the Volga region in 1917, came to the United States in 1949; he died in Los Angeles in 1967. He was the first "new" Russian emigré to make a name for himself as a novelist. After his first novel, *Denis Bushuev* (1949; in English, by Scribner, 1951), he wrote three more books, all of them published by the New York based Chekhov Publishing House: a book of stories, *Taiga* (1952), a book of stories, poems and plays, *Goluboe molchanie* (1953), and another novel, representing a sequel to his first novel, *Bunt Denisa Bushueva* (1956). Critics acknowledged Maksimov's mastery of portraiture, dramatical conflicts, and landscape-painting—especially of his beloved Volga.[22] Petr Aleksandrovich Murav'ev recently published a novel, *Vremia i den'* (1973), dealing with life in New York City and contrasting the unchecked progress of technological civilization with the slowdown in man's spiritual growth. This work was followed by a second novel, *Polius lorda*, which was serialized in *Novoe russkoe slovo* (January–March, 1976).

Vladimir Vladimirovich Nabokov (Russian pen name, Sirin) belongs to both the Russian and American literatures. Before the War, in Europe, he published many books in Russian (*Mashen'ka, Korol', dama, valet, Zashchita Luzhina, Podvig, Kamera Obscura, Otchaianie, Priglashenie na kazn', Vozvrashchenie Chorba, Sogliadatai*). During the 1940's Nabokov, for a decade, wrote in English and became an American writer. However, since the 1950's he also published several books in Russian; in addition to his collection of poems *Stikhotvoreniia*, he wrote two novels, *Dar* (1952) and *Lolita* (1967), a collection of stories, *Vesna v Fial'te i drugie rasskazy* (1956), and his reminiscences, *Drugie berega* (1954). In the last ten years six of Nabokov's earlier Russian books were reprinted: *Priglashenie na kazn'* (1966), *Zashchita Luzhina* (1967), *Korol', dama, valet* (1969), *Mashen'ka* (1974), *Podvig* (1974), and *Dar* (second edition, corrected, 1975). The early attitudes toward Nabokov among Russian critics and readers were very variegated. Only a few immediately accepted his originality and talent. Since the 1950's he has been more widely recognized, though probably few would go as far as Nina Berberova, who affirms that Nabokov is "the greatest writer in the Russian language of this century, and one of the greatest contemporary writers in any language . . . ."[23]

Nikolai Vladimirovich Narokov (pen name of Marchenko), born in a small town in Bessarabia in 1887, came to the United States in 1950; he died in Monterey, California, in 1969. He wrote two novels, *Mnimye velichiny* (1952; published also in German, French, Spanish, and twice in English: once in book-form, and once serialized in *Saturday Evening Post*) and *Mogu!* (1965). He also left behind him a manuscript of a third novel, "Liubov' Nikolaia Borisovicha." Viktor Porfir'evich Petrov, born in Kharbin, China, in 1907, came to the States in 1940. An Orientalist, whose speciality is China and Mongolia, and a Geographer, who taught Geography at American universities until his retirement in 1975, Petrov is also a writer. In Shanghai he published two volumes of stories, *Pod amerikanskim flagom* (1933) and *V Man'chzhurii* (1937), and a novel, *Lola* (1934). In Washington, Victor Kamkin, Inc., published Petrov's novel in two books *Saga Forta Ross* (book 1, *Printsessa Elena*, 1961; book 2, *Konets mechtam*, 1963), a collection of stories, *Kitaiskie rasskazy* (1962), a tale, *Kolumby Rossiiskie* (1971), a novel, *Kamerger Dvora* (1973), and another tale, *Zavershenie tsikla* (1975). At the present time Viktor Petrov is working on a historical novel, which has as its background events taking place in the Far East. As a prose-writer, Petrov deals with the life of Russians in Alaska, in California, and in China.

Arkadii Borisovich Rovner, born in Odessa in 1940, left the Soviet Union only two years ago, but he has already succeeded in publishing a book of stories, *Gosti iz oblasti,* in the United States (1975). Leonid Denisovich Rzhevskii, born in Moscow in 1905, came to America in 1963. While still in Europe, he published two novels, *Mezhdu dvukh zvezd* (1953) and *Pokazavshemu nam svet* (1960), and a collection of stories, *Dvoe na kamne* (1960). Since coming here, he has published another collection of stories and tales, *Cherez proliv* (1966), and another novel, "Sputnitsa," serialized in the almanac *Mosty* (1968-1970, Nos. 13-15). Still another novel, *Dve strochki vremeni,* is scheduled for publication by Posev. As a prose-writer, Rzhevskii sees his distinguishing trait as an attempt "to create an unconstrainedly-narrative style of author's speech, and with regard to contents—a 'syncretism' of the life's theme" (Questionnaire).

Andrei Sedykh (pen name of Iakov Moiseevich Tsvibak) was born in Feodosiia, Crimea, in 1902, and came to the States in 1942. While living in France, he wrote several books of sketches and stories: *Staryi Parizh* (1926), *Monmartr* (1927), *Parizh noch'iu* (with a foreword by A. I. Kuprin, 1928), *Tam, gde zhili koroli* (1931), *Tam, gde byla Rossiia* (1931), and *Liudi za bortom* (1933). Since his arrival in the United States, Sedykh has published the following books: *Doroga za okean* (1942), *Zvezdochety s Bosfora* (with a foreword by I. A. Bunin, 1948; 2nd ed., 1974), *Sumasshedshii sharmanshchik* (1951), *Tol'ko o liudiakh* (1955), *Zamelo tebia snegom, Rossiia* (1964), *Pod nebom Ispanii* (1964), *Zemlia obetovannaia* (1966), *Ierusalim, imia radostnoe* (1969). The first of Sedykh's American books was published by *Novyi zhurnal,* the others by *Novoe russkoe slovo.* His book in English, *This Land of Israel* (1967), went through two printings. As a prose-writer, Sedykh considers simplicity of style, lack of mannerisms, and purity of language to be his distinguishable traits (Questionnaire).

Nikolai Nikolaevich Sergievskii, who was born in Russia in 1875, is author of two historical novels, *Gishpanskaia zateia* (1941; 2nd., revised and supplemented ed., 1955) and "Kamerger i gishpanka ili Russkie v Kalifornii" (serialized in the review *Vozrozhdenie,* 1949-1950). Vladimir Dmitrievich Sokolov-Samarin, born in Orel in 1913 and living in the United States since 1951, published here three books of stories, *Peschanaia otmel'* (1964), *Teni na stene* (1967) and *Tsvet vremeni* (1969), as well as a book of travel sketches, *Dalekaia zvezda* (1972). Critics noted Samarin's constantly growing mastery over the genre of the miniature story with its delicate structure, requiring true harmony of its components and the right word.[24]

Mikhail Stepanovich Solov'ev, born in Russia in 1908, published a novel in two volumes, *Kogda bogi molchat* (1963), which earlier appeared in

English under the same title, *When the Gods are Silent* (1953), as well as in German, Swedish, Norwegian, French, Chinese, and some other languages. Solov'ev has also written a book of sketches, based on his personal experiences as a military correspondent in the Soviet Union, *Zapiski sovetskogo voennogo korrespondenta* (1954). Nikolai Ivanovich Ul'ianov, born in St. Petersburg in 1904 and living here since 1955, is author of a historical novel, *Atossa* (1952), and a book of stories, *Pod kamennym nebom* (1970). He is now finishing another historical novel that concerns the time of the first World War and the end of the Russian Empire, "Sirius," some chapters of which were published in *Novyi zhurnal* (starting with No. 43 in 1955). As a prose-writer, Ul'ianov strives for "simplicity, clarity, and forcefulness of language" (Questionnaire).

Vasilii Semenovich Ianovskii (Yanovsky), born in Russia in 1906, came to the United States in 1942. He published several novels and tales: *Koleso* (1930), *Mir* (1931), *Liubov' vtoraia* (1935), "Amerikanskii opyt" (serialized in *Novyi zhurnal*, 1946-1948), *Portativnoe bessmertie* (1953), *Cheliust' emigranta* (1957), and "Zalozhnik" (serialized in *Novyi zhurnal*, 1960-1961). He also published three novels in English: *No Man's Time*, translated from Russian by Isabella Levitin and Roger Nyle Parris, with a foreword by W. H. Auden (1967), *Of Light and Sounding Brass* (1972) and *The Dark Fields of Venus* (1973).[25]

There are a number of other prose-writers: Ol'ga Iork (pen name of Ol'ga Iurkevich), who has written a novel, *Reka vremen* (1967); Grigorii Klimov, whose popular book of sketches *Berlinskii Kreml'* (1953; preceded by a German language edition) was followed by a novel, *Imia moe legion*, a chapter of which appeared in *Grani* in 1958; Viktor Mort, author of *Znatnye puteshestvenniki* (1954), *Kheppi end* (1968), and *Mera podlosti*; Victor Robsman, who published a book of stories and sketches of a former correspondent of *Izvestiia*, *Tsarstvo t'my* (1956); Pavla Tetiukova, author of three collections of stories and tales: *Po putiam i dorogam* (1955), *Serebrianaia nit'* (1957), and *Farandola* (1960), and others. Some prose-writers, like Iurii Bol'shukhin and Iurii Krotkov, though well known to the reading public, have not yet published their fiction in book form.

On the other hand, there are a number of writers, who are not engaged, at least primarily, in fiction-writing, but whose reminiscences and autobiographical sketches are distinguished by certain literary qualities; among them are Svetlana Allilueva, Iurii Elagin, Mikhail Koriakov, Vladimir Petrov, Elena Scriabina, Aleksandra Tolstaia, Vladimir Varshavskii, and others.

It would appear from this survey that the most common narrative genre is that of the short story or tale, though the novel—including the historical novel—is also well represented. In addition to stories in various journals, many authors have also published collections of stories. Sometimes, in the same book, stories are printed with poems. A number of novels have been published first—or exclusively—in literary-political journals or even in newspapers (essentially, *Novoe russkoe slovo*). Alongside stories, tales, and novels, a very popular genre is the sketch or feature-story. The genre of literary and literature-related memoirs is also produced.

Much of the prose is autobiographical, or at least heavily based on the author's personal experience. Some authors reflect American life, a few treat life in Western Europe, but most deal with life in either prerevolutionary Russia, or more often than not, Soviet Russia—depending on whether the author belongs to the "old" or the "new" (in the case of Alla Ktorova and Arkadii Rovner—to the "newest") emigration. In addition to life under Stalin, the experiences, connected with the German-Soviet war of 1941-1945—the front, the rear, the captivity—are also of importance. Of course, the life of emigrés in Europe and America is quite heavily reflected.

The ability to handle artistically these life-experiences and literary genres varies from author to author, depending on natural gifts and acquaintance with literary techniques. As for experimentation in prose, relatively few have engaged in it; the majority have remained on traditional formal grounds, inherited from the classical Russian literature. The predominant literary "school" is that of Realism or Neo-Realism, and, in this sense, there is more common ground with the legacy of the nineteenth century than with the Modernism of the turn of the century or with Symbolism. But all these attempts at generalizations are by no means meant to substitute for the first and correct impression of a great variety of individual authors and their work.

* * *

While poetry has been written exclusively in Russian, and most fiction has been written in Russian, with only a few exceptions (whenever there were books in English, they usually were translations from Russian), literary scholarship was produced both in Russian and English. And literary scholarship quite often went hand in hand with literary criticism, and vice versa. What a literary scholar and critic wrote in response to the Questionnaire with regard to himself could often be said about others too. The difference between scholarship and criticism, then, would amount to presence or absence of footnotes; when an author uses footnotes, he produces a piece of scholarship, when not, a piece of criticism. But there is no doubt that scholarship predominates, and it is more often than not connected with academic activities at American universities. The following listing (unavoidably incomplete) indicates the authors and their works who are directly or partially related to literary scholarship and criticism.

Vera Aleksandrova (pen name of Vera Aleksandrovna Shvarts) was born in Kovno in 1895, lived in the United States since 1940, and died in New York in 1966. She has written *A History of Soviet Literature 1917-1964: From Gorky to Solzhenitsyn* (1963; 1964) and *Literatura i zhizn': Ocherki sovetskoi literatury, 1927-1945* (1969), and she was the editor of *Pestrye rasskazy: Sbornik emigrantskoi prozy* (1953) and of a collection of Soviet prose *Opal'nye povesti* (1955). Alex E. Alexander, Associate Professor of Russian Language and Literature and Chairman of the Russian Division at Hunter College, is author of *Bylina and Fairy Tale: The Origins of Russian Heroic Poetry* (1973) and translator and editor of *Russian Folklore: An Anthology in English Translation* (1975).

Metropolitan Anastasii (Aleksandr Aleksandrovich Gribanovskii), born in the government of Tambov, came to the United States in 1950, and was head of the Russian Church in Exile from 1936 until his death in New York in 1965. He wrote *Pushkin v ego otnoshenii k religii i pravoslavnoi tserkvi* (1939; 2nd ed., 1947) and *Nravstvennyi oblik Pushkina* (1956). Ivan Mikhailovich Andreev, who for many years was a Professor at the Russian Holy Trinity Monastery at Jordanville, N.Y., published a booklet on M. Iu. Lermontov (1964) and the first part of his selected lectures on Russian literature, *Ocherki po istorii russkoi literatury XIX veka* (1968). Nikolai Sergeevich Arsen'ev, Emeritus Professor of St. Vladimir's Orthodox Theological Seminary, Crestwood, N.Y., where he taught until his retirement in 1967, is author of some twenty-five books (some of them in three or four languages—English, Russian, German, French, Rumanian, or New Greek), among them: *Die Russiche Literatur der Neuzeit und der Gegenwart in ihren geistigen Zusammenhängen* (1929), *Iz russkoi kul'turnoi i tvorcheskoi traditsii* (1959), *O Dostoevskom* (1972), *Dary i vstrechi zhiznennogo puti* (1974).[26]

Nina Nikolaevna Berberova, was born in St. Petersburg in 1901, and came to the United States in 1950. Before that she lived in Paris, where she published some ten books, including three novels, a collection of tales, and a play.[27] Since 1963 she has been Professor of Russian Literature at Princeton University. In addition to Vladislav Khodasevich's *Sobranie stikhov* (1961), she edited also his *Literaturnye stat'i i vospominaniia* (1954). She published a book in French on Aleksandr Blok and his time. Her Russian autobiography, *Kursiv moi* (1972), was first published in English under the same title, *The Italics Are Mine* (1969). Marianna Sergeevna Bogoiavlenskaia, born in Helsinki in 1915, came to America in 1950. Professor of Russian Literature at Dickinson College, she is author of *Religioznaia lichnost' Gogolia v novom osveshchenii* (1960).

Boris L'vovich Brazol' (1885-1963) has written numerous speeches on Russian writers of the nineteenth century, published by the Pushkin Society (Obshchestvo imeni A. S. Pushkina) in New York City, including *A. S. Griboedov* (1945), *Pushkin i Rossiia* (1949), *Slovotvorchestvo A. S. Pushkina* (1950), *Dushevnaia drama Gogolia* (1952), *I. A. Goncharov* (1952), *A. S. Khomiakov* (1954), *Raznoudariaemost' u Pushkina i v russkoi rechi* (1955), *Tserkovnoslavianskaia i bibleiskaia stikhii v tvorchestve A. S. Pushkina* (1958), and *V. I. Dal', bessmertnyi russkii leksikograf* (1961). The same society published two volumes of his *Rechi* (Vol. I, 1943; Vol. II, 1953). The poet Iosif Brodskii made selection for and introduced an anthology, *Modern Russian Poets on Poetry* (1976).

Aleksandr Georgievich Dynnik was born in Libava, Latvia, in 1919, arrived in this country in 1966, and is currently Associate Professor of Russian at Michigan State University and author of two books, *A. I. Kuprin: Ocherk zhizni i tvorchestva* (1969) and *Russian Literature Until 1837* (1975). German Sergeevich Ermolaev, who was born in Tomsk in 1924 and arrived in the U.S.A. in 1949, is Professor of Russian Literature at Princeton University. He wrote *Soviet Literary Theories, 1917-1934: The Genesis of Socialist Realism* (1963), translated and provided with an introduction and notes for Maksim Gor'kii's *Untimely Thoughts* (1968; 1970), and edited (with introduction and notes) the Russian edition of Maksim Gor'kii's *Nesvoevremennye mysli* (1971). Ermolaev is working now on a book on Mikhail Sholokhov's art.

Tat'iana Pavlovna Fesenko, a poet and prose-writer, is co-author, with Andrei Vladimirovich Fesenko, of *Russkii iazyk pri Sovetakh* (1955) and compiler of a catalogue, Eighteenth Century Russian Publications in the Library of Congress (1961). At present she is preparing for publication a collection of her essays on books and authors, which will include a series on "Books and People of the Eighteenth Century in Russia."

Boris Andreevich Filippov, whose poetry and fiction was referred to earlier, was, until his retirement in 1975, an Adjunct Professor of Russian Literature at The American University. He wrote a book of literary sketches, *Zhivoe proshloe* (Vol. I, 1965; Vol. II, 1973), and *Leningradskii Peterburg v russkoi poezii i prose* (1973; 2nd, augmented ed., 1974). Filippov edited or co-edited a great number of books. Those which he edited alone include Nikolai Kliuev's *Sochineniia*, in two volumes (1954), *Siniavskii i Daniel' na skam'e podsudimykh: Protsess Siniavskogo I Danielia* (1966), and *Sovetskaia potaennaia muza: Iz stikhov sovetskikh pisatelei, napisannykh ne dlia pechati* (1961). Together with Gleb Petrovich Struve, Filippov edited the collected works of Anna Akhmatova in three volumes (Vol. I, Vol. II, 1968; Vol. III, 1975), the works of Nikolai Gumilev in four volumes (1962-1968), those of Nikolai Zabolotskii (1965), Nikolai Kliuev in two volumes (1969), Osip Mandel'shtam (in one volume, 1955; in two volumes, 1964, 1966; in three volumes, 1967-1971), and Boris Pasternak in three volumes (1961). Together with Evgeniia Vladimirovna Zhiglevich, Filippov edited Iurii Annenkov's *Dnevnik moikh vstrech: Tsikl tragedii* in two volumes (1966), F. M. Dostoevskii's *U Tikhona: Propushchennaia glava iz romana 'Besy'* (1964), Boris Zaitsev's *Dalekoe* (1965) and *Reka vremen* (1968), Emmanuil Rais' *Pod glukhimi nebesami* (1967), and Ol'ga Forsh's *Sumasshedshii korabl'* (1964).

Gleb Aleksandrovich Glinka, the poet, is also a literary scholar. Author of *Na perevale* (1954), he is now engaged in research on the theory of Russian versification and is preparing his memoirs for publication. Roman Borisovich Gul', whose fiction was referred to earlier, published a book of essays and reviews devoted to Soviet and emigré literatures, *Odvukon'* (1973). Roman Osipovich Iakobson (Jacobson) was born in Moscow in 1896. Cross Professor of Slavic Languages and Literatures and General Linguistics at Harvard since 1949 and Professor at Massachusetts Institute of Technology since 1957, he is author of a great number of works, including *Noveishaia russkaia poeziia, nabrosok l-yi: V. Khlebnikov* (1921) and *O cheshskom stikhe, preimushchestvenno v sopostavlenii s russkim* (1925). Primarily a linguist, he has been co-editor of the *International Journal of Slavic Linguistics and Poetics* (since 1951).[28]

Iurii Pavlovich Ivask, the poet, is Professor of Russian Literature at the University of Massachusetts and author of *Konstantin Leont'ev: Zhizn' i tvorchestvo* (1974). He has written numerous critical essays and book-reviews in journals and newspapers, and he defines his approach in this way: "I attempt to combine two methods: analytical ('formal') and 'synthetical' (mythological). On the basis of analysis of poetry I attempt to present the creative profile of the poet and writer, i.e., I create a certain myth. As literary scholar I write with footnotes, as a critic—without them. But the method is the same" (Questionnaire).

Archbishop John (Shakhovskoi) of San Francisco, who as a poet writes under the pen name Strannik, has written many books. Among those published in the last quarter of a century and having a certain relation to literature or writers are *Vremia very* (1964), *Kniga svidetel'stv* (1965), *Moskovskii razgovor o bessmertii* (1972), and, especially, *K istorii russkoi intelligentsii (Revoliutsiia Tolstogo)* (1974). In them, Archbishop John pursues "Revelation of the spiritual aspect of the creative work—philosophical, artistic, and literary" (Questionnaire). Liudmila Georgievna Keler, born in Troitsk in 1917, is Associate Professor of Slavic Languages and Literatures at the University of Pittsburgh and author of *A. A. Delvig: A Classicist in the Time of Romanticism* (1970). Irina Kirk, born in Harbin, Manchuria, in 1926, is Associate Professor of Germanic and Slavic Languages at the University of Connecticut. She published *Dostoevsky and Camus* (1973) and *Profiles in Russian Resistance* (1975). Aleksei Evgen'evich Klimov, born in Riga in 1939, came to Canada in 1949 and from Canada to the United States in 1961. At present he is teaching Russian language and literature at Vassar College. He is co-editor, with John B. Dunlop and Richard Haugh, of *Alexandr Solzhenitsyn: Critical Essays and Documentary Materials* (1973; 2nd enlarged ed., 1975).

Ivan Mikhailovich Kontsevich, born in Poltava in 1893, came to the United States in 1952, where he taught at the St. Trinity Seminary; he died in San Francisco in 1965. He wrote *Istoki dushevnoi katastrofy L. N. Tolstogo* (1960). Iurii (Georgii) Grigor'evich Krugovoi, born in Khar'kov in 1924, came to the United States in 1957. At the present time he is Professor of Russian at Swarthmore College. He has written a book in Italian, *La lotta col Drago nell'Epos eroico russo* (1967). Sergei Pavlovich Kryzhytskii (Kryzytski) was born in the government of Poltava in 1917 and came to America in 1946. He is Professor of Russian at Oberlin College. He wrote *The Works of Ivan Bunin* (1971), and edited, with introduction and commentaries, Ivan Bunin's *Okaiannye dni* (1973; 2nd ed., 1974) and *Pod serpom i molotom* (1975). Dimitrii Aleksandrovich Levitskii was born in Czestochowa, Russia, in 1907. Professor of Russian at the U.S. Government Language Training Facility in Washington, D.C., he is author of *Arkadii Averchenko: Zhiznennyi put'* (1973).

Nikolai Onufrievich Losskii was born in the government of Vitebsk in 1870 and came to the United States in 1950, where he taught at St. Vladimir's Theological Seminary; he died near Paris in 1965. Author of numerous books on philosophy, he also published *Dostoevskii i ego khristianskoe miroponimanie* (1953). Vladimir Fedorovich Markov was born in Leningrad in 1920, and he came to the United States in 1949. He is Professor of Russian Literature at the University of California at Los Angeles. He has written *The Longer Poems of Velimir Khlebnikov* (1962) and *Russian Futurism: A History* (1968; Italian translation, 1973), and he is the editor of *Die Manifeste und Programmschriften der russischen Futuristen* (1967). Currently, Markov is working on a history of Imaginism and on a commentary to the entire poetry of Konstantin Bal'mont. Vladimir Vladimirovich Nabokov, the poet and fiction-writer, was, until his retirement, Professor of Russian Literature at Cornell University. He has written *Nikolai Gogol'* (1944), and he is translator and commentator of A. S. Pushkin's *Eugene Onegin*, in four volumes (1964; rev. ed., 1970).

Nadezhda Anatol'evna Natova (Anatol'eva, Popliuiko) was born in Tashkent in 1918, and arrived in the United States in 1959. Associate Professor of Russian Literature at George Washington University, she initiated The North American Dostoevsky Society (of which she was Executive Secretary-Treasurer and now is Vice-President) and is the Executive Secretary of the International Dostoevsky Society. She has written *Dostoevskii v Bad Emse* (1971) and is the editor of B. Pasternak's *Poeziia: Izbrannoe* (1960).

Temira Andreevna Pachmuss was born in Skamja, Estonia, in 1927 and came to the United States in 1955. Professor of Russian Literature at the University of Illinois at Urbana, she wrote *F. M. Dostoevsky: Dualism and Synthesis of the Human Soul* (1963) and *Zinaida Hippius: An Intellectual Profile* (1971), and she edited *Zinaida Hippius: Collected Poetical Works* in two volumes (1971), *Intellect and Ideas: Selected Correspondence of Zinaida Hippius* (1972), *Zinaida Hippius: Selected Works* (1972), and *Zinaida Hippius as a Playwright* (1972). Another of her Hippius' books, *Between Paris and St. Petersburg: Selected Diaries of Zinaida Hippius*, has been accepted for publication by the University of Illinois Press.

Marianna Artem'evna Poltoratskaia, born in St. Petersburg in 1906, came to the United States in 1950, and died in Albany, N.Y., in 1968. She taught at several American institutions of higher learning; in 1960 she organized the Russian summer school at Windham College and was its Director until 1968, when she organized a similar school at Norwich University. She published *Russkii fol'klor* (1964) and a number of works on the Russian language. Nikolai Petrovich Poltoratskii was born in Istanbul, Turkey, in 1921 and arrived in the United States in 1955. Professor of Slavic Languages and Literatures at the University of Pittsburgh, he edited *Na temy russkie i obshchie* (1965), *Russkaia literatura v emigratsii* (1972), and I. A. Il'in's *Russkie pisateli, literatura i khudozhestvo* (1973).

Ol'ga Petrovna Raevskaia-Hughes, born in Khar'kov in 1932, came to America in 1949. Associate Professor of Slavic Languages and Literatures at the University of California at Berkeley, she is the author of *The Poetic World of Boris Pasternak* (1974) and co-editor, with Gleb Struve and Robert P. Hughes, of *A Century of Russian Prose and Verse: From Pushkin to Nabokov* (1967). Leonid Denisovich Rzhevskii, a fiction-writer, is also a philologist and literary scholar. Emeritus Professor of Slavic Literatures at New York University, he is author of *Iazyk i totalitarizm* (1951), *Iazyk i stil' romana B. L. Pasternaka Doktor Zhivago* (1962), *Prochten'e tvorcheskogo slova: Literaturovedcheskie problemy i analizy* (1970), *Tri temy po Dostoevskomu* (1972), and a collection of essays on Aleksandr Solzhenitsyn (1972; an English edition of this book will be published by Alabama University Press). As a literary scholar and critic, Rzhevskii affirms "the primacy of 'artistry' in a work of literature" (Questionnaire). Vsevolod Mikhailovich Sechkarev, born in Khar'kov in 1914, immigrated to the United States in 1957. Curt Hugo Reisinger, Professor of Slavic Languages and Literatures at Harvard University, has written *N. S. Leskov: sein Leben und sein Werk* (1959), *Geschichte der russischen Literatur* (1962), *A. Puschkin, sein Leben und Werk* (1963), *Studies in the Life and*

Work of I. Annenskij (1963), *Gogol, his Life and Work* (1965), and *I. A. Goncharov, his Life and Work* (1974).[29] As a literary scholar, Sechkarev points out his "lack of love for the approach of our fashionable American Slavicists (*nomina sunt odiosa*)" (Questionnaire).

Vladimir Il'ich Seduro was born in Minsk in 1910 and came to the United States in 1951. He is Professor of Russian at Rensselaer Polytechnic Institute. While in this country, he published the following books: *Dostoevskovedenie v SSSR* (1955), *The Byelorussian Theater and Drama* (1955), *Dostoevski in Russian Literary Criticism, 1846-1956* (1957; 2nd ed., 1969), *Les récents développements des études sur Dostoievsky en Union Soviétique (1955-1960)* (1960), and *Dostoevski's Image in Russia Today* (1975), a section of which, *Dostoevski in Russian Emigré Criticism*, was also published separately. V. Seduro has prepared another book for publication, "Dostoevski and World Theater." Andrei Sedykh, whose fiction was mentioned earlier, has also published a book of literary memoirs, *Dalekie, blizkie* (1962; 2nd ed., 1963). Ariadna Semenovna Shiliaeva (Shilaeff) was born in Blagoveshchensk in 1920 and came to the United States in 1955. Associate Professor of Russian and Chairman of the Department of Russian at Wheaton College, she published *Boris Zaitsev i ego belletrizovannye biografii* (1971) and is now working on a book on Soviet literature, with the tentative title "Literaturnoe ubiistvo i samoubiistvo."

Mark L'vovich Slonim was born in Novgorod-Severskii in 1894 and immigrated to America in 1941. Member emeritus of the Sarah Laurence College English faculty, he is now living in Geneva, Switzerland, where he had been the Director of the College's Foreign Studies Program. Among his numerous books, he singles out *The Epic of Russian Literature: From Its Origins through Tolstoy* (1950; with corrections, in 1964; reprinted), *From Chekhov to the Revolution: Russian Literature 1900-1917* (1962, reproduced, with corrections, the first ten chapters of *Modern Russian Literature: From Chekhov to the Present*, published in 1953), *Soviet Russian Literature: Writers and Problems, 1917-1967* (1967, reproduced the 1964 edition—with corrections, revisions, and new material; there were, all together, five reprints), *An Outline of Russian Literature* (1958; 1959), *Russian Theater from the Empire to the Soviets* (1961), and *Tri liubvi Dostoevskogo* (1953; in English, *Three Loves of Dostoevsky*). The first three books on this list were translated into German, Italian, Spanish, Japanese, etc.; *Three Loves* was translated into German, Italian, Spanish, Greek, etc.; and *Russian Theater* was translated into a number of other languages. At present, Mark Slonim is working on a new, revised and enlarged, 6th reprint of his *Soviet Russian Literature* for the Oxford University Press, and on his "Literary Reminiscences."

Gleb Petrovich Struve, Emeritus Professor of Slavic Languages and Literatures at the University of California at Berkeley, wrote the standard work *Soviet Russian Literature: 1917-1950* (1951; this is a revised and enlarged edition of *25 Years of Soviet Russian Literature*, 1944, which, in turn, was an enlarged edition to *Soviet Russian Literature*, 1935); there was also a new revised edition, *Russian Literature Under Lenin and Stalin* (1971; 1972); the 1944 edition was used for the French version, *Histoire de la littérature Soviétique* (1946); and the 1951 edition served as basis for the German revised, considerably enlarged, and brought up to 1957 version, *Geschichte der Sowjetliteratur* (1957, reprinted in 1964; the work was recently translated into Italian). Struve also wrote two Russian books, *Russkaia literatura v izgnanii* (1956), which is now being translated into English, and *Russkii evropeets: Materialy dlia biografii kniazia P. B. Kozlovskogo* (1950). Struve is editor of *Russkie rasskazy—Russian Stories* (a dual-language paperback (1961) and co-editor of *A Century of Russian Prose and Verse: From Pushkin to Nabokov* (1967). Together with Boris A. Filippov, Gleb Struve edited the collected Russian works of N. Gumilev (in four volumes, 1962-1968), A. Akhmatova (two volumes, 1968-1969; vol. III in the press), O. Mandel'shtam (in three volumes, 1967-1971), N. Kliuev (in two volumes, 1969), and B. Pasternak (in three volumes, 1961). Struve is also co-editor of M. Tsvetaeva's unpublished letters (1972). Since 1960, he has been co-editor with N. Riazanovskii, of *California Slavic Studies*, published by the University of California Press. On 20 April 1973, the American Association for the Advancement of Slavic Studies presented Professor Struve with an "Award for Distinguished Contributions to Slavic Studies," which summed up Professor Struve's qualities and contributions in these words: "Pioneer in studies of Soviet Russian and emigré literature, you were often the first to attract attention to new or unjustly forgotten writers. During a quarter of a century as teacher and director of research, you have inspired several generations of literary scholars. The written record of your prodigious scholarship spans the full history of Russian literature and sets an example for us all. To your students, colleagues and friends who honor you as teacher, scholar and editor, you embody a unique capacity for work, a rare degree of dedication, and a grand combination of scholarly and human integrity."

Kiril Fedorovich Taranovskii was born in Tartu, Estonia, in 1911 and came to the United States in 1958. Professor of Slavic Languages and Literatures at Harvard University, he is the author of *Ruski Dvodelni Ritmovi* (1953) and *Essays on Mandelstam* (1974). Countess Aleksandra L'vovna Tolstaia, the daughter of Lev Tolstoi, an indefatigable humanitarian and President of Tolstoy Foundation, has written *The Tragedy of Tolstoy* (trans. Elena Varneck, 1933) and a two-volume work in Russian,

Otets: Zhizn' L'va Tolstogo (1953).[30] Nikolai Aleksandrovich Troitskii, author of novellas, was, until his retirement, the Russian Bibliographer at Cornell University, and he compiled a bibliography of works of and about Pasternak, *B. L. Pasternak, 1890-1960* (1969).

Nikolai Ivanovich Ul'ianov, already mentioned as fiction-writer, taught, until his recent retirement, Russian literature and cultural history at Yale University. Of the seven books which he published while in the United States, two collections of essays are of particular importance for literary scholarship and criticism: *Diptikh* (1967) and *Svitok* (1972). As a literary scholar, Ul'ianov defines his attitude thus: "First of all, I worry lest the study of literature turn into criticism, philosophical pus or a political or religious sermon. I look after a strict fulfillment of the requirements and methods which have become stable in literary scholarship" (Questionnaire).[31] Mark Veniaminovich Vishniak, born in Russia in 1883, is author of twenty-six books and booklets in Russian, French and English, which include *Sovremennye zapiski: Vospominaniia redaktora* (1957).[32] Elena Pavlovna Vukanovich, born in Turkestan in 1916, arrived in the United States in 1959. Assistant Professor of Slavic Languages and Literatures at the University of Pittsburgh, she is author of *Zvukovaia factura stikhotvorenii sbornika Sestra moia Zhizn' B. L. Pasternaka* (1971).

Kirill Iosifovich Zaitsev (later, as a monk, Arkhimandrit Konstantin) was born in Russia in 1886 and came to the United States after World War II. Until his death in 1975 he taught at the Holy Trinity Seminary in Jordanville, New York, where he also edited *Pravoslavnaia Rus'* and *Pravoslavnyi Put'*. He wrote *I. A. Bunin: Zhizn' i tvorchestvo* (1933) and *Lektsii po istorii Russkoi slovesnosti*, in two parts, *Chast' pervaia: Do-petrovskii period* (1967) and *Chast' vtoraia: XVIII vek, Karamzin, Zhukovskii* (1968), and edited *Pushkin i ego vremia* (1937), *Shedevry literaturnoi kritiki* (1941), *Shedevry russkoi poezii* (compiled by P. Kazakov, vol. I, 1941; vols. II-III were destroyed in 1945). Viacheslav Klavdievich Zavalishin was born in Petrograd in 1915 and came to the United States in 1951. Author of *Early Soviet Writers* (1953; 2nd ed., 1971), he has now finished the first draft of another book concerning late Romantic motifs in Russian culture. As literary scholar, Zavalishin strives to ascertain the contacts between literature and art and music (Questionnaire).

Sergei Aleksandrovich Zen'kovskii was born in Kiev in 1907 and came to the United States in 1949. Professor of Russian Literature at Vanderbilt University, he is author of *Russkoe staroobriadchestvo* (1970) and co-author, with David Armbruster, of *Guide to the Bibliographies of Russian Literature* (1970). He translated, edited, introduced and commented upon *Medieval Russia's Epics, Chronicles and Tales* (1963; 2nd rev. ed., 1965; 3rd rev. ed., 1975), which was published in German as *Aus dem alten Russland: Chroniken, Epen und Geschichten* (1968). He also edited, introduced, and supplied bibliography to D. Čiževskij's books: *Comparative History of Slavic Literatures* (1971), *History of Nineteenth Century Russian Literature: The Romantic Period* (1974), and *History of Nineteenth Century Russian Literature: The Age of Realism* (1974).

Evgeniia Vladimirovna Zhiglevich-Filippova, born in Riga, Latvia, in 1921, arrived in America in 1952. She is a member of the editorial-publishing group led by Professors Gleb Struve and Boris Filippov. She is editor of E. Zamiatin's books *My* (1967), *Litsa* (1967), and *Sochineniia*, vol. I (1970), M. Zoshchenko's *Pered voskhodom solntsa* (1967), and V. Rozanov's *Izbrannoe* (1970). She has also edited books translated from or into Russian: A. Akhmatova's *Requiem* (translated into Estonian by Mariia Under, 1967, and into Latvian by Peteris Aichars, 1968), V. Kandinskii's *O dukhovnom v iskusstve* (1967), T. S. Eliot's *K opredeleniiu poniatiia kul'tury* (trans. E. V. Zhiglevich, 1968). The books edited jointly by E. V. Zhiglevich and B. A. Filippov were referred to in connection with the latter's work. At present she is working, with B. Filippov, on the second volume of Zamiatin's and the second volume of Rozanov's works; she is also working with G. Struve on an edition of M. Voloshin's works.

This list should be supplemented by at least a few more names: Petr Evgen'evich Ershov (1895-1966) is author of *Comedy in the Soviet Theatre* (1955); Zoia Osipovna Iur'eva has edited an *Anthology of Russian Symbolist Critics* to be published by Brown University; Victor Sergeevich Krupich has edited an anthology of Apollon Grigor'ev's writings; the poet and prose-writer Galina Nikolaevna Kuznetsova has written recollections about Ivan Bunin *Grasskii dnevnik* (1967); Marina Ledkovskaia is author of *The Other Turgenev: From Romanticism to Symbolism* (1973); Oleg Aleksandrovich Maslennikov has written *The Frenzied Poets: Andrey Biely and the Russian Symbolists* (1952); Aleksandr Petrovich Obolenskii published *Food-Notes on Gogol* (1972); Pavel Nikolaevich Paganuzzi is author of *Lermontov: Avtobiograficheskie cherty v tvorchestve poeta* (1967); Galina V. Selegin' published *Prekhitraia viaz' (Symvolizm v russkoi proze: Melkii bes Fedora Sologuba)* (1968); Anatolii Alekseevich Sokol'skii is author of *Russian Literature, XI-XX Centuries* and *Literaturnye otkliki i stranstviia* (1973); and Ariadna Vladimirovna Tyrkova-Williams (1869-1962) is author of *Zhizn' Pushkina* (Vol. I, 1929; Vol. II, 1948), a study of Russian folklore, "V mire chudesnogo" (serialized in *Vozrozhdenie*, 1960), and three books of memoirs: *Na putiakh k svobode* (1952), *To, chego bol'she ne budet* (1954), and "Pod'em i krushenie" (serialized in *Vozrozhdenie*, 1956 and 1958).[33] Two non-literary scholars have devoted to Russian literature special attention: Georgii Petrovich Fedotov (1886-1951), especially in his posthumous collection of essays, *Novyi grad*

(1952), and Valentin Aleksandrovich Riazanovskii (1884-1968), in his *Obzor russkoi kul'tury* (1947-1948).

There is also a group of scholars, prolific writers, whose roots remained in Europe, but who taught for a while at various American universities: Dmitrii Ivanovich Chizhevskii, Boris Genrikhovich Unbegaun, and Vladimir Vasil'evich Veidle. Leonid Ivanovich Strakhovskii (1898-1963), a poet, prose-writer, and scholar, moved later in his life to the University of Toronto and was the editor of a Russian review, *Sovremennik*, which is still in existence. On the other hand, there are a number of Russian scholars in Canada who taught or regularly teach, usually during the summer months, in the United States, the most prominent among them being Rostislav Vladimirovich Pletnev and Nikolai Vsevolodovich Pervushin, who took over, from the late Marianna A. Poltoratskaia, the directorship of the Russian Summer School at Norwich University in Vermont.

Finally, this survey suggests some tentative conclusions. As in poetry and fiction, the greatest contributions to Russian literary scholarship and criticism in the United States have been made in the last thirty to thirty-five years. Three generations of literary scholars are engaged in this effort; the oldest scholars included in this survey were born before the end of the nineteenth century, the youngest just before World War II. Those representing the older generation, though few in numbers, contributed heavily to their field, but the role of the largest group—that of the middle generation—is also notable. And there are some very promising young literary scholars.

Literary criticism, inasmuch as it can be divorced from literary scholarship, has been of lesser importance than the latter. To a great extent, critical publications were buried in journals and even newspapers and were seldom collected into books. The majority of those engaged in literary scholarship, particularly in the last quarter of a century, have been teaching at American institutions of higher learning. Hence, their publications have been often in both Russian and English (and, in some instances, in German, French, Italian, and other languages).

The areas covered by scholarly publications are very diverse: Old Russian Literature, eighteenth-century, classical Russian literature of the nineteenth century, Modernism, Symbolism, Acmeism, Futurism, Soviet literature, Emigré literature, Comparative Slavic literatures, etc. Russian nineteenth-century literature is, quite naturally, the favorite. There are many studies dealing with individual authors of both the nineteenth and twentieth centuries, prose-writers and poets. Literary genres as such have not aroused significant interest. In most instances, methodology has been "traditional," rather than Formalist, though the latter school—as well as the religious-philosophical—has its exponents too.

* * *

In view of the very limited resources which were at the disposal of immigrants for printing their books, periodicals and newspapers were often the most important outlet for their publications. In his book Ivan Okuntsov cites the following statistics concerning Russian newspapers and periodicals in the United States: in 1868, one; in 1887, two; in 1897, six; in 1907, eight; in 1917, twenty-four; in 1927, sixteen; in 1935, twenty-two.[34] He adds that, in this country, there have appeared altogether 153 Russian newspapers and periodicals.[35] Elsewhere he writes that in 1916 the half a million Russian immigrants in the United States published sixteen publications—four dailies, seven weeklies, one newspaper published twice a week, and four monthlies.[36] Still further he quotes somewhat different statistics which appeared in a Russian publication in Detroit. During the seventy-five year period from the 1860's through the 1930's there appears to have existed 188 Russian publications—sixty-eight newspapers and 120 periodicals. Of this total, ninety-three were published by various organizations and ninety-five by individuals; eighty-three political, thirty religious, twenty-five social, fourteen economic, two professional, eight humorous, fifteen literary-scholarly, and one medical.[37] Most of them were printed in New York City and Chicago.

Many of the 188 newspapers and periodicals published literary and literature-oriented materials, in particular the fifteen publications which were by nature literary-scholarly. One can imagine the total amount of literature which appeared over the years in all of them. Someday there will be, no doubt, one, two or more dissertations devoted to the study of this phenomenon. But beforehand one can question the artistic value of most of these publications. Moreover, very few of them had a prolonged life.

From the period treated in Okuntsov's book, only one publication has survived until our own days, the New York-based newspaper *Novoe russkoe slovo* (New Russian Word). Paradoxically, it is the oldest Russian daily not only in the United States, but in the entire world—including the Soviet Union. The reason for this strange situation is that the Bolsheviks, soon after they took power in Russia, closed down all prerevolutionary Russian newspapers and periodicals, with the exception of *Pravda*. But even *Pravda* is younger than *Novoe russkoe slovo*: the former begins its history on 5 May 1912, whereas the latter was started in 1910, and thus has been in existence for sixty-six years. During most of its existence, *Novoe russkoe slovo* was published by V. I. Shimkin, and, for fifty years, edited by Mark Efimovich Veinbaum (1923-1973).[38] After his death the newspaper passed into the hands of Andrei Sedykh, whose fiction was discussed earlier.

Andrei Sedykh began his journalistic career while still a high school student in Crimea, Russia. Having emigrated to France, he became, in 1922, a contributor to the Russian newspaper *Poslednie novosti*, edited in

Paris by the well known Russian historian and politician P. M. Miliukov, and was appointed in 1924 its correspondent at the French Parliament. From 1926 to 1940, he was also the Parisian correspondent of the Russian newspaper *Segodnia*, published in Riga, Latvia, and from 1927 to 1942 of the *Novoe russkoe slovo*. Having moved to the United States, he became, in 1942, a member of the editorial board and city editor of *Novoe russkoe slovo*, in 1967 its editor-administrator and companion to the editor-in-chief M. E. Veinbaum (Weinbaum), and from 1973 its editor-publisher and owner (as well as President of the Russian Literary Fund). As a journalist, Andrei Sedykh wrote several thousand articles and dispatches. As editor, A. Sedykh points to the transformation of his newspaper into a free forum, the pages of the newspaper being open "to all, except Communists, who do not recognize the freedom of press and who, consequently, cannot use it" (Questionnaire).

Novoe russkoe slovo, which, as a result of the recent newsprint shortage and the steep rise of printing costs is issued now six times a week (except Mondays), has published over the years articles, stories (and even novels), poems, book reviews, etc., by hundreds of authors, both American and European, and is inseparable from the history of Russian literature in this country and outside Russia in general.[39] While literary or literature-related materials can be found on the pages of *Novoe russkoe slovo* almost any day, there is a special section in the Sunday edition, "Literatura i iskusstvo" (Literature and Art), which has been especially appreciated by readers interested in literature.

Until a few years ago, there was another Russian newspaper published in New York City, *Rossiia*, and there still exists a third one, *Russkaia zhizn'*, published in San Francisco, but their importance for the Russian literary scene in the United States is rather marginal.

Like newspapers, Russian magazines and reviews did not last long.[40] Some of the almanac-type publications or non-periodical collections of prose and poetry had, possibly, a better chance to survive, at least in libraries.[41] Four literary periodicals deserve to be singled out: *Novosel'e*, *Opyty*, *Vozdushnye puti* and *Novyi zhurnal*.[42]

Novosel'e, a monthly literary-artistic magazine, was published and edited by the Sofiia Iul'evna Pregel'[43] from 1942 to 1950, first in New York City and later in Paris. Altogether fifty-two issues appeared (the publication place of No. 42/44 was indicated as New York-Paris instead of simply New York). *Novosel'e*'s pro-Soviet patriotic leanings during the German-Soviet War of 1941-1945 were duly noted in the Soviet *Kratkaia Literaturnaia Entsyklopediia*.[44]

Opyty, a literary journal similar in character to *Chisla* (Paris, 1930-1934), was published by Mariia Samoilovna Tsetlina in New York

City in 1953-1958. Nine issues were published. The first three (1953-1954) were edited by Roman Nikolaevich Grinberg and Vsevolod Leonidovich Pastukhov, the other six (1955-1958) by Iu. Ivask. Of the almanac *Vozdushnye puti*, edited by R. N. Grinberg in New York City in 1960-1967, only five issues were published, but they contained many important literary materials.

Still, none of these publications can be compared, either in literary importance or in longevity, with *Novyi zhurnal* (New Review). This "thick" review was conceived by Mikhail Osipovich Tsetlin (1882-1945) and Mark Aleksandrovich Aldanov (1886-1957)[45] while still in France in 1940, on their way to New York. The first issue appeared in 1942, and the review has been in existence ever since that time, for thirty-four years. Aldanov gave up his editorial duties after the fourth issue, though he remained a permanent contributor, and Tsetlin died while working on the eleventh issue. The review passed into the hands of the Harvard Russian historian and essayist Mikhail Mikhailovich Karpovich (1888-1959), who was its sole editor during the next fourteen years.[46] After his death an editorial board was created consisting of Roman Borisovich Gul',[47] whose fiction was discussed earlier, Nikolai Sergeevich Timashev (1886-1970) and Iurii Petrovich Denike (1887-1964). First the illness and then the death of his co-editors made Roman Gul' the sole editor—until a new editorial board was created in 1975, consisting of R. B. Gul' and two other writers, whose fiction was also discussed earlier, Gennadii Andreevich Andreev (Khomiakov) and Leonid Denisovich Rzhevskii.

Reviewing the history of *Novyi zhurnal*,[48] Roman Gul' singles out four periods: 1) from its founding in 1942 to the end of World War II in 1945, 2) from 1945 to the beginning of the so-called "Thaw" in the Soviet Union after the 1953 death of Stalin, 3) from the mid-fifties to the mid-sixties, and 4) from the mid-sixties till now.

The first period is characterized by an abundance of topical political articles and a poor poetry section. However, the review published the valuable fiction of I. Bunin, M. Aldanov, B. Zaitsev, V. Nabokov, M. Osorgin, V. Ianovskii and others. During the second period, beginning with the eleventh issue, the review was able to contact Russian writers, who remained during the War in Europe, and publish the fiction of B. Zaitsev, A. Remizov, N. Berberova, V. Varshavskii, G. Gazdanov, R. Gul', L. Zurov, M. Ivannikov, Iu. Margolin, I. Odoevtseva. The prose and poetry of the "new" émigrés, recent Soviet citizens—G. Andreev, P. Ershov, N. Ul'ianov, I. Elagin, O. Anstei, G. Glinka, O. Il'inskii, D. Klenovskii, V. Markov, N. Morshen—also appeared in the review. During the third period, the review was first to publish a segment of Boris Pasternak's *Doktor Zhivago*, and contacts with other Soviet writers were established. The review also penetrated into Slavic countries, satellites of the Soviet Union. The current fourth period is different in that manuscripts of Soviet writers were no longer smuggled out, but delivered directly by a number of "newest" émigrés—writers, who fled the Soviet Union or were expelled from it, such as Anatolii Kuznetsov, Iurii Krotkov, Arkadii Belinkov, Mikhail Demin, and others.

During the thirty-four years of its existence *Novyi zhurnal* has published many valuable works not only in its sections of poetry and fiction, but also in such sections as "Literature and Art," "Memoirs and Documents," "Politics and Culture," "Communications and Notes," "In Memoriam," and "Bibliography." The latter includes reviews of books in Russian, English and other languages of the world. From the very beginning *Novyi zhurnal* emphasized tolerance and non-partisanship, barring, however, totalitarian points of view, and it strove to be a literary, cultural and widely-democratic journal of high quality.

There is also a yearly journal which is of definite significance to literary scholarship and criticism—*Zapiski Russkoi Akademicheskoi Gruppy v S.Sh.A.* (Transactions of the Association of Russian-American Scholars in the USA), edited by Professor Konstantin Gavrilovich Belousov.[49] Started in 1967, it already numbers nine volumes. With the exception of volume III (1969), all issues contain works dealing with Russian literature. Especially important are volumes V (1971), devoted to Dostoevskii; VI (1972), containing papers on A. Solzhenitsyn and on Russian Acmeism; VII (1974), with papers on *Gulag Archipelago*; and IX (1975), with papers on A. Pushkin.

Also worthy of mention is a pedagogical journal, *V pomoshch' prepodavateliam russkogo iazyka*, for nineteen years (Nos. 1-48, 1947-1966) edited and published by Nikolai Pavlovich Avtonomov, first in Oregon and then in San Francisco. Though, as the title indicates, a primarily methodical linguistic publication, the journal contains a great deal of information that might be of more immediate concern to students and teachers of Russian literature. It also has published monographs and collections of articles by N. P. Avtonomov, P. E. Ershov, N. V. Pervushin, and M. A. Poltoratskaia on both language and literature. In 1967 the journal was passed to V. I. Grebenshchikov, who at that time taught at Michigan State University, and began to appear under a new, double title: *Russian Language Journal—Russkii iazyk (Izuchenie i prepodavanie).*[50]

Though this survey is concerned primarily with periodicals in Russian, we should not overlook (in addition to the already mentioned *California Slavic Studies*, edited by Nikolai Valentinovich Riasanovskii, Gleb Petrovich Struve, and Thomas Eeckman) a very important Russian-American review, published in English—*The Russian Review.*

In his "Preface" (p. 1) to the *Cumulative Index to Volumes 1-30, 1941-1971*, compiled by Virginia L. Close (Stanford, California: The Russian Review, 1972), the Editor of *The Russian Review*, Dimitri Sergeevich von Mohrenschildt, traced briefly the thirty-year history of his journal. It was started in November 1941 by a group of Russians and Americans in New York as a nonpartisan free forum of scholars and writers "of a wide variety of political views, excluding, however, those identified with the totalitarian ideologies—communism and fascism," and with a purpose designed "to interpret impartially Russia's past and present and to promote a better understanding of Russia by Americans." From 1941 to 1948 the journal was published semi-annually; since 1949, it has been a quarterly. At the beginning it was published in New York, from 1942 to 1967 at Dartmouth, in Hanover, N. H., and, in the autumn of 1967, it was moved to Stanford, California, where, since 1968, it has been sponsored by the Hoover Institution on War, Revolution and Peace. It maintained, however, as in the past, its editorial and administrative independence. The purpose of *The Russian Review* was formulated in these words: "to interpret the real aims and aspirations of the Russian people, as distinguished from and contrasted with Soviet Communism, and to advance general knowledge of Russian culture, history, and civilization." In the thirty-year period covered by the *Cumulative Index*, "more than 1000 articles by distinguished scholars, writers and leaders of prerevolutionary Russia" and some 3000 book reviews by specialists in the Russian cultural, historical, political and economic scene have been published by *The Russian Review*. The *Index* has a special section, "Literary History and Criticism," with subdivisions "Pre-1917," "Emigré" and "Translations" (pp. 60-65; plus "Poetry Translations," pp. 74-76), and very numerous alphabetical entries on individual literary persons, prerevolutionary, emigré, and Soviet.

Beginning with the thirty-third volume in 1974 *The Russian Review* has been taken over by Terence Emmons. In his "Editorial Note," he promised to "continue to pursue the aim of 'advancing general knowledge of Russian culture, history, and civilization' " and to "seek, as before, to publish material of high quality in the fields of Russian history, politics, literature and the arts."[51]

Our understanding of the Russian literary scene in the United States would be incomplete without at least a brief reference to the publishing situation.

Ivan K. Okuntsov mentions the first Russian publishing house in America (which was located at 31 East 7th Street in New York City), owned by L. Pasvol'skii, Vilchur and N. Sergievskii and soon closed down because of insufficient demand for their books; the New York City publishing house "Orion" owned by S. I. Gusev-Orenburgskii, who, together with V. Levin, published his books and several issues of a periodical *Vremennik*; and G. D. Grebenshchikov's publishing house "Alatas" in Churaevka, Connecticut, which published mostly his books and books by Rerikh and A. Remizov. There were a few other publishing houses of a homespun nature, and some of the Russian newspapers (*Russkoe slovo*, *Novoe russkoe slovo*, *Russkii golos*, *Rassvet*, *Svet*, *Pravda*, etc.) also occasionally engaged in publishing ventures.[52] We could add that the later-day periodicals (*Novosel'e*, *Opyty*, *Novyi zhurnal*, etc.) published a few books too. On the whole, however, Russian-language book publishing in this country continued to be rather rudimentary until the appearance, in the fifties and sixties, of three major publishing houses: Chekhov Publishing House, Victor Kamkin, Inc., and Inter-Language Literary Associates.

The Chekhov Publishing House (Izdatel'stvo imeni Chekhova) was established by the East European Fund with the help of a grant from the Ford Foundation and published its first book in the Spring of 1952. In his brief survey of the activities of the Chekhov Publishing House, the late editor of *Novyi zhurnal* M. M. Karpovich formulated its purpose thus: "The idea was to assist Russian émigrés, more particularly the postwar Soviet émigrés, in satisfying their spiritual needs and in finding their bearings in the western world. A closely allied purpose was to provide a medium of experience for creative writers from among the émigrés, old and new alike."[53] Though the Chekhov Publishing House discontinued its activity in April, 1956, in the four years of its existence it published over one hundred and fifty titles. According to my count, this includes eleven titles of poetry,[54] forty-three of fiction,[55] two of drama,[56] and thirty-eight of literary criticism, scholarship, and literary, or at least literature-related, memoirs and autobiographies,[57] i.e., a total of eighty-four titles—more than half of all books published by the Chekhov Publishing House. One tends to agree with Karpovich, that, though "not all of its publications have been of an equally high level of importance and literary distinction, on the whole it has been an impressive achievement. To a large degree, the Chekhov Publishing House effectively served those purposes for which it was founded."[58]

Another important publishing program supported by American funds has been led by Gleb Petrovich Struve and Boris Andreevich Filippov, with the active participation of Evgeniia Vladimirovna Zhiglevich-Filippova. Their main operation was called Inter-Language Literary Associates (Mezhdunarodnoe literaturnoe sodruzhestvo), with two auxiliaries, "Russkaia kniga" (Russian Book) and "Okno" (Window). Altogether they published over seventy titles, the majority of which were mentioned in connection with the activities of B. Filippov, G. Struve, and E. Zhiglevich, whose introductory articles, commentaries, elaborations on textual readings and versions, and bibliographies are to be found in most of the books of the Inter-Language Literary Associates.[59]

The third most important publishing house has been Victor Kamkin, Inc. (or Russkoe knizhnoe delo v S.Sh.A.), located first in Washington, D.C., and then moved, together with the huge Victor Kamkin Bookstore, to Rockville, Maryland. Viktor Petrovich Kamkin was born in St. Petersburg in 1902, and, before coming to the United States in 1949, lived in China, where he sold, published, and printed books. In 1953 he started his bookstore in Washington, D.C. After his recent death, his widow, Elena Andreevna Kamkina, took over. According to my count, in the last quarter of a century Kamkins published or republished twenty titles of poetry,[60] twenty-three of prose,[61] and eighteen of literary criticism, literary scholarship and literary or literature-related memoirs[62]—a total of sixty titles of importance to our topic. For a strictly emigré undertaking, this is, indeed, a remarkable achievement.

There are also a few other publishers.[63] And many books were published by the authors themselves. On the whole, during the last twenty-five years, quite a number of books in all three categories—poetry, fiction, and literary scholarship (and adjoining areas)—were produced in this country, most in New York City and Washington, D.C.

* * *

It seems to me that on the basis of what has been said it is already possible to draw, at least tentatively, the following conclusions (as well as to confirm the statements made beforehand, at the beginning).

(1) Of the three categories of Russian emigrés—"old," "new," and "newest"—the contribution to Russian poetry, fiction, and literary scholarship in the United States by the "old" emigration, on the whole, outweighs that of the "new," though the latter has contributed heavily, especially in poetry. The "newest" emigration is, naturally, only beginning its creative life.[64]

(2) With regard to the five "waves" of immigrants which we characterized in the introduction, the most productive were the "old" emigrés of the third "wave" and the "old" and "new" émigrés of the fourth.[65] Thus, when we speak of Russian literature in the United States, we refer mostly to that which has been created in the last thirty-five years.

(3) Poetry seems to be the area of the greatest development. While fiction is important too, drama is almost non-existent. Literary criticism is to be found mostly in newspapers and periodicals, whereas literary scholarship has resulted also in significant numbers of books. There is at least one important newspaper, *Novoe russkoe slovo*, and an extremely important periodical, *Novyi zhurnal*, which should not be overlooked by any serious student of Russian literary life. Publishing activities have brought the

492

greatest results when they were supported by American funds, as in the case of Chekhov Publishing House and Inter-Language Literary Associates; however, one cannot but wonder at the extent of the emigré non-sponsored productivity.

(4) Russian literature in the United States is—by language, content, and intent—essentially an important branch of Russian emigré literature in general. Poets write in Russian, and only in the last few years have the poems of some of them become available in English translation. The same is true of fiction; though several novels and stories were published in English translation, there is only one author, Vladimir Nabokov, who has become an "organic" part of the American literary scene. And while literary criticism continues to be in Russian, literary scholarship became, to a great degree "Americanized"—due, no doubt, to the fact that its representatives are usually professors at American institutions of higher learning.

(5) Being part of the Russian emigré literature, Russian literature in the United States has to be related to Russian prerevolutionary and Soviet literature in general and evaluated in terms of some "optimal" Russian literary criteria. Using such criteria, one could argue that Russian literature in the United States has already made a definite contribution to Russian literature in general.

(6) As for its future, it is, of course, a matter of speculation. The present Russian literature in the United States was born out of political events—the Russian Revolution and the victory of Bolshevism-Communism in Russia (and, later, the rise and fall of the Third Reich). Due to other political events, it could as easily contract as it has expanded. But for a number of Russian language authors, America is bound to remain their final home. And if the Communist rule in Russia does not come to an end in the near future—and the influx of new literary blood from the Soviet Union continues—there is sufficient reason to believe that Russian literature in the United States will continue to assert itself.[66]

University of Pittsburgh

NOTES

[1] In a letter to me Professor Struve singled out three such essays: "The Double Life of Russian Literature," *Books Abroad* (Autumn 1954), pp. 389-406; "Russian Writers in Exile: Problems of an Emigré Literature," in *Comparative Literature*, Proceedings of the Second Congress of the International Comparative Literature Association at the University of North Carolina, 8-12 September 1958 (Chapel Hill: The Univ. of North Carolina Press, 1959), pp. 592-606; and "Russian Literature," in *World Literature Since 1945; Critical Surveys of the Contemporary Literature of Europe and the Americas*, ed. Ivar Ivask and Gero von Wilpert (New York: Frederick Ungar, 1973), pp. 547-92. This last essay appeared first in the German edition of this

book, and the English text represents an expanded version of the German text. Of the three essays, the one that was published in 1973 is of more immediate importance for the topic of this paper.

[2] Fabii Zverev, "Poety 'novoi' emigratsii," pp. 71-82, English résumé pp. 368-69; L. Rzhevskii, "Khudozhestvennaia proza 'novoi' emigratsii," pp. 83-91, résumé pp. 369-70; Roman Gul', *Novyi zhurnal*, pp. 321-31, résumé pp. 384-85; Nikolai Andreev, "Ob osobennostiakh i osnovnykh etapakh razvitiia russkoi literatury za rubezhom (Opyt postanovki temy)," pp. 15-38, résumé pp. 365-66; Liudmila Foster, "Statisticheskii obzor russkoi zarubezhnoi literatury," pp. 39-44, résumé p. 366; Iurii Ivask, "Poeziia 'staroi' emigratsii," pp. 45-69, résumé pp. 367-68; C. Nicholas Lee, "Mark Aleksandrovich Aldanov: zhizn' i tvorchestvo," pp. 95-104, résumé pp. 370-71; R. Pletnev, "Russkoe literaturovedenie v emigratsii," pp. 255-70, résumé pp. 380-81. Hereafter referred to as *Russkaia literatura v emigratsii.*

[3] For a few authors this last question turned out to be a little confusing, and they answered that it is not up to them but to others to speak of their distinguishing traits. This would have been so if a self-evaluation were required involving their judgment about whether they are gifted or lacking talent, deep or superfluous, original or imitating, etc. Fortunately, most respondents accepted this question the way it was meant—as referring to external or formal characteristics. The latter are sometimes clearer to the author himself than to an "outsider." Quotations from the questionnaire are indicated parenthetically within the text, and are hereafter cited as Questionnaire.

[4] Reviewing *Vremia razluk*, Valerii Pereleshin suggested that Lidiia Alekseeva was a Neo-Classicist by temperament and by poetical training, who uses traditional meter, likes rich rhyme, and wild experimental consonances and dissonances (*Novyi zhurnal*, No. 109 [December 1972], p. 298).

[5] In his review of *Utverzhdenie* Boris Nartsissov notes the thematical and artistic growth of Nonna Belavina from 1961 through 1966 to 1974, her independence (which he thinks is rather unusual with poetesses) from the influence of Anna Akhmatova and Marina Tsvetaeva, the simplicity of her style, her approximate but sonorous rhymes, and her fresh imagery ("Poeziia Nonny Belavinoi," *Novoe russkoe slovo*, 29 October 1974).

[6] See, for example, Iurii Ivask's reviews of *Stikhotvoreniia i poemy* (*Novyi zhurnal*, No. 79 [June 1965], pp. 297-99) and of *Ostanovka v pustyne* (*Novyi zhurnal*, No. 102 [March 1971], pp. 294-97). It appears that Iosif Brodskii found a very congenial response among those associated with Ardis Publishers and the *Russian Literature Triquarterly* (hereafter cited as *RLT*), which published many of his poems in Russian and in English translation. Reviewing for the *RLT* Brodskii's *Selected Poems*, Emery George started with these enthusiastic words: "The publication of Joseph Brodsky's *Selected Poems*, in the sometimes superb translations by George Kline, last year by Harper & Row, this year, on both sides of the Atlantic, by Penguin Books, is undoubtedly *the* publishing event in Russian poetry for the West for these twin seasons" (*RLT*, No. 10 [Fall 1974], p. 422). Emery George contemplates "reminiscent work by Rilke, Apollinaire, Hollander, while seeing the strong newcomer added to their ranks. In all, Brodsky must certainly be judged, already now, to belong with the strongest in the mainstream of European verse, alongside Donne and Yeats, Holderlin and Mandelstam" (ibid., p. 423). The evaluation of Brodskii's poetry by Russian critics, though positive, never went as far as that. *RLT* also printed "A Bibliography of the Published Works of Iosif Aleksandrovich Brodskii," compiled by George L. Kline (*RLT*, No. 1 [Fall 1971], pp. 441-55).

[7] Fabii Zverev, who has a very high opinion of Ivan Burkin's poetry, sees it as light, volatile, and merry, even when the poet is sad or thoughtful (*Russkaia literatura v emigratsii*, p. 76).

[8] Reviewing *Metafory*, Victor Terras wrote that Igor Chinnov's world resembles that of Turgenev: "It is that of a 'westernized' Russian of refined culture, an aesthete who is apologetic, not boastful about it, a humanist in spite of a deep-rooted pessimism, a sceptic who has a deep respect and affection for religion and who himself *almost* believes, a realist and keen observer of life who wishes he could be a mystic and for moments becomes one, a fine intellect capable of philosophic abstraction who prefers, nevertheless, to capture, with precision and finesse, the concrete images of ordinary life" (*Slavic and East European Journal*, 15, No. 1 [Spring 1971], 81).

[9] From L. Rzhevskii's introductory article to *Pod sozvezdiem topora* (pp. 7, 18, and 6 of the manuscript).

[10] Fabii Zverev says of Gleb Glinka that, being "a master of ironical and ironical-dramatical poetry, he never tires of admiring the tragic but always so entertaining world" (*Russkaia literatura v emigratsii*, p. 73).

[11] In Oleg Il'inskii's poetry Fabii Zverev sees "sturdy, sometimes even fleshly imagery," "masterful archaisms–reminiscences," "poeticized prosiness," and an attempt to rediscover anew and rename the world around him (ibid., p. 80).

[12] In Iurii Ivask's poetry Igor Chinnov singles out "a refined sound-fabric, original rhyming," often unusual rhythmical design, "plenty of emotion, though concealed by jesting"; the first impression is that of painted toys, "but the toyful in them is only a pseudonym of the important" ("Smotrite–stikhi," *Novyi zhurnal*, No. 92 [September 1968], pp. 140 and 141).

[13] L. Rzhevskii, "Strofy i 'zvony' v sovremennoi russkoi poezii," *Novyi zhurnal*, No. 115 (June 1974), p. 137.

[14] Reviewing *Pod'em*, Victor Terras wrote that Boris Nartsissov "is a virtuoso of the driving rhythms of the Russian binary meters—further proof that a Russian poet can be modern, cosmopolitan, and Western while remaining within the formal boundaries of nineteenth-century poetry" (*Slavic and East European Journal*, 15, No. 1 [Spring 1971], 81).

[15] In this survey only collections of poems by individual authors were mentioned. For lack of space, no reference to authors' publication in periodicals and newspapers was made. As for major anthologies, only two of them, published in New York City prior to 1950, were casually mentioned—*Iz Ameriki* (1925) and *Chetyrnadtsat'* (1949). Therefore, it seems proper to list here those Russian poets who live or have lived in the United States and who were included in four major anthologies published since 1950. 1) In *Na Zapade*, comp. Iu. P. Ivask (New York: Chekhov Publishing House, 1953)–L. Alekseeva, Amari, O. Anstei, N. Berberova, A. Brailovskii, I. Elagin, O. Il'inskii, A. Kasim, Kh. Krotkova, G. Kuznetsova, I. Legkaia, V. Markov, N. Morshen, V. Nabokov, T. Ostroumova, V. Pastukhov, S. Pregel', E. Rubisova, L. Strakhovskii, G. Struve, T. Timasheva, M. Tolstaia, M. Chekhonin, I. Chinnov, G. Shirokov, A. Shishkova, V. Iurasov, and I. Iassen. 2) In *Muza Diaspory*, ed. Iu. K. Terapiano (Frankfurt am Main: Posev, 1960)–L. Alekseeva, O. Anstei, N. Berberova, I. Burkin, I. Elagin, Iu. Ivask, O. Il'inskii, V. Korvin-Piotrovskii, G. Kuznetsova, V. Markov, N. Morshen, V. Nabokov-Sirin, B. Nartsissov, S. Pregel', E. Rubisova, L. Strakhovskii, G. Struve, B. Filippov, I. Chinnov, A. Shishkova, and I. Iassen. 3) In *Sodruzhestvo*, comp. T. P. Fesenko (Washington: Victor Kamkin, Inc., 1966)–L. Alekseeva, N. All, O. Anstei, E. Antonova, N. Belavina, N. Berberova, I. Burkin, M. Vizi, N. Vorob'ev, Iu. Gertsog, G. Glinka, A. Darov, V. Dukel'skii, I. Elagin, Iu. Ivask, O. Il'inskii, V. Il'iashenko, M. Kardinalovskaia, G. Kuznetsova, G. Lakhman, I. Leg-

kaia, D. Magula, V. Markov, E. Matveeva, N. Morshen, B. Nartsissov, T. Ostroumova, G. Panin, S. Pregel', E. Raich, A. Rostovskii, E. Rubisova, K. Slavina, Strannik, G. Struve, Z. Trotskaia, B. Filippov, I. Chinnov, A. Shishkova, V. Ellis, and V. Iankovskaia. These three anthologies are, of course, in Russian (and the poets are listed here in the order in which they are in the anthologies, i.e., according to the Russian alphabet). But recently there appeared a fourth anthology, in English–*America's Russian Poets*, ed. and trans. R. H. Morrison (Ann Arbor: Ardis, Inc., 1975), which is especially important for those readers who do not know Russian. The poems are preceded by a general introduction by the editor (pp. 9-14) and followed by biographical notes on the authors (pp. 71-75). Fifteen contemporary Russian poets are represented by ninety-one poems. There are poems by Lidiia Alekseeva (seven poems), Ol'ga Anstei (two), Nonna Belavina (two), Ivan Burkin (one), Igor Chinnov (sixteen), Ivan Elagin (thirteen), Boris Filippov (two), Oleg Il'inskii (four), Iurii Ivask (twelve), Iraida Legkaia (seven), Elena Matveeva (four), Nikolai Morshen (eight), Boris Nartsissov (nine), Aleksandr Rostovskii (two), and Richard Ianin (two). R. H. Morrison indicated that the fact that some of the poets "are given more space than others is in no way a reflection on any of the poets. On the contrary, it reflects only one translator's inability to do fitting justice to the poets' at times complex and compact style" ("Introduction," p. 13).

[16] *Na Zapade*, pp. 6-7.

[17] *Russkaia literatura v emigratsii*, pp. 46 and 68. Writing a decade earlier, when some of these developments were only beginning to take more definite shape, Iu. K. Terapiano also noticed (*Muza Diaspory*, pp. 5-25) that the "Parisian note," which was dominant in Russian emigré poetry between the two world wars, came to an end after the World War II. By the early 1950's, the new generations of both "old" and "new" emigré poets, who perceived the Parisian note as decadent and fixed on the theme of death and on personal emotional experiences, began to form a new stylistic and ideological synthesis. Terapiano had no name for this new synthesis. It is possible that Iurii Ivask has now found the proper term in the "American note."

[18] *Drugaia zhizn' i bereg dal'nii*, pp. 3-6.

[19] See, for example, L. Rzhevskii's review of Roman Gul's *Bakunin* in *Novyi zhurnal*, No. 119 (June 1975), pp. 289-90.

[20] See the reviews of *Parallax* in *Novoe russkoe slovo* by N. Otradin (24 December 1972), L. Rzhevskii (4 February 1973), and Tat'iana Fesenko (4 March 1973).

[21] Iu. K. Terapiano, "*Grani*: Chast' literaturnaia," *Russkaia mysl'*, Paris, 29 June 1963. See also Olga Hughes, "Alla Ktorova: A New Face," *RLT*, No. 28 (1973), pp. 507-21.

[22] *Russkaia literatura v emigratsii*, p. 84.

[23] Nina Berberova, *The Italics Are Mine* (New York: Harcourt, Brace & World, Inc., 1969), p. 566. The editors of *RLT* and Ardis Publishers have a similar view of Nabokov's work. The literature on Nabokov is already voluminous–and constantly growing. One of the lastest additions is *A Book of Things About Vladimir Nabokov* (Ann Arbor: Ardis, 1974), which includes Liudmila A. Foster's "Nabokov in Russian Emigré Criticism" (pp. 42-53) and P. M. Bitsilli's "V. Nabokov's *Invitation to Beheading* and *The Eye*," a review article translated from *Contemporary Annals*, No. 68 (Paris, 1936), by D. Barton Johnson (pp. 65-69). For the attitude of Russian emigré critics toward Nabokov see also Gleb Struve's *Russkaia literatura v izgnanii*, pp. 278-90 and 363-64. A very helpful work is Andrew Field's *Nabokov: A Bibliography* (New York: McGraw-Hill, 1973).

[24] *Russkaia literatura v emigratsii*, p. 89.

[25] In his *Russkaia literatura v izgnanii* Gleb Struve analyzes V. S. Ianovskii's work up to early 1950's (pp. 294-97).

[26] For a biographical and intellectual profile of Professor Arsen'ev, see R. Pletnev's essay "N. S. Arsen'ev" in *Russkaia religiozno-filosofskaia mysl' XX veka*, ed. N. P. Poltoratskii (Pittsburgh, Pa.: Department of Slavic Languages and Literatures, University of Pittsburgh, 1975), pp. 176-85.

[27] Nina Berberova's activities as a poet and fiction-writer belong essentially to her European past and, for this reason, were not considered in the previous sections of this survey. On her work, see Gleb Struve, *Russkaia literatura v izgnanii*, pp. 290-92.

[28] See the three-volume collection of essays on the occasion of his seventieth birthday, *To Honor Roman Jakobson* (The Hague: Mouton, 1967), and *Roman Jakobson: A Bibliography of His Writings* (The Hague: Mouton, 1971).

[29] See "A Bibliography of the Writings of Vsevolod Michajlovic Setchkarev," comp. Stanley J. Rabinowitz, in *Mnemozina: Studia literaria russica in honorem Vsevolod Setchkarev*, ed. Joachim T. Baer and Norman W. Ingham (München: Wilhelm Fink Verlag, 1974), pp. ix-xiv.

[30] On the occasion of A. L. Tolstaia's ninetieth birthday, *Novyi zhurnal* published a salutation by its editor Roman Gul', "K devianostoletiiu A. L. Tolstoi," and an article by the editor of *Novoe russkoe slovo* Andrei Sedykh, " 'Milaia doch' i drug': 90-letie Aleksandry L'vovny Tolstoi" (No. 115, June 1974, pp. 5 and 6-18 respectively).

[31] See also V. Sechkarev, "N. I. Ul'ianov—esseist i uchenyi: K semidesiatiletiiu," *Novyi zhurnal*, No. 119 (June 1975), pp. 261-66.

[32] See also M. Vishniak's article "Sovremennye zapiski" in *Russkaia literatura v emigratsii*, pp. 353-60 (English résumé, p. 387).

[33] See her son's book, Arkadii Borman, *A. V. Tyrkova-Vil'iams po ee pis'mam i vospominaniiam syna* (Louvain–Washington, D.C., 1964).

[34] Ivan K. Okuntsov, *Russkaia emigratsiia v Severnoi i Iuzhnoi Amerike* (Buenos Aires: Seiatel', 1967), p. 311.

[35] Ibid., p. 312.

[36] Ibid., p. 319.

[37] Ibid., p. 344. Okuntsov gives as his source *Detroitskii zhuravel'*; however, he does not give full reference.

[38] Okuntsov says (p. 329) that the newspaper was founded by Ivan K. Okuntsov initially under the name *Russkoe slovo*; in 1915 it became a daily; during World War I it was taken over by L. Pasvol'skii and in 1921 by V. I. Shimkin, who gave it its present name, *Novoe russkoe slovo*. Later (p. 388) Okuntsov states that in 1921 the newspaper was published by Shimkin and Veinbaum, and edited by Durmashkin, Okuntsov and Fovitskii.

[39] The list of contributors published by the newspaper in 1975, contains some 400 names, including such authors living in Europe as A. I. Solzhenitsyn, V. E. Maksimov, A. A. Galich, A. D. Siniavskii, Z. A. Shakhovskaia (writer and editor of the Russian weekly newspaper *Russkaia mysl'*, published in Paris), etc.

[40] In her *Bibliografiia russkoi zarubezhnoi literatury 1918-1968* (Boston: S. K. Hall & Co., 1970), Vol. I, List No. 2: Journals, Collections, and Anthologies, pp. 19-88. Liudmila Foster lists a few such periodicals, among them *Bich*, ed. V. N. Il'in (New York, 1936-38), *Delo*, ed. M. Ivanitskii (San Francisco, 1951), *Zaatlanticheskii kumach* (organ of the Circle of [Russian] Proletarian Writers and Artists in North America [New York, 1925]), *Zhizn'*, ed. S. Gusev-Orenburgskii (New York, 1924-1925), etc. All of them, as the dates indicate, did not exist long. A publication

of a different nature lasted much longer: *Den' russkogo rebenka*, a yearly collection of articles and fiction (San Francisco, 1934-1953).

⁴¹ As, for example, the first collection of stories, sketches and drawings, *Dosug*, ed. N. Sergievskii (New York: The First Russian Publishing House in America, 1918); a collection of poetry and prose, *V teni neboskrebov* (New York: Kruzhok proletarskikh pisatelei i poetov v Severnoi Amerike, 1922); *V plenu neboskrebov* (New York: Kruzhov proletarskikh pisatelei v Severnoi Amerike, 1924); a collection of Russian emigré literature, *Kovcheg* (New York: Ob'edinenie russkikh pisatelei, 1942), etc. Alongside New York City, another center of literary activities was San Francisco, where the Russian Literary-Artistic Circle published at least three almanacs: *Dymnyi sled* (1925), *Kaliforniiskii sbornik* (1934), and *U Zolotykh vorot* (1957).

⁴² A fifth, *Sotsialisticheskii vestnik*, the central organ of the Russian Social-Democratic Workers' Party, founded by L. Martov in 1920, and published first in Berlin and since 1941 until its recent demise in New York, though a partisan magazine, deserves to be mentioned also, because of the numerous articles on Soviet literary developments by Vera Aleksandrova.

⁴³ S. Iu. Pregel' (1897-1972) is author of six collections of poetry, all published in Paris: *Razgovor s pamiat'iu* (1935), *Solnechnyi proizvol* (1937), *Polden'* (1939), *Berega* (1953), *Vstrecha* (1958), and *Vesna v Parizhe* (1966).

⁴⁴ See P. L. Vainshenker's entry on S. Iu. Pregel' in *Kratkaia Literaturnaia Entsiklopediia*, Vol. V (Moscow: Sovietskaia Entsiklopediia, 1968), column 956.

⁴⁵ M. O. Tsetlin is author of *Rasskazy* (Berlin, 1924), *Dekabristy: Sud'ba odnogo pokoleniia* (Paris: Sovremennye zapiski, 1933; New York: Opyty, 1954), and a book on the Mighty Five in Russian music, *Piatero i drugie* (New York: Novyi zhurnal, 1944). M. A. Aldanow (pen name of Landau), a noted historical novelist and essayist, is author of too many books in Russian and in English, French and other translations to be listed here. See C. Nicholas Lee's "Mark Aleksandrovich Aldanov: Zhizn' i tvorchestvo," in *Russkaia literatura v emigratsii* (pp. 255-70, English résumé pp. 380-81) as well as C. N. Lee's *The Novels of M. A. Aldanov* (The Hague: Mouton, 1969).

⁴⁶ On M. M. Karpovich see Serge A. Zenkovsky, "A Russian Historian at Harvard," *The Russian Review*, 17, No. 3 (October 1958), 292-300, and "Michael Karpovich 1888-1959," by Philip E. Mosely, Martin E. Malia, William Henry Chamberlin, and Dimitri von Mohrenschildt, *The Russian Review*, 19, No. 1 (January 1960), 56-60, 60-71, 71-74, 74-76 respectively.

⁴⁷ R. B. Gul' has been associated with *Novyi zhurnal* for almost a quarter of a century; in 1952 he became the secretary of the review, on the invitation of the editor M. M. Karpovich and the publisher M. S. Tsetlina. R. B. Gul's present companions are also experienced editors. G. A. Andreev, in particular, was the editor of an important almanac, *Mosty* (Nos. 1-15, 1958-1970). As editor, L. Rzhevskii is especially exacting in everything that concerns "stylistic correctness and expressiveness," and G. Andreev considers it very important that what is published be both "interesting to the reader and representing sufficient public value" (Questionnaire).

⁴⁸ Roman Gul', "Dvadtsat' piat' let Novogo Zhurnala" (*Novyi zhurnal*, No. 87 [June 1967], pp. 6-28) and "Sotaia kniga" (*Novyi zhurnal*, No. 100 [September 1970], pp. 5-6). These two articles were included in Roman Gul's *Odvukon'* (New York: Most, 1973) and, before that, in contracted form, in *Russkaia literatura v emigratsii* (pp. 321-31, English résumé 384-85).

⁴⁹ Professor K. G. Belousov, born in Russia in 1896, was, before arriving in the United States in 1947, Dean of the International University in Munich. In 1947-1948

he was one of the organizers of the New York-based Association of Russian-American Scholars in U.S.A., Inc., and since then he has been its permanent Vice President. Its first President was Professor E. V. Spektorskii (1871-1951), former Rector of Kiev University; its second President was Professor M. M. Novikov (1876-1966), former Rector of the Moscow University; its third President was Professor A. A. Bogolepov, former Prorector of Petrograd University. Since 1970 the Association has been headed by Professor N. S. Arsen'ev. Though during the twenty-eight years of its existence the Association has lost some seventy members, products mostly of pre-revolutionary Russian universities and in many instances scholars with international reputations, it had in 1975 some 180 members, representing various academic disciplines. Besides publishing its *Transactions*, the Association has organized, over the years, a dozen symposia (some of them in conjunction with Hunter College and Fordham University), including symposia on Old Russian literature (1966), religious problems in Russian literature (1967), F. M. Dostoevskii (1971), Aleksandr Solzhenitsyn (1971), Russian Acmeism (1972), *Gulag Archipelago* (1974), A. S. Pushkin (1974), and A. K. Tolstoi (1975).

[50] The last available issue (vol. 20, No. 104, Fall 1975) lists N. P. Avtonomov as Founder and Editor Emeritus, V. I. Grebenshchikov as General Editor, and Munir Sendich as the Editor of *Russian Language Journal* (hereafter cited as *RLJ*). The issue has three main sections: "Methods," "Language and Literature," and "Book Reviews" (plus a very useful "Directory of Russian and Slavic Programs and Faculty in the United States and Canadian Colleges: 1975-1976," compiled by M.S. and T.J.). In the Spring of 1975 a supplementary issue, *Toward a Definition of Acmeism*, edited by another Michigan State University Professor, Denis Mickiewicz, was published by the *RLJ*.

[51] *The Russian Review*, 33, No. 1 (January 1974), iii. One notes, however, that while the subtitle of the review ("An American Quarterly Devoted to Russia Past and Present") has been preserved, the definition of the review's purpose ("to interpret the real aims and aspirations of the Russian people, as distinguished from and contrasted with Soviet Communism") has disappeared from the review's mast-head.

[52] Okuntsov, *Russkaia emigratsiia v Severnoi i Iuzhoi Amerike*, pp. 346-47. An old publishing house still in existence in New York City is that of Nikolai Nikolaevich Mart'ianov, which published a collection of Russian poetry and prose *Chtets-deklamatov* (n.d.).

[53] Michael Karpovich, "The Chekhov Publishing House," *The Russian Review*, 16, No. 1 (January 1957), 53.

[54] Anna Akhmatova, *Izbrannye stikhotvoreniia*; *Neizdannyi Gumilev*, ed. Gleb Struve; Ivan Elagin, *Po doroge ottuda*; S. Iurasov, *Vasilii Terkin posle voiny*; Aleksei Khomiakov, *Izbrannye sochineniia*, ed. N. Arsen'ev; Nikolai Kliuev, *Polnoe sobranie sochinenii* in two volumes, ed. Boris Filippov; Osip Mandel'shtam, *Sobranie sochinenii*, ed. Gleb Struve and Boris Filippov; F. I. Tiutchev, *Izbrannye stikhotvoreniia*; and three anthologies: *Russkaia lirika ot Zhukovskogo do Bunina*, ed. A. A. Bogolepov, *Na Zapade*, an anthology of Russian emigré poetry, ed. Iurii Ivask, and *Priglushennye golosa*, an anthology of poetry behind the iron curtain, ed. V. Markov.

[55] M. A. Aldanov, *Zhivi kak khochesh'*, in two volumes, and *Kliuch*; V. I. Alekseev, *Nevidimaia Rossiia* and *Rossiia Soldatskaia*; Mikhail Bulgakov, *Sbornik rasskazov*; I. A. Bunin, *Vesnoi v Iudee i drugie rasskazy*, *Zhizn' Arsen'eva* (first complete edition), *Mitina liubov' i drugie rasskazy*, and *Petlistye ushi i drugie rasskazy*; Evgenii Chirikov, *Iunost'*; A. Damanskaia, *Miranda*; G. P. Danilevskii, *Sozhzhennaia Moskva*; Aleksandr Ertel', *Smena*; Nina Fedorova, *Sem'ia*; E. Gagarin, *Vozvrashchenie korneta. Poezdka na Sviatki*; Gaito Gazdanov, *Nochnye dorogi*; N. V. Gogol', *Povesti*

(with a foreword by V. Nabokov); S. Gusev-Orenburgskii, *Glukhoi prikhod i drugie rasskazy*; V. S. Ianovskii, *Portativnoe bessmertie*; I. Il'f and E. Petrov, *Dvenadtsat' stul'ev* and *Zolotoi telenok*; S. Iurasov, *Vrag naroda*; K. Leont'ev, *Egipetskii Golub'*. *Ditia dushi*; N. Leskov, *Soboriane*; Sergei Maksimov, *Bunt Denisa Bushueva*, *Goluboe molchanie* and *Taiga*; D. S. Merezhkovskii, *Aleksandr I i dekabristy*; D. L. Mordovtsev, *Zhelezom i krov'iu*; Vladimir Nabokov, *Vesna v Fial'te i drugie rasskazy* and *Dar*; N. Narokov, *Mnimye velichiny*; Prince V. Odoevskii, *Deviat' povestei*; Irina Odoevtseva, *Ostav' nadezhdu navsegda*; B. Panteleimonov, *Posledniaia kniga*; A. Remizov, *V rozovom bleske*; Panteleimon Romanov, *Tovarishch Kisliakov*; L. Rzhevskii, *Mezhdu dvukh zvezd*; N. A. Teffi, *Zemnaia raduga*; Anri Truaiia, *V gorakh*; N. I. Ul'ianov, *Atossa*; and two anthologies, *Opal'nye povesti* and *Pestrye rasskazy*, ed. V. A. Aleksandrova.

⁵⁶ S. Malakhov, *Begletsy. Otets* and *Letchiki*.

⁵⁷ Georgii Adamovich, *Odinochestvo i svoboda*; D. Aminado, *Poezd na tret'em puti*; I. A. Bunin, *O Chekhove*; N. N. Evreinov, *Istoriia russkogo teatra (s drevneishikh vremen do 1917 g.)*; Iu. Elagin, *Temnyi genii* and *Ukroshchenie iskusstv*; G. P. Fedotov, *Novyi grad*; S. L. Frank, *Biografiia P. B. Struve*; Gleb Glinka, *Na perevale*; N. A. Gorchakov, *Istoriia sovetskogo teatra*; Roman Gul', *Kon' ryzhii*; Georgii Ivanov, *Peterburgskie zimy*; R. V. Ivanov-Razumnik, *Tiur'my i ssylki*; Vladislav Khodasevich, *Literaturnye stat'i*; Mikhail Koriakov, *Osvobozhdenie dushi*; N. O. Losskii, *Dostoevskii i ego khristianskoe miroponimanie*; Sergei Makovskii, *Portrety sovremennikov*; Iu. B. Margolin, *Puteshestvie v stranu ze-ka*; Vladimir Nabokov, *Drugie berega*; M. Osorgin, *Pis'ma o neznachitel'nom* (with a foreword by M. Aldanov); V. Rozanov, *Izbrannoe*, ed. Iurii Ivask; Iuliia Sazonova, *Istoriia drevnerusskoi literatury*, in two books; Boris Shiriaev, *Neugasimaia lampada*; Prince S. Shchertabov, *Khudozhnik v ushedshei Rossii*; Mark Slomin, *Tri liubvi Dostoevskogo*; Fedor Stepun, *Byvshee i nesbyvsheesia*, in two volumes; Gleb Struve, *Russkaia literatura v izgnanii*; Iu. Terapiano, *Vstrechi*; Aleksandra Tolstaia, *Otets (Zhizn L'va Tolstogo)*, in two volumes; Marina Tsvetaeva, *Proza*; A. Tyrkova-Vil'iams, *Na putiakh k svobode; V.* Varshavskii, *Nezamechennoe pokolenie*; V. Veidle, *Vechernii den'* and *Zadacha Rossii*; B. P. Vysheslavtsev, *Vechnoe v russkoi filosofii*; Boris Zaitsev, *Chekhov*; E. Zamiatin, *Litsa*; and V. P. Ziloti, *V dome Tret'iakova*.

⁵⁸ "The Chekhov Publishing House," pp. 57 and 58. This Chekhov Publishing House, which discontinued its activities in 1956, should not be confused with another Chekhov Publishing House (Izdatel'stvo imeni Chekhova) started fourteen years later with the millionaire Edward Klein as its President and the British Professor Max Hayword as its editor-in-chief. When the new Chekhov Publishing House published Iosif Brodskii's *Ostanovka v pustyne*, there followed a number of polemical exchanges in connection with this "usurpation." (See especially G. Andreev, "Pod maskoi emigratsii," *Novoe russkoe slovo*, 14 July 1970, as well as M. Koriakov, "Listki iz bloknota," ibid., 26 June 1970, and Edward Klein's letter to the editor, "Ob izdatel'stve imeni Chekhova," ibid., 11 July 1970.)

⁵⁹ The name of the publishing house "Russkaia kniga" is to be found on the following books: Georgii Adamovich, *Edinstvo* (poems, 1967); Dm. Klenovskii, *Stikhi: Izbrannoe* (1967), Boris Nartsissov, *Pamiat'* (poems, 1965); Irina Odoevtseva, *Odinochestvo* (poems, 1965); Vladimir Samarin, *Peschanaia otmel'* (1964) and *Teni na stene* (1967).

⁶⁰ Ivan Elagin, *Drakon na kryshe*; N. Gumilev, *Sobranie sochinenii* in four vols., ed. G. P. Struve and B. A. Filippov; Iu. Ivask, *Khvala*; V. Korvin-Piotrovskii, *Pozdnii Gost': Stikhi* and *Poemy. Dramaticheskie poemy*; Iraida Legkaia, *Poputnyi veter*; Gizella Lakhman, *Zerkala*; Nikolai Morshen, *Dvoetochie*; Igor' Severianin, *Sobranie*

poez in four volumes (*Gromokipiashchii kubok, Zlatolira, Ananasy v Shampanskom,* and *Victoria Regia*) and Vol. V, *Poezoantrakt*; Fedor Sologub, *Odna liubov'*; M. Shipovnikov, *Iz chashchi promel'knuvshikh let* and *Pochti avtobiografiia*; A. Shpakovskii, *Na putiakh zhizni i mysli*; Iurii Terapiano, *Izbrannye stikhi*; A. Vertinskii, *Pesni i stikhi*; and *Sodruzhestvo*, an anthology of contemporary Russian emigré poetry, compiled by Tat'iana Fesenko.

⁶¹ G. Al'tshuler, *Delo Tveritinova*, in two volumes; Arkadii Averchenko, *Izbrannoe*; Nina Fedorova, *Zhizn'*, in three volumes; Tat'iana Fesenko, *Glazami turista*; B. A. Filippov, *Kresty i perekrestki*; Iurii Galich, *Kogda malinovki zveniat*; D. Kanevskii, *Na Zapad*; Alla Ktorova, *Litso Zhar-Ptitsy*; Ivan Lukash, *Bednaia liubov' Musorgskogo*; S. Mintslov, *Sviatye ozera*; Viktor Mort, *Kheppi end. Nevydumannye rasskazy*; V. P. Petrov, *Kitaiskie rasskazy, Kamerger dvora, Saga Forta Ross* and *Zavershenie tsikla;* V. Robsman, *Rasskazy i ocherki;* Vs. Solov'ev, a chronicle of four generations (each title in two books), *Sergei Gorbatov, Vol'ter'ianets, Staryi dom, Izgnannik,* and *Poslednie Gorbatovy*; A. Verbitskaia, *Vavochka*, in three books; and Ol'ga Zhigalova, *Shalaia Kassandra*.

⁶² Georgii Adamovich, *Kommentarii*; V. N. Butkov, *Tvorchestvo M. Iu. Lermontova*; K. Duble, *Nekotorye paralleli k romanu Mikh. Bulgakova Master i Margarita*; V. N. Efremov, *Ocherki po istorii russkoi literatury 19 veka*; Apollon Grigor'ev, *O natsional'nom znachenii tvorchestva A. N. Ostrovskogo*; D. P. Hitchkok, *Reading the Russian Text of the "Memoirs of a Madman" of N. V. Gogol*; I. A. Il'in, *Russkie pisateli, literatura i khudozhestvo*; V. Ivanov i M. Gershenzon, *Perepiska iz dvukh uglov*; I. Kostovskii, *Maiakovskii i mirovaia poeziia*; N. K. Koz'min, *Iz istorii russkoi literatury 30-kh godov (N. A. Polevoi i A. I. Gertsen)*; Galina Kuznetsova, *Grasskii dnevnik*; D. A. Levitskii, *Arkadii Averchenko: Zhiznennyi put'*; A. I. Nekrasov, *Kol'tsov i narodnaia lirika: Opyt parallel'nogo analiza*; Irina Odoevtseva, *Na beregakh Nevy*; Galina Selegen', *Prekhitraia viaz'. Simvolizm v russkoi proze: Melkii bes Fedora Sologuba*; Vs. S. Solov'ev, *Bol'shoi chelovek: Iz vospominanii o Dostoevskom*; M. Stepanenko, *Proza Sergeia Klychkova*; and V. Veidle, *Zimnee solntse.*

⁶³ The brothers Rausen in New York City were active as printers and publishers. Rausen Publishers produced, among other books, Asiia Gumetskaia's *Maiakovskii i ego neologizmy*. A couple of books were published by the now defunct New York-based Society of Friends of Russian Culture which was directed by the late Georgii Isakovich Novitskii (with Professor Nikolai Sergeevich Timashev as Vice-President). There is also a new publishing house, "Put' Zhizni" (The Path of Life), which was established in 1935 in the city of Pechery, Estonia, and then reestablished in New York City in 1971. Thus far, it published Boris Zaitsev's *Izbrannoe* (1973) and Iv. Shmelev's *Leto Gospodne* (1975), as well as two books by artists associated with the literary world, E. E. Klimov's *Russkie khudozhniki* (1974) and M. V. Dobuzhinskii's *Vospominaniia* (1976). Finally, it is worth mentioning that another publishing house, *Zaria*, which is directed by Sergei Aleksandrovich Zauer and located in London, Ontario, Canada, is in close contact with some of the Russian authors in the United States. It published two of Ivan Bunin's books, *Okaiannye dni*, with an introductory article and notes by the American Professor S. P. Kryzhitskii (2nd. ed., 1974), and *Pod serpom i molotom*, a collection of stories, recollections, and poems, compiled and with an introduction and notes by S. P. Kryzhitskii (1975).

⁶⁴ Having said that, one must add, that the distinction between "old" and "new" emigration becomes, with the years, less and less pronounced. It is quite possible that what happened to the "new" emigration will in time happen also to the "newest." It has already happened to those who came from the Soviet side in late forties and early fifties, and who were, for a while, called the "newest." The attempt of the present

"newest" émigrés, of the seventies, to create an independent literary-political voice by founding a new review, *Novyi kolokol*, has practically failed—only one issue was published.

[65] Concerning the Russian emigration of the first "waves," Ivan K. Okuntsov, writing in the 1930's, came to the negative conclusion that "with regard to literature it produced almost nothing essential and important" (*Russkaia emigratsia v Severnoi i Iuzhnoi Amerike*, p. 348).

[66] In the preparation of this paper every effort was made to establish the data correctly and fully. Unfortunately, this turned out to be not possible in several instances.

Rusyn-American Ethnic Literature

Paul R. Magocsi

ABSTRACT

This is the first study that deals with the belles-lettres written by Rusyn-American immigrants in the United States. The bulk of the Subcarpathian Rusyns came to this country as part of the massive immigration from eastern and southern Europe in the decades preceeding World War I. At that time, their homeland was an integral part of the Hungarian Kingdom; more specifically, Rusyns inhabited portions of several counties along the southern slopes of the Carpathian Mountains in the northeastern part of Hungary. By 1920, Rusyn-American immigrants numbered approximately 200,000, while today the original immigrants and their descendants total close to 650,000. The series of dialects they speak are classified as Ukrainian, and although in the European homeland after World War II they have generally identified themselves as Ukrainian, Subcarpathian immigrants have until today maintained themselves as an ethnic community distinct from the Ukrainian-American immigration. Only a small proportion of the Subcarpathian immigrants had more than an elementary level of education. Nonetheless, the community produced a wide variety of publications, some of which included belles-lettres. The latter category was clearly the work of amateurs. Thus, the author of the present study felt it more useful to isolate those themes that predominated in the literature and to provide a socio-historical rather than a literary analysis. Among the most frequent themes encountered were: (1) the immigrant experience (i.e., the adjustment to American society); (2) the continuing relationship with the homeland; (3) village life in the homeland; (4) the problem of national allegiance; and (5) a preoccupation with religious and spiritual concerns. As for genres, poetry, short stories, and especially short plays (usually intended for fraternal and church drama clubs) predominated. Only one novel was produced in the immigration, and that by E. Kubek, who concerned himself with life in the homeland. (PRM)

Among the territories within and immediately adjacent to the boundaries of the Ukrainian SSR, Subcarpathian Rus'[1] has provided proportionately the largest number of immigrants. Recently, it was estimated that in

503

the United States there are about 1,300,000 persons who either immigrated or are descendants of immigrants from Ukrainian territories. Of these, as many as 650,000 can trace their origin to the Subcarpathian region.[2] The Subcarpathian Rusyns, or simply Rusyns[3] as they are known in this country, underwent a specific development and have traditionally remained separate from the rest of the Ukrainian-American community. Hence, a discussion of Subcarpathian immigrant literature might best be treated outside the context of Ukrainian emigré belles-lettres.

The question of sources is a serious problem. Many literary works written by Subcarpathian Rusyns appeared over several decades in immigrant newspapers, almanacs, and other periodicals. These publications are now difficult to obtain, and for some titles complete sets are no longer available. The situation for the researcher is further complicated by the fact that there is no bibliography of Rusyn-American publications[4] and that biographical information about the authors under consideration is not readily available. Finally, scholars like A. Hartl, V. Birchak, E. Nedziel'skii, O. Rudlovchak, and Iu. Baleha, who have written extensively on literary developments in Subcarpathian Rus' during the twentieth century, seem totally unaware of the literary efforts undertaken by Rusyns living in the United States.[5]

In view of such factors, this introductory study must inevitably be limited in scope. The prose, poetry, and drama analyzed here comprise most of the belles-lettres that were published as separate volumes.[6] Some works were also drawn from periodical publications; the selection is at best representative, but by no means complete. Because of the limited quantity of material under review and the absence of accomplished authors or differing literary styles (all works are in a descriptive style that falls somewhere between late nineteenth-century romanticism and naturalism), I have decided to adopt a thematic approach and to determine how this literature reflects the ideals and environment of the community it represents. Initially, however, it would be useful to review briefly the social and cultural background of Rusyn communities in Europe and the United States.

Like most immigrants from eastern and southern Europe, Rusyns came to the United States to improve their economic status. Their homeland, located along the slopes and valleys of the Carpathian Mountains, was until 1918 an integral part of the Kingdom of Hungary. Towards the end of the nineteenth century the region experienced a series of poor harvests, a demographic increase, and the general neglect of the Hungarian government, so that Rusyn peasants had to struggle to obtain even the basic necessities for physical survival. Poverty, starvation, and illiteracy characterized their dismal situation—one that was graphically described by a contemporary Hungarian publicist:

> The sovereign stag should not be disturbed in its family entertainments. . . .
> What is a Ruthenian compared with it? . . . Only a peasant! . . . The hunting
> periods . . . last two weeks. There come some of the Schwarzenbergs, the
> Kolowrats, the Liechtensteins . . . they tell each other their hunting adven-
> tures. . . . In order that they should tell each other all this . . . 70,000 Ruthen-
> ians [Rusyns] must be doomed to starvation by the army of officials. . . . The
> deer and the wild boar destroy the corn, the oats, the potato and the clover of
> the Ruthenian. . . . Their whole yearly work is destroyed. . . . The people sow
> and the deer of the estate harvest.[7]

By 1914, about 150,000 Rusyns had settled in the United States.[8] The majority had come from the Hungarian counties of Szepes (Spiš), Sáros (Šariš), and Zemplén (Zemplin), territories which are now located in northeastern Czechoslovakia. Though employed as farmers, shepherds or woodcutters in Europe, they quickly entered the industrial work force and settled in mining and manufacturing centers in Pennsylvania, New York, New Jersey, and Ohio. Generally, Rusyns did not intend to remain in the New World, but only work there long enough to earn dollars so that they could return to the "old country," pay off a mortgage, or buy a new homestead and land. Yet, despite the "temporary" nature of their stay, they did establish several cultural and religious organizations, especially in the vicinity of Pittsburgh, Pennsylvania.[9]

The largest of these was the Greek Catholic Union of Rusyn Brother-hoods (*Sojedinenije Greko-Kaftoličeskich Russkich Bratstv*), founded in Wilkes Barre, Pa. in 1892. Other groups included the United Societies of the Greek Catholic Religion (*Sobranije Greko Katholičeskich Cerkovnych Bratstv*) and the Greek Catholic Russian Orthodox Brotherhood (*Greko-Kaftoličeskoje Pravoslavnoje Sojedinenije Russkich Bratstv*). These societies were basically insurance organizations concerned with the physical welfare of their members, though they also defended the interests of the various Rusyn churches and attempted to raise the level of immigrant culture by publishing newspapers, books, and other materials.[10]

The ideological policies of these groups reflected traditions brought from Europe, most important of which were: (1) an intense desire to protect the individual character of the Greek Catholic Church[11] or, if that were not possible, to join the Orthodox Church; and (2) the tendency to identify with the Russian or more often with an independent Carpatho-Rusyn nationality. In the second instance, the rejection of the Ukrainian national ideology was clearly pronounced. The origin of such attitudes may be traced to the homeland, which in the late nineteenth century was still in the embryonic stage of national development.

The small Subcarpathian intelligentsia, mostly Greek Catholic priests, had not yet decided on any one national orientation. In the decades following the 1848 revolution many leaders fostered association with Russian culture and the use of that language in local publications. A few others stressed the particular national character of the Subcarpathian Rusyns and favored the adoption of a language based on local dialects. Finally, there was a significant number (known as Magyarones) who opted for the dominant Hungarian civilization, explicitly supported national assimilation, and came to consider Rusyns as simply Hungarians of the Greek Catholic rite. Rusyn Magyarones were especially well represented in the hierarchy of the Greek Catholic Church, which not only succumbed to national assimilation but also began to Latinize or Magyarize the ecclesiastical service in conformity with the precepts for the Hungarian Roman Catholic Church. The reaction of many Rusyn parishioners was conversion to Orthodoxy.

Before 1918, the Subcarpathian intelligentsia had almost without exception remained immune to the Ukrainian national ideology. Indeed, there were contacts with Galicia, but these were primarily with Russophile individuals and organizations. Attempts by Galician-Ukrainian nationalists to develop relations with their Subcarpathian brethren were repeatedly rejected. Typical was the attitude of Alexander Dukhnovych, "the national awakener of the Subcarpathian Rusyns." Although he believed that the people "on the other side of the mountains are not foreign to us," he did not hesitate to express displeasure with the growth of Ukrainianism in Galicia. Commenting on Ukrainian literary efforts, he wrote: "Excuse me, brothers, if I am insulting someone, but I must state truthfully that there is nothing tasteful in your stories. . . . I don't understand by what means you suddenly change the pure Rusyn language to Ukrainian."[12] Thus, a concern to defend the Greek Catholic Church combined with a pro-Russian, pro-Hungarian, or independent Carpatho-Rusyn national orientation were the cultural elements that existed in the homeland and hence dominated the intellectual framework of Rusyn immigrants.[13]

Subsequent developments within immigrant organizations revealed the influence of ideological preconceptions brought from Europe. In the early years of the century, Greek Catholic priests found it difficult to maintain the traditions of their church, then legally under the jurisdiction of an uninformed and frequently antagonistic American Roman Catholic hierarchy. One result was a large scale conversion to Orthodoxy. These Orthodox Rusyns, who identified themselves as Russians or Carpatho-Russians, joined other Orthodox immigrants, strove to publish materials in the Russian language, and soon identified with that nationality.[14]

Rusyn lay organizations also experienced a critical period of internal dissension. For instance, the Greek Catholic Union originally included Rusyns from both Subcarpathian Rus' and Galicia, but in 1894 a Rusyn (later renamed Ukrainian) National Union was set up to accommodate nationally conscious Ukrainian immigrants, especially from Galicia. Similarly, a Galician Ukrainian-Subcarpathian Rusyn split occurred within the Greek Catholic Church. That body finally resolved the problem in 1916 by forming separate Subcarpathian and Galician branches, each with its own administrator. The Greek Catholic Union and Subcarpathian Greek Catholic Church then attempted to rid themselves of the domineering influence of the Magyarone clergy. They were successful in these efforts, and in 1918 certain lay leaders and priests joined to create the American Council of Uhro-Rusyns which proclaimed the Rusyns to be an independent nationality. The new Council succeeded in having its nationality views recognized by the United States government as well as by other immigrant groups (including some Ukrainians), and it subsequently played a decisive role in the political developments of postwar East-Central Europe.[15] The independent Rusyn orientation came to represent by far the largest percentage of immigrants from Subcarpathian Rus'.

Subcarpathian immigrant literature is at best an amateur enterprise. A high percentage of Rusyns who came to this country were either semi-literate or illiterate, and even the educated strata, primarily clergymen, were trained in a Hungarian environment and often not capable of expressing themselves freely in any standardized Slavic language. As Sigmund Brinsky unhesitatingly admitted: "I know well that I am not a writer. Not my ability, but rather love for my people urged me to do what I did."[16]

As might be expected, the immigrant experience is an important theme in Rusyn-American belles-lettres, and an examination of the texts can provide insights into the reasons for immigration, the problems of acculturation in America, and the relations with the old country. Traditionally, economic hardship was accepted as the primary stimulus that forced immigrants to leave Europe, but the literature reveals that unrequited love or social approbation were also important motivations for departure. Stefan Varzaly's[17] play, *Selska svad'ba* (The Village Wedding), provides one possible scenario. Fedor, the poor young hero, has to have some financial security before marrying. Thus, he follows the advice of his future father-in-law to live in America "a few years, and when you earn something, come back home . . . buy yourself land and become a farmer."[18] However, in two short stories by Emilij A. Kubek[19]—"Paschal'nyj dar" (The Easter Gift) and "Komu što Boh obical" (God Promised Different Things to Different People)—two young suitors flee to America because in both instances they are embarrassed to remain at home. One of them returns from the army to find his sweetheart already married, the other decides to leave because his proposal for marriage was seemingly ignored. Thus, America becomes a refuge, an emotional safety valve, where distraught persons can expurge their guilt or shame.

The direct relationship of immigrants to American society is not a focal point except in a few of Kubek's short stories. In his "Paschal'nyj dar," one gets a slight feeling for working-class living conditions, but it is in

"Palko Rostoka" that the ideals of immigrant life are most clearly displayed. Palko, or Paul Smith as he has become, has worked for seventeen years in an automobile factory. He is fully trusted by the owner, who appoints him foreman, as well as by the workers who elect him union vice-president. In the course of a strike, Paul defends the integrity of the boss and asks: " 'Where in the world have you heard that any capitalist would help striking workers?' "[20] The moral is clear: work hard and like Paul you might become a foreman, get your own house and car, and maybe even become a partner in the firm.

If settings that relate Rusyn immigrants directly to American society are rare, the literature does abound with episodes that delineate the internal problems of immigrant existence. The most persistently recurring theme is drunkenness. Like other immigrants, Rusyns reacted to the alienation they encountered in the New World by drowning themselves in alcohol, though they seemed to have had trouble holding it down. Valentine Gorzo[21] wrote a three-act drama, *Fedorišinovy* (The Fedorišins), based on an actual episode "in the life of American Rusyns." The play centers on Hryc Fedorišin, a chronic drunkard who terrorizes his wife and five children. He is forbidden by the court to live at home, defies the order, and finally, in the course of an argument, is shot dead by his oldest son. Throughout, the brutality and crudeness of the father is stressed and the cause of the tragedy placed on the "stinking," "accursed alcohol."[22] Virtually all the immigrant authors deal with the problems of drunkenness. Kubek's four volumes symbolically begin with a poem, "Dobryj tato" (Good Daddy), a rather pathetic account by a child who laments the fact that his father is always in a bar. Similarly, Kubek's hero, Marko Šoltys, is at the beginning of the novel left destitute because of a drunken father and is compelled to promise his dying mother that he will never touch alcohol.[23] Even New Year's greetings in a poem by Brinsky are accompanied by a warning not to drink too much.[24] Indeed, America's prohibition experiment did not bode well for Rusyn immigrants: in this unfortunate "draj kontry" our Ivan had to turn to "munšajn."[25]

Immigrant contact with the homeland is also a subject that frequently recurs. One variant, as in several poems by Brinsky, recalls letters sent from America. If the family in the old country wanted dollars, the immigrant needed in exchange information about his former society. To maintain himself in the New World, he pleaded for psychological sustenance. There seemed to be an almost desperate desire to know "što novaho doma?"—what's new at home. Is the neighbor's daughter married, is grandma all right, do the gypsies still play, does the brook still flow? "Write me about everything that happens."[26]

Certain aspects of Rusyn-American political activity were also made evident in the literature. In 1918, the immigrants played a crucial role in the process that led to the incorporation of Subcarpathian Rus' into Czechoslovakia. Subsequently, they regretted their decision and repeatedly sent protests to the League of Nations and the Czechoslovak government, but their economic contribution to the province did not decrease. For even if their countrymen had for a brief time

> Received life,–
> And a golden fate,–
> Holy freedom,

they were nonetheless

> All poor over there,
> Barefoot and in rags.[27]

Thus, the immigrants in America who were "of the same blood and bones" were asked to contribute to the material uplifting of their "brother Rusyns" at home. Kubek also informs us that groups of immigrants "from the free land, the land of Washington" returned home to "see if our Rusyns are really free?"[28] Elsewhere, the same author describes the return from America of the politically conscious Ivan, who is distraught because "his people are suffering from the Czechs and especially from the Slovaks."[29]

Yet despite their awareness of the far from ideal situation in Subcarpathian Rus', many individuals in the Rusyn immigrant community could not help but long for the supposed joys of rustic village life that they knew in their youth. In a poem published in 1958, Peter J. Maczkov[30] (perhaps unconsciously reflecting the disillusionment of environmentalists in this country) feels convinced that

> There is where you can drink clean water morning and evening,
> There is where clothes are made at home;
> There is where there are no factories, mines, dust, smoke,
> There is where every peasant is the 'lord' of his own household.[31]

This rather simplistic vision, most likely prompted by an old-age flight into sentimental melancholy, was poignantly questioned thirty-five years earlier in a poem by Kubek entitled: "Ci lem viditsja mi?" (Does it only seem so?). Here the dilemma of the first-generation immigrant who has established roots in the United States is best expressed.

> Now my thoughts gaze below the Carpathians,–
> My homeland I can't forget;
> Although in my youth luck did not shine on me
> And a struggle with want often occurred,
> I was a host to misery in the homeland;
> Still my homeland is dear to me even now.

The final refrain expressed the unsettling vacillation of the immigrant who does not know if he can or if he should return.

> Are the evenings, the summers, the land, the resting places
> more beautiful there?
> Or does it only seem so to me?[32]

There are several aspects of the immigrant experience that are not dealt with by Rusyn-American writers. For instance, there was no reference, not even indirect, to the ecclesiastical struggle, either with the American Roman Catholic hierarchy, the Orthodox converts, the Galician-Ukrainian faction, or the non-celibate traditionalists. Again surprising is the total lack of concern with the Ukrainian and Slovak national activists. Ecclesiastical controversies and encounters with self-conscious Ukrainian and Slovak immigrants were (and in many cases still are) the dominant feature of Rusyn life in the United States, yet the authors under consideration did not consider it appropriate or necessary to refer to such problems.[33]

Besides the immigrant experience, stories dealing with village life in the homeland are well represented. An analysis of the characters portrayed provides an insight into the style, ideals, and shortcomings of Rusyn civilization. As in most peasant and bourgeois societies, material concerns, particularly attachment to the land, are uppermost in the minds of most individuals. For example, the hero of Kubek's novel, *Marko Šoltys*, is driven to fulfill his dying mother's last request: " 'Swear to me my child that you will remain honest, good and stolid your whole life . . . and so that I can rest in peace, buy back the family land.' "[34] To be sure, great sacrifices were needed in order to achieve such goals and consequently the theme of personal happiness vs. material security pervades much of the immigrant literature.

In Varzaly's play, *Selska svad'ba*, a greedy mother wants at all costs to have her daughter marry a lazy, though rich, young man. The maiden's distress is summed up in the first scene: "My mother values richness more than the future of her daughter. So that our parcel of land can be joined to the rich man's, my mother is ready to give me to slavery, give me to that drunkard."[35] Such an attitude is again made evident in the anonymous play *Arendarj v klopot'i* (The Tenant in Trouble). In an extended scene, a returning immigrant, Ivan, decides to propose marriage to his childhood sweetheart. Her parents are first consulted, they consent, but their concern is only on how much the wedding will cost. A detailed discussion of food and alcohol follows. Then Ivan asks the daughter for her hand, but instead of the expected blush or outburst of joy, the girl calculatingly responds:

> Oh, I am so happy! Pray to God that it [the wedding] takes place as soon as possible. Then I will be certain that our property will not fall into Jewish hands![36]

This negative attitude towards Jews is another characteristic of Rusyn immigrant literature. As in *Arendarj*, there was always the fear that the land of the overtaxed Rusyn peasant would someday fall into the hands of the local moneylender, invariably a Jew. Alongside Jews stand lawyers, judges and women—the pantheon of evil characters in Rusyn-American writings. Stefan F. Telep[37] composed a short satire for children, *V sudi* (In Court), in which the forces of law and order are ridiculed. Typical of the dialogue is a query by the judge directed to an oft-convicted criminal: "As I see by your record, you have been associating with bad company for a long while." To which the accused replied: "As long as I can remember I've always had business with lawyers and judges."[38]

Women are also disparagingly treated. In almost all instances describing male-female relationships, the courtship stage is marked with promises by the suitor that he will give his fiancée everything in life. After marriage, however, the standard characterization reveals a disrespectful husband who treats his passive wife as chattel and can only address her as the old lady (stara) or grandma (baba). In a lighter vein, Julius Dobra's *Oženilsja s ňimoju* (I Married a Dumb Woman) combines the negativism expressed toward both lawyers and females. A judge marries a speechless woman, arranges a successful operation, and then is driven wild by his chattering companion. To make his marriage tolerable, he has himself made deaf—a solution that should not seriously affect his profession because he will not have "to hear all the lies of lawyers and the deformations of the accused."[39]

The problem of national identity had always been of prominent concern to Rusyns in Europe and the United States.[40] On this question, immigrant writers adopted basically two orientations. They identified either: (1) with the Subcarpathian region, and in some cases suggested the existence of an independent Rusyn nationality; or (2) with Russia and accepted the view that their people were part of the Great Russian nation. Themes of *lokalpatriotismus* prevail in the poetry of Brinsky, Kubek, and Maczkov, who offer unlimited praise for the villages, rivers, and mountains "of holy Rus'...under the Beskyds."[41] The Prešov Region of northeastern Czechoslovakia is most often described, and Orestes Koman has left us a kind of tour of this area in his short story, "Jak stalsja Vasko šustrom?" (How Vasko became a Shoemaker).[42] A rather extreme instance of local pride is found in Ivan Ladižinsky's book-length eulogy on immigrants from Kamjonka (*kamjonskij narod*), a small village in the westernmost portion of the Prešov Region.[43] This tendency toward ethnopolitical fractionalization was later underscored as a danger by Maczkov who called on former residents of Szepes, Sáros, Abaúj, Zemplén, Ung, Ugocsa and Máramoros Counties to join together as Rusyn brothers into one "great family."[44]

If Ladižinsky has shown special allegiance to a few villages south of the Carpathians, he is at the same time one of the few who unequivocally identified both himself and his "Carpatho-Russian" people (Karpatorossy) with the Great Russian nation. In a decidedly nationalistic poem, he declared:

> We will avenge our enemies.
> Arise my people,
> Let the earth tremble
> In a struggle for what is our own;
> Let the whole world know
> How we love what is ours;
> If possible—we will die
> For all that is Russian.[45]

This author also composed several other poems that propounded the idea of unity with Russian civilization.[46] Like Ladižinsky, Kubek could simultaneously praise the local region and laud the virtues of "Matuška Rossija,"[47] while Koman wrote a short story, "Košikari u Carja Nikolaja" (The Basketweavers at Tsar Nicholas' Court) which was concerned with emphasizing the existence of close relations between the people "from the Carpathians, the land of Koriatovych" and the Russian tsar.[48]

In general, political commentary is at a minimum in the works under analysis. We already mentioned the brief criticism against the Czechoslovak regime offered by Kubek, but the only other instance of a political stance was that adopted by Koman. Writing in the 1950's, this author attacked "the red tyrant," Khrushchev, and criticized "the pressure of the red regime" in the homeland where "the Communists have forbidden religious processions (*otpusty*) and have refused to allow the walls and windows [of the churches] to be repaired."[49] Elsewhere, he lamented the death of Tsar Nicholas II and his family, who were not, as other émigrés, "lucky enough to get our of that red paradise! "[50] Actually, this anti-Communist attitude is an exception in Rusyn-American belles-lettres, since most works were published before World War II, a time when the Soviet regime had not yet established itself south of the Carpathians.

On the other hand, spiritual concerns continued to loom large in Rusyn-American life and literature. Since many authors were priests, religious themes were abundant. In a sense, all the immigrant writings are didactic in character, but beyond that a large number are solely religious in inspiration. Koman dramatized the birth of Jesus in a three-act play, *Viflejemskaja noč* (The Night of Bethlehem),[51] while Jurion Thegze moralized on Christ's adolescence in a short story, "Vo cerkvi Jerusalimskoj" (In the Church of Jerusalem).[52] Brinsky also wrote several poems praising the Virgin Mary, Christ, and various church holidays, while the layman Maczkov's volume of poetry is dedicated exclusively to religious subject matter. Maczkov's writings are less concerned with revealing how faith may sustain the individual than with the presentation of eulogies dedicated to the various saints, religious places, and contemporary Rusyn-

American hierarchs. As for the trials and tribulations of everyday life, an anonymous poem in a journal published by a Rusyn fundamentalist sect in Vermont seemed to promise what many immigrants hoped for—an afterlife in heaven for the faithful:

> Everything there will be free from all sorrow
> Closed off by gates from [this earthly] life; . . .
> Enmity will cease, peace will reign,
> And freedom for all will be forever.[53]

Despite our concern with thematic content, perhaps a few words about the aesthetic value of Rusyn immigrant literature are in order. One gets the overall impression that, with the exception of Kubek, Rusyn authors never had a clear conception of the works they were composing. Hence, many stories get off to a good start but end with a situation that is hardly related to what preceded it. For instance, Telep's short play, *V sudî*, is basically a scene in a court room that includes satirical exchanges between the judge and the plaintiff; suddenly, it ends with an unexpected eulogy on Rus', the Rusyn language, and the Rusyn way of life. Similarly, in *Arendarj v klopot'i*, the focal point throughout the first two acts is the problem of marriage, yet the third act concludes with a slapstick and rather boring episode in which the local Jewish innkeeper hides in a barrel to protect himself from the bridegroom.

Generally, the character sketches are clearly delineated though flat, i.e., they are limited in psychological depth. Kubek cannot be accused of writing aimlessly since his stories are almost always well conceived units; moreover, he frequently depicts in a convincing way complex characters. Nonetheless, his narrative does tend to be choppy and it often seems that individual episodes are strung together without consideration for smooth transitions. As pointed out above, however, these immigrant writings represent only an amateur effort at literature, so that aesthetic criteria should not perhaps be applied too stringently.

There is one area, though, in which Rusyn-American literature has undeniable value. I refer to language.[54] A noted Hungarian linguist remarked that the United States is a "museum of languages," a place where immigrants from all over the world still speak and write languages as they existed during the late nineteenth century. In most cases, this stage of linguistic development is no longer evident in the country of origin. Despite the occasional use of literary Russian, the language used in Rusyn immigrant literature is lexically and morphologically based on the dialects of the Subcarpathian region. Since today the language used there is heavily influenced by either Russian, Ukrainian, or Slovak, and since in the past local authors strove to write in either literary Russian, Ukrainian, or Magyar, Rusyn-American literature is one of the few places where the older spoken forms have been preserved. Thus, words or constructions like *bandurka* (potato), *dahde* (somewhere), *falatka* (piece), *id* (toward), *kaprul'a* (dirt in the eye, a dirty person), *kapur* (gate), *klikati* (to name), *kortit mene* (I am curious), *maštalna* (cowshed), *merkuvati* (to be careful), *obist'a* (property), *valal* (village), *žadaliste* (you asked), have already or are now rapidly disappearing from use in Europe. Inevitably, there are also American-English calques—*burder* (boarder), *dviženije obrazy* (moving pictures), *kurtina* (curtain), *majna* (mine), *Oj boj ja holoden* (Oh boy, I'm hungry), *porč* (porch), *rum* (room)—although these are relatively rare. On the other hand, the language does contain many eastern Slovak dialectal words—*apo* (father, from the Hungarian *apa*), *kadi* (to where), *kel'o* (how much), *zat'al* (meanwhile)—which reveal (as do place names found in the texts) that most of the authors came from the Prešov Region. In any case, Rusyn-American literature is a linguistic preserve waiting to be tapped by the specialist interested in dialects or the history of language.[55]

This brief survey of selected writings has revealed the thematic nature of Rusyn immigrant literature. Life in America or in the "old country" and national and religious subjects were the most common themes. Admittedly, this was a literature of amateurs, produced in most cases by well-meaning individuals who wanted to raise the cultural level of their brethren, not produce literary masterpieces. Furthermore, the literature enjoyed only restricted circulation and because of its limited aesthetic value had no discernible impact on literary activity in the homeland. Nonetheless, these Rusyn-American literary efforts do bear witness to the viable independent existence of this immigrant group and will continue to have value as sociohistorical and linguistic documents.

Harvard University

NOTES

[1] This term is meant to describe all territory inhabited by Rusyns living south of the Carpathian Mountains—regions which today comprise the Transcarpathian Oblast' of the Ukrainian SSR and the Prešov Region (*Priashivshchyna*) in northeastern Czechoslovakia. Subcarpathian (below the Carpathians) suggests geographical location; Rus', the national and religious affiliation of the people. In historical literature, the region has been variously called Ugro-Rus', Ruthenia, Carpatho-Russia, and Carpatho-Ukraine. For further reading see Paul R. Magocsi, "An Historiographical Guide to Subcarpathian Rus'," *Austrian History Yearbook*, IX-X (Houston: Rice University, 1973-1974), 201-65.

[2] These figures are only approximations based on church membership, a relatively reliable statistical source. The exact number of Orthodox believers with roots in Subcarpathian Rus' (here estimated at 310,000) is particularly difficult to determine. Paul R. Magocsi, "Carpatho-Rusyns," *Harvard Encyclopedia of American Ethnic Groups* (Cambridge, Mass.: Harvard Univ. Press), forthcoming.

[3] The Rusyns have been known by many different names: Uhro-Rusyns, Ruthenians, Carpatho-Russians, and Carpatho-Ukrainians. The name Rusyn was most fre-

515

quently employed by the inhabitants and cultural leaders of Subcarpathian Rus', and only recently has the present-day official designation, Ukrainian, come to be widespread among the population. In the United States, with the exception of a few recent newcomers who have opted for Carpatho-Ukrainian (Zakarpatets'), the vast majority use the names Rusyn, Carpatho-Russian, or the less specific term, "Slavish." In July, 1918, the American Council of Uhro-Rusyns recognized Uhro-Rusyn or Rusyn as the only correct names for their people and these forms are used by most of the authors under consideration in this study.

⁴ A research project is presently underway at Harvard University that will result in the publication of five monographs. Included is an extensive bibliography and survey of documentation on Carpatho-Rusyns in the United States, being prepared by Edward Kasinec. See Richard Renoff and Stephen Reynolds, eds., *Proceedings of the Conference on Carpatho-Ruthenian Immigration, 8 June 1974*, Harvard Ukrainian Sources and Documents Series, No. 2 (Cambridge, Mass.: Harvard Ukrainian Research Institute, 1975), pp. 5-20.

⁵ The one exception is Dmitrii Vergun who in a published lecture on Subcarpathian literature included two paragraphs on immigrant literary activity. See his "Karpatoruská literatura (Stručný přehled)," *Osm přednášek o Podkarpatské Rusi* (Prague: n.p., 1925), p. 55. However, even the prolific Rusyn-American writer, Joseph P. Hanulya, failed to include any references to immigrant literature in his survey, *Rusin Literature* (Cleveland: n.p., 1941).

⁶ The author is grateful to the many individuals who supplied important data, but especially to Msgr. Basil Shereghy and Reverend Stephen Veselenak, O.S.B. of McKeesport, Pa., who provided most of the rare materials that made this study possible.

⁷ M. Bartha, *In the Land of the Kazars* (1901), cited in Oscar Jaszi, *The Dissolution of the Habsburg Monarchy* (Chicago: Univ. of Chicago Press, 1966), p. 235.

⁸ The estimates regarding Rusyn immigration range from 6,299 to 500,000. Cf. Oleksander Mytsiuk, "Z emihratsii uhro-rusyniv pered svitovoiu viinoiu," *Naukovyi zbirnyk Tovarystva "Prosvita,"* XIII-XIV (Uzhhorod, 1937-1938), 21-32, and Ladislav Tajtak, "Pereselennia ukraintsiv skhidnoi Slovachchyny do 1913 r.," *Duklia* 9, No. 4 (Prešov, 1961), 97-103.

⁹ On the early history of Rusyn immigration, see "Amerikanskaia Rus'," *Illiustrovannyi russko-amerikanskii kalendar na god 1926* (Philadelphia: "Pravda," 1925), pp. 80-87; John Masich, "Highlights in the Glorious History of the Greek Catholic Union of the U.S.A.," *Jubilee Almanac of the Greek Catholic Union*, LXXI (Munhall, Pa., 1967), 33-74; Walter G. Warzeski, *Byzantine Rite Rusins in Carpatho-Ruthenia and America* (Pittsburgh: Byzantine Seminary Press, 1971), pp. 95-128; Peter Kokhanik, *Nachalo istorii Amerikanskoi Rusi*, 2nd ed. (Trumball, Conn.: Karpatorusskoe literaturnoe obshchestvo, 1970), pp. 479-514.

¹⁰ The Greek Catholic Union still publishes the *Amerikansky russky viestnik* (1892-1952), later renamed the *Greek Catholic Union Messenger* (1952-present). The United Societies sponsored *Rusin* (1910-1917) and now *Prosvita* (1917-present), while the Greek Catholic (now United) Russian Orthodox Brotherhood of America issued *Narodna obrana* (1916), renamed *Russky viestnik-Russian Messenger* (1917-present). All titles in this study reproduce the Latin script form as in the original. Transcriptions of dialectal titles from the Cyrillic alphabet follow the Library of Congress pattern for Ukrainian with these additions: ѣ = î; ы = ŷ.

¹¹ The Greek Catholic (Uniate) Church, or Catholic Church of the Byzantine Rite, was established by the Union of Brest (1596) for the Orthodox population of Poland and by the Union of Uzhhorod (1646) for Subcarpathian Rus'. The new church

recognized the supremacy of the Pope and was incorporated into Rome's hierarchical structure, although it was permitted to retain most of its eastern traditions, such as marriage of priests and use of the Slavonic liturgy and Julian Calendar.

[12] From an article in *Viestnik . . . Rusinov avstriiskoi derzhavy*, No. 11 (Vienna, 1863), cited in Kyrylo Studyns'kyi, "Aleksander Dukhnovych i Halychyna: studiia," *Naukovyi zbornyk Tovarystva "Prosvita,"* III (Uzhhorod, 1924), 92. The Ukrainians most active in trying to develop contacts with Subcarpathian Rus' were Mykhailo Drahomanov—see his *Avstro-rus'ki spomyny: 1867-1877* (L'viv: n.p., 1889-1892), pp. 386-436 and *Spravy Uhorskoi Rusy* (L'viv: n.p., 1895)—and Volodymyr Hnatiuk, who published six volumes on Subcarpathian ethnography and numerous other studies concerning the territory. For the negative reactions to these efforts by contemporary Subcarpathian leaders like S. Sabov, I. Sil'vai and Iu. Stavrovskii-Popradov, see Evgenii Nedziel'skii, *Ocherk istorii karpatorusskoi literatury* (Uzhhorod: Izd. Podkarpatorusskago Narodoprosvietitel'nago Soiuza, 1930), note 2, pp. 256-57. Even the eventual Ukrainophile, Avhustyn Voloshyn, later Premier of Carpatho-Ukraine (1938-1939), at first castigated "that horrible plague of Ukrainianism (*vikrainizma*) and radicalism which has recently spread in Galicia, which introduces continual disputes, and which alienates the Rusyn from his church, from his language, and even from his Rusyn name," *Mîsiatsoslov* (Uzhhorod, 1909), cited in ibid., note 2, p. 247. For valuable insight into certain aspects of the problem, see Michal Danilák, "Styky haličských a zakarpatských Ukrajincov v 2 polovici XIX storočia," in *Zhovten' i ukrains'ka kul'tura* (Prešov: KSUT, 1968), pp. 35-47.

[13] Not until after World War II did nationally conscious Ukrainian immigrants arrive from Subcarpathian Rus'. For the most part, they have remained estranged from the older Rusyn-American groups and have associated rather with the Ukrainian immigrant community. Nevertheless, their New York-based organizations, the Carpathian Research Center and Carpathian Alliance, which publishes the monthly *Vistnyk Karpats'koho Soiuza* (1970-present), maintain a distinctly regional profile. Some Subcarpathian immigrants (especially from the Prešov Region) belong to the Lemko Union (Yonkers, N.Y.), an organization that represents Lemkians, the westernmost branch of Rusyns who lived in Galicia on the northern side of the Carpathians. The Union, which sometimes claims that Lemkians make up an independent national group, publishes a newspaper in a Galician Lemkian dialect, *Karpatska Rus'* (1927-present).

[14] The largest "Russian" organizations set up by or including large numbers of immigrants from Subcarpathian Rus' are the Mutual Aid Society (*Obshchestvo Vzaimopomoshchi*, est. 1895), which still publishes the newspaper *Svit—The Light* (1916-present), the Society of Russian Brotherhoods (*Obshchestvo Russkikh Bratstv*, est. 1900), which continues to issue *Pravda*, now entitled *The Truth* (1900-present), and the American Russian National Brotherhood (*Amerikanskoje Russkoje Narodnoje Bratstvo*, est. 1912) which sponsored *Rodina* (1927-1945) and *Brotherhood-Bratstvo* (1927-1949). These organs were joined in 1959 by another publication, *Svobodnoe slovo Karpatskoi Rusi*, edited by the Subcarpathian immigrant, M. Turianitsia. All of these periodicals have included poems, plays and short stories, though by far the majority of immigrant authors are from Galicia, not Subcarpathian Rus'.

[15] A Pittsburgh lawyer, Gregory I. Zsatkovich, was the Subcarpathian immigrant most responsible for pressing the idea of an independent Uhro-Rusyn nationality. As guiding spirit of the American Council of Uhro-Rusyns, he met with President Wilson and Thomas G. Masaryk, the future president of Czechoslovakia, and almost single-

handedly conducted the American side of the negotiations that led to Subcarpathia's incorporation into the new Czechoslovak state. In 1920, Zsatkovich was appointed the first governor of Subcarpathian Rus'. In a recent comparative study–Joseph P. O'Grady, ed., *The Immigrant's Influence on Wilson's Peace Policies* (Lexington, Ky.: n.p., 1967)–Zsatkovich's extraordinary successes were repeatedly praised. On Rusyn-American political activity, see Victor S. Mamatey, "The Slovaks and Carpatho-Ruthenians," in ibid., pp. 224-49 and Paul R. Magocsi, "The Political Activity of Rusyn-American Immigrants in 1918," *East European Quarterly*, 10, No. 3 (Boulder, Colo., 1976), 347-65.

[16] *Stichi* (Homestead, Pa.: Vyd. Sojedinenija Gr. Kaftoličeskich Russkich Bratstv, 1922), p. 3. Very Reverend Sigmund Brinsky was born in 1881 in Mat'aška (Sáros County), eastern Slovakia. Like his father and grandfather, Sigmund was ordained a Greek Catholic priest in 1908 after completing his studies at the Seminary in Prešov. He came to the United States before World War I, served as a parish priest, and published many articles and poems in the *Amerikansky russky viestnik*. For a brief discussion of his literary activity while still in Europe, see Olena Rudlovchak, "Literaturni stremlinnia ukraintsiv Skhidnoi Slovachchyny u 20-30kh rokakh nashoho stolittia," in *Zhovten' i ukrains'ka kul'tura*, p. 162.

[17] Very Reverend Stefan Varzaly (1890-1957) was born in Ful'anka (Sáros County), eastern Slovakia. He completed the gymnasium and teacher's college (1911) in Prešov. Subsequently, he attended the Prešov Seminary and was ordained a Greek Catholic priest in 1915. Reverend Varzaly was a village priest in the homeland, and after emigrating to the United States in 1920 continued such duties in New Castle and Rankin, Pennsylvania. Being a married priest, he adamantly opposed the celibate policies of the Pittsburgh Greek Catholic Diocese and because of his views was suspended in 1931 and five years later excommunicated. He was a founding member (1932) of the Committee for the Defense of the Eastern Rite and acted as its chief spokesman for several years. He joined the anti-celibate, traditionalist group of excommunicated priests led by Orest Chornock, who established in 1938 the American Carpatho-Russian Orthodox Greek Catholic Church. In 1945, Varzaly split with Bishop Chornock and associated himself for a while with a group that came to be known as the Carpatho-Russian People's Church. While editor (1930-1937) of the *Amerikansky russky viestnik*, he published several poems and polemic articles in opposition to celibacy. Under his direction, the publications of the Greek Catholic Union adopted the view that the Rusyns were not an independent nationality, but rather "a branch of the great Russian ethnos." Varzaly was the founding editor of *Vistnik* (1936-195?).

[18] Stefan Varzaly, *Selska svad'ba: veseloihra iz žizni podkarpato-russkaho naroda* (Homestead, Pa.: "Amerikansky russky viestnik," n.d.), p. 6.

[19] Reverend Emilij A. Kubek (1859-1940) was born in Rafejovce (Sáros County), eastern Slovakia. He completed theological studies at the Prešov Seminary, was ordained a Greek Catholic priest in 1881, and was an active cultural leader in local Rusyn villages. Among his many publications before coming to America is the monumental polyglot dictionary *O-szláv-magyar-ruthén (orosz)-német szótár a szentirás olvasásához* (Uzhhorod: Unio könyvnyomdarész., 1906). In 1904, he emigrated to the United States and served as a parish priest. Reverend Kubek was clearly the most prolific and talented Rusyn-American writer; he published a four volume collection, *Narodny povísti i stichi* in 1922, and continued to compose short stories and poems that appeared in the publications of the Greek Catholic Union.

[20] *Narodny povísti i stichi*, I (Scranton, Pa.: "Obrana," 1922), 33-34. With the exception of *Marko Šoltys*, all the works of Kubek mentioned in this study are found in volume I.

518

²¹Very Reverend Valentine Gorzo (1869-1943) was born in Bilky (Bereg County), in the Transcarpathian Oblast' of the Ukrainian SSR. He completed gymnasia studies in Uzhhorod and Mukachevo, attended the Uzhhorod Seminary, and was ordained a Greek Catholic priest in 1892. He came to the United States in 1905 and was appointed to a large parish in McKeesport, Pennsylvania, where he served as spiritual advisor (1908-1943) to the United Societies (*Sobranije*). As legal prosecutor of the Pittsburgh Diocese, he was a loyal defender of the Bishop during the controversies of the 1920's and 1930's. As a founding member of the American Council of Uhro-Rusyns, Reverend Gorzo participated in the delegation which met with President Wilson in October, 1918. He continually maintained a concern with the homeland and was a patron of the Podkarpatskii Bank in Uzhhorod. His publications included *Osnovna amerikanska istorija* (1924) and *Ťahary svjaščennika* (1925) as well as many translations of liturgical books.

²²Valentine Gorzo, *Fedorišnovy: drama . . . iz žit'a Amerikanskich Rusinov* (McKeesport, Pa.: Sobranije Greko Katholičekich Cerkovnych Bratstv, 1925).

²³Emilij A. Kubek, *Marko Šoltys: roman iz žit'ja Podkarpatskoj Rusi*, 3 vols., in his *Narodny povísti* (1923), vols. II, III, IV.

²⁴"Pozdrav na novyj hod" (Greetings for the New Year), in Brinsky, *Stichi*, pp. 145-51.

²⁵From the Brinsky poem "Suchota" (Dryness), in ibid., pp. 154-55.

²⁶Brinsky, "Pis'mo do kraju" (The Letter to the Old Country), in ibid., pp. 54-56.

²⁷Brinsky, "Brat'a Rusiny" (Brother Rusyns), in ibid., pp. 22-25.

²⁸"Pozdravlenije dl'a krajevoj Rusi" (Greetings for the Old Country Rus'), Kubek, *Narodny povísti*, I, 112-13.

²⁹"Komu što Boh obical," ibid., pp. 180-81.

³⁰Peter J. Maczkov (1880-1965) was born in Livov (Sáros County), eastern Slovakia. His formal education was limited to attendance in the elementary school of his native village. He came to the United States in 1898 and worked for many years as a laborer in Pennsylvania and Ohio; he later became a salesman and served on the clerical staff of the U.S. Steel Corporation. Maczkov educated himself and became a prolific writer and cultural worker. He was assistant editor of the *Amerikansky russky viestnik* (1914-1936), editor of the *Amerikanskij russkij sokol* (1918-1936), and editor of *Children's World-Svit Ditej* (1917-1932). Besides the collection of poems discussed here, Maczkov wrote a reader for parochial school children, *Novyi bukvar'* (Homestead, Pa.: n.p., 1921), and a guide for becoming a citizen, *The Citizen's Primer* (1915).

³¹"Tam selo moje rodnoje" (My Native Village Over There), in Peter J. Maczkov, *Vinec nabožnych stichov*, 2nd ed. (Munhall, Pa.: n.p., 1958), p. 134.

³²Kubek, *Narodny povísti*, I, 189-90.

³³Beyond the realm of belles-lettres, however, there does exist a large polemic literature written by Subcarpathian immigrants. A few illustrative titles include: Josif P. Hanulya, *Cija pravda? Katholikov li ili ne-Katholikov?!* (1922) and his *Orthodoxy, Schism and Union* (Cleveland: n.p., 1935); G. Kotubii and I. E. Bora, *Istoricheskaia kometa ili raskrytie pokhristianizirovaniia iazychestva: temnyk viekov* (Proctor, Vermont: n.p., 192); Michael Yuhasz, *Wilson's Principles in Czechoslovak Practice: the Situation of the Czechoslovak People Under the Czech Yoke* (Homestead, Pa.: n.p., 1929); P. I. Zeedick and A. M. Smor, *Nase stanovisce* (Homestead, Pa.: n.p., 1934); Peter G. Kohanik, *The Biggest Lie of the Century—"the Ukraine"* (New York: n.p., 1952) and his *Highlights of Russian History and the "Ukrainian" Provocation* (Perth Amboy, N.J.: n.p., 1955); Sevastiian Sabol, *Katolytstvo i pravoslaviie* (New York: n.p., 1955).

³⁴Kubek, *Narodny povísti*, II, 39.

³⁵Varzaly, *Selska svad'ba*, p. 4.

³⁶*Arendarj v klopot'i: komedija iz sel'skaho žit'a* (Perth Amboy, N.J.: Vostok Publishing Co., 1929), p. 26.

³⁷Stefan F. Telep (1885-1965) was not from Subcarpathian Rus', but born in Pielgrzymka, a little village just north of the Carpathians in the Austrian province of Galicia, now part of Poland. He attended a parochial elementary school in his birthplace and in 1903 emigrated to the United States. He settled in Mayfield, Pennsylvania, and worked for about a decade in the local coal mines. Then he bought a hand printing press, began to support himself as a printer, and published his own editorials, poems, and plays, one of which was *Boh svídok: trahykomediia v 4 aktakh yz amerykanskoho zhyt'ia* (Mayfield, Pa.: The Author, 1929). In 1928, Telep, together with his two sons, initiated *The Mayfield News*, a paper which was in circulation for close to thirty-five years. He was also a founding member of the fraternal organization, Lubov, and author of a reader for elementary parochial schools, *Russkii bukvar'* (Mayfield, Pa.: The Author, 1938).

³⁸Stefan F. Telep, *V sudí: stsenychnŷi obrazok dítei* (Mayfield, Pa.: The Author, 1944), p. 10.

³⁹J. Dobra. *Oženilsja s ňimoju* (Homestead, Pa.: "Amerikansky russky viestnik," n.d.), p. 15. Julius Dobra was born in Ung County near Uzhhorod, and, after coming to this country, he served as a cantor in the Greek Catholic (Byzantine Rite) Cathedral in Homestead, Pa. During the 1930's, he set up a cantor's school at the cathedral.

⁴⁰For an analysis of this problem, see Paul R. Magocsi, *The Shaping of a National Identity: Subcarpathian Rus' 1848-1948* (Cambridge, Mass.: Harvard Univ. Press, 1977).

⁴¹The Beskyds are a range of the Carpathians. The quotation is from "Brat'a Rusiny" (Brother Rusyns) by Brinsky, in *Stichi*, p. 22. See also his "Vo našem valal'i" (In Our Village), "Malenkoje selo" (Little Village), and "Bo vir' Topl'a" (Believe me, oh Topl'a River), in ibid., pp. 57-58, 73-76, 161-64. Also, "Pod obrazom Duchnoviča" (Under the Image of Dukhnovych), "Pozdravlenije dl'a krajevoj Rusi" (Greetings for the Rus' Country) by Kubek, *Narodny povísti*, I, 86-90, 112-13; and "Tam selo moje rodnoje" (My Native Village Over There), "Moje selo L'ivov mnohi l'udi znajut" (Many People Know My Native Village Livov) by Maczkov, in *Vinec*, pp. 135-39.

⁴²*Kalendar' Greko Kaftoličeskaho Sojedinenija v S.Š.A.*, LV (Munhall, Pa.: n. p., 1951), 25-26, 42-45. Reverend Orestes Koman (1894) was born in Beloveža (Sáros County), eastern Slovakia. He attended the Prešov and Budapest Seminaries and was ordained a Greek Catholic priest. After emigrating to the United States in 1921, he acted as Spiritual Advisor (1944-1969) to the Greek Catholic Union and from 1923 to 1974 served as parish priest in Elizabeth, New Jersey.

⁴³Ivan A. Ladižinsky, *Karpatorossy v Evropi i Ameriki: primir Kamjonka* (Cleveland: n.p., 1940). Very Rev. Ivan Ladižinsky (1905-1976) was a native of Jarabina (Orjabina) (Szepes County), eastern Slovakia. He attended the Prešov Seminary and was ordained a Greek Catholic priest. During the 1920's, he was an elementary school teacher in the Prešov Region and emigrated to the United States in 1930. Being a married priest, he was one of those who left the Pittsburgh Diocese and joined Bishop Chornock's American Carpatho-Russian Orthodox Greek Catholic Church. In 1938, Reverend Ladižinsky was elected vice-president of the Cleveland-based American Russian National Brotherhood and appointed editor of its official organ, *Rodina*. Three years later he headed the Carpatho-Russian Unity, a political organization that published the monthly, *Jedinstvo* (1942-1943), which protested Hungary's occupa-

tion of Subcarpathian Rus' during World War II. For several years until his death, he was a parish priest in Duquesne, Pennsylvania.

[44] Peter J. Mączkov, "My–Sojedinenije!" in *Kalendar' Greko Kaftoličeskaho Sojedinenija v S.S.A.*, LVII (Munhall, Pa.: n. p., 1953), 39-41.

[45] "Narode moj" (To My People) in Ladižinsky, *Karpatorossy*, p. 118.

[46] "Spasibo" (Thanks), "Molitva" (A Prayer), "Na Novyj hod" (For the New Year), ibid., pp. 110, 116, 126-27.

[47] "Svobodna Rossija–1917" (A Free Russia–1917), in Kubek, *Narodny povísti*, I, 168-170.

[48] *Kalendar' Greko Kaftoličeskaho Sojedinenija v S.S.A.*, LVI (Munhall, Pa.: n. p., 1952), 28-32. The allusion to Koriatovych refers to a prince from Podillia who crossed the Carpathians (according to legend, leading 40,000 people) in 1395 and received the fortress of Mukachevo from the King of Hungary. Koriatovych has subsequently been hailed as one of the first great heroes of the Subcarpathian Rusyns.

[49] These citations are taken from Koman's short stories, "Vaňko Onufer," ibid., LXV, 25, and "Medzi-Peci," ibid., LVIII, 30.

[50] Košikari u Carja Nikolaja," ibid., LVI, 32.

[51] *Kalendar' Sojedinenija*, XXXIX (Homestead, Pa., 1934), 65-72.

[52] Jurion, *Vo Cerkvi Jerusalimskoj i Petrova Denna Platna* (McKeesport, Pa.: "Prosvita," 1922). Very Reverend Jurion Thegze (1883-1962) was a native of Bereg County, Transcarpathian Oblast'. He attended the Uzhhorod Seminary and was ordained a Greek Catholic priest in 1905. In 1912, he came to the United States where he served as a parish priest among other places in Whiting, Indiana. His literary efforts include the short story, *Zahraj miňi Cigane* (Homestead, Pa.: n.p., 1922).

[53] "Pokoi" (Peace) in *Prorocheskoe svietlo*, IV (Proctor, Vermont, 1922), p. 5. For information on this little-known Rusyn settlement, see Paul R. Magocsi, "Immigrants from Eastern Europe: The Carpatho-Rusyn Community of Proctor, Vermont." *Vermont History*, 42, No. 1, (Montpelier, Vt., 1964), 48-52.

[54] One grammatical standard was composed for Rusyn-American writers by Joseph P. Hanulya, *Hrammatyka dlia amerykanskykh rusynov* (McKeesport, Pa.: "Prosvita výdav. spolechnosty," 1918). This text, printed in Cyrillic, strove to impose Russian vocabulary and morphology on the dialects as spoken in Subcarpathian Rus'. The authors discussed in this study disregarded the Hanulya grammar, wrote in dialect, and with the exception of Telep, published in Latin script.

[55] The language used in the influential newspaper *Amerikansky russky viestnik* has been analyzed by Charles E. Bidwell, *The Language of Carpatho-Ruthenian Publications in America* (Pittsburgh: University of Pittsburgh Center for International Studies, 1971). The Harvard project (mentioned in note 4) includes a study on the language of Carpatho-Rusyn immigrant publications being undertaken by Professor Michał Łesiów. For the status of the language today, see the chapter by Paul R. Magocsi on Carpatho-Ruthenian in *The World's Written Languages: A Survey and an Analysis of the Degree and Modes of Usage*, Vol. 1, *The Americas* (Quebec: Centre international de recherches sur le bilinguisme, Université Laval, 1977), forthcoming.

American-Serbian Literature

Peter D. Bubresko

ABSTRACT

American-Serbian literature, from its remote origin to the present time, is as fundamentally poetic as its source of inspiration—the Serbian soul. Mauriac's idea that "only poetry enables us to capture the human truth" is the basic concept of a valid comprehension of life. The inadequacy of the photographic imprint of reality by intelligence, "small thing on the surface of ourselves" [Barrés], is certain. Hence, the intuitive perception of existence does not cease to deepen in its flow with earthly and celestial responsiveness. Rejecting the limitations of determinism, Serbian ethnic literature eliminates the falsity of life in a static image of the world. The nostalgic feelings toward the Old Country, the gradual process of adaptation to the new environment, anguished war memories and postwar scars, inflicted by change, rehabilitation, and challenge, constitute the main themes of American-Serbian literature in its prosperous growth. From Jovkich's traditional Romantic militancy in the very beginning of the century, to the fierce modernism of the contemporary Tesich and Simic, the continuity prevails. The literary vein reflected in the less productive period between World Wars never dried out, but was sustained by the inexhaustible poetic impulse and the ennobling impact of suffering. Arriving from the native land under traumatic circumstances, American Serbs expanded their capacities under the serene skies of America. The grafted branches extended from the wholesome tree in the New World, reaching forth in the convulsive search for freedom and dignity across "the nine seas." (PDB)

A century ago, Serbians began to immigrate to the United States, primarily to escape political pressure in their enslaved provinces. In many cases economic reasons also stimulated them in the exodus to the New World. Like all immigrants from Europe, the Serbs were motivated at that time by the spirit inherent in the following lines:

> For the first time, the Europeans had a chance to free themselves, just by crossing the Atlantic within a few weeks, of the secular feuds which divided them; for the first time, they relegated the problem of property and the

522

procession of hates in the background; for the first time, since prehistoric times, the most dangerous enemy of man was, not the human being, but nature.[1]

The oldest Serbian settlements were founded along the West Coast and Gulf of Mexico between the 1860's and 1880's. The first Eastern Serbian Orthodox Church consecrated to Saint Sava, today a landmark of California, was erected in 1894 in the old mining town of Jackson. The second church, Saints Constantine and Helen, was blessed in 1895 in Galveston, Texas. Coming from Dalmatia, Bosnia, Hercegovina, Lika, Srem, Banat, Backa, Southern Serbia—provinces annexed by Austro-Hungary—and the old Serbian kingdom of Montenegro, the people felt nostagically attracted to the California and Texas coasts because of the maritime landscapes and warm climates that were similar to that of the Adriatic. The revolt against imposed tyranny, narrowness of native horizons clouded by frequent wars, and suffering under the centuries-old Ottoman yoke considerably accelerated the migration across the Ocean.

Moreover, to escape compulsory military service and political and religious persecution, the young men fled to "this American asylum" in the wake of decisions of the Berlin Congress in 1897:

Everything here tended to regenerate them: new laws, a new mode of living, a new social system, the power of transplantation, like all other plants, they have taken root and flourished! Formerly they were not numbered in any civic list of their country; here they rank as citizens. This country is now that which gives them land, bread, protection and consequence.[2]

In search of a better life and spiritual freedom, the immigrants came in waves to the exotic shores of the new continent. The eagerness to surpass their human condition through their growth on a fertile soil, to conquer life in its brightness and opulence, inspired the young Serbians in their fateful decisions to help themselves and their families to emerge from enrooted poverty. Often, they toiled for several years to earn the fare as passengers in steerage for the transatlantic voyage. Without formal education or with only elementary instruction, these resolute and intelligent peasants proved themselves capable of rebuilding their lives in the New World. They asserted themselves from the beginning as an energetic ethnic minority, constructively included in the total culture of the adopted country they ardently loved. Fused with it, they became within a generation true, loyal Americans.

With an enviable vigor, rejuvenated on the American soil, "an immense reservoir of youthfulness," they began immediately to organize themselves under two flags; American and Serbian banners are seen in communities throughout the United States. Sporadically, parishes and fraternal organizations started to expand. Cultural activity with emphasized interest in literature developed in the larger colonies. This literary zeal, manifested often in the bud, stemmed from an inborn enunciative talent, and a strong ambition to attest the value of their race. They were also inspired by Serbian popular poetry, whose tradition was very alive and influential. The national treasure, epic poetry, renowned in European countries, nourished their embryonic literary concepts expressed through dailies, monthly reviews, almanacs and calendars. An intense theatrical activity was a part of their cultural achievements indispensable to the spiritual needs and pride of American Serbs for their identity in the melting pot.[3]

They succeeded in establishing themselves in America in varied professions ranging from farming, industrial work and mining to the intellectual attainments symbolized by Nikola Tesla (1856-1943), inventor of universal renown. "Father of the Wireless," Tesla migrated to the United States in 1884, where he was recognized for his outstanding scientific contributions (about nine hundred patented inventions). The Nobel Prize in Physics shared with Edison in 1915 was one of the many honors bestowed upon him. Mauriac's lines alluding to the immigrants in general are descriptive of American Serbs:

> Although this continent was populated by Europeans, they acquired here some new salient traits. During three centuries, America was characterized by a mobile and unstable frontier oriented toward the West. On this extreme fringe of civilization, crudeness of life, struggle against wilderness and Indian, abundance of land, and necessity for mutual help created a type of man: pioneer, generous, independent, violent, who only recognized the inequality created by physical force and hardships. In such an environment, men arrived from different countries, finally became alike.[4]

Experiencing rejuvenation on the dynamic American soil,

> All possessed a spirit of free cooperation, which scarcely existed in Europe. The jealousies were gradually minimized on the frontier because the immigrants felt equal confronted with the same danger. The government being unable to reach them, the pioneers governed themselves. The neighbor was not an adversary, but an associate. Inspired by such circumstances, their gaiety and goodwill surprised and continues to bewilder Europeans, accustomed to quarrels around the steeple. That is why a certain ease in their freedom was noticeable as a new phenomenon.[5]

Because of the new conditions, a Spartan life prevailed among the immigrants. A testimony of a prominent American Serb underlies the merits of the Serbian pioneer parents in the new land:

> Our parents were kin to poverty all their lives, but departed the richest in spiritual wealth. They were universally loved and respected. And they are worshipped and mourned today, ten, twenty, and thirty years after death, by sons and daughters who appreciate the priceless legacy they bequeathed us: a legacy of self-sacrifice; of pride, industry, thrift and independence.
>
> . . . .
>
> The history of the future is bound to record their patriotism, valor, devotion and dedication, prudence, wisdom, and fidelity to Christian ideals.[6]

Once the building of the first churches in California and Texas was accomplished, the organizational life was accelerated. The first Serbian Benevolent and Literary Society was founded in 1880 in San Francisco. The newspapers *Liberty* (1901-1902) and weekly *Serb Independence* (1902-1908) appeared there under the editorship of Veljko Radojevich (1868-1956). One description of him reads:

> The sage and dean of Serbian journalism in U.S.; born in the village Podi (near Herceg-Novi). Coming in America 1900, [he] brought to his fellow immigrants a literary ability, unblemished character and an abundance of energy for cultural work. He contributed to most of the Serbian and Croat publications throughout the land; for two years [he] edited San Francisco's *Liberty*, and his own *Serb Independence* for six years. His writings have true national character, deep-rooted national philosophy, interpretation of the original language as found and thought by Vuk Karadzic (1787-1864, author of Serbian grammar and collector of Serbian folk songs).[7]

In the early 1900's the Serbians were coming in waves to the Eastern seaboard. In the beginning, immigrants in the East as well as the West worked in mines, steel mills, railroads and the fruit farms in California. The Serbian Benevolent Society Unity (Jedinstvo), founded in Chicago in 1897, was closely linked with Serbia.[8] The emigration of Serbs to the eastern parts of America was intensified particularly by the annexation of Bosnia and Hercegovina by Austro-Hungary in 1908 and by the beginning of World War I. Due to the stabilization of numerous Serbian communities in these regions, the fraternal societies were often unified. The various clubs, sport associations "Soko" (The Falcon), "Prosveta" (Enlightment), and the first Serbian Fraternal Federation (1903), were already in existence.

Through an energetic process of adaptation to the New World, they preserved their national heritage; immersed in the new total culture Serbs assimilated readily and effectively. Alexis de Tocqueville points out:

> In America, the principle of people's sovereignty is not at all hidden or sterile as it is in some other nations; this principle is recognized by customs, proclaimed by laws; it spreads with freedom and reaches without difficulties its last consequences.[9]

After World War II, about fifteen thousand new immigrants from the European refugee camps reinforced the old emigration with their intellectual capacities and fervent patriotic zeal. Due to the new blood, American-Serbian literature was enriched considerably and secured for its future evolution.

* * *

The first American-Serbian poet, Proka Jovkich-Nestor Zucni, lived in San Francisco and Oakland at the beginning of the century (1903-1911). The epithet "the poet-torch" underlines the character of his poetry; his work was greatly influenced by the tempestuous events at the turn of the century in his native land menaced by war. Under the impact of Maxim Gorki and due to the resemblance of their lives, he coined the pseudonym Nestor Zucni, which denotes the bitterness of existence. This literary Bohemian earned his bread first as a typographer and then as an editor of the daily *Serb Independence* in San Francisco. Creator of the new sensibility in patriotic poetry, his poems of exile and national struggle were enflamed. The literary revolt, pronounced in his verses, inspired the Promethean "Poem to a Beggar":

> I am neither born to be offered
> As a sacrifice to the ancestral law,
> Nor to be tortured by the stagnant life,
> On a pale prairie in plebeian crowd's sight.[10]

In the following militant stanza, the poet rejects both repulsive egoistic motives and enslavement to rooted conventionality:

> I wouldn't be able to live at home,
> Nor reduce my universe to onion plants,
> I prefer life where suffering, bitterness,
> Anxiety and revolt reign.[11]

Sounding like a bugle on the battlefield, these lines are permeated by spite for humiliating cowardice:

> What! I should restrain my rage
> Looking at these miserable beings pale and bent,
> At their dirty, calloused hands,
> And staring anguished eyes! [12]

He shuns away from the pusillanimity of shabby despair on the edge of life caused by a wreck:

> I am not the poet of an abject outcast,
> Who creeps slowly, cowardly, in the dust,
> Burying his pride at the bottom of the heart.
> No! I am the soul of the revolted ones![13]

Paul R. Radosavljevich (1889-1953), Ph.D., Pd.D., Serbian born educator, studied in his native land, then in Austria, Germany and Switzerland. Member of the American Psychological Association, he taught for about three decades at New York University. Author of many books in his field, Radosavljevich also published in 1919 the masterpiece *Who Are the Slavs?*,[14] which introduced him into belletristics. In this very informative study, he presented the Slavic soul perceived in all its depth and creativity. Among varied aspects of the Slav race, he emphasized in particular the Serbian popular poetry under anonymous authorship, which actually supplants an unwritten ancient history of Serbian people and is the expression of their "glowing poetical spirit," the creator of its knightly charac-

526

ters and chivalrous enterprise. The vitality of these original legendary poems, and of their patriarchally suggestive power to preserve spiritual values from oblivion and to illustrate heroic deeds, stems mostly from the Serbian secular resistance to Asiatic barbarism:

> But the most important of the Slavic popular literature is the Serbian Popular Poetry—a branch of literature that still survives among the Serbs, though it is almost extinct in all other nations. Much of this poetry is of unknown antiquity, and has been handed down by tradition from generation to generation. The Slavic genius of the Serbian people has created all sorts of "unwritten literature," without recurring to the "printer's devil." They have the reputation of being a poetical nation. To-day there are thousands of Serbian legends, fairy-tales, ballads and songs.[15]

Enthusiasm for the folk poetic heritage of Serbia, discovered by Alberto Giovanni Battista Fortis (1743-1803), spread rapidly through Europe during the expansion of Romanticism. This Italian traveler and naturalist published in his *Viaggio in Dalmazia* (Travels in Dalmatia, 1774), both in the Serbian original and Italian, "Hasan-aginitza" or "The Wife of Hasan Aga," one of the finest Serbian songs:

> The celebrated Pole, whom Goethe called "The Poet Laureate of the World," Adam Mickiewicz (Polish Longfellow), in his enthusiastic courses on Serbian cycles of rhapsodies at the College de France (Paris, in 1840-1842) says the following about this song: "The Christian idea was never in verse expressed so beautifully and directly, yet with its full mysticism, as in the song 'Tzar Lazar Chooses the Heavenly Kingdom.' " In his *Les Slaves* (I, 334) Mickiewicz says: "The Serbs, that people engrossed in its past, and destined to become the musician and the poet of the entire Slavic race, does not even know that it should one day become the greatest literary glory of the Slavs." It was not because he was himself a Slav, that he sang the unbounded praises of this beauty so enthusiastically, but because he understood the moral of this beauty.[16]

The echo of Serbian poetry resounded at once in Germany, cradle of Romanticism, "when the Turkish hurricane swept away the Serbian Empire (1389)"[17] on Kosovo Field:

> The Great German philologist, Jakob L. K. Grimm (1785-1863), a great friend of national literatures, became an enthusiastic admirer of Serbian poetry. He began immediately to bring out these songs, paying a tribute of unstinted admiration to this poetry. He translated some of the Serbian folk-songs. In 1824 he writes: "I have three volumes of Serbian poems, and not one among them that is not excellent! German folk-poetry will have to hide before it." He admits that the Serbian ballads are far superior to the German *Nibelungenlied.*[18]

Among many admirers of this poetic harvest, Grimm celebrated fervently the Serbian cultural heritage, created spontaneously by the innate poetic impulse, and inspired "by the tradition instead of the printed page":

> When Jacob L. K. Grimm read the Serbian ballads he wrote: "The Serbian national poetry deserves indeed general attention. . . . The wealth and the beauty of Serbian popular poems would if well known astonish Europe. . . . In them breathes a clear and inborn poetry such as can scarcely be found among any modern people. . . . Europe will learn the Serbian language just because of the Serbian ballads."[19]

In addition, Radosavljevich, in a documented outline of Serbian mythic poetry, stressed Goethe's prophetic views on bright perspectives for this spiritual wealth of mystic Old Serbia, which elevates the soul as a precious part of the nation's intellectual life:

> J. W. Goethe (1743-1832), the great "citizen of the universe," translated that simple, but powerful tragedy of domestic life, the Hasan-aginitza; also wrote articles of Serbian popular poetry in his *Ueber Kunst und Alterthum*, an art journal.[20]

The expanded popularity of the Serbian songs was noticeable in other European countries and in Great Britain:

> But this interest was not confined only to Germany. The French literary world was equally appreciative. Madame de Staël (1766-1817) had already (in 1797) shown her sympathy for the Serbian race and its songs.[21]

Neither did the British men of letters remain indifferent to these songs—they translated them and popularized them.[22] It is rightly said that the Serbs are not the soldiers of the King who have gone to war, but the soldiers of an Ideal.[23]

Yovan Dutchich, considered the greatest modern poet in Yugoslavia, studied in his country, Geneva and Paris. During the formative years, he was greatly influenced by Parnassians and Symbolists, whose doctrinal ideas and techniques he transplanted in his native soil. In *Imperial Sonnets*, he recreated the patriotic deeds of Serbian people. His masterfully executed prose poems are entitled *The Blue Legends*. His letters from different countries, *Cities and Chimeras*, are rich in historical reminiscences, cultural observations and literary allusions. *The Love Poems and Adriatic Sonnets* explore the labyrinth of the human heart and the dramatic past of the classical Dalmatian coast. The numerous essays and *The Treasure of Tzar Radovan* abound in philosophical reflections and poetically contemplative moods. Due to his enviable success and membership in the Serbian and the Rumanian Royal academies and in the PEN club in London, Dutchich's pre-war renown was well founded in European literary circles. At the outbreak of the war in 1941, Ambassador Dutchich escaped from Madrid to the United States, where he developed a feverish literary activity in Gary, Indiana which continued to the end of his life in 1943.

A manuscript note from New York expressed the impulsive impressions of the America which fascinated the poet:

All that I read or heard about the United States wasn't sufficiently suggestive to give me an image of this country. Everybody is expressing an opinion concerning the New World from the point of view of his respective nation, as a fanatic believer in his own philosophy of life and finally as an European proud of his ancestry. However, the evaluation of the American people shouldn't be based entirely on the comparison with other parts of the world. I found America considerably greater than seen in my dreams and projected in my visions. . . .

Fifth Avenue fully reflects the American genius: taste, charm, style, joy of life, and many other wonders which demonstrate the ever changing enthusiasm and dynamism of America whose creative spirit is never immobilized. . . .

On these stories, I didn't have the impression that I was on a new continent but on a new planet. The expression *The New World* is very appropriate in this case. The newness of life in all its aspects is quite evident here. . . .

I felt the poetry of American life, convinced that neither world peace nor war are imaginable without an engagement of America in the crucial issues of our time. The first morning in New York, I became aware of the fact that if I didn't see America, my existence would never be complete.[24]

Dutchich's lyrics, published in America on the eve of his death in 1943 and characterized by transcendental depth, stress the fusion of the emotional and cerebral fibers, a dominating principle of all his poetry. In this intellectualization process he tried to "assimilate all the heart's phenomena with those of thought" (Dutchich) in a verse of an astonishing fluidity and suggestive images. By reason of their concision and multiple spiritual shades, *Lyrical Poems*,[25] permeated by the mystery of earthly human destiny, appeared as the conclusive exploratory involvement in life and its sudden turn of fortune.

In the poem entitled "The Road," Dutchich expresses the anguish caused by the impenetrableness of the eternal celestial enigma engulfing life from the cradle to the grave:

> I would like to go upstream
> To discover the source and the mouth!
> But finally the night surprised me,
> And always thicker thorns erupting in darkness.[26]

The more our insights deepen, always humanly limited, the more the thickness becomes obstructive:

> Where is the sparkling well,
> What is the first truth so remote?
> There is no road leading in these regions!
> The river is becoming deeper, darker.[27]

The human race is plagued by insatiable curiosity and restlessness under the cruel blows from the tenebrous horizons:

> As a famished flock of migratory birds
> Crossing the radiant ocean from one shore to another,

> Landing on the thorny field, whipped by the breeze,
> Menaced by the mute threatening clouds. [28]

"The Pious Poem" reaffirms religious faith, under staggering temptations, emerging purified from convulsion inflicted by life's revolutionary changes:

> All my conceived thoughts are blasphemous,
> But under your breath my strings vibrate:
> I don't see the road I follow,
> While my eyes overflow with your greatness. [29]

The reconquered belief sounds triumphal in the poem "To God," which is a hymn to divine inconceivable greatness:

> I built the imaginative white churches in your name;
> While praying I kept ringing the bells;
> I sobbed for Thy magnanimous son;
> And chased the infamous devil from your cross. [30]

The creative mission of poetry being sacerdotal, Dutchich stresses its preponderance and multiplicity in different engagements through life in "The Poem":

> The Lord sowed me always,
> I am a new word and symbol everywhere—
> In white bread the first seed,
> The corner stone in a fortified tower.
>
> An atom of dust on a deserted road,
> The solar circle and image,
> Spark in the eye of a poor man,
> Bitter tear shed by a martyr. [31]

Dutchich's last book of poetry, written in America (in Cyrillic characters) at the end of his life, bears an imprint of man's perplexity, accumulated anguish and crystallized faith in God in the midst of a dynamic cosmos. The expanded vision of the human reach is distilled through experience, painfully acquired wisdom and some intuitive approaches to existence. The thought in struggle with itself doesn't cease to oscillate because of its inability to humanize the unknown. In an effort to inflict transcendent meaning upon all manifestations of life, he proceeds by the juxtaposition of moods often contradictory in his perception of the universe. The emotional intensity here is the foundation which gives the impetus to his lyrical meditations.

Count Sava Vladislavich: A Serbian Diplomat at the Royal Court of Peter The Great and Katherine The First [32] is the title of this exhaustive monograph solidly documented about a Serbian "who occupied a distinguished position among Russian diplomats in the eighteenth century. During two and a half decades, he took part in all important events of the Russian empire." [33]

A Path along the Road (historical evocations), *My Fellow Travelers* (literary portraits), *The Mornings seen from Leutar* (philosophical essays) are the last three works of Dutchich published in America in Serbian.[34]

It is relevant to note that these posthumous Dutchich works have been published in Yugoslavia (1969) in a series entitled *Assembled Works of Yovan Dutchich.*[35] This edition stirred a very long and violent controversy, still sporadically alive and bitter, because of the author's strong anti-communist convictions.

Michael Pupin, "poet-scientist," lived in the United States from 1874 to 1935. The year 1889 marks the beginning of his celebrated academic career at Columbia University, where Pupin Institute is a foundation well deserved by this great American Serb and scientist of universal renown. His autobiography, *From Immigrant to Inventor,*[36] relates all phases of his fascinating life on both sides of the Atlantic. The Pulitzer Prize, bestowed upon the distinguished pedagogue in 1925, was a worthy recognition for a vividly traced portrayal of a great human destiny. Personally acquainted with Presidents Harding and Wilson, he played an important role in relations between his native country and the United States after World War I.

Freeman J. Dyson, of the Institute for Advanced Studies at Princeton, writes in the introduction to Pupin's autobiography:

> The book has two major themes. One is the experience of the European immigrant coming to the United States, with his gradually growing awareness that he belongs to two cultures whose ends are not always reconcilable. The other is the experience of a student of physics. . . . In describing these various experiences, Pupin makes the spirit and texture of a past age come to life. . . . In particular, his descriptions of the scientific atmosphere in the different countries he visited have an absolutely authentic touch.[37]

Discussing the unorganized energy of the sun through space, the inventor injects the poetic fibre into the scientific block with religiosity. He proves that both the poet and the scientist are closely related through their creative affinity. As to the terrestrial phenomena under the impact of the sun, Pupin emphasizes the miraculous order as soon as the diffused solar rays reach the earth. These lines in the purely poetical transposition would be reminiscent of Baudelaire's "Correspondences," that is, of the invisible mysterious links between earth and sky the poet has to perceive:

> But their fate and destiny are fixed and determined as soon as they arrive on mother earth and are caught by the leaves, the blossoms, and the ripening fruit of the fields, meadows, and orchards, and by the endless nets of the all embracing oceans.
>
> The chaotic, non-coordinated energy-swarms are thus imprisoned and made to work together with a definite aim and for a definite purpose. The joys and beauties of our seasons will tell you the story of this wonderful transformation of primordial energy from chaos of the young stars, white hot with joy of life, to the cosmos of the old, cold, and moribund earth.[38]

This approach, both scientific and poetic, to the structural intricacy of the universe, leads the author to the concept of a coordination of many millions in America, eager to eliminate hatreds and suspicions: Our blessed country is destined to become the first ideal democracy in the world.[39]

Bishop Nicolai Velimirovich, reputable theologian as well as literary figure, lived in America from 1946 until his death in 1956. Widely known in England as an inspired preacher during World War I, later he distinguished himself in America as a penetrating literary critic and essayist. His book entitled *The Life of St. Sava* (written in English) is a romanticized biography of the founder of the independent Serbian Orthodox Church in the twelfth century. The sanctified hero and his turbulent time are depicted vividly with solid documentation and rich local color in recreation of the far removed past:

> Once upon a time there lived a boy prince, very intelligent, rich and fair looking. All the doors of worldly pleasures and success were open before him. But something within himself turned him away from all those things after which millions of human beings are feverishly striving. He renounced all vanities and allurements of the world and one day secretly fled away from the royal court, and settled in a desert place as a poor stranger intent only upon enlightening his soul by fulfilling God's will to perfection.[40]

The sacred mission of the greatest Serbian saint is announced concisely in the epitome, with a Biblical simplicity in its narrative tone:

> Many years later this worldly prince, led by God's hand, returned from the desert to his native country as a prince of the church and forever the spiritual leader of his nation. Being childless, he became the father of many and many millions of his spiritual sons and daughters through the centuries.
>
> This happened over seven hundred and fifty years ago. And the torch of spiritual light he lit among his people is still burning and the number of his spiritual children in Christ constantly increasing.
>
> In our generation his people for love of him are building churches, dedicated to his name on all five of God's continents, where they have been dispersed by a stroke of destiny.[41]

Milan Petrovich lived in the United States from 1949 to 1963. A great soul anguished by his long captivity in Germany and the convulsiveness of life in exile, he expressed himself movingly in the collection of poems under the title *The Petrified Tears*,[42] written in Serbian (Cyrillic characters). The flow of sadness inflicted by his disastrous fate deepens his insight into the human condition and colors an enthusiasm inspired by the earthly and heavenly wonders in "Melancholy":

> Only the singing birds dispel my gloom!
> When the star in May sparkles in rosy dawn,
> I knit the small nests for the lark and nightingale.
> Every sad day they fly to me,
> As I am Pan's child.
> Two birds from the grove are healing me with milk.
> O, how deep is the anguish in the far away world![43]

In Petrovich's verses, the inner drama is deciphered with an exceptional perceptivity. The harshness of reality and its encroachment on the poet's destiny are well interpreted psychologically, through abundant imagery and great rhythmic variations, and can be only partly captured in translation. Petrovich's original poetic idiom reaches a perfect prosodical form in versification. The scenes from nature, still and live, attract the poet's attention and stimulate his delicate involvement in surrounding life. In the poem entitled "A Duckling," he expresses a closeness to the enlivened landscape that he suggestively depicts:

> Leaving the nest she dove into the river,
> Unwilling to wait for her small sibling
> Which slowly, on top of a low hill,
> Rocks around the home on a circular path. . . .

> I caught the duckling with a fish from the river,
> And took her to the berth next to the mother and sister,
> Looking how, in a green shrub,
> They sisterly offer each other the tiny fish from the beak.[44]

Far from being bookish and anemic, Petrovich's Romantic poetry is vitalized by frequent refuge to a childhood and native climate nostalgically missed. The rejuvenated nature, emerging from hibernating somnolence, elates his imagination with a bucolic chastity in the poem under the title "The Spring":

> Beautiful as an angel under the rainbow's arch,
> A child greeted me with hand and smile,
> Led me on the path along the white lilies,
> And first strawberries, rosy and ripe.

> While the child picked the scarlet berries and flowers,
> A little bird perched in front of him,
> Cheered the child with a song and flew away in a bush
> With a small strawberry in his tiny beak. . . .

> How happy am I in the early spring, when a child,
> Beautiful as an angel under the rainbow's arch,
> Takes me by his tender hand
> In the flowers not yet plucked.[45]

Ljubica Grkovich-Boljanich, in her life of ups and downs, went to Yugoslavia first at the age of two for a short period of time. Then, she went again at the age of sixteen, when she finished her secondary studies. Those contacts with the ancestral land affected her innate sensitivity and intensified her unquenchable thirst for expanded horizons. Deeply influenced by Serbian poetry and the patriarchal climate of the Old Country, her uprooted life was later permeated by the fatalistic moods and pessimistic, violent agitation in a night "thick as the resin." Once harbored in Gary, Indiana, her home town, she vividly participated in the social and cultural life of a large and prosperous American-Serbian community, proud of her friendship with Yovan Dutchich whose poetry ravished her.

One of her favored themes, poverty, inspired the poem "On the Road," in which she expresses her philanthropic dream in confrontation with misery:

> Tonight, I will depart on a long journey. . . .
> But I shall go from star to star
> And everywhere gather the golden dust,
> then, at once, the same night, sprinkle the gold
> on the terrestrial paths, trampled under the food of miserable beings.[46]

In the love poem bearing the title "The Blooming Branches," the intoxication of nature in its rebirth corresponds to the awakening of human passions and fertility of dreams:

> The blooming branches
> are knocking on my window through the night:
> a gold drop pours
> in every wound
> in every flower
> and all lilies rave tonight about the first love.[47]

In her book of poems, *The Swan's Songs*,[48] written in Serbian (Cyrillic characters), the most frequent themes are solitude, fatality, and nostalgic feelings, stimulated by the changes of environment in the beginning of her nomad experience, which injected the spleen, *le mal du siècle*, in her conception of life. In "Every Night," the poetess sadly remembers Bosnia, the central Yugoslav province, whose landscape is imbued with the poetry of the soil and with the oriental sensuality reflected in its folklore. This elemental poetical harvest spread abundantly across the mountains and valleys is accumulated through the tumultous centuries of captivity under the Ottoman yoke:

> Every night, from the blue distant regions
> the memories revive and a strange song resounds.
> So many sorrows will rush upon me
> while the ancient fountain from Bosnia
> whispers in my dream.[49]

Under the impact of despair and a loss of vitality, in the poem "The Thoughts," she feels the corrosive effect of disenchantment inflected by the cruelty of human destiny:

> The moonlight weaves the golden net
> the foolish thoughts fly
> and fall trapped.
> With a sad accompaniment of rain
> they expire more silently
> but still hopeful enough.

> The silver pours from firmament
> the water roars far away
> while the blood ferments in my veins.
> All my joys fall and rise
> and like in a vigorous oak
> I feel inside a worm eating up my life.[50]

The tenderness and inexpressible gratitude for parental love are stressed in her gently simple stanzas. "To My Mother" is a glowing hymn to the maternal affection evoked in a poignant way:

> I am unable
> to depict your image
> with colors and light.
> There is only a pale, frail word
> to be my confession,
> whisper and my cry . . . .[51]

Yovan Kontich lived in America from 1946 to 1965 in Pittsburgh, Pennsylvania and in Chicago, where he edited the daily *The American Srbobran* and the weekly *Liberty*, organs of the Serb National Federation and the Serbian National Defense respectively. Later he was editor of the literary monthly review *Serbian Historical and Cultural Association* "Njegos" in Chicago. In his adopted country, Kontich published two books of short stories inspired by the psychological agony of the fighters in a war without a truce: *Through the Fire and Tears*[52] and *On the Road to Exile.*[53]

A former commander in the army of General Michailovich, Kontich vividly evokes the Yugoslav guerrilla and the continuation of his struggle in the world. Concisely structured and written in a picturesque, sober style, these stories illustrate the ethical values of Serbs in a heroic revolutionary movement. "That's America"[54] recreates the destiny of an immigrant, a judge by profession, who with stoicism endures the initial hardships of adaptation to the new environment. And he generously helps relatives to preserve familial pride and to pursue the struggle against despotism. In this chronicle we follow the militant state of mind experienced by the Serbian fighters dispersed throughout the world, often under unbelievable circumstances:

> He reserved for himself only the most indispensable, sending the rest to his wife and parents. In the beginning, he would ship some things for the house and for his closest relatives, since he realized from their first letters that they were deprived of everything. Even of bread. . . . In every package, in a discreet way, he enclosed some jewelry. At the first, trinkets which bring happiness, and then some valuable jewels. Two goals were in his mind: to help his parents and his beloved wife; to secure their financial independence, but also to provoke envy and respect of those who reproach his decision (to leave for America).

> In spite of a long captivity, which sharply wrinkled his face and left deep scars in his soul, he wasn't preoccupied with himself . . . .[55]

In the story under the title "The War without a Truce,"[56] Kontich's style is vivacious and full of metaphoric images in a vibrant succession:

> Krsto was an interpreter in the legation of Montenegro. He spoke a few languages. Krsto went into the world young, a moustache scarcely visible. As vigorous as a pine, of a generosity inherent to maternal tears, and as fresh as the breaking dawn in the mountains. In Corinthia he mastered Italian and German, while in Constantinople he learned Turkish. The languages stuck to his vital intelligence and remained there as imprints in wax. All this knowledge and experience were acquired accidently. And so lightly.[57]

Anka Godjevac-Subbotich, born in Serbia, has lived in New York City since 1941, where her husband, former envoy of Yugoslavia in London, became a lawyer and university professor. Educated in her native land, Germany, and in France, this jurist with a European reputation excels equally in her literary creativity. Besides the numerous articles and essays published in many dailies and reviews here and in Europe, Anka Godjevac-Subbotich gives public lectures at different American and Canadian universities and colleges. *From Three Continents*,[58] a book written in Serbian (Cyrillic characters), abounds in perspicacious observations of an enlightened traveler with cosmopolitan experience. Poetically inclined, she succeeds in detecting the essential traits of scrutinized reality with a human warmth and an impulsive originality:

> New York seen from the air resembles a lazy somnolent alligator, struck against a rock along the coast. Having lived for years on the sixteenth floor in a building in the heart of New York, I acquired the habit of observing the city from an aerial perspective. Perched on my observatory, I used to look at it in winter and summer, day and night. The street, which is protected by the pent-roofs for safety reasons, is not visible from my apartment. Unable to reach my floor, the tumult coming from the street is not heard. I see and hear only the planes, and that's why they appear to be closer than the passing cars. Comparable to the fast silver fish, the aeroplanes swim across the celestial basin above my head. On the horizon, through the park I see the edge of New York, unparalleled in its beauty on five continents.[59]

This global vision of New York is colored by some memories harvested in Europe which emerge suddenly:

> All these sights create the impression that I have been anchored for years on a yacht in one of New York's harbors. The sea air coming up to my terrace intensifies the illusion. The other complices in this refuge are the light effects along the horizon of this immense city, which are extracting from my memory and bringing to me the silhouettes of all great European cathedrals, to the point that I don't know whether I am in Paris, Florence or Munich. I particularly like to contemplate the moon's sickle in its cosmic march, hooked on a steeple instantaneously and with a touch of slight irony. During the half-curfew imposed in war, Central Park and its western periphery recreated the

authentic ambient prevailing in Maupassant's novels at the end of the last century: streets poorly illuminated by lanterns, crowded with old carriages carrying women dressed in long skirts and large hats. All these evocations stimulate my feelings that I am not totally drifted from the Old World and sunk in the New one. However, what is incontestable, at the first sight of the night from my light house, I did irrevocably fall in love with this monstrous city.[60]

Bozidar Purich came to America from London (1957), where he was the president of the Yugoslav government in exile during World War II. Educated in Belgrade and Paris, he served as a diplomat for almost ten years in the United States (Washington, D.C., San Francisco, and Chicago). From the time of his arrival in this country, Purich held the position of the executive secretary of Serbian National Defense in Chicago and editor of the weekly *Liberty*. At the present time, he is on the editorial staff of *The American Srbobran* (Serbian Edition in Cyrillic characters), a daily published in Pittsburgh, Pennsylvania, in collaboration with the talented journalists, Yovan Bratich and Yovan Jovetich. In Yugoslavia Purich is particularly known as the author of the book of poetry *Galant Feasts* (1920); in America he excels in literary criticism.

In 1952, Purich published a series of articles dedicated to Dutchich in *The American Srbobran* (Serb Sentinel), trying to evaluate the poet as the creator of some audaciously innovative trends in Serbian poetry under the influence of French and classical literatures:

> Having assimilated all that the French culture was able to offer, Dutchich traced its eternal models in ancient Rome and Athens. Through long acquaintance with the Greek philosophers and poets he drew a conclusion that there is nothing new in the world, in the realm of thoughts, emotions and experiences—that everything was experimented with and analyzed prior to our time. The first monotheist and the first communist were discovered by Dutchich in the pagan world. The individual way in which this eternally same truth is expressed constitutes the unique new element.
>
> *Cities and Chimeras* written so poetically are worthy of the splendid Greek spirit and wisdom. Through all these literary strolls, Dutchich has preserved his character: nothing that would be contrary to his emotional life, taste and conviction affected him; he never was victimized by any lie, pose or infection. He always came back home with the same honesty characteristic of his native Hercegovina, fully experienced in the psychological domain and in the human depth, eager to leave a legacy of a rich treasure to his people. Our greatest contemporary poet, in essence a modern humanist, encyclopedist and moralist, Dutchich like Dositej (the celebrated Serbian writer in the eighteenth century) before him, shall be a man of enlightenment.[61]

The wealth of his life, multiple experience on the cultural plane, the depth of his literary heritage and the preeminence of his seigneurial personality place Purich, *homme honnête*, on the highest level in the Serbian culture in America today.

Mateja Matejich of Ohio State University is the gifted author of a collection of verse under the title *The Poems*[62] (written in Serbian, Cyrillic characters), published in 1964 with an introduction by Bozidar Purich. A priest also, Matejich is a prominent poet of purely Christian inspiration, intellectually powerful and convincing.

"On the Eve of the Publication" is a loose translation of the title of the poem that stands at the threshold of the collection:

> Like the young widows, in black veils,
> I am sending you, daughters of sorrow, to the people,
> To lament with them at every requiem,
> Eager to see your tears consoling those in agony.[63]

Revealing his conception of poetry in a bold and original way, the author is advising his *off-springs* to reject flattery and shabbiness. And, alluding to human hostility, they should come back home with broken wings symbolizing their mutual affinity. Being ennobled by suffering during the war and its aftermath, he is exceedingly vulnerable to human indifference and perfidy, as expressed in "The Encounters":

> My hand seeks another hand
> to grasp with a squeeze
> rooted in the heart,
> but encounters convulsive fingers.
>
> Sometimes, my soul is well
> overflowing, luminous, serene
> but without an outlet to flow,
> then all this strength withers,
> and the whole life fades,
> or, to bypass death,
> crumbles in droplets—
> in tears saturated with bitterness.[64]

The totality of exalting joy, "given to us by the whole thickness of life" [Giono], evaporates if not immediately shared, communicated without speculative restraint.

In "My Destiny," deceived by the depoetized present, the poet tries to find refuge in the past, but he is unable to dissipate the stormy clouds on his horizons:

> In a crowd, I am a clown like many others
> Who laughs boisterously and rejoices lightly,
> Then whips himself with sorrow and suffocates in tears
> In the subsequent prolonged nights.
>
> In my memory pure as a saint,
> The past entices only a sad smile
> Then in my soul, in twilight,
> A frozen sea of ruins sparkles.[65]

The impermeability of human destiny is masterfully evoked in the poem entitled "The Eyes," whose prophetic capability is inferior to spiritual insight:

> Two insatiable desires nourished by images,
> two rapacious hands always empty and full,
> two warm abysses, two alive wells—
> are my eyes.
> As from a nest, my glance
> like a butterfly lands and carelessly wanders—
> that's how I observe.
> And when the desire to see erupts,
> to plunge deeper and soar higher,
> I enslave the glare
> and close my eyes . . . .[66]

The diversity and the challenge of Matejich's themes are impressive: resurrection of the past, introspective investigation of the inner life, pessimistic war memories, duplicity of human nature, flow of life, cult of spirituality, and patriotism, never weeping, but lucid, virile and enlightened. "Fruits of solitude," a volume of poetry in manuscript deals predominantly with the transcendental philosophy which is one of his poetically creative obsessions.

Dragoslav Dragutinovich, former officer in the Yugoslav Royal Army, born in Belgrade, spent almost a decade in German captivity and European refugee camps. Armed with the wisdom extracted from his tragic experience, he arrived in America in 1949 to face an orientation in the New World. Stoically, Dragutinovich went through all the phases of a stormy life, which required the highest patriotic and ethical values. Revealing purity of soul and firmness of character under all circumstances cruelly imposed by destiny, he succeeded in becoming an historian of Golgotha of Serbia through a crucial period of almost forty years. His abundant literary output is impressive: three collections of short stories and three books of poetry, which is an unequaled success these days among American Serbs. The poet expresses impressions, feelings, symbolic visions and life's sound philosophy. Dragutinovich's poetry ranks among the best. It encompasses prewar explosiveness, horrors of the war and prison camps, Serbian nationalist resistance on the native soil, and many vicissitudes of the postwar period through the world. Always documented, this poetic chronicle detects a historical matter psychologically complex, seized in spontaneous immediacy by a lucid and talented witness.

His analysis of the prisoner's life is a series of moving events and details crystallized mostly through close observation. Saved from the voracity of time, they loom on every page of *Vibrations of the Soul.*[67] In a misanthropic mood, deceived by depraved human nature, the poet distrusts his fellowman. In the poem entitled "Despair," he stresses solidity and constancy of nature, opposed to the moral fragility of man:

Today, I believe in the fragrant flower
which blossoms through the garden of good
and evil human beings,
in quiet clouds on the azure skies
spreading joy above all fields,
and I believe in the innocent young bird
on a leafy branch
singing for all the same song heard yesterday.[68]

The inborn love for nature, passionately cultivated in his poetry and prose, is gently expressed in the poem "The Break of Day." The obscurity yields to the vigor of the penetrating light. As a salutary relief, dawn spreads its blessings after the violent nocturnal agitation. It is a deep contemplative poem immersed in a glimpse of a landscape poetically evoked:

As soon as dawn scatters its invigorating locks,
the shepherd of God's flock heralds the new day
and shelters the stars in a gilded pasture.
On the illuminated earth life erupts
sparrows chirp
men chatter
the wheat whispers, and the pines spread
their heavenly scent.[69]

"The Twilight" sheds the spiritual peacefulness inspired by an idyllic landscape, and a mythologically jubilant atmosphere created "when the solar spearmen disappear behind the hill":

The noise of the day calmed.
Above the ripe fields
awakened stars wove the golden veil.
On the river,
mutely, above the water,
accompanied by discreet reflections,
white birch trees dance
as naked nymphs.[70]

An incompleteness of involvement in the external, concrete world is caused by the lack of contact with nature and its rejuvenation in "Prisoner's Spring." A landscape being "a state of mind" experience in the "metallic paddock" affects the enslaved observer in a way comparable to a sterilized plant:

I see
the lukewarm sun warms the cold earth,
sowing God's blessings across the ploughed spaces,
and I hear the voices

of birds
and children.

They say that's how spring begins . . . .

. . . .

As yesterday, everything is deserted around here.

The spring did neither smile at me
nor rekindle my sad soul,
nor wipe up the gray wintry shadow.[7 1]

"A Dreamy Desire" suggestively revives the earthly life alienated from chastity. Eager to "relax under God's wing" far from "the stench, mouldy prisoner's hut," the poet views life behind 'the grave as the only salutary port:

I dream about solitude, heights, and celestial
azure . . .
Willing to escape from the mire,
to flee from the new hell called Earth,
and find peace somewhere far away,
where the muddy feet don't touch the soil,
where truth shines, love reigns,
and justice still lives.[7 2]

The elegiac tone of his filial appeal "Don't Wait for Me" denotes a life devoid of joy and perspective. As an insurmountable hindrance interposed between the poet and his mother, the hellish uncertainty fatally stands:

Don't spin the wool, my old mother,
gray because of me,
in vain you wait on the edge of the village,
with a face stricken by the nostalgic ardor. . . .
don't pray for me on Sundays
don't kneel beneath our icon. . . .

Between us the absence is triumphant,
the ice accumulates under the unknown trellis.
We don't welcome anymore the swallows and Aprils,
the cherry's snow doesn't sift on our beaten tracks.[7 3]

Among our youngest writers, Steve Tesich is one of the most prominent. Born in Yugoslavia in 1942, he moved at the age of fourteen with his family to the United States. He studied at Indiana University (where he earned the B.A.), in the Soviet Union (on an NDFL Fellowship), and at Columbia University (where he earned the M.A. in Russian Literature). Tesich has written short stories, a novel and a play, *The Predicators*, done as a workshop production at the American Academy of Dramatic Arts in New York City. The author's other play, *The Carpenters*, was recently produced by the American Place Theatre and televised nationally. In *The Carpenters*, conceived in existentialist gloom, Tesich depicts the decay of a modern decadent family. The impenetrableness of this labyrinth without exit is reminiscent of Zola's *L'Assommoir* and its vulgarity of atmosphere:

> We're no better than a couple of rooms. . . . two extra rooms. . . . and rooms can't talk to one another or hear one another.
>
> . . . .
>
> We were happy because we hoped. We based all our hopes on the family. We were a couple of people living together waiting for a family to come along and make us one. . . . Then we got a family and we reversed ourselves completely and started looking back to those happy days when it was just two of us. Our hopes were excuses and our happy memories are lies.[74]

Eroded by sloth and other vices, inherited and developed, the family sinks into a laxity of morals. Due to these evils, the infernal abyss between parents and children becomes an open pit. Revealed in the absolute lack of communication and an unavoidable boredom, the initial blemish spreads fatally. And the numerical expansion of Carpenters finally equals the shrinking of all moral principles to the total annihilation of the family. Progressive oblivion of honesty and a light sociological inquest into filth are shaded by the naturalistic and existentialist moods of pessimism and paralysis.

The other renowned representative of our younger generation is Charles Simic, born in Belgrade in 1938. The early migration to Paris with his mother at the age of ten and then a year later to America to rejoin his father was beneficial to his eventful adolescence. Simic studied at Chicago University (1956-1959) and at New York University until 1961. After his U.S. military service in France as an American soldier (1961-1963), he received the B.A. in 1964 and became a graduate student at New York University.

The very diversified professions that he experienced in his youth deepened the poet's contemplative bent. The last in a series is his teaching career in English at California State University in Hayward. Profusely translating from Russian, French and Serbo-Croatian, he steadily cultivates an invigorating contact with foreign literature on a comparative basis.

Prolific poet *par excellence*, Simic has published an enviable number of books of verse in English. His poems, seen in reputable anthologies, underline Simic's eminent standing in America's literature of today. Numerous contributions to the reviews of the avant-garde enhance his dynamic contemporaneity. In the multiplicity of his subdued lights, Baudelaire's spleen is often detectable. The thickness of daily sameness and heredity's phantom—"secluded spider"—loom often through his well balanced stanzas:

> Is it in my life, that walk
> Under the flowering plums:
>
> Their lazy rustling,
> The earth a censer.

Meadows tipped by the wind
A deep breath and they enter:

Airy, softly untangled webs
Of an unknown long secluded spider;

And you by my side, inaudible.
It was simply like that.[75]

Well interwoven in an original pattern, a mixture of Surrealistic and Symbolist elements lends to his poetry a charm of clarity, in spite of its modern structure. Spared of excesses imposed by the European movement, Simic impresses his reader with logical interpretations in spite of innovative trends. Automatic writing, psychical automatism, lack of aesthetic preoccupations and of control exercised by reason, all these defects of the revolutionary school are not in Simic's spectrum. Neither are Surrealistic experimentation based on corrupting dreams, nor allegorical political implications.

The opacity of Surrealism, often hermetic, dissipates under impact of many Symbolist touches projected from his volatile imagination. In "Stone,"[76] Simic dreams about his metamorphosis in a stone, where he would be fortified against indiscreet glances and humiliations of a carnivorous crowd. This isolationism alludes to the Parnassian impassibility and fiercely sacred pride, and explains the poet's eagerness to decipher the "bewildered fishes" probing the inner vibration of the stone. The defiant solidity of the rock and its stoic muteness intrigue the poet confronted with an ontological phenomenon of an apparently petrified mystery:

I have seen sparks fly out
When two stones are rubbed,
So perhaps it is not dark inside after all;
Perhaps there is a moon shining
From somewhere, as though behind a hill—
Just enough light to make out
The strange writings, the star-charts
On the inner walls.[77]

* * *

The inclusion of brief selections from all authors in this review may prove useful as an initiation into this ethnic heritage. These excerpts illustrate principal facets of the Serbian contribution to the total American literature. The arrangement of authors is mainly chronological. It roughly represents, in order of birth, their most significant influence on the literary evolution of American-Serbian literature.

The section devoted to each author begins with a biographical sketch and a succinct critical commentary to make him more accessible. The deliberately limited number of writers is imposed by the requirement of this review and its bicentennial spirit. For the same reason, regretfully, other authors of talent and justified popularity have been omitted from this essay. The history of the war itself, its martyrdom, and the very valuable political outline of accelerated events connected with the struggle of the Serbian people are also excluded with deep regrets due to the concision required.

Texas Tech University

NOTES

[1] André Maurois, *Histoire des Etats-Unis 1492-1828* (New York: Editions de la Maison Française, 1943), p. 11. This and subsequent translations are mine, with the exception of the excerpts from Govorchin, Karlo, Roucek, Radosavljevich, Pupin, Velimirovich, Tesich and Simic.

[2] J. Hector St. John de Crèvecoeur, *Letters from an American Farmer*, quoted in Gerald Gilbert Govorchin, *Americans from Yugoslavia: A Survey of Yugoslav Immigrants in the United States* (Gainesville: Univ. of Florida Press, 1961), p. 3.

[3] Karl Malden, Academy Award recipient for the Best Supporting Actor in *A Streetcar Named Desire*, had his first stage experience in Gary, Indiana, in the American-Serbian theatre where his father, Peter Sekulovich, was one of the leading performers.

[4] Maurois, p. 13.

[5] Ibid., pp. 13-14.

[6] Milan Karlo, "Our Pioneer Parents—The Legacy They Left Us," *Almanac American Srbobran* (Pittsburgh: Serb National Federation, 1963), pp. 82-90.

[7] Joseph S. Roucek, *Slavonic Encyclopaedia* (New York: The Philosophical Library, Inc., 1949), p. 1069.

[8] During the Balkan War in 1912-1913 and World War I in 1914-1918, American Serbs proved their devotion to the native country by sending 20,000 volunteers in the struggle against tyranny.

[9] Alexis de Tocqueville, *De la Démocratie en Amérique* (Paris: Union Générale d'Editions, 1963), p. 54.

[10] Proka Jovkich-Nestor Zucni, "Chant à la guenille" (Poem to a Beggar), *Anthologie de la Poésie Yougoslave des XIXe et XXe siècles*, ed. Miodrag Ibrovac (Paris: Libraire Delagrave, 1935), p. 242.

[11] Ibid.

[12] Ibid.

[13] Ibid.

[14] Paul R. Radosavljevich, *Who Are the Slavs?* 2 vols. (Boston: The Gorham Press, 1919).

[15] Ibid., I, 315.

[16] Ibid., I, 329.

[17] Ibid., I, 332.

[18] Ibid.

[19] Ibid., I, 330.

[20] Ibid., I, 331.

[21] Ibid., I, 333.

[22] Ibid., I, 334.

[23] Ibid., I, 352.

[24] Manuscripts in possession of Leposava Dutchich, Gary, Indiana.

[25] Yovan Dutchich, *Lyrical Poems* (Pittsburgh: Serb National Federation, 1943).

[26] "The Road," ibid., p. 14.

[27] Ibid.

[28] Ibid., p. 15.

[29] "The Pious Poem," ibid., p. 17.

[30] "To God," ibid., p. 27.

[31] "The Poem," ibid., p. 40.

[32] Yovan Dutchich, *Count Sava Vladislavich: A Serbian Diplomat at the Royal Court of Peter the Great and Katherine the First* (Pittsburgh: Serb National Federation, 1942).

[33] Ibid., p. i.

[34] Yovan Dutchich, *Assembled Works*, Posthumous Manuscripts, comp. and ed. Yovan Djonovich and Peter D. Bubresko (Chicago: Palandech's Press, 1951).

[35] Yovan Dutchich, *Assembled Works: The Morning Seen from Leutar*. Vol. IV is entitled *My Fellow Travelers* (Sarajevo: "Svjetlost," 1969; Belgrade: "Prosveta," 1969). Vol. VI is entitled *A Path Along the Road* (Sarajevo: "Svjetlost," 1969; Belgrade: "Prosveta," 1969).

[36] Michael Pupin, *From Immigrant to Inventor* (New York: Scribner's, 1960).

[37] Ibid., p. v.

[38] Ibid., p. 385.

[39] Ibid., p. 397.

[40] Bishop Nicholai D. Velimirovich, *The Life of St. Sava* (Libertyville: Serbian Eastern Orthodox Diocese, 1951), p. ix.

[41] Ibid., pp. ix-x.

[42] Milan M. Petrovich, *The Petrified Tears* (Trieste, Italy: Serbian Eastern Orthodox Parish, 1962).

[43] Ibid., p. 85.

[44] Ibid., p. 133.

[45] Ibid., p. 86.

[46] Ljubica Grkovich-Boljanich, "On the Road," *The Swan's Songs* (Chicago: Palandech & Sons, 1961), p. 23.

[47] "The Blooming Branches," ibid., p. 30.

[48] Grkovich-Boljanich, *The Swan's Songs*.

[49] "Every Night," ibid., p. 42.

[50] "The Thoughts," ibid., p. 29.

[51] "To My Mother," ibid., p. 53.

[52] Yovan Kontich, *Through the Fire and Tears* (Pittsburgh: American Srbobran, 1946).

[53] Yovan Kontich, *On the Road to Exile* (Chicago: "Obod" Printing & Publishing, 1956).

[54] "That's America," ibid., p. 181.

[55] Ibid.

[56] "The War Without a Truce," ibid., p. 162.

[57] Ibid., p. 162.

[58] Anka Godjevac-Subbotich, *From Three Continents* (Melbourne, Australia: Unification Printers and Publishers, 1961).

[59] Ibid., p. 110.

[60] Ibid., pp. 110-11.

[61] Bozidar Purich, "Yovan Dutchich: Literary Portrait," *The American Srbobran*, Serbian Edition, 15 January 1952, p. 3.

[62] Mateja Matejich, *The Poems* (Munich: Iskra, 1964).

[63] "On the Eve of the Publication," ibid., p. 11.

[64] "The Encounters," ibid., p. 33.

[65] "My Destiny," ibid., p. 50.

[66] "The Eyes," ibid., p. 31.

[67] Dragoslov Dragutinovich, *Vibrations of the Soul* (Melbourne: Unification Printers and Publishers, 1968).

[68] "Despair," ibid., p. 86.

[69] "The Break of Day," ibid., p. 20.

[70] "The Twilight," ibid., p. 19.

[71] "Prisoner's Spring," ibid., p. 112.

[72] "A Dreamy Desire," ibid., p. 119.

[73] "Don't Wait for Me," ibid., p. 96.

[74] Steve Tesich, *The Carpenters* (New York: Dramatists Play Service, Inc., 1971), pp. 34-55.

[75] Charles Simic, *White* (Berkeley: New Rivers Press, 1972), p. 27.

[76] Charles Simic, *The Major Young Poets*, Al Lee, ed. (New York: World Publishing Co.; 1971), p. 85.

[77] "Stone," ibid., p. 85.

Slovenian-American Literature

Giles Edward Gobetz

ABSTRACT

The Slovenian-American literary orientations, themes, and accomplishments are manifestations of the "Old World" traits transplanted to America and gradually integrated into American literature and culture. The ideological literary "camps," which had prevailed in Slovenia, have to a considerable extent survived in America, especially among the immigrant authors, and have been used as a basis for the classification of the Slovenian American *literati* along an ideological continuum, ranging from religious and Catholic literature, through a substantial middle-range area of relative ideological neutrality, to progressive, socialist and, finally, radical literary orientations. The leading Slovenian American authors Frederic Baraga, Bernard Smolnikar, Etbin Kristan, Louis Adamic, Frank Mlakar, Karl Mauser, James Rausch, and Joseph Kalar have gained national and international recognition. The Slovenian American *literati*, being influenced by the Slovenian, American, and other cultures, have, in turn, exerted an influence on American literature, culture, and politics. Starting in the 1680's with the travel and ethnographic reports of the Slovenian missionary and explorer Anton Kappus and culminating in the religious and Slovenian-Indian literature in the nineteenth century, Slovenian American literature has reached its modern, secular culmination toward the middle of the twentieth century in the highly influential works of Louis Adamic and the Dostoevskian literary expression of Frank Mlakar, both of whom dealt with predominantly Slovenian and other ethnic themes and helped to popularize the view of America as a Nation of Nations—a view which has recently been expanded and transcended by James Rausch's work, *A Family of Nations: An Expanded View of Patriotism . . . A New Dedication to Humanity.* (GEG)

The Slovenians, or the Slovenes, are the westernmost Slavic poeple who currently number a little over 1,800,000 in their native land, Slovenia, the northernmost republic of Yugoslavia, and close to a million (including about 500,000 in the United States) in all other countries. Because of their small size and centuries of political subjugation, the Slovenians have been

547

relatively little known in America and the world.[1] Who, then, are the Slovenians and what are some of their historic and cultural characteristics which may have influenced their literature in the New World?

According to Bernard Newman, the noted English author,

> Slovenia's masters ranged from Charlemagne to Napoleon, but the people clung tenaciously to their own culture and language. . . . The Slovenes used to share with the Scandinavians the reputation of being the best-read people in the world—the number of books read per head of the population was four times the British figure. . . . It was manifestly impossible for a small people to gain and hold its freedom when surrounded by acquisitive great powers, but the Slovenes, determined to secure the greatest possible degree of home rule, concentrated on cultural rather than on political liberty. It was a miracle of survival almost without parallel. The boundaries of Slovenia have never been based on physical features; they rest upon the moral strength of its people.[2]

In De Bray's *Guide to the Slavonic Languages* we read that "literacy in Slovenia reaches almost 100 per cent and their beautiful literature is often characterized by a gentle melancholy or a positive and constructive optimism."[3] Louis Adamic tells us that in Slovenia "most of the streets are named after poets, essayists, novelists, dramatists, and grammarians,"[4] and R. H. Markham, an American author who spent some time in Slovenia, compares the coffee houses in Slovenian cities with the reading rooms in American public libraries.[5]

In their millenium-long struggle for survival as a distinct nationality group the Slovenians apparently have concentrated on their Slovenian language and, since the early days of the Protestant Reformation, also on their literature as the crucially important vehicles of their national consciousness and culture and their primary means of survival as a distinct people. This situation gave the Slovenian *literati* a somewhat disproportionally important position in the Slovenian society at home. To a great extent, this same orientation has also been transplanted to America, especially among the Slovenian-born immigrants.[6]

Among other factors which have played an important role in the Slovenian national consciousness and prestige is their early democracy, which flourished in their northernmost province of Carinthia many centuries before the world-famous Magna Carta of 1215 came into being. This ancient Slovenian democracy and the ritual of the installation of the dukes of Carinthia were described in superlative terms by many famous historians and philosophers, among them Aeneas Silvius Piccolomini who later became Pope Pius II, and Jean Bodin whose book, *Les six livres de la Republique*, published in 1576, has frequently been considered as the greatest work in political science published since Aristotle's *Politics*.[7] According to this ritual, which was described by Piccolomini as "something unique and unheard of in other lands" and by Bodin as being "without an equal in the world," the newly elected Duke of Carinthia was installed and recognized as the ruler of this northernmost region of Slovenia only after he had publicly and solemnly promised his electors and subsequent subjects that he would be a good judge, a just and courageous protector of his country, and a compassionate supporter of widows and orphans.[8]

As shown by Joseph Felicijan, Bodin's book was read by Thomas Jefferson, who initialed Bodin's description of the ancient Slovenian Carinthian democracy. The democratic ritual which was practiced in Carinthia between the seventh and early fifteenth centuries represented an early concrete historical precedent of the social contract theory—*the* theory which provided the ideological, legal, and moral justification for the American Declaration of Independence and subsequent revolution. Since Jefferson initialed a text and made marginal notations only when he considered it as being of exceptional significance, Felicijan maintains that Jefferson singled out this democratic Slovenian ritual as a historical precedent of the social contract theory and as one of the important elements on which the Declaration of Independence was based.[9]

On the other extreme is a conservative evaluation by a Harvard historian Crane Brinton who concedes to Slovenians a minor, but a real role in the development of our Western democratic institutions. In Brinton's opinion,

> ... the picturesque Slovenian ceremony was reasonably well known to political philosophers, and indeed through Bodin known to Thomas Jefferson. This Slovenian ceremony was a part of a complex tradition, a minor variable but a real one, in the cluster of ideas that ... went into the making of modern Western democratic institutions.[10]

Another founding father of our Nation, Benjamin Franklin, was also somewhat dependent on a modest Slovenian writer, grammarian, and translator, Janez (in Slovenian), Johann (in German) or John (in English) Primec (or Primic), who not only discussed Franklin in Slovenian, but also translated him into German, and thus helped to popularize the thought of this wisest American in several European countries in the early years of the United States of America.[11]

Similarly, a number of prominent American writers and poets heard and recorded the voice of Slovenia, among them Henry Wadsworth Longfellow whose *Hyperion: A Romance* includes "The Story of Brother Bernardus," based on the life and works of the Slovenian American immigrant writer and scholar, Bernard Smolnikar, who advocated a universal Church, a world government, and universal peace and justice before, during, and after the American Civil War and whose works in English and German have been preserved at Harvard and other leading centers of learning.[12]

After this sketchy introduction of Slovenia and a few examples of cross-fertilization between America, one of the greatest and politically most powerful countries, and Slovenia, one of the smallest and politically most subjugated countries, both of which, however, have hungered for freedom and progress, let us now take a glance at Slovenian writers and poets who lived and worked in America and at their role in American literature and culture.

* * *

As might be expected, the earliest contributions made by the Slovenian American writers consisted of travel reports and ethnographic works. The earliest known such Slovenian contribution is that of Mark Anton Kappus (1657-1717), a Slovenian professor and missionary who was one of the three principal explorers in *Viages a la Nacion Pima en California* (Travels to the Nation of Pima in California) in 1694.[13] Kappus also wrote *Enthusiasmus sive solemnes ludi poetici* (Enthusiasm, or Solemn Poetical Plays, 1708), consisting of 276 chronograms and representing an early attempt in America at combining poetry, history, and ethnography. In 1701, according to Herbert E. Bolton and other authorities, Kappus sent to Europe, together with various reports, also the very first geographic map which informed the world that California was not an island, as it had been believed until then, but a solid part of the American mainland.[14]

The second most famous Slovenian American ethnographic work is a book about the American Indians, written by the Slovenian immigrant missionary and the first Bishop of Marquette, Frederic Baraga (1797-1868). This book was first published in 1837 in simultaneous German, French, and Slovenian editions.[15] It was followed by a similar, but more comprehensive work on the Indians of North America, *Die Indianer in Nord Amerika*, written in German by the Slovenian missionary, Franc Pirc (or Franz Pierz, 1785-1880), and published in St. Louis in 1855. Travel and ethnographic reports, published in books and in Slovenian, American, Austrian, and other magazines, journals, and newspapers, continued throughout the nineteenth and twentieth centuries, ranging from Baraga and Pirc to our contemporaries Joseph Grdina,[16] Andrew Kobal,[17] and Jim Klobuchar.[18]

The modern Slovenian American culmination of this genre of literature was reached with *The Native's Return*, by the Slovenian immigrant author Louis Adamic (1899-1951),[19] which was the Book-of-the-Month Club selection for February of 1934 and, according to Henry A. Christian, became an instant success and transformed Adamic into a national celebrity.[20] Thus Adamic presented, for the first time, a glimpse of Slovenia to the larger American reading public.

As one might assume, the Slovenian literary traditions have been, to a considerable degree, transplanted to America and have exerted a strong influence on the Slovenian-born immigrant *literati*. In addition to a high value placed on literature and a relatively high status awarded by the

Slovenian society to its writers and poets, Slovenia has also been characterized by an unusually pronounced emphasis on ideological distinctions among the so-called "camps" or "schools." The conservative Catholicism and innovative liberalism has been the strongest ideological subdivision in the Slovenian literature, as well as in economics, politics, and other aspects of the Slovenian national life. This strongly pronounced ideological continuum, ranging from the religious and Catholic-inspired literature on the one hand, through the relatively "neutral" writings toward the middle, to progressive (liberal), socialist, and radical orientations at the left side of the continuum, has also characterized the Slovenian American ethnic literature, particularly that of the Slovenian-born *literati*.[21]

Among the oldest and perhaps the most persistent of these ideologically based categories is the Slovenian Catholic religious literature, whose first and most prolific Slovenian American representative was Bishop Frederic Baraga. During his busy American career as missionary, bishop, and scholar (1831-1868), Baraga wrote a large volume of meditations and several prayer books, epistles, and pastoral letters in the Otchipwe (Ojibway) and Ottawa Indian dialects, and in the Slovenian, German, and French languages.[22] Several generations of Slovenian American missionaries and priests, as well as nuns and laymen, continued to contribute to this genre of literature up to the present time, among them Kazimir Zakrajšek, O.F.M. (1878-1958), with his many prayer books, meditations, and religious booklets and articles;[23] Bishop Gregory Rožman (1883-1959), whose serialized spiritual thoughts and articles appeared in many Slovenian Catholic magazines, almanacs, and newspapers;[24] and our contemporaries, Joseph Vovk, best known for his translations into Slovenian of religious poetry, psalms, and hymns;[25] Joann Birsa, Edward Krasovich, Valentine Spendov, O.F.M., Frank Perkovich, and many others who have helped to popularize Slovenian religious songs, often in English translation, and music in America;[26] and Fortunat Zorman, O.F.M., current editor of the Slovenian language *Ave Maria* magazine and of an annual almanac of the same name, published by the Slovenian Franciscan Fathers of Lemont, Illinois.[27]

Among the noteworthy contributions to the Slovenian American religious literature one should also mention such works as John C. Gruden's *The Mystical Christ*, published in London, England, and St. Louis, Missouri, in 1936; George Trunk's translation from Slovenian into English of France Veber's theodicy text, *There Is a God* (1942); Anthony Merkun's ecumenical work, *Cirilmetodijska ideja* (The Cyril-Methodian Idea, 1952), and Charles Wolbang's continuous series on the Slovenian Catholic Missions throughout the world, published in *Ameriška Domovina*, the Cleveland-based Slovenian daily newspaper.[28]

Although nearly all of the aproximately 500,000 Slovenians now living in the United States are Catholic (practical or nominal, as the case may be), Slovenian Americans have also contributed to non-Catholic religious literature in America. Thus, Andreas Bernardus Smolnikar (1795-1869), a Slovenian immigrant who had started his career as a Catholic priest and theologian, later became an ardent, anti-Catholic religious reformer who spread his ideas not only as an orator at numerous American religious and civic affairs and in conferences with American political and civic leaders, but also as a prolific writer of works advocating a universal religion and a world government, with universal justice and peace, the emancipation of women and slaves, and utopian socialism. The author of at least seven books, a dozen booklets, and a large number of articles and epistles,[29] Smolnikar was a blend of brilliance and eccentricity, a founder of several millennial communities, and a very colorful person who became the subject of several literary essays by Longfellow and others and was referred to, probably half-seriously and half-jokingly, as the "thirteenth apostle."[30]

A century after Smolnikar, Joseph L. Mihelic, a Slovenian American professor of Old Testament, Literature, and Languages at Dubuque Theological Seminary, has gained distinction as a Presbyterian theologian and writer who, in addition to other works, contributed over forty articles to the *Interpreter's Bible Dictionary* and the *Encyclopedia Britannica*.[31]

The Slovenian religious writers are followed on the ideological continuum by those Catholic *literati* who dealt with secular themes from a Catholic point of view or wrote under the Catholic label. From several scores of these Catholic Slovenian American writers and poets only a few leading names can here be mentioned, among them the following missionaries and priests: Oton Skola, O.F.M. (1805-1879), a talented writer, poet, and painter; Ivan Čebul (1832-1898), author of essays, articles, and poems in Slovenian, English, French, Greek, and Indian languages; Msgr. Joseph Buh (1833-1922), founder and vicar general of the Diocese of Duluth, writer and editor of *Amerikanski Slovenec* (The American Slovenian); Simon Lampe, O.S.B. (1865-1939), writer, educator, and an authority on the Otchipwe language; George Trunk (1870-1973), writer, historian, translator, and painter (who was at the time of his death the oldest Catholic priest in America); Andrew Smrekar (1871-1939), poet, writer, and a prolific translator who, among other works, translated Shakespeare into Slovenian; Hugo Bren, O.F.M. (1881-1953), theologian, writer, translator, and editor; Kazimir Zakrajšek, O.F.M. (1878-1959), author of numerous short stories, novelettes, dramas, and plays, and founder and editor of *Ave Maria*, a monthly magazine and annual almanac; John Oman (1879-1966), contributor to Catholic Slovenian American magazines and newspapers;

Bernard Ambrožič, O.F.M. (1892-1973), editor and author of numerous short stories and novelettes; Alexander Urankar, O.F.M. (1902-1952), poet; Vital Vodusek (1906-1973), best known for his collections of poems, *Pesmi* (Poems, 1928) and *Poezije* (Poetry, 1937); and Edward Surtz, S.J. (1909-1973), writer, scholar, and literary critic, and an internationally known authority on St. Thomas More.[32]

Among the living Slovenian American Catholic priests and nuns (1976), the following leading authors of secular works from the Catholic point of view stand out: Msgr. John L. Zaplotnik, the most prolific biographer of Slovenian American missionaries and contributor to numerous Slovenian and American magazines, journals, almanacs, and newspapers;[33] Basil Valentin, O.F.M., former editor of *Ave Maria* in America and current editor of *Misli* (The Thoughts) in Australia, a novelist, storyteller, children's author, and poet;[34] William Furlan, best known for his book *In Charity Unfeigned* (1952); Bishop James S. Rausch (Slovenian on his mother's side), general secretary of the National Conference of Catholic Bishops and of the United States Catholic Conference, author and editor of influential works on human rights, the Catholic Church, American society, and international affairs;[35] Sisters Bernard Coleman and Verona LaBud, authors of *Masinaigans: The Little Book* (1972); and Sister Lavoslava Turk, contributor to Catholic magazines and papers and author of *Pesem šolske sestre* (The Song of a School Sister), a collection of short stories, published in 1974.

Among laymen, several Slovenian American writers and poets have been classified as Catholic authors. Included in this category are Anton Klinc (1862-1949), writer and editor of *Narodna Beseda* (Our Nation's Voice) and *Nova Domovina* (New Homeland); James Debevec (1887-1952), humorist, writer, and editor of *Sloga* (Harmony), *Glas SDZ* (Voice of SDZ), and *Ameriška Domovina* (American Home); Louis Pirc (1888-1939), writer and editor of *Nova Domovina* and *Ameriška Domovina*; Ivan Zupan (1875-1950), editor of *Glasilo KSKJ* (The KSKJ Herald) and poet, best known for his collection of poems *Iz življenja za življenje* (From Life for Life, 1935); John Jerich (1894-1973), editor of *Amerikanski Slovenec* (The American Slovenian), *Baragova Pratika* (Baraga's Almanac), and *Novi Svet* (The New World), and author of numerous essays, articles, and a collection of short stories;[36] and Zdravko Novak (1909-1971), author of such novels as *Pota božja* (God's Ways, 1957) and *Utrinki* (Fragments, 1959), of several dramatizations, and of over 200 short stories and articles.[37]

Among the living Slovenian American Catholic *literati* (1976) the following names stand out: Stanley Zupan, former English editor of *Glasilo KSKJ*, of *Marquette News*, and of *Skyline*, the literary quarterly of Cleveland College, a talented author of short stories and essays; Ivan Račič, former editor of *Amerikanski Slovenec*, writer, and musician; Marie Prisland, writer and columnist, widely known for her book of "collections and recollections," *From Slovenia to America*, published in 1968; Ferry Bukvic,. storyteller and novelist, best known for his novel *Brezdomci* (The Homeless, 1948), a penetrating analysis of the uprooted victims of war; Fred Orehek, editorial writer for *The Chicago Tribune* and author of short stories and portraits of Slovenian Americans; Ludvik Puš, author of two books of memoirs, including *Klasje v viharju* (Harvest in the Tempest, 1970); Mirko Javornik, author of several neorealist works; and Milena Soukal, Rose Mary Prosen, Marian Jakopič, and Eric Kovačič, poets.[38]

The most prolific living Slovenian American Catholic writer and poet is Karl Mauser (1918-), who came to America in 1950 as a refugee and has gained international recognition as author of over twenty novels, of several dramas, and a large number of novelettes. His many short stories and poems have been published in Slovenian magazines, almanacs, and newspapers in both Americas, Europe, and Australia.[39]

Closer to the "middle range" or "neutral" orientation of the ideological continuum we also find, in addition to hundreds of Slovenian American authors in such fields as science, education, medicine, and related areas, several Slovenian American *literati*, among them: Frank Sakser (1876-1961), writer and essayist and editor of *Glas Naroda* (The People's Voice) and of *Slovensko-Amerikanski Koledar* (Slovenian American Almanac); Frank Kerže (1876-1961), author of many novelettes, essays, short stories, and poems, and editor of the humorist magazine *Komar* (Mosquito), *Glasilo SNPJ* (The SNPJ Herald), and of the literary magazine *Čas* (Time); Anton Terbovec (1882-1962), humorist, essayist, storyteller, and editor of *Nova Doba* (New Era); Dr. Frank J. Kern (1887-), editor of *Glasnik* (The Herald) and *Clevelandska Amerika* (Cleveland's America), and author of an English-Slovenian Dictionary (*Angleško-slovenski besednjak*, 1919), of an English-Slovenian Reader (*Angleško-slovensko berilo*, 1926), of many articles on health and medicine, and of a very valuable book of memoirs, *Spomini*, published in 1937; Ivan Zorman (1889-1957), composer and the leading Slovenian American poet, widely known among Slovenians for his collections *Poezije* (Poetry, 1919), *Pesmi* (Poems, 1922), *Lirični spevi* (Lyric Poems, 1925), *Slovene Poetry* (1928), *Pota ljubezni* (The Pathways of Love, 1931), and *Iz novega sveta* (From the New World, 1938).[40]

Others in this category are Janko Rogelj (1895-1974), editor of *Enakopravnost* (Equality) and author of numerous articles, essays, and poems, including three collections of short stories and poems; Vatro Grill (1899-1976), editor of *Enakopravnost*, columnist, translator, and author of a book of memoirs, *Med dvema svetovoma* (Between Two Worlds, 1976); Andrew Kobal (1899-) who, in addition to his many scientific works, wrote two books on his world-wide travels, numerous short stories and essays, and fifteen dramas; Ivan Jontez (1902-), editor of the literary magazine *Cankarjev Glasnik* (Cankar's Herald) and a talented novelist, storyteller, and poet, best known for his books *Senca preko pota* (A Shadow Across My Path, 1940), *Jutro brez sonca* (Morning Without Sun, 1949), and *Trouble on East Green Street* (1956); Anthony J. Klancar (1908-), essayist, translator, and journalist; Frank Mlakar (1913-1967), an exceptionally gifted storyteller, poet, and novelist whose book, *He, the Father* (1950), transformed him into a nationally known writer; Ben Kocivar (1916-), former senior editor of *Look* magazine, writer, and commentator; Robert Debevec (1918-), a talented author of short stories and articles, as well as of two legal books; William Horvat (1919-), former editor of *Journal of American Aviation Historical Society*, widely known for his book *Above the Pacific* (1966); and Dr. Bernard Jerman (1921-), scholar, biographer, and literary critic, best known in America and England for his book, *The Young Disraeli* (1960).[41]

A more comprehensive overview should also discuss such writers, poets, reporters, or translators as Joseph Ambrožič, John Arnež, Paul Borstnik, Mary Frankovich Cassidy, Jim Debevec, Frank Dolence, Robert Dolgan, Anthony Garbas, John Gottlieb, Janko Grampovčan, Joseph Gregorich, William Heiliger, Jacob Hocevar, Mary Grill Ivanush, Frances Jazbec, Richard Juvancic, Ivan Kapel, Joseph Kess, Frank Kolaric, Edward Krasovich, Rado Lencek, Corinne Leskovar, Ludwig Leskovar, Vinko Lipovec, James Mally, John Sesek-Nielsen, Albina Novak, Tony Petkovsek, Josephine Petrič, Julia Pirc, Ludwig Potokar, Edwin Primoshich, Antoine Rezek, Elsie Rudman, Antoinette Simcic, Frank Sodnikar, Rado Staut, Frank Suhadolnik, Rick Sustaric, Bogumil Vošnjak, Joseph Zelle, and, especially, Nada Skerly, former *Time* magazine reporter and an award-winning writer on the aged; Stanley Modic, current executive editor of *Business Week* and former editor of *Our Voice*; and Margot Klima, editor of *Our Voice* and executive editor of the *Clevelander* magazine.[42]

Many works of Louis Adamic are ideologically "neutral" (i.e., neither rightist nor leftist, neither pro-Catholic nor pro-Socialist), while some of his books have been classified as progressive, socialist, or leftist, depending on the values and orientations of groups or persons who provided the label. Adamic came to America at the age of fifteen and has become the best known Slovenian American writer. Henry A. Christian compiled an impressive but, inevitably, incomplete list of 564 titles written by Adamic, including books, pamphlets, articles, forewords, and other contributions. Christian also lists over 500 items by other American and European authors, dealing with the life and works of Louis Adamic.

Among Adamic's most important works are the following books: *Dynamite: The Story of Class Violence in America* (1931), *Laughing in the Jungle: The Autobiography of an Immigrant in America* (1932), *The Native's Return: An American Immigrant Visits Yugoslavia and Discovers His Old Country* (1934), *Grandsons: The Story of American Lives* (1935), *Cradle of Life: The Story of One Man's Beginnings* (1936), *The House of Antigua: A Restoration* (1937), *My America: 1928-1938* (1938), *From Many Lands* (1940), *Two-Way Passage* (1941), *What's Your Name?* (1942), *My Native Land* (1943), *A Nation of Nations* (1945), *Dinner at the White House (1946), and Eagle and the Roots* (1952). Adamic was also editor of *Common Ground* and of the *Peoples of America Series*. A master of prose and a very influential popular historian, sociologist, social philosopher, critic, and reformer, he has gained national and international fame, as well as criticism and hostility which ultimately cost him his life.[43]

In our present overview, Adamic represents the transition from the "neutral," "middle range" orientation to the progressive and socialist camps—a somewhat ambiguous position which he shares with a number of other authors, such as Kerže, Grill, Rogelj, and Jontez. The leaders of the progressive and socialist camps (where the two labels have often been used interchangeably) were Etbin Kristan (1867-1953), editor of *Svoboda* (Freedom), *Rdeči Prapor* (Red Standard), and *Zarja* (The Dawn) in Europe, and of *Ameriški Družinski Koledar* (American Family Almanac), *Proletarec* (The Proletarian) and *Cankarjev Glasnik* (Cankar's Herald) in America, and author of many volumes of poems, short stories, dramas, novels, and novelettes;[44] Joseph Zavertnik (1896-1929), editor of *Glas Svobode* (The Voice of Freedom), *Proletarec, Glasilo SNPJ, Slovenski Delavski Koledar* (Slovenian Workers' Almanac), and *Prosveta* (Enlightenment), best known for his comprehensive volume *Ameriški Slovenci* (American Slovenians, 1925); Martin Konda (1872-1922) and Frank Medica (1875-1955), editors of *Glas Svobode* and *Mir* (Peace);[45] Ivan Molek (1882-1962), editor of *Glasnik* (Herald) and *Prosveta*, storyteller, translator, and author of *Dva svetova* (Two Worlds, 1932), *Veliko mravljišče* (The Huge Anthill, 1934), and *Sesuti stolp* (The Tower That Collapsed, 1935);[46] Frank Zaitz (1888-1967), editor of *Ameriški Družinski Koledar, Majski Glas* (The Voice of May), and *Proletarec*, and a prolific author of essays, short stories, and articles about Slovenian Americans;[47] Frank Magajna (1895-1971), novelist, satirist, and translator into Slovenian from English and French;[48] Katka Zupančič (1889-1967), who wrote over 300 poems, five dramas, and 137 short stories and articles;[49] Jack Tomsic (1897-), a worker-poet whose poems were published in various progressive magazines and papers and appeared in a collection, *Pognale so na tujih tleh* (They've Grown in a Foreign Land, 1968); and Anna Krasna

(1900-), former editor of *Glas Naroda*, translator, and author of numerous short stories, novelettes, and poems, including a collection of poems, *Za lepše dni* (For a Better Future, 1950).[50]

Many authors of the progressive-socialist orientation also contributed their short stories, novelettes, poems, and articles to *Ameriški Družinski Koledar* (American Family Almanac, 1915-1950), *Majski Glas* (The Voice of May, 1933-1945), *Cankarjev Glasnik* (Cankar's Herald, 1937-1943), and *Mladinski List* (The Voice of Youth, 1922-). In addition to Krasna, Kristan, Molek, Zaitz, and Zupančič whom we have already mentioned, the following writers were among the leading contributors to these publications: Frank Alesh, Louis Beniger, Vincent Cainkar, Angelo Cerkvenik, Frank Česen, Josip Chesarek (the father of four-star United States General, Ferdinand J. Chesarek), Josip Durn, Anton Garden, Filip Godina, Oscar Godina, Erazem Gorshe, Louis Jartz, Louisa Jartz, Joseph Jauh, William Jereb, Zdenka Mihelich, Mary Jug-Molek, Louis Kaferle, Mirko Kuhel, Donald Lotrich, Ludwig Medvesek, Milan Medvesek, Zvonko Novak, Joško Oven, Matt Petrovich, Charles Pogorelec, Leo Poljšak, Lou Serjak, Anton Shular, Joseph Šircel, Joseph Siskovich, Joseph Snoy, Frank Taucher, Fred Vider, Jacob Zupančič, and Nace Žlemberger.[51] Exceptionally prolific contributors were also Ivan Zorman, of a predominantly "neutral" or "middle range" ideological orientation, and Ivan Jontez, who started his writing career as a socialist, created some of his major works as a "neutral" novelist and poet, and moved with one of his novels to a conservative-rightist position.[52]

Finally, the lone representative of the extreme radical pole of the Slovenian American ideological continuum is Joseph Kalar (1906-1972), associate editor or contributing editor of *New Masses, Left Front, International Literature*, and *The Anvil*, one of America's foremost revolutionary writers and poets.[53]

This inevitably incomplete overview of the Slovenian American literature—the literature of a numerically small and relatively unknown ethnic group—reveals a strong literary involvement in all areas of the ideological continuum, ranging from the religious literature by Bishop Baraga, the current official candidate of the American Catholic Church for sainthood, to the radical literature of Joseph Kalar, one of America's foremost revolutionary writers, poets, and editors. One suspects that a more detailed analysis would show a more or less normal curve distribution, with most contributions falling into the middle-range area, characterized by a relatively "normal," "neutral" or moderate orientation, showing a persistent decrease as one moves to the more extreme positions on the far right or left.

* * *

As has already become apparent, the Slovenian American *literati* deal with a considerable variety of themes. Kappus, Baraga, Franc Pirc, and several other missionaries created some of the early works on the American Indians; Adamic was a foremost writer on American ethnic groups— and on his native Slovenia and Yugoslavia; Klobuchar takes us to the little known American mountain ranges and hidden trails in search of beauty, courage, and a deeper humanity; and with Grdina and Kobal we visit Greece, Turkey, Israel, the Soviet Union, Bulgaria, Pakistan, India, Korea, Japan, and Formosa. With Baraga we can pray and meditate in the Indian, English, and Slovenian languages, or we can immerse ourselves into theological writings by Smolnikar, Gruden, and Mihelic, each representing a completely different theological orientation. We can enjoy Vodusek's Slovenian poetry about St. Francis, Fortunat Zorman's religious writings in *Ave Maria*, and visit with Wolbang Slovenian missionaries in Zambia, on Madagascar, in Thailand, or in Japan.[54]

We can take nostalgic trips to Slovenia with almost all Slovenian immigrant writers and poets, including Franc Pirc, Kristan, Ivan Zorman, Adamic, Mauser, Valentin, Prisland, Rogelj, and Jakopič. With the humorist Terbovec we can laughingly visit the American West, we can walk occasionally in the seventeenth century footsteps of Kappus, or we can descend with Molek to the "graveyards of the living" where Slovenian and other miners were contributing their sweat, their health and, not infrequently, their lives for a better America. With Baraga, we can plead for God's mercy and love; with Smolnikar, for a universal church, world government, and universal peace. We can unite our voices with Kristan and Molek, advocating better working and living conditions for the working class, after we have visited in their works the vividly painted scenes in mines and factories, in bars and hospitals. Milena Soukal takes us to the "Temples of Peru" in her sensitive search for brotherhood and love, while Kalar "prays" to thunder to put an end to exploitation and oppression. With Mauser we watch how John Kovach, abandoned and alone, dies next to his machine at the Cleveland Twist Drill, in the heart of the Slovenian ethnic neighborhood which also inspired Mlakar's Dostoevskian, powerful story. With Bukvic we analyze the uprooted and alienated man of the modern world. With Krasna we visit the "black villages" and with Katka Zupančič we revolt against man's inhumanity to man. With Smolnikar, Kristan, Adamic, Mauser, and Rausch we dream highly different dreams about a new humanity and a better world. Finally, we visit Jontez who had traveled the whole continuum. Paralyzed with a stroke, he reads to us his swan song: "There is a time for everything." His face is pale. His voice trembles. We pretend to be staring at the shelves filled with books, the poet's only possession. In America one is not supposed to cry!

Yes, the themes differ. There is a tremendous variety. There is, as *The Cleveland Plain Dealer* of 2 September 1956, reported, "an unexplored field of literature." There are the many voices of the many American ethnic groups. There are the many voices within each ethnic group—a rich, unexplored field of literature.[55]

* * *

Occupationally, the Slovenian American *literati* represent a wide range of strata. As far as we know, Adamic alone made his living as a writer. In harmony with the Slovenian literary tradition, a large proportion of Slovenian missionaries and priests, ranging from obscure chaplains to famous bishops, were actively involved in literary pursuits. Quite a number of Slovenian American *literati* worked as editors and reporters of Slovenian ethnic newspapers, among them Kristan, James Debevec, Louis Pirc, Zaitz, and Molek, while others occupied editorial or reporting positions with the American magazines and newspapers, as, for instance, Klobuchar, Kocivar, Orehek, and Skerly.

The following illustrations may suggest the wide range of occupations held by the Slovenian American *literati*: Smrekar was a chaplain; Trunk, a pastor; Franc Pirc and Čebul, missionaries; Baraga and Rausch, bishops; Kalar, a lumberjack; Mauser (a former seminarian whose books are widely read in German, French and Spanish translations) and Tomsic, factory workers; Mlakar was a coal miner, businessman, and reporter; Rogelj, an insurance representative; Grill and Robert Debevec, lawyers; Kern, physician; Stanley Zupan, a banking executive; Zorman, a composer and music teacher; Borstnik, a radio announcer; and Bren, Bukvic, Jerman, Kobal, John Modic, Nielsen, Prosen, and Surtz, university professors.[56]

The Slovenian immigrant *literati* failed to form a single, relatively permanent, unifying organization of their own, although many of them occupied leading positions in numerous Slovenian cultural, fraternal, educational, social, and other organizations. Those who were ideologically close to each other frequently formed small, informal circles or joined Slovenian language or university clubs, library clubs, and similar groups. The ideologically opposed or "incompatible" *literati* usually either ignored each other or competed for the souls of readers, although there were notable exceptions, such as Vodusek, a Catholic priest and a sensitive poet who was a friend and admirerer of Kristan, a leading progressive and socialist writer; or Ivan Zorman, a moderate, "middle-range" poet and essayist who cultivated friendship and cooperation with the *literati* belonging to Catholic, neutral, progressive and socialist camps. Several *literati* have also considerably changed their ideological orientations in the course of their writing careers—for instance, Louis Pirc, from progressive to Catholic-clericalist; Jontez, from socialist to neutral and, in one work, to conservative; Kern, from socialist to neutral; Adamic, from neutral to progressive and, some would say, leftist, etc.[57]

A glance at the Slovenian American literature reveals that it was published in both Americas, in several European countries, and even in Australia by a large number of Slovenian magazines, journals, almanacs, and newspapers. Several Slovenian American authors also appeared in American and international periodicals: *American Mercury*, *Family Digest*, *True*, and *Sports Afield* (Robert Debevec); *The Saturday Evening Post* (Adamic, Kobal); *Look* (Kocivar); *Time* and *Life* (Skerly); *Family Circle*, *Skyline*, and *Golf Digest* (John Modic); *Skyline* (Stanley Zupan, Klancar); *Moreana*, *Philological Quarterly*, *Renaissance News*, etc. (Surtz); *Esquire*, *Common Ground*, etc. (Mlakar); *Journal of American Folklore*, *The American Slavic Review*, *The Slavonic Review*, etc. (Klancar); *New Masses*, *International Literature*, *Left Front*, *The Anvil*, etc. (Kalar); and *Harper's Magazine*, *The Living Age*, *The American Parade*, *American Mercury*, *New Republic*, *Reader's Digest*, *Saturday Review of Literature*, *American Scholar*, etc. (Adamic).[58]

Books by the Slovenian American *literati* have been published by a considerable number of Slovenian publishing establishments in the United States (Ameriška Jugoslovanska Tiskovna Družba, Ave Maria Press, Prosvetna Matica, Triglav, Equality Printers, etc.); Slovenia (Mohorjeva Družba, Slovenska Izseljenska Matica, Državna Založba Slovenije, etc.); Austria (Mohorjeva Družba v Celovcu); Italy (Mohorjeva Družba v Gorici); Argentina (Slovenska Kulturna Akcija, Baraga Editorial, Svobodna Slovenija); and elsewhere. Occasionally, Slovenian authors have resorted to "Samozaložba," where they served as their own publishers and distributors.

The Slovenian American literature written in English has been published by a large number of American and, occasionally, British publishers, ranging from Harper Brothers, Herder, and Vanguard Press to Yale, Princeton, Oxford, and the University of Chicago Press. Works by Slovenian American writers have also been published by various publishers in Austria, Germany, Switzerland, France, Spain, Sweden, and other countries by their respective native publishers.

While the bulk of Slovenian American literature has been written in Slovenian and the works in English are a close second, the Slovenian missionary *literati* were remarkably polyglot and often wrote with equal facility in the Slovenian, English, German, French, Latin, and Indian languages. As a rule, other Slovenian *immigrant* writers were also fluent in many languages, especially in Slovenian, German, Italian, and English, while a few knew seven to ten languages, and Merkun studied and considerably mastered no fewer than twenty-seven languages.[59] In most instances, however, it can be said that missionaries wrote in several languages to reach as many faithful as possible for religious purposes and the immigrant writers other than missionaries usually wrote predominantly or exclusively in Slovenian to perpetuate in America the Slovenian language and heritage. And the American-born *literati* of Slovenian descent wrote almost exclusively in English, although some of them continued to show a preference for Slovenian themes (e.g., Mlakar), viewed often in the light of American, rather than Slovenian values. Thus a substantial number of *literati* wrote only in Slovenian, among them Zaitz, Grdina, Kerže, Ambrožič, Rogelj, Vodušek, Jakopič, and Mauser. Others wrote only in English, for instance, Mlakar, Kocivar, Robert Debevec, and Kalar. While Adamic came to America at fifteen and wrote a few minor pieces in Slovenian, all his major works were in English. Some *literati* wrote with equal facility in English and in Slovenian, among them Ivan Zorman, Klancar, Krasna, Jontez, Grill, Kern, Zaplotnik, and Prisland. Zakrajšek wrote mostly in Slovenian, but he also edited a religious magazine and wrote a number of minor works in Slovak. Kristan wrote mostly in Slovenian, but also produced a book and several articles in German. When one counts works in original languages and translations, the Slovenian American literature has been published in at least the following languages: Slovenian, English, Otchipwe (Indian), Ottawa (Indian), German, Spanish, French, Latin, Italian, Croatian, Serbian, Slovak, Czech, Greek, Arabic, Portuguese, and Finnish.[60]

* * *

At this time it is still much too early to evaluate properly the impact and contributions of the Slovenian American literature. We may, however, make a few tentative observations.

The *literati* have, undoubtedly, helped to preserve the Slovenian heritage in America and among Slovenian minorities in European and other countries. Their works had an educational and recreational value for their compatriots. The literary achievements of their Slovenian fellow-citizens have often been a source of pride to the uprooted immigrants and their descendants. Translations from and to English have stimulated literary and cultural cross-fertilization, starting with Primec's translation of Benjamin Franklin from English to German—and we may be just entering an era of increased activity of this kind, as also suggested by the Bicentennial edition of an *Anthology of Slovenian American Literature*, published by *Slovenski Ameriški Institut*—The Slovenian Research Center of America.[61]

The Slovenians have also made a considerable contribution to American Indian literature. Albert J. Nevins writes in *Our American Catholic Heritage* that "Bishop Baraga was the first of the American bishops to issue his pastoral letters in Indian."[62] Rudolph P. Cujes points out that a volume of over 700 pages of Baraga's meditations, *Katolik Enamiad*, first published in the Otchipwe language in 1850, was reprinted in 1939, in the period of the Indian cultural revival, and that missionaries and scholars are still using Baraga's Indian dictionaries and grammars. Similarly, the writings about the Indians by various Slovenian authors remain an important contribution to American Indian history, just as the Indian songs, recorded by Baraga and several other Slovenian missionaries, survive as examples of American Indian folklore and literature.[63]

In other areas, some contributions are still relatively unknown and invisible and call for further research and documentation. Thus, for instance, John Modic, a Slovenian American, translated Johann Nestroy's play, *Einen Jux will er sich machen.* Thorton Wilder adapted this English translation for *The Merchant of Yonkers*, later rewritten as *The Matchmaker*, and finally resulting in *Hello, Dolly!*[64] Other contributions have become visible and even acclaimed, although the Slovenian background of their creators has seldom been mentioned. Thus, for instance, Bernard Jerman's *The Young Disraeli* was described by *Punch* of 14 December 1960, as "an absorbingly well-written book" and by the *Times Literary Supplement* of 23 December 1960, as "a work of genuine and exuberant scholarship." In 1971, American, British, French, and German scholars and writers jointly dedicated a "Festschrift," *Moreana: Meliora*, to Edward Surtz, the Slovenian American writer and scholar of international fame.[65]

While the quality of the Slovenian American literature was undoubtedly uneven, several Slovenian writers had their works published in some of America's most prestigious periodicals, as we have already indicated. At least three Slovenian American writers (Adamic, Mlakar, and Kalar) were included in Edward J. O'Brien's *The Best Short Stories.* Adamic was frequently reprinted by *Reader's Digest*, one of his books was the Book-of-the-Month Club selection and was reprinted in *Modern Classics* edition; he was also included in Argentina's collection of "Obras famosas," or "Famous Works."[66] Mauser, while practically unknown to American readers, went through a number of editions in German and Spanish translations, was published in French as a "great Catholic writer" in the collection *La Pensée Universelle* (The Universal Thought), and was included in the international collection *Gigante* among the "giants of world literature."[67] Frank Mlakar received several awards for poetry and plays, but gained national recognition with his novel, *He, the Father*, which was acclaimed by *Time* magazine as "a powerful Dostoevskian story."[68] Kalar was included in Jack Conroy's *The Anvil Anthology*,[69] and Robert Debevec's story, "Long Shot to Kill," a factual account of the shooting of a Confederate general by a Union soldier, first published in *True* magazine, was aired on national television in the General Electric True Series.[70] Debevec's success on television reminds us of another "unexplored field of Slovenian ethnic literature," of such scriptwriters and television producers as Daniel Hrvatin whose "Cleveland's Moon Shot" has brought him national publicity,[71] and Jerome Turk, who has become nationally and internationally known for such creations as "Concepts in Communication," "Listening in on Latin America," "The Many Faces of Mary," "Some Beloved Child," and the United States of America multimedia travel show which was seen at Expo '70 at Osaka, Japan.[72]

If it is true, as Gunnar Myrdal maintains, that the greatest American dilemma is a moral dilemma—the dilemma of transforming the American Dream into reality,[73] then we may say that in this noble effort the Slovenian American writers have played a remarkable role. Bishop Baraga had been fighting for the preservation of Indian cultures and writing books, grammars, and dictionaries in Indian languages a century before the American government adopted a more humane and pluralistic orientation toward these first Americans.[74] Brewton Berry discusses Adamic as the leading exponent of cultural pluralism and cultural democracy in America,[75] a view which has gained official recognition in the United States Congress in 1972 and which has become increasingly popular and powerful today.[76] Finally, Bishop Rausch puts Adamic's America as a Nation of Nations into a world-wide, universal context in his book *A Family of Nations: An Expanded View of Patriotism . . . A New Dedication to Humanity.*[77]

As we are entering the third century of our history as a Nation, we may unite our voices with that of the Slovenian poet Oton Župančič:

> Forge me on thy anvil, Life!
> Am I flint—then I shall flash.
> Am I steel, then I shall sing.
> Am I glass, then let me crash![78]

Let us hope and pray that America will never crash, that she will always flash as one of the great lights of freedom and that, strong as steel, she will continue to sing in its many voices—this our Nation of Nations in the Family of Nations!

Kent State University

NOTES

[1] Primož Kozak, *Slovenia* (Belgrade: Yugoslav Review, 1974), pp. 1-16, 81-112, 209-22. See also Milko Kos, *Zgodovina Slovencev* (Ljubljana: Slovenska Matica, 1955); Bogo Grafenauer, *Zgodovina slovenskega naroda*, 5 vols. (Ljubljana, Zadružna Zveza, 1956-1962); and John A. Arnez, *Slovenia in European Affairs* (New York: Studia Slovenica, 1958).

[2] Bernard Newman, *Unknown Yugoslavia* (London: Herbert Jenkins, 1960), pp. 198-99.

[3] R. G. A. De Bray, *Guide to the Slavonic Languages* (London: Dent and Sons, 1951), p. 365.

[4] Louis Adamic, *The Native's Return* (New York and London: Harper and Brothers, 1934), p. 29.

⁵ R. H. Markham, *Tito's Imperial Communism* (Chapel Hill: Univ. of North Carolina Press, 1947), pp. 10-11.

⁶ Adamic, pp. 29-31; Grafenauer, V, 179-204.

⁷ Joseph Felicijan, *The Genesis of the Contractual Theory and the Installation of the Dukes of Carinthia* (Celovec: Družba sv. Mohorja, 1967), p. 25.

⁸ Felicijan, pp. 53, 73-74, 81; and Kos, pp. 86-89. Facsimile of Bodin's text, initialed by Jefferson, appeared in Felicijan, p. 15.

⁹ Felicijan, pp. 5, 9-10, 15.

¹⁰ Crane Brinton, rev. of *The Genesis of the Contractual Theory*, by Joseph Felicijan, *The Catholic Historical Review*, 54, 4 (1969), pp. 657-58.

¹¹ Helfried Patz, "Geschenke der Slowenen an die Welt," *Steirische Berichte*, 9, 5 (1965), p. 135.

¹² Henry Wadsworth Longfellow, *Hyperion: A Romance* (Cambridge: The Riverside Press, 1893), pp. 360-72; Andreas Bernardus Smolnikar, *Denkwürdige Ereignisse im Leben des Andreas Bernardus Smolnikar* (Cambridge: Folsom, Wells and Thurston, 1838); *Proclamation of the True Union* (Donnely's Mill, Pa.: Perry Co., 1862); *The Great Encyclic Epistle* (Baltimore: S. S. Mills, 1865); etc. See also "Bernard Smolnikar," in Alfonz Gspan, ed., *Slovenski Biografski Leksikon*, X (Ljubljana: Slovenska Akademija Znanosti in Umetnosti, 1967), pp. 392-96.

¹³ "Marko Anton Kapus" in Izidor Cankar, ed., *Slovenski Biografski Leksikon*, III (Ljubljana: Zadružna Gospodarska Banka, 1928), pp. 426-27; and Erik Kovačič, "Pater Kapus–prvi slovenski misijonar v Severni Ameriki," *Ave Maria Koledar 1970* (Lemont: Slovenski Frančiškani, 1970), pp. 89-95.

¹⁴ Herbert E. Bolton, *Rim of Christendom* (New York: Russell and Russell, 1960), p. 464.

¹⁵ Frederic Baraga, *Geschichte, Character, Sitten und Gebräuche der Nord-Amerikanischen Indier* (Ljubljana: J. Klemmens, 1837); *Abregé de l'Histoire des Indiens de l'Amerique Septentrionale* (Paris: La Societé de Bons Livres, 1837); and *Popis navad in zadržanja Indijanov polnočne Amerike* (Ljubljana: J. Klemmens, 1837).

¹⁶ Mila Šenk, "Štiri knjige Jožeta Grdine," *Slovenski Izseljenski Koledar 1968* (Ljubljana: Slovenska Izseljenska Matica, 1968), pp. 247-49; and 'Jože Grdina 80-letnik," *Ameriška Domovina*, 3 March 1972, p. 2.

¹⁷ Andrej Kobal, *Svetovni popotnik pripoveduje*, 2 vols. (Gorica: Mohorjeva Družba, 1975-1976).

¹⁸ Klobuchar's books include *The Zest (and Best) of Klobuchar* (1967), *The Playbacks of Klobuchar* (1969), *True Hearts and Purple Heads* (1970), *Will America Accept Love at Halftime?* (1972), *Where the Wind Blows Bittersweet* (1975). More detailed information can be found in *Slovenian Research Center of America Archives* in Willoughby Hills and Kent, Ohio. Hereafter cited as *SRCA Archives*. Each archive contains multiple data, such as *vitae*, bibliographies, clippings, copies, photographs, etc.

¹⁹ See note 4.

²⁰ Henry A. Christian, *Louis Adamic: A Checklist* (Kent: Kent State Univ. Press, 1971), p. xxvi.

²¹ Arnez, pp. 142-43; Ivan Prijatelj, *Kulturna in politična zgodovina Slovencev, 2* vols. (Ljubljana: Akademska Založba, 1838); and Dr. Anton Kacin, "Dr. Anton Mahnič," in Dr. Rudolf Klinec, ed., *Zgodovina goriške nadškofije* (Gorica: Mohorjeva Družba, 1951), pp. 79-106.

²² Rudolph P. Cujes, *Ninidjanissidog Saiagiinagog: Contributions of the Slovenes to the Socio-Cultural Development of the Canadian Indians* (Antigonish: St. Francis Xavier Univ. Press, 1968), pp. 58-92.

[23] Fortunat Zorman, "Pokojni p. Kazimir," *Ave Maria Koledar 1959* (Lemont: Slovenski Frančiškani, 1959), pp. 128-31; and *SRCA Archives*.

[24] Dr. Filip Žakelj, ed., *Duhovne misli škofa dr. Gregorija Rožmana* (Celovec: Družba sv. Mohorja, 1969); and *SRCA Archives*.

[25] *Cerkvena poezija: psalmi, slavospevi in cerkvene himne* (Celovec: Družba sv. Mohorja, 1952); *Jezus Kristus: Premišljevanja*, trans. Albin Škrinjar, I (Trst: Samozaložba, 1962), and II, 1963.

[26] Joann Birsa, *Glory to God: A Collection of Slovenian Hymns in English Translation* (Denver: Holy Rosary Church, 1971); Valentin Spendov, O.F.M. *Organ Music in Slovenia* (Rome, Pontificio Istituto di Musica Sacra, and Lemont: Ave Maria Press, 1973); and Alfred Fischinger, "Važen prispevek k cerkveni glasbi," *Amerikanski Slovenec*, 23 July 1975.

[27] M. T., "P. Fortunat Zorman 60-letnik," *Ameriška Domovina*, 2 Dec. 1974.

[28] *SRCA Archives*.

[29] Longfellow, pp. 360-72; John L. Zaplotnik, "Kako je Kamničan snoval komunski raj v Ameriki," *Ave Maria Koledar 1947* (Lemont: Slovenski Frančiškani, 1947), pp. 115-27; and Dr. Janez Stanonik, "Andrej Bernard Smolnikar," *Slovenski Izseljenski Koledar 1962* (Ljubljana: Slovenska Izseljenska Matica, 1962), pp. 170-74.

[30] Gspan, p. 395.

[31] *SRCA Archives*.

[32] J. M. Trunk, *Amerika in Amerikanci* (Celovec: Samozaložba, 1912), pp. 544-605; Bernard Coleman and Verona LaBud, *Masinaigans: The Little Book* (St. Paul: North Central Publishing Co., 1972), pp. 281-303; P. Bazilij, "Viharnik je omahnil," *Misli* (Nov. 1973), pp. 307-09; Germain Marc'Hadour, "Reverendo atque amando Patri Edwardo Surtz, S. J., amici Thomae Mori s.p.d.," *Moreana: Meliora*, 4 (1971), n.p.; and *SRCA Archives*.

[33] Coleman and LaBud, p. 303. In addition to numerous articles and essays, Msgr. Zaplotnik wrote two books: *De vicariis foraneis* (Washington: The Catholic Univ. of America, 1927); and *Janez Čebulj: misijonar v Ameriki* (Groblje: Misijonska Knjižnica, 1928). He also translated various literary works from English into Slovenian.

[34] One of Valentin's works, on "Rural Scenes in Slovenia," appeared in Dr . Ferdinand Kolednik's French translation as *Le petit Tonček du Potok: Scenes da la vie rurale en Slovenie* (Montreal and Paris: Apostolat de Presse, 1961).

[35] James S. Rausch, *The Family of Nations* (Huntington: Our Sunday Visitor, 1970); *Human Rights* (New Orleans: National Council for Catholic Laity, 1973); *The Right to Live* (St. Paul: College of St. Thomas, 1974); *Christian Values in Today's Society* (Cincinnati: Archidiocese of Cincinnati, 1975); and *Research in the Church* (Washington: Catholic Univ. of America, 1975).

[36] "Learning About America," *The Cleveland Press* 5 May 1939; "Družina Ivana Zupana," *Novi Svet*, June, 1941, pp. 167-68; "Pred 20 leti je umrl Jakob Debevec," *Ameriška Domovina*, 3 March 1972; "Zadnje slovo Johna Jericha," *Amerikanski Slovenec*, 17 Oct. 1973; and *SRCA Archives*.

[37] Zdravko Novak, "Slovenska zdomska knjižnica," *Ameriška Domovina*, 22 March 1971; Pavle Borštnik, "Pogreb pokojnega g. Zdravka Novaka," *Ameriška Domovina*, 8 Dec. 1971; and *SRCA Archives*.

[38] "Library Board Fetes Mrs. Prisland," *The Sheboygan Press*, 24 Sept. 1963; Dr. Tine Debelja, "Panorama slovenskih leposlovnih ustvarjlacev v emigraciji," *Zbornik Svobodne Slovenije 1955* (Buenos Aires: Svobodna Slovenija, 1955), pp. 231, 234-36; and *SRCA Archives*.

[39] Debeljak, p. 231; Janez Sever, "Karel Mauser," a series of articles published in *Ameriška Domovina*, Nov. 1952; "Karel Mauser petdesetletnik," *Glas Slovenske Kulturne Akcije*, 28 Aug. 1968; and *SRCA Archives*.

566

⁴⁰Jože Bajec, "Biografije," *Slovenski Izseljenski Koledar 1967* (Ljubljana: Slovenska Izseljenska Matica, 1967), pp. 308-21; "Frank Kerže," in Izidor Cankar, ed., *Slovenski Biografski Leksikon*, III (Ljubljana: Zadružna Gospodarska Banka, 1928), p. 452; "Frank J. Kern," *Slovenski Biografski Leksikon* III, 444; Theodore Andrica, "Slovenian Poet Reared in U.S. Gains Fame," *The Cleveland Press*, 24 Sept. 1929; and *SRCA Archives*.

⁴¹"Janko N. Rogelj," Gspan, p. 121; Bajec, pp. 316-17; Debeljak, p. 235; "Frank Mlakar," in William Coyle, ed., *Ohio Authors and Their Books* (Cleveland: The World Publishing Co., 1962), p. 450; John M. Urbancich, "Success Comes Easy to Bob Debevec," *The Euclid News Journal*, 16 March 1972; "Journal Editor Selected," *AAHS Newsletter*, May, 1968; "Books of Interest," *The National Review*, 27 Aug. 1960, p. 121; and *SRCA Archives*.

⁴²"Jože Ambrožič," *Čas* (1923), p. 332; Debeljak, p. 236; Ludvik Potokar, *Zapiski* (Cleveland: Krog, 1951); Frank Česen, "Odlomek iz zgodovine St. Clair Avenije," *Slovenski Izseljenski Koledar 1970*, pp. 307-08; and *SRCA Archives*.

⁴³Christian, pp. i-xlvii, 1-142; "Louis Adamic," in Stanley J. Kunitz and Howard Haycraft, eds., *Twentieth Century Authors* (New York: The H. W. Wilson Co., 1942), pp. 4-5; and *SRCA Archives*.

⁴⁴Joža Mahnič, "Obdobje moderne," in Lino Legiša, ed., *Zgodovina slovenskega slovstva*, V (Ljubljana: Slovenska Matica, 1964), 292-307; and Cvetko A. Kristan, "Etbin Kristan: borec za boljšo bodočnost delovnega ljudstva," *Prosveta*, 17 Sept. 1970.

⁴⁵Frank Zaitz, "Jože Zavertnik: njegovo življenje in delo," *Ameriški Družinski Koledar 1930* (Chicago: Jugoslovanska Delavska Tiskovna Družba, 1930), pp. 149-61; Bajec, pp. 320-21; and *SRCA Archives*.

⁴⁶"Ivan Molek," in F. K. Lukman, ed., *Slovenski Biografski Leksikon*, V (Ljubljana: Zadružna Gospodarska Banka, 1933), 149; and Cvetko A. Kristan, "Ameriški slovenski književnik Ivan Molek," *Rodna Gruda*, Sept. 1957, pp. 190-91.

⁴⁷Bajec, pp. 318-19; and *SRCA Archives*.

⁴⁸France Adamič, "France Magajna," *Naši Razgledi*, 5 Nov. 1971, p. 643; and I. S., "France Magjna: kmet in pisatelj," *Rodna Gruda*, Nov., 1971, p. 32.

⁴⁹Jože Bajec, "Bibliografija del Katke Zupančič," *Slovenski Koledar 1974* (Ljubljana: Slovenska Izseljenska Matica, 1974), pp. 318-25.

⁵⁰Jože Bajec, "Jubilej Ane Praček-Krasne," *Slovenski Izseljenski Koledar 1971*, pp. 206-07; and "Bibliografija Anne P. Krasne," *Slovenski Koledar 1975*, pp. 270-77.

⁵¹Ivan Molek, "Petdesetletnica slovenskega časnikarstva v Ameriki," *Ameriški Družinski Koledar 1941*, pp. 28-36; Jože Bajec, "Petinsedemdeset let slovenskega časnikarstva v ZDA," *Slovenski Izseljenski Koledar 1967*, pp. 273-307; and *SRCA Archives*.

⁵²Correspondence by Ivan Zorman and Jontez, *SRCA Archives*.

⁵³Edward J. O'Brien, ed., *The Best Short Stories* (Boston: Houghton Mifflin Co., 1934), pp. 357, 362.

⁵⁴At the time of this writing, no library has a complete collection of all Slovenian American literary works. Among the best existing collections are those of the Slovenian National Library on St. Clair Avenue, Cleveland, Ohio; Slovenian Research Center's Collection, Willoughby Hills and Kent, Ohio; Franciscan Library, Lemont, Ill.; the SNPJ Collection, Burr Ridge, Ill.; the Library of Congress, Washington, D.C.; and the National and University Libraries, Ljubljana, Slovenia.

⁵⁵Such literature provides a good illustration of how little known and unexplored Slovenian ethnic literature has been in America. While some of their writers have become well known in several European countries, they have received practically

no publicity in America. Some leading American papers have willingly publicized Slovenian card parties or "eating affairs," but have stubbornly refused to mention the literary and other accomplishments of Slovenian Americans, thus helping to perpetuate the image of ethnics as a blue-collar, lower-class people. .

[56] In Slovenia, as well as among Slovenian Americans, it would be difficult to find a single occupation or profession whose members have not attempted to write prose or poetry. Students of literature and of sociology may eventually profit from a careful examination of these materials, both published and unpublished.

[57] See note 21 and *SRCA Archives.*

[58] Christian, pp. 1-66; and *SRCA Archives.*

[59] Trunk, pp. 545-46, 553, 556, 565; Coleman and LaBud, pp. 282, 285, 287, 290; Edward Gobec, *Love Moves Mountains* (Bedford: The Home Press, 1960), p. 30; and Giles Edward Gobetz, "The Ethnic Ethics of Assimilation: Slovenian View," *Phylon: The Atlanta Univ. Review of Race and Culture,* 17, 3 (Fall 1966), 271.

[60] *SRCA Archives.*

[61] A detailed analysis of the role of the Slovenian ethnic writers, poets, dramatists, and translators, based on survey data, book reviews, and personal documents, is currently in progress and will be published at a later date.

[62] Albert J. Nevins, *Our American Catholic Heritage* (Huntington: Our Sunday Visitor, 1972), p. 149.

[63] Cujes, pp. 58-96; and *SRCA Archives.*

[64] Correspondence and copies in *SRCA Archives.*

[65] *Moreana: Meliora,* 4 (1971). See also "Fr. Edward L. Surtz Dies," *The Cleveland Press,* 20 Jan. 1973.

[66] Christian, pp. 70, 72.

[67] Karel Mauser, *Kaplan Klemens,* trans. Bernhardt Strauss and Gerold Schmid (Luzern: Rex Verlag, 1955); *El capellán,* trans. José I. Belloch Zimmermann (Barcelona: Luis de Caralt, 1961); *Yerné, le fils du défunt,* trans. Ferdinand Kolednik (Paris: La Pensée Universelle, 1974); etc.

[68] "Books," rev. *Time,* 7 Aug. 1950, p. 72. See also Coyle, p. 450; Joseph Zelle, "Slovenian Colony Here Is Background for Novel," *Cleveland News,* 19 July 1950; and Nelson Algren, rev. of *He, The Father, New York Times,* 30 July 1950, p. 12. The author gratefully acknowledges valuable information on Mlakar which has been supplied by Viola Mlakar, Helen Perusek, Rose Marie Prosen, and Edward Pekovnik, and will be more fully utilized in future publications.

[69] "Collar," in Jack Conroy and Curt Johnson, eds., *Writers in Revolt: The Anvil Anthology* (New York: Lawrence Hill and Co., 1973), pp. 91-96.

[70] Urbancich, p. 5; and *SRCA Archives.*

[71] Mark, "Cleveland's Moon Shot," *Variety,* 11 Dec. 1963; and *SRCA Archives.*

[72] Bob Seltzer, "Best Location Pays Off," *The Cleveland Press,* 12 July 1967; and *SRBA Archives.*

[73] Gunnar Myrdal, *An American Dilemma* (New York: Harper and Row, 1944), pp. lxxi, 1-25.

[74] Cujes, pp. 58-92; Nevins, p. 149; and Giles Edward Gobetz, Jože Goričar, and Peter Jambrek, "Yugoslav Sociology," in Raj P. Mohan and Don Martindale, eds., *Handbook of Contemporary Developments in World Sociology* (Westport and London: Greenwood Press, 1975), p. 281.

[75] Brewton Berry, *Race Relations: Interaction of Ethnic and Racial Groups* (Boston: Houghton Mifflin Co., 1951), p. 13.

[76] Hon. Richard Schweiker, "Implementation of Schweiker Ethnic Studies Bill," *Congressional Record,* Vol. 118, No. 155, 30 Sept. 1972.

568

[77] See note 35.

[78] Oton Župančič, "Forge Me on Thy Anvil," in Janko Lavrin and Anton Slodnjak, eds., *The Parnassus of a Small Nation* (Ljubljana: Državna Založba Slovenije, 1965), p. 91.

Ukrainian Literature in the United States: Trends, Influences, Achievements

Dmytro M. Shtohryn

ABSTRACT

In order to present an adequate view of Ukrainian literature in the United States and its contribution to American cultural life, I have divided this paper into four principal parts. The first part gives a brief historico-social background of the Ukrainian immigration to the United States and the beginnings of religious, social and cultural activities of Ukrainian communities. There was no coordination of Ukrainian literary activities in the United States until the 1950's. The immigrants after World War II were the first to bring from the Ukraine a tradition of organized literary life. Part two of this paper concerns various literary organizations and their publications that have been instrumental to the growth of Ukrainian literary life in this country. The main part of this paper is devoted to the literary activities of four generations of writers. While the literary works of writer-pioneers dealt primarily with the life of Ukrainian immigrants in America, the writings of the second generation of Ukrainian authors dealt with events and socio-political activities in the Ukraine itself. These works were written during the period of World War I, the independence of the Ukraine, and the time between the two world wars. The new wave of Ukrainian immigration to the United States after World War II included many authors who represented all genres of Ukrainian literature and literary trends which were influential not only in the development of modern Ukrainian literature but of European and American literature as well. The young generation of authors, primarily poets, known as the New York Group, started its activities in 1955. This group is a natural phenomenon of the Ukrainian ethnic group in this country and represents a vital continuity of the Ukrainian literary process. The development of Ukrainian literary criticism in America is divided into literary scholarship and critical evaluations of works of single authors or groups. This paper concludes with an emphasis on the achievement of Ukrainian literature in the United States and its contribution to the American literary treasure. (DMS)

The year 1976, which marks the Bicentennial of the United States, has an additional significance for the Ukrainian community in this country.

This date is generally regarded as the Centennial of the arrival of the first Ukrainian settlers in America, in the eastern states. The development of Ukrainian cultural activities and the growth of Ukrainian literature in the United States began soon after the immigrants' arrival.

The purpose of this article is to give a general picture of the literary activities and production of Ukrainian authors in this country from their beginning in the 1890's to the present time. In observing this development we shall try to answer several fundamental questions: What is Ukrainian literature in America? Is it a part of the literary heritage of the Ukraine? Is it a literary product written and published in the vernacular and meaningful only to the Ukrainian ethnic group in the United States, or is it some sort of a cultural bridge between America and the Ukraine? And finally, is it only an emigré literature in this country of both a Ukrainian-American and Ukrainian emigré literary process? In other words, we shall attempt to characterize it from the literary and social points of view and to determine its place in the framework of American literature, as well as to show its role in the development of modern literature in the Ukraine. In an effort to meet these objectives, I divide this article into the following main parts: (1) brief historico-social background, (2) literary organizations and their publications, (3) four generations of writers, and (4) literary criticism.

In spite of the fact that Ukrainian literature in the United States began to develop in the 1890's, there has as yet been no comprehensive study of this process, nor a scholarly evaluation of its representatives. There are, however, several general outlines, surveys and critical descriptions dealing with single literary groups, as well as analyses of various authors' works. The earliest among them was in Ivan Franko's survey of Ukrainian literature, published in 1904, in which this distinguished Ukrainian poet and scholar showed his interest in the literary activities of his countrymen in America.[1] A brief description of the development of Ukrainian American literature from its beginning to the 1930's was published by Omelian Reviuk in the jubilee book of the Ukrainian National Association in 1936.[2] Also valuable in this respect are the studies and critical surveys of Hryhorii Kostiuk,[3] Roman Kuchar,[4] Yaroslav Chyz,[5] as well as an anthology of Ukrainian poetry in the West, edited by Bohdan Boichuk and Bohdan Rubchak, which includes critical descriptions of a number of contemporary authors living in the United States.[6] All of these publications and other such works have been taken into consideration in the preparation of this article.

* * *

Although some sources, particularly the studies of Yaroslav Chyz,[7] Luka Myshuha,[8] and Wasyl Mudryi[9] indicate that Ukrainians were in

America as early as the beginning of the seventeenth century, the major waves of Ukrainian immigrants started in the second half of the nineteenth century and came in ever increasing numbers during the following decades until the 1950's. The first Ukrainian immigrants were primarily farmers, most of them coming from small villages; they had little formal education. Finding themselves in the industrial urban surroundings of the eastern states, without skills or knowledge of the English language, the immigrants usually performed the hardest and lowest-paying jobs. Hence, it was quite natural that they sought mutual help and protection in the strange environment of their new homeland. First, they organized Ukrainian churches and fraternal societies. These societies proved to be fundamental in the establishment of the religious, social and cultural activities of the Ukrainian community in various parts of the country for years to come. Those who came to North Dakota, Wisconsin, Montana and other central states were in a better situation. Having farming experience, they were able to start new Ukrainian farm settlements even with Ukrainian names, such as "Ukraina"[10] and "Kyiv"[11] and to organize their religious and social life as well. At the present time there are nearly one and a half million Ukrainian Americans.[12] Most of them are organized into hundreds of local societies and more than sixty-five nationwide organizations, which have branches in various cities. The activities of these organizations range widely from the scholarly research conducted by the Ukrainian Academy of Arts and Sciences in the U.S.,[13] and Shevchenko Scientific Society[14] and other scholarly professional societies[15] to youth education provided by hundreds of Saturday and Sunday schools and five nationwide youth organizations, or social and political activities within the framework of other societies, including the Ukrainian National Association. This association is the oldest Ukrainian fraternal insurance organization, and, with nearly 500 branches, it is instrumental in assisting numerous cultural projects and political actions.[16] The activities of all these organizations are usually coordinated by the Ukrainian Congress Committee, the principal representative of Ukrainians in the United States.[17] Most Ukrainians in America belong to four religious denominations. The Ukrainian Catholic, Ukrainian Orthodox, Ukrainian Evangelical and Ukrainian Baptist churches together number approximately 400 parishes and congregations. There are about thirty full-day Ukrainian Catholic elementary schools, five high schools, two junior colleges, two theological seminaries, one college,[18] and three chairs and a research institute at Harvard University founded by the Ukrainian community.[19] In speaking about the Ukrainian press in America, I should stress that, although the newspaper *Alaska Herald–Svoboda*, edited by the Ukrainian immigrant Rev. Agapius Honcharenko, included some articles about the Ukraine and its history as early as in 1867,[20] the first Ukrainian newspapers to closely reflect the socio-cultural activities and working conditions of the early Ukrainian settlers were *Ameryka* (America), *Svoboda* (Liberty), and were issued by the fraternal and insurance organizations in the 1880's and 1890's. These newspapers provided the settlers with practical advice about building their new lives in this country.[21] In addition, these newspapers included news from the Ukraine and often reprinted literary works of distinguished Ukrainian authors. At the present time there are nearly 250 Ukrainian periodical and serial publications in the United States, including two dailies and seven weeklies; 328 of them are published in Ukrainian and over thirty in English.[22]

* * *

There was no coordination of Ukrainian literary activities in the United States until the 1950's.[23] The immigrants after World War II were the first to bring from the Ukraine a tradition of organized literary life. They have founded various literary art clubs, which, since that time, have been instrumental not only in holding literary critical conferences, but also in providing frequent occasions for literary meetings, called "Authors' Evenings" for the reading of new works by the authors themselves. The Ukrainian Writers' Association in Exile, "The Word," might be considered the most important of these societies. Founded in 1954 with its seat in New York, the Association unites Ukrainian authors (writers in all genres and literary critics) in diaspora, a hundred of whom live in the United States.[24] Its serial publication *Slovo* (The Word) is devoted primarily to new literary works and criticism, including the proceedings of its conferences. Another active group, The Ukrainian Cultural Workers' Association, consists of persons in fields of the humanities and arts, including writers and literary critics living in the United States and Canada.[25] The Association's official irregular publication, *Estafeta*, which started in 1970, is devoted mainly to literary topics. Its title was evidently taken from a poem by Lina Kostenko, the leading modern poetess of the young generation in the Ukraine, who, after a bitter attack by the Soviet authorities, has remained in silence since 1964. Ukrainian children's writers and critics have organized a separate society, The Federation of Writers for Youth and Children, uniting almost all authors in this literary field in diaspora, but with the predominant number of them in the United States. In fact, this society was founded in Germany in 1946, and later resumed its activities in this country. Since the 1950's this group, which has approximately forty members, has published, with the assistance of the Ukrainian National Association, the monthly magazine for children *Veselka* (The Rainbow) and, for parents, collections of educational theoretical articles entitled *My i nashi dity* (We and Our Children). The philological sections of the Shevchenko Scientific Society and the Ukrainian Academy of Arts and Sciences in the U.S., and the Literary Section of the Ukrainian Research Institute at Harvard provide studies on literary topics, usually published in their serial publications or conference proceedings.[26] Besides, there are smaller literary groups like *Svitannia* (The Predawn) and *Volosozhar* (Pleiades). They issue their irregular publications with the same names. Two literary foundations[27] and six literary art clubs in New York, Philadelphia, Detroit, Chicago, Minneapolis, and Los Angeles provide a forum for oral presentations and critical evaluations of writings by particular authors. While the membership of all the societies which have been mentioned consists predominantly of writers and critics who started writing in the Ukraine in the 1920's-1930's or during the emigration after World War II in the 1940's, the New York Group of poets unites almost all modern authors of the younger generation who were brought up and educated in the United States or other countries outside Ukraine.[28] In fact, this group is not an organized body with an adopted constitution or formal membership, and in this respect it might be compared to the Kievan Neoclassical group of poets of the 1920's. Having something of a Bohemian background, it was initiated in 1955 in New York and since 1958 has published the annual *Novi Poesii* (New Poetry), a collection of new original poetical works by its members and translations of Western European and especially modern American authors.[29] As all other societies, the group unites young authors of Ukrainian origin in exile; some of them write in both Ukrainian and English. Besides the official publications of these literary groups and organizations, there are at least nine other serials and periodicals (including four annual almanacs) which offer their pages for literary works and criticism. The bimonthly *Kyiv*, for example, was the first one in the United States that, under the editorship of Bohdan Romanenchuk (a literary scholar and bibliographer), managed to be a tribune of almost all literary artists in North America from 1950 to 1964. A weekly supplement to the daily *Svoboda* was similar in its scope, but it was published separately as *The Sunday Edition* in New Jersey and edited in 1952 by the writer and scholar, Vasyl' Chaplenko.[30] In 1962 in Detroit a new non-periodical journal *Terem* (The Tower) was started under the firm of the Institute of Ukrainian Problems and the editorship of Iurii Tys-Krokhmaliuk, a writer and military historian. Each issue of this publication is devoted to a separate subject concerning culture, a literary group, or even a single author. And finally the quarterly *Ovyd* (Horizon) in Chicago and three politically oriented monthly journals, *Suchasnist'* (Contemporary Times) in Munich, *Vyzvol'nyi shliakh* (The Liberation Path) in London, and *Novi dni* (New Days) in Toronto, devote a predominant part of their issues to problems of Ukrainian literature, including that in America.

* * *

The first literature of the early Ukrainian immigrants was poetry, based primarily on their rich folklore, expecially folk songs which they brought from the old country. In fact, the variety of genre used was rather limited, and only poetry and short stories were developed to any extent. The first poets were mostly Ukrainian Catholic priests who, at the same time, played a leading role in establishing the organized life of the newcomers.[31] One of them, Father Hryhorii Hrushka (1860-1913), the founder and the first editor of the newspaper *Svoboda* (1893-1900), and co-founder of the Ukrainian National Association, might be considered the first such poet. His poems, which were published in *Svoboda* as early as 1895, usually had a moral character and were often similar to his church sermons. Hrushka used them as ingredients in his articles in order to call the readers' attention to the main question of these articles. Formally his poems were just simple rhythmical verses with feminine rhyme in the second and fourth lines of each stanza. In other words, they were exact mimicries of Ukrainian folk songs of the Carpathian region, called *Kolomyiky*. A few verses by Hrushka will illustrate this poetical structure:

> Hei, brattia, do chynu,
> Ne hodyt'sia spaty,
> Vzhe sontse zpoludnia,
> Pora i nam vstaty
>
> I vziatys' do pratsi
> Ta shchyroho trudu
> Vo imia nauky
> Dlia nashoho liudu.

In English these lines read:

> Begin, brothers, to act,
> Don't shamefully sleep,
> Afternoon already is here,
> It's time to awake.
>
> It's time to get busy,
> Begin work in earnest
> In the name of education
> For all our people.[32]

Besides this sort of verse Father Hrushka also published several longer poems, such as *Mainers'ka syrota* (Miner's Orphan), *Pisni rus'koho mainera* (Songs of Rusyn, i.e., Ukrainian Miner), *Povorot mainera na rodynu* (Return of a Miner to His Homeland), and a short story *Syla voli* (Will-power).[33] All of them describe the bitter fate of Ukrainian miners in Pennsylvania and other states, as well as life's tragedies among the first Ukrainian settlers in America, particularly those who left their families in the old country. Hrushka's works, written in easy, simple form, met exactly the psychological needs of early Ukrainian immigrants. On the other hand his writings influenced the whole group of Hrushka's contemporaries who followed his footsteps in the form and content of their literary works. This group included S. Sosenko, Iu. Syrotiuk, I. Boiko, P. Tymkevych, K. Kuryllo, and perhaps the most talented poet and the first satirist, Sava Chernets'kyi.[34] The latter became one of the principal contributors to the development of Ukrainian literature in Canada before he moved to the United States.[35] Having completed at least the secondary school level in the Ukraine, Chernets'kyi was very active in the social-cultural life of Ukrainian communities in Canada and later in this country. As a poet he showed in his writings a remarkable skill and ability in versification. According to some literary critics a number of his poems indicate that he was a master of form and that he possessed a real poetic inspiration. One such work is the poem *Psalom 140* (Psalm 140), which was written under the influence of the greatest Ukrainian poet, Taras Shevchenko. It reads:

> O free us, merciful God,
> From unjust people,
> From oppressors, lawless tyrants,
> Omnipotent hangmen;
> From those damned foes,
> Who sharped their teeth
> And seek to destroy us.
> Free us, we pray,
> Save us from them.
> For You are our only hope,
> Destroyer of evil.
> For You only know well
> That we follow You;
> Only You saved our people
> In time of perilous battle . . . .[36]

For his satiric verses Chernets'kyi used the pen name Chalyi, under which he published several collected volumes of poems and short stories.[37]

Publishing his short story "Willpower" in 1896, Hryhorii Hrushka also began this particular genre of Ukrainian literature in America. Among the other short story writers that should be mentioned is the Ukrainian Catholic priest Stepan Makar, one of the editors of weekly *Svoboda* at the end of the nineteenth century. His story "American Boy," published in 1899, treats the problem of assimilation and accompanying demoralization faced by the children of many Ukrainian immigrants. A similar theme was presented by another priest, Nestor Dmytriv,[38] in his stories *Sviatyi vechir v Amerytsi* (Christmas Eve in America), *Vyishla za menonita* (She Married a Mennonite), and "Assimilation." Iuliian Chupka also treated this theme in the stories entitled *Obrazky z Ameryky* (Pictures from America).[39]

Mykhailo Biela, perhaps under the influence of Ukrainian authors in Canada, wrote several stories in which he pictured the encounter between Ukrainian and other emigré cultures in America and the struggle among them on the grounds of family life.[40]

All these writings were directed primarily towards the needs of Ukrainian settlers and their conduct of life in the new country. Hence they usually included material of a Christian, moral, or patriotic nature. The significance of these works was rather more social than literary.[41] Observing the development of the early Ukrainian literary movement in America, Franko, in his critical survey mentioned earlier, stated that most of the authors discussed above had not yet really contributed to Ukrainian literature. Their writings are interesting because they reflect the life and social conditions of Ukrainians in America, but they could not meet literary artistic standards.[42] This strict judgment by Franko was written in 1904. In Iuliian Bachyns'kyi's criticism, published in his book *Ukrains'ka imigratsiia v Z.iednanykh Derzhavakh Ameryky*, in 1914, the literary evaluation of these writers was more favorable, indicating the formal and stylistic achievements of some authors. This critic also stressed the significance of Ukrainian classic works, especially the writings of Taras Shevchenko, Ivan Franko, Lesia Ukrainka, Iurii Fed'kovych and other distinguished Ukrainian writers, which were often reprinted in Ukrainian periodicals in America and thus played an important role in influencing the writing of the immigrant authors.[43]

While the literary works of writer-pioneers dealt primarily with the life of Ukrainian immigrants in America, the writings of the second generation of Ukrainian authors dealt with events and socio-political activities in the Ukraine itself. These works were written during the period of World War I, the independence of the Ukraine, and the eventful political and social struggles in the Ukraine between the two world wars. Thus, those historical activities, as well as their principal figures and heroes appeared as the main topics in literary works, especially in Western Ukraine and abroad. On the other hand, the flourishing development of Ukrainian literature in the Ukraine itself brought to the scene a number of distinguished writers whose creative, critical and translated works brought world acclaim to Ukrainian literature. Most of these authors were also represented in publications of the Ukrainian community in the United States. In addition, one of the modern Ukrainian poets, Alexander A. Granovsky (1887-1976), whose works were still being evaluated in the Ukraine, came to the United States during World War I.[44] He continued his writings together with his educational duties as professor and researcher in entomology at the University of Minnesota, positions from which he retired in the 1950's. This poet should be recognized as a central figure in Ukrainian literature in the

United States during the second phase of its development, i.e., from the late 1910's to the early 1940's. Having started as a lyric poet and a member of the group of modern poets in the Ukraine,[45] Granovsky published three separate collections of his poetry in Kiev in 1910-1914, and was appreciated not only by contemporary critics but also by Serhii Iefremov, one of the Ukraine's leading literary historians, in his history of Ukrainian literature.[46] In America, Granovsky switched the theme of his poems to the patriotic topics which were in keeping with his later political activities as one of the leaders of the Ukrainian liberation movement outside the Ukraine during the period between the two world wars.[47] During the last twenty-five years Granovsky has published four other volumes of poetry in which, among poems dedicated to his fatherland and its political struggle, one may notice pure lyric reminiscences, philosophical thoughts, and original pictures of nature composed in carefully selected poetical form with traditional meters and stanza structure, including sonnets. Some of these poems indicate that their author closely watched the development of Ukrainian literature in the Ukraine and abroad, and especially works of his contemporaries, the great masters Maksym Ryl's'kyi and Pavlo Tychyna in Kiev,[48] or Ievhen Malaniuk and Oleh Kanyba-Ol'zhych in Prague.[49] Granovsky was perhaps the first Ukrainian poet in the United States who, in his lyric expressions such as "Minnesota," "Mississippi," and "V Skeliastykh Horakh" (In the Rocky Mountains), presented the beauty of American nature and landscape,[50] or compared America and Ukraine from the ideological point of view, as he did in the poem *Amerytsi* (To America).[51] He also translated into Ukrainian over thirty American-Indian songs, prayers and lamentations which represented seventeen different tribes.[52] Finally, it was Granovsky who, in poetical verse, gave an original definition of the identity of Ukrainians in America:

> I have been often asked—how can I love
> Two countries, as my fatherland, so dearly?
> To share my soul with them, my life, and love . . .
> And faithful be to both—how could it be, really?
>
> But it is so! Indeed—I love them both!
> America I love—as though my wife,
> With whom I share my happiness and life—
> Why shouldn't I love her till the last breath?
>
> I love Ukraine as well! As a faithful son
> Loves Mother. She that gave me life, first kiss!
> To both I owe creative thoughts and bliss—
> For their future greatness under the sun!
>
> My love to both of them is true and strong
> And my devotion to the cause-sincere,
> I see no conflict in my love, no fear—
> For liberty of both I sing my song!

578

> With freedom here—in stature grows each man
> With dignity to share in fullest measure,
> So dear to him his priceless native treasures—
> With love to both! What more can one demand?
>
> And you, my friends, have kept this guiding light—
> To see America as true, as love,
> Enriched with cultures, visions, and the lore—
> For human destiny and freedom fight![53]

Granovsky was joined by a number of other poets in the trend toward patriotic writings dedicated to the Ukraine and the stormy events of its revolution and post-revolutionary time. Their poems were in accord with the general national feeling of the predominant part of Ukrainian society in this country, enlarged as it was by newcomers, particularly veterans of the Ukrainian National Army after World War I. Dmytro Shtohryn,[54] Anastasiia Rybak, Kateryna Malanchuk, Maria Sarabun, Petro Turchyn-s'kyi, Dmytro Zakharchuk,[55] and, from the younger generation, Mykola Horishnyi and others cultivated in their poetry the idea of Ukrainian independence with a parallel expression of admiration for liberty and democracy in America. The most productive of these poets were Matvii Kostyshyn (1888-1976) and the Ukrainian Orthodox priest, Stepan Musiichuk, (1894-1952). Kostyshyn was like an official poet of Ukrainian immigration, publishing shorter and longer poems on almost all occasions and national festivities.[56] His poetry usually bore a tone similar to that in the following verses:

> My people of the Cossack blood . . .
>
> Look at Ukraine, at the wide steppes,
> There you shall find downcast sorrowful graves,
> Which for truth and freedom filled the rows,
> They will remind you of the blood days of fight . . .
>
> Do not forget falsehood, do not forget . . . .[57]

Rev. Musiichuk was the author of over 700 verses, among them the anthems of the Ukrainian Women's League of America and the Ukrainian National Association, the first stanza of which reads:

> Lykui, Vkraino, storono kokhana,
> Pryvit Tobi zza moria shlemo svii.
> Lykui, Zamors'ka Vitchyno prybrana,
> Shcho nas pryniala za svoikh ditei.

Its English translation is

> Glory to you, Ukraine, our dear motherland,
> From overseas we send you our greetings.
> Glory to you, our adopted motherland
> That accepts us as your own children.[58]

Close to these poets were Mykola D. Velychko (pen name Marko Skrytyi), the author of original lyrics and translator of Polish, German, English and Russian authors,[59] and Ivan Muliarchyk, who expressed (in poems and stories) philosophical thoughts, especially in his *Oborona muzy* (Defense of Muse), *Sonet, Bohy i liude* (Sonnet, Gods and People),[60] and *O tempora, o mores.*[61]

From the social and patriotic point of view, this poetry accomplished its purpose, but with the exception of Granovsky and, to some extent, Musiichuk, its real contribution to literature remains debatable. Simple standard verses without original ideas or esthetic features, they were written in order to meet the need of particular days, but not the need of the ages. According to Omelian Reviuk this was, perhaps, the reason that many Ukrainian periodicals in America often offered their pages for authors in the Ukraine[62] where, after World War I, new individuals with artistic talent and fresh ideas with modern trends came to literature.

The new wave of Ukrainian immigration to the United States after World War II represented a colorful complex. This group of people, numbering over a hundred thousand (mostly political emigrants), went through the stormy events of the war and the camps for displaced persons in Western Europe, finally finding their permanent homes in America. In their number were thousands of highly educated and qualified individuals, including hundreds of literary workers. Many of the latter were recognized by literary criticism in the Ukraine, but later were persecuted and even exiled to Soviet or German concentration camps for their ideas or national conception. Thus, only in the United States were they able to use their talents fully. A number of these authors were the leading members of Ukrainian literary circles in the Western Ukraine and abroad, especially in the Prague Group in Czechoslovakia, or in the Warsaw Group in Poland. With command of other European languages and knowledge of world literature, they represent all genres of Ukrainian literature and literary trends which were influential not only in the development of modern Ukrainian literature but of European and American literature as well. In fact, after World War II, and before coming to the United States, Ukrainian writers, while living in occupied zones of Western Germany, were active in the Artistic Ukrainian Movement (Mystets'kyi Ukrains'kyi Rukh) organized in Germany and popularly called MUR during the second half of the 1940's.[63] It was headed by such persons as the writer Ulas Samchuk, the literary scholars, George Shevel'ov (Iurii Sherekh), and Hryhorii Kostiuk, and other prominent literary figures.[64] Besides its various periodical and serial publications, this society provided an excellent forum for literary conferences and discussions of further paths toward developing a so-called great Ukrainian literature in the free world.[65] Thus, the Ukrainian Writers'

Association in Exile, "The Word," with Hryhorii Kostiuk as its president, simply superseded MUR in New York. Seeking new opportunities for its work, the Association was able to establish close cooperation with Ukrainian authors who had come to America earlier and to assume literary relations with other ethnic societies, expecially the Polish Literary Institute, the Institute of Jewish Research, Bulgarian Writers in Exile, and the Jewish Section of the PEN Club in New York. Several Ukrainian writers became members of the International PEN Club and were active at its congresses.[66]

While the novel was quite poorly represented among previous Ukrainian writers in the United States, since the 1950's this genre has had perhaps the largest number of authors. Thematically these works range from historical, social, and family chronicles to descriptions of the life and struggles of the Ukrainian people under the Soviet regime, from fictional biographies, autobiographies and memoirs to pictures of social and family life in America. Most of them bear all of the main hallmarks of realism (novels by Fotii Meleshko, Halyna Zhurba, Maria Strutyns'ka, Sofia Parfanovych, Oleksii Kobets', Volodymyr Nestorovych, and others), and Neorealism, with some romantic colors, represented by Iurii Tys-Krokhmaliuk, Hryhorii Luzhnyts'kyi and Anatol' Halan. Mykola Ponedilok (1922-1976), who began writing in the United States, specialized in the tragic-lyric novel, sketch and story, picturing with sincere narration Ukrainians of the prewar, war, and postwar periods, including their life in America.[67] The late Todos' Os'machka (1895-1962), first representative of existentialism in Ukrainian poetry, created a remarkable naturalistic picture in his novel *Rotonda dushohubtsiv* (Red Assassins), a work (translated into English and French) depicting the suffering of Ukrainians in the Soviet Union.[68] Like Os'machka in his prose is Vasyl' Barka, particularly in his novel *Zhovtyi kniaz'* (The Yellow Prince).[69] Dokiia Humenna, the most productive contemporary Ukrainian novelist and author of twenty-one volumes, began by writing short stories in the 1920's. After harsh accusation by official Soviet criticism for her so-called bourgeois nationalistic tendencies, she remained silent from the 1930's until the 1940's. Thus, most of her novels were written abroad, primarily in the United States. Principally a realist and psychological novelist in her earlier works, Humenna moved to a new and original genre, which is characterized by Kostiuk as a "mythological-historical-retrospective vision." In this genre Humenna recreates a picture of Eastern Europe in general and of the Ukraine in particular during their prehistoric ages.[70] Three of her books are devoted to descriptions of America and of the American-Ukrainian community.[71] F. Maliar and especially Olexa Izars'kyi, according to Kostiuk, are inclined toward the psychological-analytical realism of Gabriel Marcel, Marcel Proust and Ernest Hemingway, and they search for "depth in a sensual and extrasensual world." This search is particularly apparent in the novel *Kyiv*.[72] Iaroslav Kurdydyk occupies a special place among modern Ukrainian novelists in America; he is a master of miniatures.[73] Bohdan Nyzhankivs'kyi is a master of dialogue and, at the same time, one of the leading representatives of satire in poetry.[74] Other satiric writers that should be mentioned are Ivan Kernyts'kyi (for his collections of short stories, *Tsyhans'kymy dorohamy* and *Pereletni ptakhy*, and a novel *Heroi peredmistia*), and the late M. Ponedilok (for his collections of stories, *Vitaminy* and *Sobornyi borshch*).

Edward Kozak is a distinguished painter and the editor of the only Ukrainian satirical-humorous monthly in North America, *Lys Mykyta*. He is the author of many humorous feuilletons published in this journal under his pen name Hryts' Zozulia. Some of them were issued in the separate collected volume under the title *Hryts' Zozulia* in 1973. Other represent-atives of this genre are Ivan Eventual'nyi, pseud. (collection of stories, *Proty shersty*), Stepan Vusatyi, pseud. (collection of stories, *Emigratsiia v pokhodi*), and Zosym Donchuk (satiric novels, *Hnat Kindratovych* and *More po kolina*). Donchuk in his novel *Sokolova dochka* (The Sokil's Daughter), as well as Daria Iaroslavs'ka in the novel *Ii N'iu-Iork* (Her New York), Ol'ha Savyts'ka, in the novel *Z ptashynoho hnizda* (From the Bird's Nest), and Liubov Kolens'ka, in her novel *Samotnist'* (Loneliness) give psychological-realistic pictures that are based on the lives of Ukrainians in the United States. These works concern both individuals and families with problems involving generation gaps. Iaroslav Kurdydyk, Oleh Lysiak, Iurii Tys-Krokhmaliuk and Liubomyr Rykhtyts'kyi bring to their novels the topic of the Ukrainian liberation movement during World War II, especially the Ukrainian Insurgent Army.

Ukrainian drama has not had an opportunity for successful development in the United States. Lack of a permanent professional theater and access to film or television production has caused the neglect of this genre. Hence, among approximately 2,200 titles published during the last twenty-five years, only about fifty (including more than thirty children's plays) were of the dramatic genre.[75] Leonid Poltava is first among the playwrights; he has published seven plays and four opera librettos (two of the latter *Anna Iaroslavna* and *Lys Mykyta* were successfully staged). Bohdan Boichuk, Iaroslav Hrynevych, Petro Mirchuk, Pavlo Savchuk, Vasyl' Chaplenko and Anatol' Iuryniak should also be considered as distinguished contributors to this particular genre.

Artistic sketches and memoirs are presented in Ukrainian-American literature during the postwar period by such authors as D. Humenna, Iosyp Hirniak, the late Fedir Dudko, Viktor Prykhod'ko, Mykhailo Ostroverkha, and others.

Poetry is the most flourishing genre in Ukrainian literature in the United States. Its growth was assured by such senior poets as the neo-romantic, Roman Kupchyns'kyi (1894-1976), the poet of the Ukrainian National Army and the Ukraine's independence, 1917-1920; Ievhen Malaniuk (1897-1968), a leading authority in Ukrainian poetry abroad after World War I, who envisioned the Ukraine as a "steppeland Hellas." He wrote twelve volumes of poetry and six volumes of critical essays. Malaniuk began as a symbolist and later developed a neoclassical style which is quite notable in his poem *Kamin'* (A Stone):

> Look at the stone. It holds its peace:
> On faith and wisdom it is bent.
> The world may thunder, wars increase,
> Blood gush and boundaries be rent—
> But cold and bare for all to see
> It marks the crossroads.
>
> Cars rush on
> And footsteps pass it leisurely.
> All pass it by.
>
> Like truth to con
> It stands there unconditional
> With just a hint of scorn expressed.
> That stony laughter at them all
> The passing throngs have never guessed.[76]

Bohdan Kravtsiv (Krawciw; 1904-1975) is, of course, one of the leading members of the senior poets' group. He served as editor of many periodicals, serial and monographic publications in the Ukraine and abroad. He also translated R. M. Rilke into Ukrainian. As a poet Kravtsiv was a representative of romanticism in his early poems, and neoclassicism in the later works, including the following sonnet:

> The grated, stained-glass window, guard-house style,
> An echo of the organ's voice remembers;
> The smoke of incense rises from the embers,
> And fusty chophouse odours stir the bile.
>
> Here groups of captive criminals are spread—
> The murderer, the wounder and the wencher;
> The smug, fat chaplain gives them words of censure
> In ugly sermonizing, tritely said.
>
> While I behold: Christ passes down the nave
> And to the thief and murderer he bends
> And utters a compassionate "My brother!"
>
> His all-forgiving hands are stretched to save—
> To eager lips and eyes his touch extends
> And to the broken heart's bewildered smother.[77]

The most productive member of this group is Sviatoslav Hordyns'kyi, who, in addition to his twenty volumes of original poetry and translation of Western European (English, Spanish, German, Portuguese, and French) authors, especially of Francois Villon into Ukrainian, is the author of numerous essays and articles on literary and art topics. He is also an editor of many periodicals and monographs. As an artist-painter, Hordyns'kyi "has the reputation of a Ukrainian Michaelangelo," renowned in religious painting and ornamentation of over fifty churches in the United States, Canada and Europe.[78] Hordyns'kyi, who was born in 1906 and educated in French art schools, started as a romanticist and later adopted a neo-classical style. The expressionistic trend in Ukrainian literature was represented by the late Todos' Os'machka (1895-1962), who died in Long Island. The poet left seven volumes of poetry and two volumes of translations of Oscar Wilde and William Shakespeare.[79] Vasyl' Barka might be considered a leading surrealist in Ukrainian poetry not only in the United States, but in other countries, including the Ukraine itself. Here are a few lines of his carefully constructed poetry (published in seven volumes):

> . . . Then darkness fell, a time of utter darkness.
> At once the entire state of earthly life
> Was trembling with the tears of sinless roses
> And the warm song: Hosannah in the highest!–
> Was born from the joy of spirit and of body.[80]

There are a number of other important poets. Ostap Tarnavs'kyi is presently the President of the Ukrainian Writers' Association in Exile, "The Word." He has written four volumes of poetry and one volume of essays, and he has translated French, English, American, German, and Polish poets.[81] Vadym Lesych, pseud. (V. L. Kirshak), has written ten volumes of poems and translated T. S. Eliot and J. R. Jimenez. Other writers are Hanna Cherin' (Anna Pan'kiv), with her inclination to impressionistic compositions, Marta Tarnavs'ka, Oleksa Veretenchenko, Leonid Poltava, Iryna Shuvars'ka, and Petro Karpenko-Krynytsia. The latter also belong to those Ukrainian poets who picture American Indians in their poetry. Krynytsia has devoted an entire collection of his poems, *Indiians'ki baliady* (The Indian Ballads), to an original poetic admiration of the life and the style and traditions of these people. It is interesting to note that in some ballads Krynytsia followed the formal traces of the early works of the late Ukrainian symbolist poet, Pavlo Tychyna.[82]

Authors of stories for children and young people continue to write in the traditional manner, and they attract, with their traditionally illustrated publications, the youngsters, especially those who grow in a family which preserves Ukrainian traditions. The most productive in this field are Roman Zawadovych, V. Barahura and Lesia Khraplyva, authors of a number of volumes of poetry and short stories, and children's comics as well. Marie Halun-Bloch writes only in English and thus not only for Ukrainian teenagers but for general readers of this age. Her novels *Marya*,

Aunt America, The Two Worlds of Damian, and *Bern, Son of Mikula*, based on Ukrainian history and on the family life of Ukrainians in America, are interesting to American youth because of the works' easy style and new and unknown pictures and heroes. And finally, another author of books designed for young people, Iryna Lavrivs'ka, recently published a quite original work, based, as she stated, on historical sources. It is a novel entitled *Pershyi kozak v Amerytsi* (The First Cossack in America),[83] which might be compared with American Western stories related to the pioneer's life and their first contacts with Indians. The young generation of authors, primarily poets was introduced to Ukrainian-American literature without the usual generation gap, and the activity of the New York Group, which started in 1955, could be considered as a natural step towards the vital continuity of the literary process. It was just a group of good friends from the United States, Canada, France, Germany, and Brazil, who according to their spiritual leader, Bohdan Boichuk, "barefoot tried to climb the Olympus of Ukrainian literature," offering their poetry, free from the traditional limits determined by the cannons of poetical form.[84] In other words they presented their lyrical expressions which united in conglomerate the poet's feelings, erotic experience and even *Weltanschauung*. They presented a novel without a plot, intrigue and personages, a play without action; they presented a new form of creation, close to abstractionism. It should be mentioned, however, that in world literature these ideas are not new, and the authors of the New York Group, former students of world literature (including Ukrainian and American) and today educators in different countries, were able to be acquainted with rich sources that influenced their poetical conception. For example, I would like to mention two poems written in Ukrainian, a poem *Idealizovana biohrafiia* (Idealized Biography) by Iurii Tarnavs'kyi,[85] which created a sort of revolution in the Ukrainian poetical process in the 1960's and B. Boichuk's poem *Zaklynannia* (Invocation).[86] Here we should mention not only the similarity between them, but, and this is rather important, their close relation with the American poet E. E. Cummings, especially his poem *Love*.[87] On the other hand, in some poems of the ideological character of another member of the New York Group, an American poetess Patricia Warren, who also became a known Ukrainian author under the pseudonym Patrytsiia Kalyna, we may observe some traces of the archeological poems of the late Ukrainian poet and scholar, Oleh Kandyba-Ol'zhych, who died in a German concentration camp.[88] Another contribution of the New York Group of authors to Ukrainian and American literatures is apparently their constant translation of Western European and American poets into Ukrainian and of Ukrainian authors into English, German and other Western tongues.[89] Close to the New

York Group in form but different in their philosophical concept of the world are the writings of dissident, young Ukrainian authors in the Soviet Ukraine, who might be called spiritual emigrants, because almost all their works have been published outside the Soviet Ukraine, especially in the United States. Many of them are translated into English and thus are available to the American public. Their main theme, which might even be called their poetical religion, involves a quest for a liberation of the human soul and for universal love, for the love of the individual, of the nation, of mankind. At the same time the search for truth and service to truth unites both groups.

* * *

Any discussion of the development of Ukrainian literary criticism in America might be divided into literary scholarship and the critical evaluations of works of single authors or groups. The literary scholars, usually members of the older and middle generations, follow the methods appropriate to their research, which they have chosen before or immediately after coming to this country. For example, George Shevel'ov, a creator of a formula for the national style in Ukrainian literature,[90] is a good example of a writer who uses the philological, aesthetical, and, to some extent, comparative methods.[91] George Kostiuk utilized in his critical works sociological and aesthetical methods. One of the oldest Ukrainian critics, Luka Lutsiv, continues his specialization in literary portraits in his monographs, and in literary evaluations in his periodical contributions to *Svoboda*. In this method, he is also followed by young critics, B. Boichuk and B. Rubchak.[92] Ostap Tarnavskyi, in his essays on world literature, Kievan Neoclassicists, Ernest Hemingway, America's Myth, T. S. Eliot, and others, applied historico-philosophical methods,[93] while John Fizer introduced to the criticism of Ukrainian modern literature an emotional-phonological classification, based primarily on the theoretic formula of John Crowe Ransom, presented in his study *The New Criticism* and partly in *The World's Body*.[94] Wolodymyr Zyla applies in his literary studies both philological and comparative methods.[95] And finally Bohdan Romanenchuk continues his research based on a bio-bibliographical method, especially in his short encyclopedia of Ukrainian literature.[96] The critical evaluation has a larger number of workers. All of these scholars, as well as the linguist and writer Vasyl' Chaplenko, the writer and educator Roman Kuchar (pen name, R. Volodymyr), the critic Kornylo Krups'kyi, and others specialize in this particular kind of literary criticism. Contributions of Ukrainian authors in the United States to Ukrainian ethnic literature continue proving that American literature is a treasure in which ethnic literatures (including Ukrainian) have their recognized but not yet acknowledged place. On the other hand, translations of American authors into Ukrainian

586

and vice versa have begun to build a bridge between American and Ukrainian literatures.

University of Illinois at Urbana-Champaign

NOTES

[1] Ivan Franko, "Iuzhnorusskaia literatura," *Entsyklopedicheskii slovar*, ed. I. E. Andreevskii (St. Petersburg: F. A. Brokhauz, I. A. Efron, 1904), 41(81), 325, col. 2.

[2] Omelian Reviuk, "Nashi literaturni i mystets'ki nadbannia v Amerytsi," *Propamiatna knyha, vydana z nahody soroklitn'oho iuvyleiu Ukrains'koho narodnoho soiuzu*, ed. Luka Myshuha (Jersey City, N.J.: Ukrains'kyi narodnyi soiuz, 1936), pp. 343-50.

[3] Hryhorii Kostiuk *Z litopysu literaturnoho zhyttia v diiaspori*, offprint from the journal *Suchasnist'* (Munich, 1971).

[4] Roman Kuchar, "The Traditional and the Contemporary in Ukrainian Emigré Literature," *The Ukrainian Review*, 19, No. 1 (Spring 1972), 66-81.

[5] Yaroslav J. Chyz, "The Ukrainian Immigrants in the United States," *Kalendar Ukrains'koho robitnychoho soiuza na rik 1940*, vol. 29, 97-128.

[6] Bohdan Boichuk, ed., *Koordynaty; antolohiia suchasnoi ukrains'koi poezii na zakhodi*, 2 vols. (Munich: Suchasnist', 1969).

[7] Chyz, p. 98, and "Vistky pro ukraintsiv v Amerytsi pered Horozhans'koiu viinoiu," *Kalendar Ukrains'koho robitnychoho soiuza na rik 1937*, vol. 26, 101.

[8] Luka Myshuha, "Ponad piv stolittia v novomu sviti," *Iuvyleinyi al'manakh, 1894-1944, vydanyi z nahody piat' desiatlitn'oho iuvyleiu Ukrains'koho narodnoho soiuzu*, ed. Luka Myshuha (Jersey City, N.J.: Ukrains'kyi narodnyi soiuz, 1944), p. 2.

[9] Vasyl Mudryi, "Ukrainian Immigration in the U.S.A.," *Guide to Ukrainian-American Institutions, Professionals and Business*, comp. & ed. Wasyl Weresh (New York: Carpathian Star Publishing Co., 1955), p. 5.

[10] Joseph Zelechivsky, "Ukraine, North Dakota," in his *Golden Jubilee Souvenir: 50th Anniversary of the Holy Priesthood, 1919-1969* (Manville, R. I.: n.p., 1969), p. 14.

[11] Yaroslav J. Chyz, "Ukraintsi v Nort Dakoti i Montani," *Kalendar Ukrains'koho robitnychoho soiuza na rik 1939*, vol. 28, 93.

[12] According to Volodymyr Kubijovyč, in "Number of Ukrainians in the World," *Ukraine: A Concise Encyclopaedia* (Toronto: Univ. of Toronto Press, 1963), I, 249, there are 1,100,000 Ukrainians in the United States, while the Ukrainian Congress Committee of America claims that there are 2,000,000 Ukrainian Americans. Cf. *Twenty Years of Devotion to Freedom: Survey of Purposes and Activities of the Ukrainian Congress Committee of America on the 20th Anniversary of Its Existence* (New York: Ukrainian Congress Committee, 1960), p. 5.

[13] The Academy's official serial publication *Annals* started in 1951, and *Visti UVAN* (News of UAAS) in 1970.

[14] The Society continues to publish its serial publications *Zapysky* (Notes), which started in L'viv, 1892, *Khronika* (The Chronicle) since 1900, and *Dopovidi* (Papers) since 1957.

[15] Here should be mentioned such societies as the Ukrainian Historical Society, Ukrainian Medical Association of North America, Ukrainian Engineers' Society of America, Ukrainian Artists Association in the U.S.A., etc. All of them publish their periodicals or irregular serial publications.

[16] Roman Slobodian, "Ukrains'kyi narodnyi soiuz v tsyfrakh," *Ukraintsi u vil'nomu sviti: iuvileina knyha Ukrains'koho narodnoho soiuzu, 1894-1954*, ed. L. Myshuha and A. Drahan (Jersey City, N.J.: Ukrains'kyi narodnyi soiuz, 1954), p. 45.

[17] Wasyl Weresh, "Ukrainian Congress Committee of America, Inc.," in his *Guide to Ukrainian-American Institutions, Professionals and Business*, pp. 136-49.

[18] *Ukrainian Catholic Archeparchy of Philadelphia: the Directory* (Philadelphia: Ukrainian Catholic Archeparchy, 1975), pp. 33-149.

[19] *Harvard Ukrainian Studies Newsletter*, Vols. 3-6 (various issues).

[20] Theodore Luciw, *Father Agapius Honcharenko: First Ukrainian Priest in America* (New York: Ukrainian Congress Committee of America, 1970), p. 176.

[21] Yaroslav J. Chyz, "Pivstolittia ukrains'koi presy v Amerytsi," *Kalendar Ukrains'koho robitnychoho soiuza na rik 1939*, vol. 28, p. 118. The first Ukrainian newspaper biweekly *America* was edited and published by the Ukrainian Catholic priest Ivan Volians'kyi in Shenandoah, Pa., 1886-1890.

[22] Oleksander Fedyns'kyi, *Bibliohrafichnyi pokazhchyk ukrains'koi presy poza mezhamy Ukrainy*, vol. 5-6, 1970-1971 (Cleveland, Ohio: Ukrains'kyi muzei-arkhiv, 1972), pp. 5-35.

[23] A need for such a coordination was evident even in 1904; cf. "Potreba literatury," *Slovo*, No. 6 (Scranton, Pa.: Vyd-vo im. A. Bonchevs'koho, 1904), pp. 6-9.

[24] Kostiuk, *Z litopysu literaturnoho . . .*, p. 6, and the information received from Mr. Roman Malanchuk, Secretary of the Association, 26 January 1976.

[25] "Asotsiiatsiia diiachiv ukrains'koi kul'tury," *Estafeta*, No. 1 (January 1970), pp. 246-48.

[26] The Institute's Literary Section was organized on 30 May 1976; cf. "Prof. B. Romanenchuk ocholyv novozasnovanu konferentsiiu," *Svoboda*, 8 June 1976, p. 1, col. 1-2, p. 5, col. 5-8.

[27] The Ivan Franko Literary Foundation in Chicago and the Ukrainian National Women's League of America Literary Foundation in New York.

[28] Kostiuk, pp. 38-41. See also Kuchar, p. 75.

[29] Bohdan Boichuk, "Iak i poshcho narodylasia N'iu-Iors'ka hrupa," *Terem*, No. 2 (March 1966), pp. 34-38.

[30] This weekly was published in Ukrainian under the title *Svoboda: nedil'ne vydannia*.

[31] Reviuk, pp. 344-46.

[32] Ibid., p. 345. Translation mine.

[33] Ibid.

[34] Ibid.

[35] Yar Slavutych, "Ukrainian Poetry in Canada: A Historical Account," *The Ukrainian Review*, 22, No. 1 (1975), 111.

[36] M. I. Mandryka, *History of Ukrainian Literature in Canada* (Winnipeg: Ukrainian Free Academy of Sciences, 1968), p. 40.

[37] S. Chalyi, *Vesela chytanka z obrazkamy*, Part 2., enlarged ed. (Scranton, Pa.: Vyd-vo Ukrains'koi knyharni, 1916).

[38] Rev. Nestor Dmytriv is usually called the "Ukrainian-American Nestor," which means a chronicler of Ukrainians in America; cf. note to Nestor Dmytriv, "Z pochatkiv nashoho zhyttia v Amerytsi," *Iuvyleinyi al'manakh, 1894-1944*, p. 246.

[39] Iuliian Chupka's four short stories "Obrazky z Ameryky," written under his pen name Buz'ko, were reprinted from *Svoboda* and published separately as the first Ukrainian book in the United States: Buz'ko, *Obrazky z Ameryky* (Shamokin, Pa.: Vydavnytstvo chasopysu "Svoboda," 1896); cf. Iaroslav J. Chyz, "Iuvylei ukrains'koi

presy i knyzhky v Amerytsi," *Kalendar Ukrains'koho robitnychoho soiuza na rik 1937*, vol. 26, 137-38.

[40] Reviuk, p. 349.

[41] Ibid., p. 344.

[42] Franko, p. 325, col. 2.

[43] Iuliian Bachyns'kyi, *Ukrains'ka imigratsiia v Z'iednanykh Derzhavakh Amerky* (L'viv: Druk. Naukovoho tovarystva im. Shevchenka, 1914), pp. 465-72.

[44] "Oleksander Nepryts'kyi-Granovs'kyi," *Samostiina Ukraina*, No. 10 (1967), p. 11. Here and elsewhere in this article the reader may encounter two different spellings of the same name (e.g., Granovs'kyi and Granovsky). One version is a direct transliteration from the Ukrainian, and the other version is based upon the Latin-alphabet spelling.

[45] Granovsky published most of his early poetical works in *Ukrains'ka khata* (Kiev), a journal which represented the modern trend in literature.

[46] Serhii Iefremov, "Na pochatku novoho viku," in his *Istoriia ukrains'koho pys'menstva*, 4th ed., rev., II (Kyiv-Leipzig: Ukrains'ka nakladnia, 1919), 314.

[47] Vivian Throp, "Dr. Alexander Granovsky, Prominent Ukrainian-American," *The Trident*, 4, No. 9 (November 1940), 4-13.

[48] Alexander Granovsky, "Zoloti vorota" (The Golden Gate), in his *Osinni uzory: poezii* (New York: Zhyttia i mystetstvo, 1957), p. 59.

[49] Granovsky, "Neolit," ibid., p. 119.

[50] Granovsky, *Iskry viry: poezii* (New York: Zhyttia i mystetstvo, 1953), pp. 75-77.

[51] *Osinni uzory*, p. 61.

[52] Granovsky, "Z indiians'kykh pisen'," in his *Iskry viry*, pp. 111-40.

[53] Granovsky, "I Love Them Both," Irene T. Granovsky, *Who We Are: A Genealogy of Our Family* (St. Paul: n.p., 1974), pp. 122-23. Irene T. Granovsky stated that this poem was written to commemorate the 50th anniversary of the International Institute of St. Paul (1970), ibid, p. 122. In fact, the first three stanzas of this poem were translated from Granovsky's Ukrainian poem "Pytaete mene," written in 1951 and published in his *Iskry viry*, p. 26.

[54] Dmytro Shtohryn, *Dolia Ukrainy* (Philadelphia: Druk. Rus'koho syryts'koho domu, 1917). The author dedicated this volume to the fighters for liberty of the Ukraine.

[55] Dmytro Zakharchuk, *Ridnyi krai: poezii* (Northhampton, Pa.: n.p., 1934). In addition to this collected volume, the author published at least four other volumes of poetry, short stories, and novels.

[56] "Matvii Kostyshyn, trubadur amerykans'koi Ukrainy, pomer na 88 rotsi zhyttia," *Svoboda*, 18 February 1976, p. 1, cols. 1-2; p. 6, cols. 3-4.

[57] Matvii Kostyshyn, "Ne proshchai" (Do Not Excuse), *Propamiatna knyha, vydana z nahody soroklitn'oho iuvyleiu Ukrains'koho narodnoho soiuzu*, p. 411. Translation mine.

[58] Stepan Musiichuk, "Hymn Ukrains'koho narodnoho soiuzu," *Ukraintsi u vil'nomu sviti*, p. v. Translation mine.

[59] Marko Skrytyi, *Pisni shchyroi liubovy* (New York: Nakl. Sichovoho bazaru, 1920).

[60] Ivan Muliarchyk, *I. Religiinist' ta bezkonfesiinist': diial'og. II Poezyi* (Detroit: n.p., 1930), pp. 26-30.

[61] Muliarchyk, *Smikh pralisa* (Detroit: n.p., 1937), pp. 22-24.

[62] Reviuk, pp. 345-46.

[63] Iurii Sherekh, "Ukrains'ka emigratsiina literatura v Evropi 1945-1949: retrospektyvy i perspektyvy," in his *Ne dlia ditei: literaturno-krytychni statti i esei* (New York: Proloh, 1964), pp. 226-74.

[64] Ulas Samchuk, a leading Ukrainian writer, wrote seventeen volumes of novels, several of them translated into English, French, German and other languages. Samchuk was the President of MUR. George Yury Shevel'ov (pen name Iurii Sherekh), one of the leading Ukrainian linguists and literary scholars, is presently professor of Slavic languages at the Columbia University. He has written approximately eighteen volumes of works on linguistic and literary topics and over 400 essays, articles and book reviews. His bio-bibliography was published in the Festschrift *Symbolae in honorem Georgii Y. Shevelov* (Munich: Universita Libera Ucrainensis, 1971), pp. 5-35. Hryhorii Kostiuk, one of the leading Ukrainian literary scholars and history researchers, is author of seven monographs and editor of many separate and serial publications. He is also the author of numerous literary essays, articles and book reviews. The bibliography of Kostiuk's works has been published in *Slovo*, vol. 5.

[65] The papers and discussions of those conferences were published in *MUR: zbirnyk* No. 1-3, 1946-1947; and in various issues of *Svitannia* and *Orlyk*, 1947.

[66] Kostiuk, pp. 12-16.

[67] Mykola Ponedilok wrote seven volumes of novels and humorous short stories, and three plays.

[68] Todos' Os'machka, *Rotonda dushohubtsiv: opovidannia* (Winnipeg: Trident Press, 1956). Os'machka is the author of three other volumes of novels, seven volumes of poetry, and translator from English and German into Ukrainian.

[69] Vasyl' Barka is the author of seven volumes of poetry, two novels, two volumes of essays, and two volumes of literary criticism. The novel *Zhovtyi kniaz'* was published in Munich, 1963.

[70] Kostiuk, pp. 20-21.

[71] Dokiia Humenna, *Bahato neba: zbirka narysiv* (New York: Slovo, 1954); *Vichni vohni Al'berty* (Edmonton: Vyd. zakhodom Petra Pausha, 1959); and *Sered khmarosiahiv: Niu-iors'ka mozaika* (New York: Slovo, 1962).

[72] Kostiuk, p. 30.

[73] Iaroslav Kurdydyk, *Etiudy-miniiatury* (Toronto: Nasha slava, 1955).

[74] Bohdan Nyshankivs'kyi (Babai), *Virshi ironichni satyrychni i komichni* (Buenos Aires: Iu. Serediak, 1959).

[75] This information is given according to several bibliographical sources, especially Bohdan Romanenchuk, *Bibliohrafiia vydan' ukrains'koi emigratsiinoi literatury 1945-1970* (Philadelphia: Kyiv, 1974); Nataliia Chaplenko, *Bibliohrafiia vydan' zhinochoi tvorchosty poza mezhamy Ukrainy* (Philadelphia: Soiuz ukrainok Ameryky, 1974); and *Kataloh knyzhok Ukrains'koi knyharni v Edmontoni*, 1961-1976.

[76] *The Ukrainian Poets, 1189-1962*, selected and translated into English verse by C. H. Andrusyshen and Watson Kirkconnell (Toronto: Univ. of Toronto Press, 1963), pp. 412-13.

[77] Ibid., p. 453.

[78] Mandryka, p. 230.

[79] Boichuk, *Koordynaty*, II, 7.

[80] *The Ukrainian Poets*, p. 438.

[81] Boichuk, II, 175; also Ostap Tarnavs'kyi, *Samotnie derevo* (New York: Slovo, 1960), pp. 39-91.

590

[82] Petro Karpenko-Krynytsia, *Indiians'ki baliady* (New York: n.p., 1968).

[83] Iryna Lavrivs'ka, *Pershyi kozak v Amerytsi: opovidannia dlia molodi*. (Toronto: Vyd-vo Homin Ukrainy, 1975).

[84] Boichuk, "Iak i poshcho . . . ," p. 36. Members of the New York Group are Bohdan Boichuk, Bohdan T. Rubchak, Patrytsiia Kalyna, Iurii Tarnavs'kyi, Zhenia Vasyl'kivs'ka, Ema Andiievs'ka, Vira Vovk, Oleh Koverko, Iurii Kolomyets', and Marko Tsarynnyk.

[85] Iurii Tarnavs'kyi, *Idealizovana biohrafiia: poezii* (Munich: Suchasnist', 1964).

[86] Bohdan Boichuk, "Zaklynannia," *Novi poezii*, No. 11 (1969), pp. 28-38.

[87] E. E. Cummings, "Liubove, tvoie volossia ie tsarstvo," *Novi poezii*, No. 1 (1959), pp. 60-61.

[88] *Novi poezii*, No. 11 (1969), pp. 40-46.

[89] Ibid., No. 1-11 (1959-1969).

[90] Iurii Sherekh, "Styli suchasnoi ukrains'koi literatury na emihratsii," *MUR: zbirnyk*, No. 1 (1946), pp. 54-81; and his "V oboroni velykykh: polemichna stattia," *MUR: zbirnyk*, No. 3 (1947), pp. 11-26.

[91] Iakiv Hurs'kyi, comp., "Bibliohrafiia prats' Prof. D-ra Iuriia Shevel'ova, 1934-1968," *Symbolae in honorem Georgii Y. Shevelov*, pp. 7-35.

[92] Boichuk, *Koordynaty*, I and II.

[93] Ostap Tarnavs'kyi, "Mit Ameryky," "Dukh sumnivu i beznadii," "Potseibichnyi mit Hemingveia," "Populiarnist' poezii," in his *Tuha za mitom: esei* (New York: Kliuchi, 1966), pp. 38-54, 65-72, 121-26.

[94] John Fizer, "Vstupna stattia," Boichuk, *Koordynaty*, I, pp. xiii-xxxii.

[95] Mandryka, pp. 210-14.

[96] Bohdan Romanenchuk, *Azbukovnyk: korotka entsyklopediia ukrains'koi literatury*, 2 vols. (Philadelphia: Kyiv, 1969-1975).

The American Yiddish Writer: From Cahan to Singer

Daniel Walden

ABSTRACT

Coming out of the medieval orthodoxy of the shtetl East European past, trying to break through to modernity, Mendele Mokher Seforim, I. L. Peretz, and Sholom Aleichem were the first major writers in Yiddish to lead their people into the nineteenth century. In the United States, David Pinski and Sholom Asch, disciples of Peretz, were among the earliest to try to bridge the gap between the two cultures. Pinski, a playwright in Eastern Europe, succeeded here with *The House of Noah Edon* (1929), a genealogical novel of three generations describing the reluctance of the children and grandchildren to follow the old ways; Asch, preoccupied with messianic redemption, ultimately turned out three Christological novels. Meanwhile, a younger group, called "Die Yunge," combined a romantic view of the past with a proletarian outlook. Isaac Raboy's *Mr. Goldenberg* (1913) and *The Jewish Cowboy* (1942) dealt with North Dakota, while Joseph Opatoshu's *Romance of a Horse Thief* (1917) was followed by many books, including *Lost Persons* (1932), and an historical trilogy. At the same time Abraham Goldfaden, David Kessler, Jacob Adler, and Maurice Schwartz dominated the theatre while M. L. Halpern, H. Leivick, Mani Leib and Jacob Glatstein were the most renowned poets. But, above all were Abraham Cahan, editor of the Yiddish daily, *The Forward* for four decades and author of *Yekl* (1896), and *The Rise of David Levinsky* (1917; both in English), and Isaac Bashevis Singer, author of novels and short stories, and the most famous Yiddish writer since World War II. However, it must be said that Cahan's fame was linked to his ability to move *The Forward* in an Americanized direction, and write immigrant novels in English; Singer, whose major outlet is the *New Yorker* magazine, is similarly famous because he is widely known in English translation. The fact is that the Yiddishkeit of the past is fading away—in spite of the romance of *Fiddler on the Roof* and the renewed interest in the colleges—and with it is going one of the most remarkable cultural phenomena the world has ever seen. (DW)

By the middle of the nineteenth century, in the Pale of Settlement in Eastern Europe, the central fact for the Jew was the recognition that to be a Jew was the fundamental environing condition on one's life. All values arose from where one was forced to live; that is, in the shtetl. All traditions were bound up in the shtetl, the shtetl was the embodiment of the Jewish community, and from the shtetl came one's prestige (or *yikhus*). To be a Talmud Khochem or a Yeshiva Bokher was the one sure way to gain status. After several hundred years of constraint and pogroms and despair, however, broken only by the influence of the Hasidic movement and the importation of the Haskalah (the Jewish Enlightenment), it was clear that aspirations could only be satisfied within the shtetl. What more natural response for Jews, who were not and could not be citizens, than to turn their energies inward. They lived in a world of their own. They required everyone to be a *mentsh*—even God. They assumed that all men were innocent, free of the Sins of the Fall, and though good and evil existed and it was believed that man was free to choose which, he would always choose what was morally and ethically right.

In the grip of reality, all Jews were potential victims of the repressive governments that surrounded them. Thus, in view of the Jewish tradition of learning, of testing and self-examination, it is not surprising that these conditions would be reflected in the literary tradition. After all, the Eastern European Yiddish writer had an identity crisis. The result, expressed by I. L. Peretz, is that the notion of a shared historical consciousness created a new type, a Jew from Eastern Europe: "Is there a people, a wander-folk without fixed borders . . . that lives, suffers, and does not perish; that is weak, attached by the greatest and the strongest and does not surrender—then must such a people see differently, feel differently, have a different view of life, a different conception of the future of the world, of life, and of man."[1] The result was a literary reflection of this culture that bore the weight of the past and gave values to what Matthew Arnold called "sweetness and light." Where there were no dominant or heroic figures in the present, the writers turned to a Biblical and/or mythical past or to a present saturated with the personalities of those who existed, "as they could." The most sensitive and perceptive voices in the nineteenth century were Mendele Mokher Seforim, I. L. Peretz, and Sholom Aleichem.

Mendele Mokher Seforim, the grandfather of Yiddish literature, was known for his ability to reflect the ethos of his people. In a story called "The Calf," for example, he exposed and criticized the people's tendency to believe in omens, and the efficacy of cheder training all day long. "To make a real person," that is, one admired by a traditional mother, the boy had to attend Hebrew school all day long. When he romped out in the air with his calf, when his cheeks grew red and healthy, he was criticized by his mother. "Is it really God's will that a human being be cooped up?" the boy wondered. "Is a virtuous Jewish child a pale and refined child?" he asked.[2] Beset by rules and regulations that no longer went well in the nineteenth century, because a few windows had been opened to the Western and secular world, the boy could no longer easily distinguish between dreams and reality, between what was and what ought to be. Mendele's stories reflected these concerns, for he held that "a literature which does not concern itself with the people and their needs and is not influenced by them cannot hope to have any influence on them."[3] In the ideal sense, happiness comes from a good heart and good deeds.

For Sholom Aleichem, who early developed a talent for mimicking the characters who patronized his father's tavern, most important was the realization that "A Kasrelik is not merely a starving man, a luckless fellow; he is, if you please, a poor man not downcast by his poverty. On the contrary, he makes a joke of it. 'How do we earn our living? Just as you see, ha ha. One lives . . . .' "[4] With so many questing after so little, with fantasies on every hand, what mattered was chance and luck. In this bed of despair the real source of his good spirits was "humor." "Not to cry, out of spite," he said was his philosophy. In turn, his prescription was "only to laugh!" In his story, "On Account of a Hat," Sholom Shachnah (nicknamed Rattlebrain), an absent-minded and usually unsuccessful real-estate broker, was on his way home after consummating a deal. Having sent a wire to his wife—"Arriving Home Passover Without Fail"—he went to sleep in the railway station after paying the porter to awaken him. Suddenly awakened from a deep dream he seized his neighbor's hat, an official's hat, and found that everyone now deferred to him and called him your excellency. When he noticed that he was wearing the wrong hat he rushed off the train, back to the station, only to have the train pull out. His only thought now was that the porter had awakened the wrong person. " 'Twenty times I tell him to wake me,' Shachnah screamed, 'and I even gave him a tip, and what does he do, that dumb ox, may he catch cholera in the face, but wake the official and me he leaves asleep on the bench.' "[5] The same kind of humor is seen in Sholom Aleichem's "Eternal Life," where a young man needing to register for military service tries to do a stranger a favor by burying the man's wife; the young man winds up being accused of murder. From that time on he disliked all those Jewish hypocrites who *said* they were God-fearing but would not help a stranger in need.[6]

The stories of Isaac Laybush Peretz, the father of Yiddish literature, suggest that in Yiddish was hidden "the weeping of our parents, the outcries of many generations, the poison and the bitterness of history." In "Bontsha the Silent," his best known story, after a lifetime of being taken advantage of, Bontasha is told by the Supreme Judge that he can have anything he wants, and all he asks for is a hot roll each morning. Bontsha's "eternal meekness" is his heritage. On the other hand, in "Devotion Without End," a fable expressing shtetl values in Yiddish literature, a young man who has been led astray by the devil, and thus forgotten all his Talmudic training, is saved by the woman he loves who sacrifices herself for him and is then saved by the Lord because of her "devotion without end."[7]

All three of these classic Yiddish writers were involved with the people they wrote about. Characteristically they felt a bond of sympathy with the downtrodden, the helpless. Caught up in a community without leverage and forced to struggle against external temptation, they were drawn to the heroism of the anti-heroic hero, the little man, the schlemiel, poor but proud. Their stories and novels, criticizing the hold of medieval Judaism, the corruptions within and the dangers from without, reflected the voice of the people. Therefore, they were terribly popular and loved until well into this century.

Among the disciples of Peretz were David Pinski, Abraham Reisin, and Sholom Asch. It was through Peretz that the Jewish intellectual was brought back to his heritage. Sholom Asch, one of the most talented of Peretz's disciples, was known primarily as the writer of plays and novels sympathetic to the Jewish community. Suddenly, in mid-career, he authored a trilogy of Christological novels: *The Nazarene* (1939), *The Apostle* (1943) and *Mary* (1949). According to Asch, his purpose was to enrich the accepted Jewish tradition with the usually unacceptable teachings of Jesus of Nazareth. That he fell out of favor with the people was to be expected. That he returned to their good graces is testimony to the lasting power of his plays, *The Messianic Age*, and *God of Vengeance*, and the novels *Motke the Thief* and *America*. More important was David Pinski, writer, poet, and playwright, also influenced by Peretz, who published first in Poland and then, from the turn of the century on, in New York. Oscillating between his need to foster socialism as a panacea and his later conviction that Jews had to struggle for personal and national dignity, he carved out a career rich in Yiddishkeit; but he is remembered today chiefly as the author of *The House of Noah Edon* (1929), written in English, a genealogical novel of three generations. That he wrote in English after three decades of authorship in Yiddish indicates his realization that Yiddish was no longer as universal a language as it had been. That Noah, at the end, was left with no one to continue the ancestral ways, points to Pinski's central metaphor, that of Noah adrift in the flood. With one of his children dead, amidst a ruined marriage, and two grandchildren killed in a suicide pact, Noah was left with death, despair and no hope.

With the onset of large scale immigration to the New World of millions of Eastern European Jews, the Old Country began to crumble. With the destruction of six million Jews in the Holocaust, the United States became the stronghold of Yiddish culture. Unfortunately, even as the forces of acculturation here whittled down the strength of Yiddishkeit so the later creation of the state of Israel and its choice of Hebrew as *the* official language, dealt Yiddish another blow. Yiddish, since the tenth century the language of the Diaspora, was finally engaged in its greatest trial as a living language.

The environment of the 1880's and the 1890's was and was not conducive to the development of an American Yiddish literature. On the one hand, the writers, having been uprooted from their Eastern European home, were suffering the effects of culture shock; on the other hand, as with most immigrants, they were eager to adjust, no matter what the cost. The popular song, "A brivele der mamen" (A Letter to Mama) was a reflection of that yearning. Meanwhile socialist and anarchist writings duplicated the political patterns established in Eastern Europe. But out of this pandemonium came the first American Yiddish writers, Morris Rosenfeld, Yehoash, Abraham Reisin, Mani Leib, Abraham Liessin, H. Rosenblatt, and David Pinski. In them was the essence of generations past, mixed with the sweat and tears and joy of Jewish America. They went into the factories and on the farms, they wrote of their experiences, and they created a new Yiddish literature.

The first major literary movement was called "Die Yunge," and was a protest against the Old World and against the sentimentalized Yiddish being written and spoken. An affirmation of love for America, this movement was also a united stand against the mediocrity and irresponsibility existing in the Jewish community. The literature of this movement was true to itself. In the works of H. Leivick, writing of Siberia in New York, Jewishness suffused every line. The same was true of the work of Issac Raboy who wrote of farms and cows and horses and prairies, and of the works of M. L. Halpern, Mani Leib, Aaron Leyeles, Jacob Glatstein, and others. It was a question of content and form and rhythm, especially rhythm. America has a rhythm, of course, as does every country. The inner rhythm comes from feeling at home here, of feeling the streets and buildings, the people, the wood, the concrete, the distances, the breadth and beat of life, the ideas Americans hold sacred. The inner rhythm also comes from a people's spiritual resources, folk resources, and it comes from an individual's attempts to liberate himself, to find himself, to find a justification in Jewish life. The writers I have mentioned all sought and found these depths. Based on the pillars of Yiddish literature, they flourished. They carried on their shoulders the past and the present, the accumulation that has made a consummate body of epics, novels, poems, plays, and stories about life and people that we call Yiddish literature in America.

Morris Rosenfeld's "The Sweatshop," for example, spoke of the tension between the old and the new. But the poems of Yehoash (Solomon Bloomgarten) showed his fears; They told of his love, too, for his people. In contrast, M. L. Halpern was anxious about the disappearing values of his people, caught up as they were in the acquisitive society. In a more grim vein, however, he wrote of the larger universe:

> The city begins not far from my house.
> On a stone, outside in the night,
> An old God sits and weeps.
> For all the doors have been closed to him. . . .
> Over us—the pain of the world.
> It cries through the window and curses
> The star which had been awaited
> And, with light, deceived us once more.[8]

Coming on the heels of "Die Yunge" were two movements that proved congenial to the young immigrant intellectuals. One, called the Introspectivists (the Insichisten), arose in 1919 following the lead of Aaron Leyeles, N. B. Minkoff and Jacob Glatstein in founding a magazine titled *In Sich*. Unlike the "Die Yunge" group, the Insichists emphasized poetry as the means by which one interpreted the environment, in accord with one's individual *Weltanschauung*. As they collectively put it in 1920: "The world exists for us only insofar as it is mirrored in us, insofar as it touches us. The world is a non-existent category, a fiction, if it is not related to us. It becomes a reality only in us and through us."[9] In short, they believed only in what the inner will created, as seen in their innovative style. Their content was wedded to their form.

Of the *In Sich* group, Glatstein was the most talented. Although he began to write when he was fourteen, a few years before he arrived in America, and published his first story in 1914, not until 1921 did his first volume of verse come out. Called simply *Jacob Glatstein* it invoked Buddha, Brahma and Nirvana. In *Free Verses* (*Frei Versen*, 1926) he began to deal with Jewish themes, and in the 1930's, after a return visit to his home in Lublin, Poland, he became preoccupied with the misery and suffering of the Jews. Indeed, the more he tasted the New World and felt the shadow of Hitler, the more he believed we might as well have remained in the ghetto. For what he had in mind, as he put it in *Homecoming at Twilight* (1940), was the almost unchanging attitudes he had experienced: "They hate us for observing the sabbath," he wrote, "and they hate us for violating the Sabbath. They hate pious Jews and they hate free-thinking Jews who eat lobster. They hate our capitalists and they hate our beggars. They hate our reactionaries and they hate our radicals. They hate Jews who earn bread and those who die three time a day from starvation."[10]

Through it all Glatstein, realizing that his audience was becoming ever smaller, wrote in Yiddish because it was a personification of the fate of his people, the secret of the relation between meaning and reality. In his poem "1919," he spoke of the disappearance of Yankel (presumably himself) and yet he also saw the future, what was to be. "How much destruction can a people suffer," he asked, "and still believe in rebuilding?" He realized that it was his fate to suffer.

Independent of the Introspectivists but also following on the heels of the "Die Yunge" group were a group of independents. Head and shoulders above all others in this category was H. Leivick. Born Leivick Halpern, early influenced by socialist ideas, he spent four years in Siberia but escaped and somehow got to New York in 1913. Supporting himself by working as a paperhanger, his first volume of poetry, *Locked In* (*Hintern Schloss*, 1918) spoke of the nature of pain.

In 1920 *The Golem*, Levick's most famous poetic drama, was published. Using an historical legend of a robot, he detailed the price necessary for a Messianic age. With the realization that the sheer mechanical power of the robot was too inhuman for a Messiah, and thus not appropriate, he made the Messiah a young beggar traveling with Elijah the prophet. In short order, several more plays appeared, capped by *Chains* (*Kehten*, 1929) which marked his break with communism and his questioning of bad means to get to good ends. And then midway through the 1930's he wrote *Ballad of the Denver Sanatorium*, and after visiting the death camps, *I Was Not In Treblinka*, *A Wedding in Fernwald*, and *In The Days of Job*. Near the end of his life, in *The Father's Shadow* (*Dem Tatens Shuttn*, 1953), he pleaded with God: "Save yourself, O God, return with us to our little land, become once more the Jewish God." He realized that unbelief and scepticism were dangerous. At least if he were within the community, even in a Hasidic community, he would pray with a handful of genuine old-fashioned Jews and sense a breath of God's nearness. He knew the dark side, and yet he saw the possibilities:

> Hour by hour I walk the streets of the Jewish East Side,
> And in the fiery whiteness my eyes paint fantastic turrets,
> Elongated columns soaring up over the ruined stalls,
> Up to the emptied sky of New York.
> Turrets hung all over their parapets with signs flashing and glowing:
> *Here Lies the Jewish People.*[11]

Although the Yiddish theatre is virtually non-existent in the 1970's, it was a thriving medium until the 1940's, with a rich tradition dating back to the 1870's. It was in Jassy, Romania, in 1876, that Abraham Goldfaden's first musical presentation took place. As with the earlier writers, he too took his work seriously, in social terms. "Every true, loyal Jew," he wrote in the 1880's, "must strive to help with thoughts and deeds, with propaganda and organization, to save his people, to work for its liberation and independence, to rescue it from discouragement, and to pour into its bitter cup at least a few drops of faith in a better future."[12] In the New World, to which he and Boris Tomashefsky, Joseph Lateiner, Jacob Adler, Jacob Gordin, David Kessler and I. J. Singer came, their work was appreciated. They were celebrated as if they were almost Gods. But gradually, as they and their audiences were Americanized, the plays and musicals showed the influence. When *The Jewish King Lear* (*Die Yiddishe Kenig Lear*, 1892) was an enormous success, a sequel was written, the Jewish Queen Lear, called *Mirele Efros*, 1898, which was equally successful. With the rise and fall of Maurice Schwartz's Yiddish Art Theatre, Yiddish theatre took its last major plunge, never to recover.[13]

On the eve of World War II, a new movement called Young Vilna arose. Coming out of a tradition in which Vilna had been the intellectual and cultural center of Eastern Europe, the Jerusalem of Lithuania, the major voices were Isaac Meier Dick, Eliakhum Zinser, Abraham Cahan, and Abraham Reisin; more recently, we have Abraham Sutzkever, and Chaim Grade, the first of whom now lives in Israel. Grade is known to Americans for *The Synagogue Courtyard* (1958), *The Well* (1962) and especially *The Agunah* (1961), a novel about a woman whose husband is missing but she cannot get a Jewish divorce because it cannot be established that he is dead. In the process, Grade unveiled a rich panorama of Jewish religious life in Vilna and the struggle between traditionalists and innovators in the 1930's. Sutzkever, whose poems date from the inception of World War II, has been concerned with the advantages of liberty for which he and his family yearned. Failing to find light, beauty and freedom, however, he conjured them up. The problem is that both Grade and Sutzkever are in Israel. The poets still writing in America are not well known. Eliezer Greenberg and Ephraim Auerbach, for example, should be better known but their renown bears a direct relation to their availability in English. As with all translations, something is lost in the translation. Yiddish, influenced by the environing culture, by the fate of Jewishness, and in addition, being essentially plebeian, a culture of *folkmessen*, is held by the tension between the traditional and secular forces that gave it life. In this context, it seems to me, Yiddish literature is part of the Western tradition, especially in the works of Abraham Cahan and Isaac Bashevis Singer.

Abraham Cahan more than anyone else has best dramatized the losses and gains of the transition to the New World. Arriving in this country from Vilna in 1882, he wrote stories and novels that were classic accounts of the crisis of ethnic identity confronted by the Eastern European Jews as they poured into New York from the 1880's through World War I. At an early age his mother told him, "You have a mirror before your eyes." Taking this seriously, he embraced Russian culture, atheism and socialism only to find that they effected a transformation that influenced his entire life. Because of his passion for humanity he overlooked the pogroms in the Ukraine; he could not see the forest for the trees. His solution then was socialism. Only later did he realize that there was a difference between a knee-jerk revolutionary who mouthed universal sounding platitudes and one who really cared for the welfare of the people, his people.

In the 1880's New York City was moving uptown, as a new breed of millionaires, rough-necks, political leaders, and ethnics emerged. At the same time sweatshops and dumbbell, coldwater flat tenements proliferated. Meanwhile Cahan became a worker, a political activist, and a writer and editor. Realizing that Yiddish papers at that time appealed to readers in a kind of literary Yiddish, he decided to write Yiddish as it was spoken. His decision not only transformed the *Forward (the Forverts)* but made it the most popular Yiddish daily in the world. He encouraged a letters-to-the-editor column, known as the *Bintele Brief*, and he wrote a thinly disguised socialist sermon each week under the pen name of the "proletarian preacher." His first essay on literature, "Realism," in 1889, dealt with man's nature and Spencer's social darwinism, and asserted that sensations are a form of cognition. He rejected the idea that the sole end of art is to afford pleasure. In this he was a link from the past, but he was also true to his own convictions. From 1891, when his first fiction appeared, it was clear that he was a "realist" and that he was involved with his people and its problems. When his first novel in English appeared, called *Yekl the Yankee*, W. D. Howells, the Dean of American letters, liked it enormously but suggested the name be changed to *Yekl: A Tale of the New York Ghetto*. His collection *The Imported Bridegroom and Other Stories* was also well received. But it was with the appearance of *The Rise of David Levinsky* (1917), written in English, that Cahan's rise to maturity was established in literary terms. It is still considered the best immigrant novel ever written. It is, as John Higham pointed out, a novel in which Cahan successfully combined the distinctively American theme of success with a Jewish subject and a Russian artistic sensibility.

All through these years Cahan was the editor of the *Forverts* and an active socialist. Caught up with the idea that the old spirit of idealism (the *neshomah yeseroh*) was gone, he wrote a number of tales at the turn of the century exploring this concept. In "Fanny and her Suitors," written in English, and later translated into Yiddish, he wrote of a socialist editor's talks with a worker named Fanny. In the same year his "Autobiography of an American Jew" was published serially in *McClure's*. From these two tales, especially from the "Autobiography" came *The Rise of David*

Levinsky. Concerning a young man's business success, and the cost of success, the novel relates David's Americanization to his unsuccessful love life and his loneliness. At the end David laments his present station, power, and worldly happiness, because he can never forget "the days of his misery." In David's words, "I cannot escape from my old self. My past and my present do not comport well. David, the poor lad swinging over a Talmud volume at Preacher's Synagogue, seems to have more in common with my identity than David Levinsky, the well-known cloak manufacturer."[14]

Was David really unhappy? Did he regret his choice of a career? Of course David was unhappy. But he relished his unhappiness; he would have made the same decision had he to do it all over again. The fact is that David, egotistical, aloof, reserved, controlled, powerful, was the man he wanted to be. He had chosen success, he had pursued the American Dream. He was also enmeshed in a schizophrenic existence, caught between the realization of what he had lost and what he had wanted to gain.

What had Cahan accomplished? Editor of the *Forverts* from 1903 till his death, he played a crucial role in the acculturation of the Jews in America. Author of novels and short stories, almost always dealing with the problems of acculturation, he is remembered today as the author of *The Rise of David Levinsky*. Realizing, as he wrote in *The Education of Abraham Cahan*, that "America lives more in one day than Russia does in ten," he transmitted that celebration of America to his people.[15] As a socialist he believed that to influence people you must first become a live man (a *mensch*). To do this he popularized Yiddish and taught his people how to grow. He realized, as it is said in "Rabbi Eliezer's Christmas," "This isn't Russia ... it's America, the land of machines and of 'hurry up ... and there you are.'" There you are! He made his peace with America. He adapted. In the doing he became a fine writer who influenced several generations of Americans, in part because he wrote *The Rise of David Levinsky* in English and because adaptation was an essential message. The primacy of an audience and accommodation were as important as felicity to Jewish life. In more recent times Isaac Bashevis Singer has taken the same path, although he continues to write in Yiddish.

When I. B. Singer was a child he recalled his father's warnings against reading the works of Peretz. "Everybody who read such books," his father said, "sooner or later became a worldly man and forsook the traditions." He was right. When his older brother moved out and into the Bohemian life, Isaac was entranced, but managed to hold onto the duality of Bohemia and tradition for himself. "Even in my stories," Singer has written, "it is just one step from the study house to sexuality and back again." From age thirteen to seventeen he lived with his mother in the little town of Bilgoray, a town that had remained unaltered since the middle ages. From this experience came his feeling for and belief in demons, spirits, magic and the like. While he studied Torah and Talmud he also dipped into the Cabala. While he pored over Spinoza he hummed a Hasidic tune. While he read Dostoevsky he delved into mysticism. While he pursued free inquiry he resisted orthodoxy. In short, as his life became saturated with that special apocalyptic and messianic flavor that gave to *Satan in Goray* its urgent fervor and fever, so he fed on the tension that built. In that little town he had a chance to see the past as it really was. "Time," he says, "seemed to flow backward." He "lived Jewish history."[16]

Composed in 1933, published in 1935 in Yiddish and translated into English in 1955, *Satan in Goray* was impelled into being by the closeness of Hitler, his unsuccessful marriage to a woman who chose communism in Russia over Singer, and the international success of his brother's play, "Yoshe Kalb." In 1935 Singer followed his brother to America. When he first arrived here, Singer felt that he had no roots, that Yiddish had no future, that the existence of the Jewish people was imperiled. As a result, he had a "real case of literary amnesia." He could not write for a number of years. Looking back, he realized that "One has to get a very great blow to act in such a way."[17] After his second marriage, and particularly after his brother's death in 1944, he was able to write again. Since then he has poured forth an unending stream of short stories and novels, all in Yiddish, which have invariably been translated into English. Thus in English he is known to those who read the *New Yorker*, *Esquire*, *Harpers*, *Cosmopolitan*, *Partisan Review*, *Commentary*, *Playboy*, *Saturday Evening Post*, *Chicago Post*, and more.

Most important, it must be said that Singer uses the past, he dwells in the past, a past replete with demons and devils who vie with men and women and God. But Singer uses the devil both as the alter ego of God, and, psychologically and artistically, to credit and to release another secret sharer, man's secret and unconscious desires. At base, the devil is used to revive moral choice, to give added dread and urgency to moral dilema, and to make personal choice a mode of self-creation and self-destruction.[18] Whether clothed in modern American dress or in the framework of the past, his concerns are attractive to Americans in the 1960's and 1970's because he reflects their anxieties as he mirrors the tensions of his experiences. In a recent story, "Tanhum," in the *New Yorker* (17 November 1975), Tanhum berated himself for not praying fervently enough or devoting himself sufficiently to Jewishness, "and he warred eternally with evil thoughts." At the same time, the questions, "What was the sense of robbing one person to give to another?" and "Had the greed for money and honors so blinded him that he didn't know the wrongs he committed?" sound suspiciously contemporary, in spite of the nineteenth century context.[19] Singer is a highly moral man, interested in moralism in literature. Certainly, as Gimpel the Fool knew, there was a difference between a world which deceived him and a life without complications, without ridicule and without deception. Having been sinned against so much, Gimpel clearly saw that his faith and innocence were ways to measure the corruption and meanness that surrounded him. So with Tarhum. At least in that way everything was still possible.

For all that, as Irving Howe has written, Singer is really not in the mainstream of Yiddish literature. "It's hardly a secret," says Howe, "that in the Yiddish literary world Singer is regarded with a certain suspicion. . . . One reason is that 'modernism' signifies a heavy stress upon sexuality, a concern for the irrational, expressionist distortions of character, and a seeming indifference to the humane ethic of Yiddishism."[20] Singer, according to Milton Hindus, "is utterly at variance with the warmhearted humanitarianism characteristic of the Fathers of Yiddish literature, I. L. Peretz, Sholom Aleichem, and others."[21]

Ironically, Singer, the only living Yiddish writer who is known to millions, is not in the mainstream, judged by those in the mainstream. The question arises then: What is the direction of Yiddish and Yiddish literature? This question becomes especially apparent if those who are most popular are known only in translation and those who are known to the few are known only in Yiddish? Is it time, as in Singer's "The Little Shoemakers," for Jews to celebrate the fact that they have not become idolators? Is it time, with Jacob Glatstein, to

> . . . secure ourselves
> With a bit of fence.
> Not a ghetto, God forbid,
> Just a quiet wall.
> Let's sit here, by ourselves,
> And with common sense
> Let's find a way to mend
> Our wasted hands.[22]

Or is it time to affirm what has happened, and revel in the positive, recognizing that nothing stands still, that Yiddish literature in America is like nothing else in the history of the Jews.

As early as 1928, and probably much earlier, the future of Yiddish and Yiddish literature was being debated. Some commentators prophesied the imminent demise of the culture. Certainly there are facts to support this thesis, if one looks at the number of those in each census who put down "Yiddish" as their mother tongue, or the declining number of Yiddish publications. As Samuel Goldenberg, a well-known actor, put it in 1928, the cause of the decline was the "merciless grinding of the wheels of

American industrialism."[23] The immigrant, for whom Yiddish was his first language and an economic asset, has disappeared, replaced by the need to hold English to be supremely important.

Will Yiddish survive? In the universities, Yiddish is now being taught, and its appeal is on the rise. In the Hasidic communities, Yiddish is still the first language and will remain so. But considering how clearly the Hasidim are cut off from the mainstream Jew and the American culture, it is virtually certain that Yiddish will not survive as the carrier of culture in the way it has. And certainly the romanticized version of the past seen in presentations like "Fiddler on the Roof" will do little to help. The fact is that nothing can compete with the pressures generated by the need to be American.

In the end, then, one has to admit that most of the great figures who wrote in Yiddish were born and brought up in Eastern Europe but moved here and died here, and most of what is now known to the general public is known through translation. A *few* remember Mendele, Sholom Aleichem and Peretz, but *many* know Cahan and Singer, and precisely because one wrote in English and the other is known in English. Yiddish, of course, has a great deal to give to the world. Indeed, the poets and writers, *if* adequately translated, *would* be discussed with the intensity that students of literature now reserve for European, English and American writers. But that is the point. Yiddish literature must be translated and translated well. After all, our "Western" tradition includes Egypt, Greece and Rome, and our literary tradition includes Dostoevsky, Turgenev, Cervantes, Balzac, Mann, Freud, the Bible and so on, all through translation. In short, it seems to me that, rather than lament the passing of Yiddish and Yiddish literature as a major living language, it is time to celebrate its arrival, to celebrate its virtues and values that will be known to all in English. For my part, I look forward to that time when, as part of our Western heritage, we will all be as familiar with Mendele, Sholom Aleichem, Peretz, and Glatstein, as we now are with Cahan and Singer. That day is overdue. That day, I hope, will dawn tomorrow.

Pennsylvania State University

NOTES

[1] Peretz' statement is quoted in Josephine Knopp, *The Trial of Judaism in Contemporary Jewish Writing* (Urbana: Univ. of Illinois, 1975), p. 20.

[2] Mendele Mokher Seforim, "The Calf," in Irving Howe and Eliezer Greenberg, eds., *A Treasury of Yiddish Stories* (New York: Viking, 1954), pp. 97-111.

[3] Quoted by Charles Madison, *Yiddish Literature, Its Scope and Major Writers* (New York: Frederick Ungar, 1968), p. 42.

[4] Madison, *Yiddish Literature, Its Scope and Major Writers*, p. 69.

[5] *A Treasury of Yiddish Stories*, p. 117.

604

[6] Sholom Aleichem, "On Account of a Hat," in *A Treasury of Yiddish Stories*, pp. 111-18; in Madison, *Yiddish Literature, Its Scope and Major Writers*, pp. 61-98.

[7] I. L. Peretz, "Bontsha the Silent," and "Devotion Without End," in *A Treasure of Yiddish Stories*, pp. 223-31, 118-50.

[8] M. L. Halpern, "Pain of the World," trans. Nathan Halper, in Irving Howe and Eliezer Greenberg, eds., *A Treasury of Yiddish Poetry* (New York: Holt Rinehart and Winston, 1969), pp. 110-11.

[9] Quoted in Sol Liptzin, *History of Yiddish Literature* (New York: Jonathan David, 1972), p. 312; this work is the single most important source for students of Yiddish literature.

[10] Ibid., p. 320.

[11] H. Leivick, "Here Lives the Jewish People," trans. Cynthia Ozick, in *A Treasure of Yiddish Poetry*, pp. 120-21.

[12] Liptzin, *History of Yiddish Literature*, p. 77.

[13] Ibid.; also see David Lifson, *The Yiddish Theatre in America* (New York: Thomas Yoseloff, 1965).

[14] Abraham Cahan, *The Rise of David Levinsky* (New York: Grosset and Dunlap, 1917), p. 530.

[15] Abraham Cahan, *The Education of Abraham Cahan* (Vol. 1-2 of 5, originally published in 1926-1931), trans. Leon Stein, A. P. Conan, and Lynn Davison (Philadelphia: Jewish Publication Society, 1969), p. 244.

[16] J. Blocker and R. Elman, "A Conversation with I. B. Singer," *Commentary*, 36 (November 1963), 368-69; I. B. Singer, *In My Father's Court* (New York: Farrar Straus, 1966), p. 240; Irving Buchen, *Isaac Bashevis Singer and the Eternal Past* (New York: New York Univ. Press. 1968), p. 9.

[17] Buchen, pp. 19-20.

[18] Buchen, pp. 207-08.

[19] Isaac Bashevis Singer, "Tanhum," *New Yorker*, 51 (17 November 1975), 41-48.

[20] Irving Howe, "Isaac Bashevis Singer, Storyteller," *Encounter*, 26 (March 1966), 64-65.

[21] Milton Hindus, rev. of *The Family Moskat, New York Times Book Review*, 14 March 1965, p. 4.

[22] Jacob Glatstein, "Come Now Let's," in *A Treasury of Yiddish Poetry*, trans. Chana Faerstein, p. 326.

[23] Quoted in Uriah Zevi Engelman, "The Fate of Yiddish in America," *The Menorah Journal* 15 (July 1928), 29.

Luncheon Presentation

America in European Eyes– An Amalgamation of Images

Peter Boerner

ABSTRACT

Although the images of America held by various European authors or national literatures have been described in separate studies, no attempt has been made to interpret these views in an all-European context. In order to demonstrate that the Europeans' views of the new world were formed under the impact of influences transcending national boundaries, I discuss four of the most significant images of America held by various sections of the European reading audience during the early nineteenth century: America, the golden land; America, a country without culture; America in romantic embellishment; and the United States as a prototypical democratic society. All these images were expressed in the various European literatures, although the direction of interest in America shifted at times from one country to another: in France, for example, Rousseau had a particularly strong impact; Germany excelled in the production of emigration literature; and in England the derogation of America as a place without culture held sway longer than on the continent. The major images of America, favorable and unfavorable, romantic and realistic, utopian and condescending, coexisted with each other in the European consciousness during the period under consideration here. These images interacted as well: a dialectic relationship between myth projection and specific knowledge, between the ideal and the real, created a strong connection between them. (PB)

Talking about the ethnic literatures of America, as we have done here for three days now, has meant, in many instances, discussing how Old-World views became fused into a new consciousness. The emphasis has been on what happened to the views of the European emigrants after their arrival in this country, or on tracing these views as they were handed on from the immigrants to their descendents growing up in ethnically colored environments.

The case I should like to make here is that the "many voices" of the immigrants from Europe more often than not sang songs based on essentially the same set of old melodies reflected in common literary traditions.

Analysts of American history have discussed the similar circumstances of emigrants from the various European countries, and art critics have commented on the Europeans' pictorial images of the New World without regard for their national origins,[1] but literary scholars seem to have considered views of America predominantly within the context of separate national units. Excellent studies have been written, for example, by Gilbert Chinard and Durand Echeverria on the French, Harold Jantz and Lawrence Marsden Price on the German, Allan Nevins on the English, and Dieter Boden on the Russian images of America,[2] but no attempt has been made to consider them in the broader context of all European literatures. One anthology, *Spektrum Amerika*, compiled by the Austrian publisher Wulf Stratowa,[3] offers a fascinating array of opinions from more than a hundred European authors, dating from the Romantic period to our time, yet does not indicate what these authors might have in common.

In order to demonstrate that also in literature many of the views of the New World were formed under the impact of influences transcending national boundaries, I have chosen out of the vast assortment of images of America four to discuss in detail: America, the golden land; America, a country without culture; America in romantic embellishment; and the United States as a prototypical democratic society.

Although my case is meant to include all European literatures, for practical purposes I shall base my remarks on the literatures of those countries for which scholars have studied the images of America most thoroughly: England, France, Germany and Russia. And to provide a temporal frame for my investigation I shall concentrate on the period from 1825 to 1835, during which European interest for America underwent a number of significant changes. Widespread disillusionment after the Napoleonic wars with their wake of economic depression and political restoration, the establishment of the United States as an autonomous political entity, and the increased availability of information about its westward expansion, induced many Europeans to consider America in a new light. Throughout much of the eighteenth century they had still viewed it as an interesting but faraway land or merely an objective for commercial ventures. Now, however, it seemed to invite their personal involvement. So marked was the change in the Europeans' attitude, in fact, that mass emigration began: in 1827 for the first time the total of emigrants reached five figures, more than 16,000. By 1832 this number had doubled.[4]

With this time focus in mind, I should like to turn to the four European images of America I have selected for consideration here.

The most prevalent image held by the Europeans about America was that of a *golden land*, where material needs would be satisfied. Dreams of a

wondrous place beyond familiar shores had existed in the popular awareness for centuries, and the discovery of America had seemed to substantiate them in many minds. These dreams were kept alive more or less intact
during the next three hundred years.[5] Reports by eyewitnesses, from Ves-
pucci's *Mundus Novus* to the learned accounts of the French Jesuit Lafi-
tau, extolled the new continent's richness of natural resources as well as its
remarkable beauty. Typical for many voices was Michael Drayton's ode
"To the Virginian Voyage," written in 1606. It praised America as an
earthly paradise

> Where Nature hath in store
> Fowle, Venison and Fish,
> And the fruitfull'st Soyle
> Without your Toyle
> Three Harvests more
> All greater than your Wish.[6]

During the eighteenth century, increased knowledge about actual conditions in America, as well as the sceptical attitudes of the Enlightenment,
began to lead to a more realistic appraisal, but in the early nineteenth
century the concept of a golden land was revived in books and pamphlets
written for potential emigrants. These publications appealed mainly to
the lower classes, offering, for example, a discussion by a French pastor in
1803 of "Le Pour et le contre" of beginning a new life in America,[7] or
calling for the foundation of a truly Swabian colony in Virginia.[8] Over
thirty such reports appeared in Germany alone between 1826 and 1836,
and in England and Scandinavia there were hardly fewer.[9] Most of them
were written by people who had been in the United States and recognized
the great opportunities for settlement there. Whether with the aim of
making some profit from the emigrants, or just from a desire to be of
help to their fellow citizens, they spoke enthusiastically about their experiences. Outstanding among these evangelists of the New World was a West-
falian surgeon named Gottfried Duden. In 1829, after what he said was a
four-year stay overseas, he published a book of more than three hundred
pages with the cumbersome title *Bericht über eine Reise nach den westlichen Staaten Nordamerikas und einen mehrjährigen Aufenthalt am
Missouri, in Bezug auf Auswanderung und Überbevölkerung, oder: Das
Leben im Innern der Vereinigten Staaten und dessen Bedeutung für die
häusliche und politische Lage der Europäer* (Report on a Journey to the
Western States of North America and a Stay of Several Years on the
Missouri, With Regard to Emigration and Overpopulation, or, Life in the
Interior of the United States and Its Significance for the Domestic and
Political Situation of Europeans).[10]

In the form of letters addressed to friends in Germany, Duden offered
detailed information about living conditions in the New World. He talked

about climate, flora and fauna, opportunities for crop cultivation, methods and costs of settling. He also gave much practical advice, of use to a farmer or craftsman. According to him, there was work for whomever sought it, and whoever worked was sure to find material independence. Often there was even more abundance than one could manage. "There is so much game, such as deer, turkey, quail, wild dove, pheasant and snipe," Duden claimed, "that a good shot can easily supply a large family with meat. The hunter who secures a deer rarely takes all of it home with him. He is satisfied to have the hide and the hind quarters, and hangs the rest on a tree for anybody else, who may wish to take a roast. . . . The garden supplies the best kitchen vegetables. Peas and beans prosper beyond all expectation. Also pumpkin, lettuce, and other vegetables are planted. Everything thrives without fertilizer, and indeed after twenty years just as well as during the first."[11]

In almost literal repetition of Michael Drayton's praise of 230 years earlier, Duden had set down what his contemporaries were eager to hear. For those who pondered the idea of beginning a new life in America, his book became daily reading. Cheap editions were produced and distributed, and, according to a prominent historian of German emigration, thousands of people, whose heads Duden had turned ("denen er den Kopf verrückt hatte"), readied themselves for the long journey to the Missouri.[12] There began to be talk about an epidemic of emigration fever.

But there were also reports from disappointed settlers that things were not as rosy as they had sounded in Duden's book. When a pamphlet pointing out the discrepancies between Duden's descriptions and the reality of American life appeared, he felt compelled to publish a "Selbstanklage wegen seines amerikanischen Reiseberichtes, zur Warnung vor fernerm leichtsinnigen Auswandern öffentlich verkündet" (Self Chastisement with regard to his American Travel Report, Publicly Announced as a Caution Against Further Thoughtless Emigration).[13] He admitted to having done a little bit of window dressing, but pointed out that the emigrants had preferred to read only the inviting parts of his book and to ignore what he had said about the difficulties of settling and cultivating virgin soil.

Although such controversies stirred public discussion for a time, in the long run the appeal of the almost utopian descriptions was more powerful than the critical voices. To escape depressing economic and political conditions in their homelands, Europeans turned to the United States in ever increasing numbers, paying little heed to warnings about the risks of emigration.

America did not only fulfill the material dreams of many Europeans. The immaturity and rawness they found there tended to engender feelings of superiority or disdain, which are reflected in the image of America as a *land without culture*. In order to understand this point of view, we have to remind ourselves that the discovery of America involved not only adventure and exploration, but also the intellectual comprehension of the new continent.[14] The prospect of controlling apparently limitless riches fed European arrogance. The inhabitants of the world overseas were construed to be not fully developed humans, but animal-like beings with no sexual or moral restraint. Montaigne's essay on cannibalism reflected this widely accepted view. In spite of some remarkable exceptions, such as Las Casas' protestations against the conquistadores' oppression of the native population, a strong Eurocentric attitude prevailed. Long after the discovery of America, many Europeans had difficulty placing it in a cosmography which was basically the same as it had been before Columbus. Thus in 1560, a Parisian lawyer and *homme de lettres*, Estienne Pasquier, observed that "this America which we call new lands does not fit into the world view of the classical authors."[15] For him, as well as for most of his contemporaries, America was a "phenomenon quite outside the range of Europe's accumulated experience and of its normal expectation."[16]

Even two hundred years later, this viewpoint found expression in the physiocrats' theory that the transatlantic climate might in the long run prevent human beings from prospering there. Buffon and de Pauw stirred a discussion among the philosophers by asserting that people and animals transplanted to America would eventually be thwarted in their growth and degenerate. The small aboriginal population of the New World was cited as evidence in support of this theory.[17]

By the time of the American declaration of independence and the subsequent establishment of the United States, patronizing attitudes had lost much of their credence on the European continent, but in Britain they were maintained long into the nineteenth century. Resentment over the colonists' severance of their ties with England remained fresh in many minds, and in the period we are considering here, negative reactions still prevailed. Many leading newspapers of the time, such as the *Quarterly Review* and *Blackwood's Edinburgh Magazine*, as well as so-called travel reports, played on the theme of old-world superiority.

A literary reflection of this "Tory condescension," as Allan Nevins has called it,[18] is Frances Trollope's *Domestic Manners of the Americans*, published in 1832. Most of the observations contained in this book were based on the author's stay in Cincinnati, at that time still an uncouth, undisciplined town, filled with the odor of large pork-packing plants, and completely lacking in attractive buildings or cultural institutions.[19] The vapidity and comfortlessness of boarding-house life; sharp dealing in business; boastfulness and lawlessness on the part of many; the hysteria, coarseness and irreverence of the frequent revivals—all this shocked the lady from England and nourished her already not too positive views of America. The chief distinction between her homeland and the United States was, as she saw it, the latter country's lamentable want of refinement. One of the few literary conversations she conducted in Cincinnati did nothing to discourage her in her disaffection: her partner attacked Byron for his immorality, thought Pope's *Rape of the Lock* inadmissible to family circles because of its very title, and proclaimed " 'Shakespeare, Madam, is obscene, and thank God, we are sufficiently advanced to have found it out!' "

Mrs. Trollope's experiences were such as to move her to declare of the Americans: " 'I do not like their principles, I do not like their manners, I do not like their opinions.' " And she announced further that she " 'never saw an American man stand or walk well.' " Her generalizations provoked some heated responses. Among liberals she was felt to be a censorious harridan, and there were calls for objective evaluations of life in the United States. Although most of the forthcoming reports were dull, and have since been consigned to oblivion, one, at least, deserved mention. It was written by Godfrey T. Vigne, a London barrister who had travelled through the Great Lakes region in the same year as Mrs. Trollope's book came out. He asserted that much of the discussion concerning America, at least in England, had been influenced by political considerations, and that the virtues of America might become more apparent if politics were left aside. As if to repudiate Mrs. Trollope, he urged his readers not to base their views on the criteria of any third party: "I advise you to go to America: . . . You will be able to form an opinion whether the state of society there be more or less enviable than that to which you have been accustomed. . . . Canvass the pretensions of the Americans, and then judge for yourself."[20]

The third complex of images I should like to talk about is closely connected with the phenomenon of *European Romanticism.* If anything is common to the views of America I have discussed so far, it is that they developed in the general awareness, out of century-old dreams, hopes or prejudices. No individual had unmistakably put a stamp on them.

This changed with the advent of Rousseau. Although America had played no role for him when he developed his primitivistic philosophy, it served him—and even more his fast growing number of followers—as the embodiment of their theories. What better prototype for the "bon sauvage" than the native American Indian, sprung supposedly from the virgin forests of Ohio and Mississippi, untouched by European civilization? Rousseau's child of nature came to life in the works of many French writers.

Among them were Chamfort's play *La Jeune indienne* (1764) and Sauvigny's *Hirza ou les Illinois* (1767), or the immensely popular novel *Inkle et Iarico*, subtitled *Histoire américaine* (1778). The other literatures of Europe were not immune and began producing translations of these French works, followed by their own creations. The Russian poet Ivan Andreevich Krylov even conceived an opera, *The Americans* (1788), in which he contrasted the disorder of the Old World with the beautiful harmony of existence in the wilderness overseas.

The extent to which the views of America emanating from Rousseau's thought became accepted by the third quarter of the eighteenth century can be seen in the proclivity of many travellers to the New World to recognize there what corresponded to their expectations. Thus Saint John de Crèvecoeur, in his *Letters from an American Farmer* (1782), descried in the new land a close approximation to the original state of nature, and he extolled the pleasures of living there. Likewise Vasilij Baranshchikov, who had been stranded in Puerto Rico in 1787 while on a Russian merchant mission, raved about the lush scenery of the island and the healthy simplicity of its inhabitants.[21]

As reports of this sort grew popular among the educated throughout Europe, a good number of them became tempted to discover for themselves the wonders of the New World. In Germany, the belief in the miraculous powers of the American environment grew so strong that it was frequently recommended as a "Besserungsanstalt," a reform institution, where the otherwise ineducable could be turned into decent human beings. In his younger years, Goethe reflected in *Wilhelm Meisters Lehrjahre* on the possibilities of such an endeavor, and Schiller thought about dramatizing the career of a European adolescent who was exposed to transatlantic surroundings.

The tenor of these concepts of America was preserved well into the decade I have used as a framework for my investigation. Chateaubriand's *Atala* and *René*, with their glorification of the scenic grandeur and human innocence of America, were eagerly assimilated by European youth. Cooper's "Leatherstocking" tales appealed to a widespread affection for the noble Indian and the honest settler, a fact attested to by the impressive sales figures of French, German, Italian and Russian translations.[22]

In addition to such audience reactions there were many creative responses, in literature as well as in the fine arts. Eugène Delacroix, Francisque-Joseph Duret and Cesare Mussini movingly depicted the American Indian as a symbol of grace, love and sincerity.[23] Lermontov intended to write a tragedy portraying the struggle between Indian savages and their white oppressors, using *Atala* as a point of departure. The Dekabrist poet Barjatinskij described the elegiac complaint of an aging Natchez on the death of his son, with magnificent rivers and "profound savannas" as background settings.[24] German authors began to imitate Cooper's tales within a few years of their publication, as evinced by Leopold Schefer's *Waldbrand* (1827) and Carl Spindler's *Der Jesuit* (1829), whose hero discovers an Indian utopia in Paraguay. Ernst Willkomm, in his novel *Die Europamüden* (1838), combined a feeling of malaise about life in Europe with a vision of America as a last retreat for men of good will.

While such concepts of America served many of the "enfants du siècle" as vehicles for the expression of their hopes and frustrations, they often did not survive the test of exposure to reality. When Alexis de Tocqueville, for example, went to the United States in the summer of 1831, "plein des souvenirs de M. de Chateaubriand et de Cooper,"[25] he was looking forward to finding true nobility of character in the native inhabitants of America, but the only Indians he met had already been corrupted by their contact with whites. The experience caused Tocqueville to divest himself of his Romantic preconceptions.

Tocqueville recovered from his shock and incorporated his observations into his book on American democracy (to which I shall return shortly), but there were others who simply were not able to reconcile their dreams with reality. An almost archetypical case was the Austrian poet Nikolaus Lenau, who journeyed to Pennsylvania and Ohio at about the same time as Tocqueville, full of utopian aspirations and personal *Weltschmerz*. Lenau found himself, however, incapable of adjusting to the harsh living conditions he encountered and, denouncing the New World as a "land without nightingales," he fled home again after only a short stay, disillusioned, depressed, and bitter toward everything American.

Just as America served to embody their primitivistic ideas for Rousseau and his followers, for others it offered encouragement to express more rational views, in which the United States was depicted as a *prototypical democratic society*.

While it might be possible to make a case that, already in the sixteenth century, concepts of America as the "City of God" incarnate reflected desires for a land offering freedom from capricious government, this image received its strongest stimulus when enlightened philosophers found in the New World the perfect locus for their visions of the future of humankind. From Voltaire's praise of the "bon Quaker" in the *Lettres philosophiques* (1734), to Abbé Raynal's celebration of America as a province of tolerance and liberty in his *Histoire philosophique et politique des deux Indes* (1770), there were many variations on this theme.

The colonies' struggle with the British crown added new dimensions to these concepts. Events leading to the declaration of independence evoked a groundswell of sympathy in all parts of Europe. Particularly to the bourgeoisie and the lower classes, America—now the United States— seemed to promise political and religious privileges they would never be granted at home. America appeared to them to be the epitome of a new order.[26] Popular periodicals like Schubart's *Deutsche Chronik* asserted that "over there" were people "who feel they are not meant to live in slavery, and with noble distaste throw off the yoke of a tyrannical government."[27] Climaxing these tendencies were attempts to idolize the leaders of the American Revolution, who, it was felt, would blaze a path toward liberty for the people of all nations. In France, reverence for Benjamin Franklin was immense, particularly after his encounter with Voltaire at the Academy of Sciences. And, as we know from Herder's *Briefe zu Beförderung der Humanität*, a similar enthusiasm developed in Germany.[28] Voicing sentiment in Russia, the *Moskovskie Vedomosti* proclaimed that Franklin would be respected as a god because he had been responsible for changes, in physics as well as in politics, that would guide humanity into a new age.[29]

Much of this popular belief in the United States was reflected in the emigration literature which developed in the early nineteenth century. In Gottfried Duden's *Bericht*, which I discussed as a paradigm, America was depicted not only as a land where the material needs of man would be met, but almost as a political utopia. A new life would begin for everybody who went there, Duden asserted, a life of liberty and happiness. Similarly, Charles Sealsfield, who came to the United States as a political refugee from Bohemia, in an eyewitness report of 1827 claimed that in America anybody could succeed because there were no class distinctions. It was no longer a place for European dropouts, but an asylum for anyone who wanted to express his ideas without coercive restriction, the only country in the world devoid of "tyranny, superstition, and prejudice."[30]

Although during the first two decades of the nineteenth century the image of America as a land of freedom and tolerance had been kept alive mostly in the popular awareness, with the appearance of Tocqueville's *De la démocratie en Amérique* in 1835, it was brought back into the realm of intellectual discussion.

Like the works of Duden and Mrs. Trollope, Tocqueville's book was inspired by first-hand experience in the United States. But while the Dudens and Trollopes had travelled without ever taking off their differently colored spectacles, Tocqueville was willing to amend his views. The information he collected proved useful to him when, on his return to France, he became involved in the debate which was developing there over the suitability of democracy as a form of government. Out of this discussion grew his thesis that the United States offered proof of the viability of a democratic constitution. He saw in America the prototype of a democracy that, in time to come, would be embraced by Europe as well. He foretold what kind of language and literature a democracy would inspire and what effect it would have on manners and morals. He was realistic enough to apprehend a day when slavery would threaten America with civil disorder, and he sensed the problems of administering justice fairly; but he also determined a basic drive for continued improvement to be the essence of democratic institutions. In concluding the first part of his work, Tocqueville went so far as to predict that the concept of the democratic society exemplified by the United States would prove to be as strong a rallying point as religion had been in the Middle Ages.

While Tocqueville's importance in the formulation of a new European image of America can hardly be overestimated, we must be aware that among his contemporaries were thinkers of similar persuasions. In a lengthy monograph Bernhard Fabian has enumerated distinguished politicians and scholars of the pre-Victorian period who concurred with Tocqueville's views, among them Basil Hall and Gustave de Beaumont.[31] In Germany, Hegel, and Goethe in his later years, expressed equally positive sentiments. Hegel, lecturing in the summer of 1830 on *Die Philosophie der Geschichte*, addressed himself to the situation of the new nation by observing the differences in progress between North and South America, the former becoming an industrialized, democratic state, while the latter continued to rely on the exploitation of the soil and people. He hailed the United States as "the land of the future where, in the ages that lie before us, matters of world importance will be revealed." It was "a land of desire for all those weary of old Europe's historical arsenal."[32] Goethe found America to be much better off than "unser Kontinent, das alte," because of its freedom from worn-out traditions and its potential for constructive growth.[33]

With this optimistic reference to America as the land of the future, I bring my survey to a close. Please allow me to add a few observations about the character of the images which I have discussed.

First of all, I should like to emphasize that none of these images was the monopoly of any one particular literature. America, the golden land; America, a country without culture; America in romantic embellishment; and the United States as a prototypical democratic society—in one way or another each of these views was expressed in the works of English, French, German and Russian authors. The direction of interest in America differed at times from one country to another: in France, Rousseau had a particularly strong impact; Germany excelled in the production of emigration literature; and in England feelings of superiority over the former colonies held sway longer than on the continent. But whatever differences there were among the images of America expressed in the literatures of Europe, they seem to me to have been not fundamental, but merely variations of the same themes.

Second, the studies investigating the concept of America in separate national literatures, which I mentioned at the outset of my discussion, are all chronologically ordered and consequently tend to give us the impression that there was a neat succession of images, moving from the mythical to the more rational, from the primitive to the sophisticated. Without denying the merits of this evolutionary approach, I should like to point out that a method which stresses the symbiosis of various European images of America can be equally illuminating. The views of the New World should be painted not only as a panorama of successive or superimposed pictures, but also as a set of constant images which appear to a greater or lesser degree at all times. At the least, I hope I have been able to demonstrate that some of the major images of America, favorable and unfavorable, romantic and realistic, utopian and condescending, coexisted with each other in the European consciousness during the period I have considered here.

Moreover, these images interacted. A dialectic relationship between myth projection and specific knowledge, between the ideal and the real, has created a strong connection among the various views. Lenau's experience served as an example: although he came to America cherishing high romantic expectations, his distress when they clashed with reality gave further impetus to the already existing feelings of Old-World superiority.

Third, nearly all scholars who have studied concepts of the New World with regard to particular authors or national literatures have stressed that these concepts evolved out of the Europeans' concerns about their own affairs, and were imposed on the faraway continent. Hildegard Meyer, for example, in a book on German views of America in the nineteenth century, maintained that, in the images she investigated, it was not "Amerika an sich" that was reflected, but the "cultural, political or economic needs" of the holders.[34] Wolf-Dieter Bach, who recently addressed himself to the same topic, also observed that German thoughts on America mirrored primarily German experiences, and consequently suggested that one should talk about the "Amerika in uns," the America which the Germans found in themselves.[35] Raymond Buckberger and Dieter Boden, who investigated the images of America in France and Russia, have expressed similar views.[36]

Although I assumed a comparable stance in an earlier study dealing with national images in European literatures, I have found I must retreat somewhat from that position.[37] Scholarship has neglected, it seems to me, to take into account the image-generating capacity of the New World itself. While in many cases America served as a vehicle for European views, it also created new images. Europeans did not only *dream* of a "golden land": but there actually *was* a vast continent, rich and sparsely populated, to substantiate their dreams. America was not merely a receptacle for European visions of religious and political freedom: events like the colonists' declaration of independence acted as catalysts in the formation of the image of the United States as a free land. Considering the European views of America to be simply outgrowths of European intellectual trends, or reflections of European social history, seems to me to be another, although perhaps unconscious, form of Eurocentrism.

In closing, I should like to express the hope that the investigations that now exist will serve as a basis from which to develop a more comprehensive synopsis of the European images of America, one that would give consideration not only to the historical genesis of these images but to their constant intermingling as well. Many voices, from Carlyle and Dickens, to Kafka, Thomas Mann, Jean-Paul Sartre and Jean-François Revel, Maxim Gorki, Johan Huizinga and Luigi Barzini, testify to the continued vigor of the views I have discussed here.

Indiana University

NOTES

[1] Cf. Hugh Honour, *The New Golden Land. European Images of America from the Discoveries to the Present Time* (New York: Pantheon Books, 1975).

[2] Gilbert Chinard, *L'Amérique et le rêve exotique dans la littérature française au XVIIe et au XVIIIe siècle* (Paris: Hachette, 1913); Durand Echeverria, *Mirage in the West. A History of the French Image of American Society to 1815* (1957; rpt. New York: Octagon Books, 1966); Harold Jantz, "Amerika im deutschen Dichten und Denken," in *Deutsche Philologie im Aufriss*, ed. Wolfgang Stammler, 2nd ed. (Berlin: Erich Schmidt, 1962), III, columns 309-372; Lawrence Marsden Price, *The Reception of United States Literature in Germany* (Chapel Hill: The Univ. of North Carolina Press, 1966); Allan Nevins, *America Through British Eyes* (New York: Oxford Univ. Press, 1948); Dieter Boden, *Das Amerikabild im russischen Schrifttum bis zum Ende des 19. Jahrhunderts* (Hamburg: Cram, de Gruyter, 1968).

[3] *Spektrum Amerika*, comp. Wulf Stratowa (Wien: Manutiuspresse, 1964).

[4] Manfred Henningsen, *Der Fall Amerika* (München: List, 1964), p. 131.

[5] Cf. Gilbert Chinard, "The American Dream," in *Literary History of the United States*, ed. Robert E. Spiller et al., 3rd ed. (New York: Macmillan, 1963), pp. 192-215.

[6] *The Works of Michael Drayton*, ed. J. William Hebel, II (Oxford: Blackwell, 1961), 363.

[7] Louis Bridel, *Le Pour et le contre ou Avis à ceux qui se proposent de passer dans les Etats-Unis de l'Amérique* (Paris: Levrault, 1803).

[8] *Neu-Württemberg. Ein Vorschlag zur Gründung einer württembergischen Kolonie im nordamerikanischen Freistaate Virginien. Mit allgemeinen Notizen über die nord-*

amerikanische Union und Kaufs- und Pachtanträgen über dortige Ländereien (Heilbronn: n.p., 1833).

⁹ A bibliography of "Auswandererliteratur" is offered by Hildegard Meyer, *Nord-Amerika im Urteil des Deutschen Schrifttums bis zur Mitte des 19. Jahrhunderts* (Hamburg: Friederichsen, de Gruyter, 1929), pp. 141-53.

¹⁰ Gottfried Duden, *Bericht über eine Reise nach den westlichen Staaten Nordamerikas und einen mehrjährigen Aufenthalt am Missouri, in Bezug auf Auswanderung und Überbevölkerung, oder: Das Leben im Innern der Vereinigten Staaten und dessen Bedeutung für die häusliche und politische Lage der Europäer* (Elberfeld: Samuel Lucas, 1829).

¹¹ "Gottfried Duden's 'Report,' 1824-1827," trans. William G. Bek, *The Missouri Historical Review*, 12 (1918), 163-79 (quote from 171-74).

¹² Rudolf Cronau, *Drei Jahrhunderte deutschen Lebens in Amerika* (Berlin: Reimer, 1924), p. 268.

¹³ Published as an appendix to Duden's book *Die nordamerikanische Demokratie und das von Tocqueville'sche Werk darüber, als Zeichen des Zustandes der theoretischen Politik* (Bonn: Eduard Weber, 1837), pp. 84-104.

¹⁴ My observations on the Europeans' negative attitudes toward America in the sixteenth and seventeenth centuries are based on Alain Clément, "Amerika als die Herausforderung des Westens," in *Sprache im technischen Zeitalter*, 56 (1975), p. 325-30.

¹⁵ *Les Oeuvres d'Estienne Pasquier* (Amsterdam: Libraires associez., 1723), II, 55.

¹⁶ J. H. Elliot, in a paper presented at the "International Conference on First Images of America: The Impact of the New World on the Old," held at the University of California at Los Angeles, in February 1975. Here quoted from Alain Clément, p. 326.

¹⁷ Cf. Gilbert Chinard, "Eighteenth Century Theories on America as a Human Habitat," *Proceedings of the American Philosophical Society*, 91 (1947), 27-57.

¹⁸ Nevins, pp. 79-102.

¹⁹ These and the following references to Mrs. Trollope's book are based on Nevins, pp. 82-83.

²⁰ Godfrey T. Vigne, *Six Months in America* (London: Whittaker, 1832), II, 273-76.

²¹ Boden, p. 21.

²² For the extensive literature concerning the European reception of Cooper see Karlheinz Rossbacher, *Lederstrumpf in Deutschland* (München: Wilhelm Fink, 1972), pp. 109-14.

²³ Reproductions in the catalogue of the exhibition *The European Vision of America*, ed. Hugh Honour (Cleveland: The Cleveland Museum of Art, 1975), nos. 274-75; Hugh Honour, *The New Golden Land*, pp. 221-23.

²⁴ Boden, p. 108.

²⁵ *Oeuvres et correspondance inédites d'Alexis de Tocqueville*, ed. Gustave de Beaumont (Paris: Michel Lévy, 1861), I, 175.

²⁶ Echeverria, pp. 39-78; Boden, pp. 31-48; James Taft Hatfield and Elfrieda Hochbaum, "The Influence of the American Revolution Upon German Literature," *Americana Germanica*, 3 (1899-1900), 338-85; Henry Safford King, "Echoes of the American Revolution in German Literature," *University of California Publications in Modern Philology*, 14 (1929), 23-193.

²⁷ Thomas Pilz, *1776-1976. Zweihundert Jahre deutsch-amerikanische Beziehungen* (München: Heinz Moos, 1975), p. 30.

[28] Cf. Albert R. Schmitt, *Herder und Amerika* (The Hague: Mouton, 1967), pp. 148-77.

[29] Boden, p. 37.

[30] *Die Vereinigten Staaten von Nordamerika nach ihrem politischen, religiösen und gesellschaftlichen Verhältnisse betrachtet* (Stuttgart: Cotta, 1827), p. iii.

[31] *Alexis de Tocquevilles Amerikabild. Genetische Untersuchungen über Zusammenhänge mit der zeitgenössischen, insbesondere der englischen Amerika-Interpretation* (Heidelberg: Carl Winter, 1957).

[32] *Vorlesungen über die Philosophie der Geschichte*, ed. Eduard Gans. 2nd. ed. (Berlin: Duncker und Humblot, 1840), p. 107.

[33] "Den Vereinigten Staaten," from *Zahme Xenien* (1827).

[34] Meyer, p. 5.

[35] Wolf-Dieter Bach, "America rasa. Vom Mythos des Neuen Anfangs," *Sprache im technischen Zeitalter*, 54 (1975), 126-46.

[36] Raymond Léopold Buckberger, *La Republique américaine* (Paris: Gallimard, 1958); foreword to the American edition by Peter F. Drucker, *Image of America* (New York: Viking, 1959), p. ix; Boden, p. 189.

[37] "National Images and Their Place in Literary Research: Germany as Seen by Eighteenth-Century French and English Reading Audiences," *Monatshefte* 67 (1975), 358-70.

Selected Bibliography

This bibliography, compiled by the speakers of the Symposium, is prepared for the convenience of readers of ethnic literatures who wish to make further study of the ethnic authors and their literary trends. The bibliography does not pretend to be complete. It includes (a) the most significant or important works of each ethnic literature, and (b) a selected list of historical, critical or biographical materials for further reference.

AMERICAN-ARMENIAN LITERATURE

Literary Works

Antreassian, Jack, ed. *Ararat: A Decade of Armenian-American Writing*. New York: Armenian General Benevolent Union, 1969.

Arlen, Michael J. *Passage to Ararat*. New York: Farrar, Straus & Giroux, 1975.

Hagopian, Richard. *Faraway the Spring*. New York: Charles Scribner's Sons, 1952.

Housepian, Marjorie. *A Houseful of Love*. New York: Random House, 1957.

Saroyan, William. *The Daring Young Man on the Flying Trapeze and Other Stories*. New York: Random House, 1934.

_____. *The Time of Your Life*, a Play. New York: Harcourt, Brace, 1939.

_____. *My Name is Aram*. New York: Harcourt, Brace, 1940.

_____. *Razzle-Dazzle*. New York: Harcourt, Brace, 1942.

Sourian, Peter. *The Gate*. New York: Harcourt Brace Jovanovich, 1965.

Surmelian, Leon Z. *I Ask You, Ladies and Gentlemen*. New York: E. P. Dutton, 1945.

Historical Works

Boyajian, Zabelle C. *Armenian Legends and Poems*. New York: Columbia University, 1959.

de Morgan, Jacques. *The History of the Armenian People: From Remotest Times to the Present Day*. Trans. Ernest F. Barry. Boston: Hairenik Press, n.d.

"Armenian Soviet Socialist Republic." *Encyclopaedia Britannica*. Fifteenth Edition, Macropaedia. Chicago: Encyclopaedia Britannica, Inc. 1974. II, 24-27.

Housepian, Marjorie. *The Smyrna Affair*. New York: Harcourt Brace Jovanovich, 1971.

Morganthau, Henry. *Ambassador Morgenthau's Story*. Plandome, N.Y.: New Age Publisher, Rep. 1974.

CHICANO LITERATURE

Acuña, Rodolfo. *Occupied America: The Chicano's Struggle Toward Liberation*. San Francisco: Canfield Press, 1972.

Meier, Matt S. and Feliciano Rivera, eds. *Readings on La Raza: The Twentieth Century*. New York: Hill and Wang, 1974.

Castañeda Shular, Antonia, Tomás Ybarra Frausto and Joseph Sommers, comps. *Literatura chicana: texto y contexto*. Englewood Cliffs, N.J.,: Prentice-Hall, Inc., 1971.

Hinojosa-S., Rolando R. *Estampas del valle y otras obras*. Berkeley: Quinto Sol Publications, 1973.

Hundley, Jr., Norris, ed. *The Chicano.* Santa Barbara: Clio Books, 1975.
Lamb, Ruth S. *Mexican Americans: Sons of the Southwest.* Claremont, California: Ocelot Press, 1970.
Ludwig, Ed and James Santibáñez, eds. *The Chicanos: Mexican American Voices.* Baltimore: Penguin Books, Inc., 1971.
McWilliams, Carey. *North From Mexico.* New York: Monthly Review Press, 1961.
Rivera, Tomás. *". . . y no se lo tragó la tierra" ". . . and the earth did not part."* Berkeley: Quinto Sol Publications, 1971.
Ruiz, Ramón Eduardo. *The Mexican War: Was It Manifest Destiny?* New York: Holt, Rinehart and Winston, 1963.
Simmen, Edward, ed. *Pain and Promise: The Chicano Today.* New York: New American Library, 1972.
Meier, Matt S. and Feliciano Rivera. *The Chicanos: A History of the Mexican Americans.* New York: Hill and Wang, 1972.
Tyler, Gus, ed. *Mexican-Americans Tomorrow.* Albuquerque: University of New Mexico Press, 1975.
Valdez, Luis and Stan Steiner. *Aztlán: An Anthology of Mexican American Literature.* New York: Alfred A. Knopf-Vintage Books, 1972.

CHINESE-AMERICAN LITERATURE

Berssenbrugge, Mei. *Summits Move with the Tide.* Greenfield Center, New York: Greenfield Review Press, 1974. (poems)
Chang, Diana. *The Frontiers of Love.* New York: Random House, 1956. (novel)
Chin, Frank, Jeffery Chan, Lawson Inada, and Shawn Wong, eds. *Aiiieeee! An Introduction to Asian-American Writing.* Washington, D.C.: Howard University Press, 1974. (anthology)
Chu, Louis. *Eat a Bowl of Tea.* New York: Lyle Stuart, 1961. (novel)
Kuo, Alexander. *The Window Tree.* New Hampshire: Windy Row Press, 1971. (poems)
Lowe, Pardee. *Father and Glorious Descendant.* Boston: Little, Brown & Co., 1943. (novel)
Wang, David Rafael. *The Goblet Moon.* Vermont: Stinehaur Press, 1955. (poems; limited edition of 50 copies)
_____. *The Intercourse.* Greenfield Center, New York: Greenfield Review Press, 1975. (poems)
_____. *Rivers on Fire.* Dunkirk, New York: Basilisk Press, 1976. (poems)
Yau, John. *Crossing Canal Street.* New York: Bellevue Press, 1975. (poems)

CROATIAN-AMERICAN LITERATURE

Bašić, Jakov. *Hrastov čvor.* [U.S.A.]: The Author, 1969.
Bonifačić, Antun. *Sabrane pjesne.* Chicago: The Author, 1974.
Ivezić, Zlata. *Srebrne suze.* Chicago: The Author, 1974.
Kesterčanek-Vujica, Nada. *Koluti vremena.* New York: The Author, 1969.
Lojen, Stjepan. *Uspomene jednog iseljenika.* Zagreb: Znanje, 1963.
Lorkovic, Hrvoje (pseud. Rok Remetic). *Karakteristika.* Hills, Iowa: The Author [1972].
Lujić, Mile. *Legende i stvarnosti.* Chicago: The Author, 1970.
Prpić, George J. *The Croatian Immigrants in America.* New York: The Philosophical Library, 1971.
_____. *Posljednji svibanj.* Rome: Ziral, 1973.

Prpić, George J. and Hilda Prpić. *Croatian Books and Booklets Written in Exile.* Cleveland: Authors in Co-operation with ISEES, John Carroll Univ., 1973.
Raspudić, Gracian. *Braća Golemci.* Chicago: The Franciscan Press, 1964.

CZECH-AMERICAN LITERATURE

Havlasa, Jan. *Pet kalifornských povídek.* Prague: Bělský a Ježek, 1910.
Hostovský, Egon. *Dobročinný večírek.* New York: Moravian Library, 1958.
——————. *Listy z vyhnanství.* Chicago: České národní sdružení, 1941.
——————. *Pulnoční pacient.* New York: Universum Press, 1959.
——————. *Tři noci.* New York: Společnost pro vědy a umění, 1964.
——————. *Všeobecné spiknutí.* Toronto: 68 Publishers, 1973.
Matějka, Ladislav, ed. *Kulturní sborník rok.* New York: Moravian Library, 1957.
Němeček, Zdeněk. *Bloudění v exilu.* Lund, Sweden: Sklizeň svobodné tvorby, 1958.
Radimský, Ladislav. *Evropan na Manhattanu.* Lund, Sweden: Sklizeň svobodné tvorby, 1958.
——————. *Naší mládeži: Napsáno v New Yorku 1968.* Rome: Vigilie, 1973.
Rechcígl, Miloslav, Jr., ed. *The Czechoslovak Contributions to World Culture.* The Hague: Mouton, 1964. (Sponsored by the Czechoslovak Society of Arts and Sciences in America.)
——————. *Czechoslovakia Past and Present I, II.* The Hague: Mouton, 1968. (Sponsored by the Czechoslovak Society of Arts and Sciences in America.)
Wellek, René. *The Age of Transition.* New Haven: Yale Univ. Press, 1965.
——————. *Essays on Czech Literature.* The Hague: Mouton, 1963. (Sponsored by the Czechoslovak Society of Arts and Sciences in America.)
——————. *A History of Modern Criticism: 1750-1950.* New Haven: Yale Univ. Press, 1955- . (To date, four volumes have been published.)

ESTONIAN-AMERICAN LITERATURE

Aspel, Alexander. "Ice, Stars, Stones, Birds, Trees: Three Major Postwar Estonian Poets Abroad." *Books Abroad*, 47 (Autumn 1973), 642-52.
Estonian Poetry and Language: Studies in Honor of Ants Oras. Ed. Viktor Kõressaar and Aleksis Rannit. Stockholm: Estonian Learned Society in America, 1965.
Harris, E. Howard. *Estonian Literature in Exile.* London: Boreas Publishing Co., 1949.
Ivask, Ivar, "Baltic Literatures in Exile: Balance of a Quarter Century." *Journal of Baltic Studies*, 3 (1972), 1-17.
——————. "Recent Trends in Estonian Poetry." *Books Abroad*, 42 (1968), 517-20.
Mägi, Arvo. *Estonian Literature: An Outline.* Stockholm: Baltic Humanitarian Association, 1968.
Mägi, Arvo, Ristikivi, Karl, and Bernard Kangro. *Eesti kirjandus paguluses 1944-1972.* With an English summary [and bibliography]. Lund: Eesti kirjanike kooperatiiv, 1973.
Matthews, W. K., comp. and trans. *Anthology of Modern Estonian Poetry.* Gainesville: University of Florida Press, 1953.
Oras, Ants. *Estonian Literature in Exile: An Essay.* With a Bio-Bibliographical Appendix by Bernard Kangro. Lund: Estonian PEN-Club/Eesti kirjanike kooperatiiv, 1967.
——————. *Estonian Literary Reader.* Indiana University Publications, Uralic and Altaic Series, 31. Bloomington, Ind.: Indiana University, 1963.

Rannit, Aleksis. "Dry Radiance: Selected Poems." Trans. Henry Lyman. In *New Directions in Prose and Poetry*, 25. Ed. J. Laughlin (New York: New Directions, 1972), pp. 146-71.
_____. *Line*. Trans. Henry Lyman. Zürich: Adolf Hürlimann, 1970.
Terras, Victor. "The Poetics of Aleksis Rannit: Observations on the Condition of the Emigré Poet." *Journal of Baltic Studies*, 5 (1974), 112-16.
Willmann, Asta. "The Perceptional World of Aleksis Rannit." *Yearbook of the Estonian Learned Society in America*, 4 (1964-1967), 32-50.

FRANCO-AMERICAN LITERATURE

General

Belisle, Alexandre. *Histoire de la Presse Franco-Américaine et des Canadiens-Français aux Etats-Unis*. Worcester, Mass.: Les Ateliers de l'Opinion Publique, 1911.
Rumilly, Robert. *Histoire des Franco-Américains*. Woonsocket, R.I.: L'Union Saint-Jean-Baptiste d'Amérique, 1958.
Therriault, Soeur Mary-Carmel. *La littérature française de Nouvelle-Angleterre*. Montréal: Fides, 1946.
Chassé, Paul-P. *Les Poètes franco-américains de la Nouvelle-Angleterre, 1875-1925*. Somersworth, N.H.: L'Abbaye de Thélème, 1968.

Prose Fiction

Kerouac, Jack. *The Town and the City*. New York: Harcourt Brace Jovanovich, 1950.
Metalious, Grace. *No Adam in Eden*. New York: Pocket Books, 1967.
Robichaud, Gérard. *Papa Martel*. New York: All Saints Press, 1962.

Poetry

Dion-Lévesque, Rosaire. *Les Oasis*. Rome: Desclée & Cie, Editeurs Pontificaux, 1930.
_____. *Quête*. Québec: Editions Garneau, 1963.
_____. *Vita*. Montréal: Editions Bernard Valiquette, 1939.
Chassé, Paul-P. *La Carafe enchantée*. Somersworth, N.H.: Abbaye de Thélème, 1968.
_____. *Et la mer efface . . .* Somersworth, N.H.: Abbaye de Thélème, 1964.

GERMAN-AMERICAN LITERATURE

Bauschinger, Sigrid, et al., eds. *Amerika in der deutschen Literatur: Neue Welt-Nordamerika-USA*. Stuttgart: Reclam, 1975.
Billigmeier, Robert H. *Americans from Germany: A Study in Cultural Diversity*. Belmont, California: Wadsworth, 1974.
Deutsch-Amerikanische-200-Jahr-Feier: Staats-Herold Almanach 1976. New York: Staats-Herold Corp., 1975.
Faust, A. B. *The German Element in the United States*. 2 vols. New York: The Steuben Society of America, 1927.
Friebert, Stuart. *Nicht hinauslehnen: Gedichte/Poems*. Munich: Delp, 1975.
Fries, Adelaide L. *The Road to Salem*. Chapel Hill: Univ. of North Carolina Press, 1944.
German-American Studies: A Journal of History, Literature, Biography and Genealogy (Published semi-annually by Institute of German-American Studies, Cleveland, Ohio.)

Harbaugh, Henry. *Harbaugh's Harfe: Gedichte in Pennsylvanisch-Deutscher Mundart.* Philadelphia: Reformed Church Publications Board, 1902.

Jordan, Mildred. *One Red Rose Forever* (A partly fictionalized account of the career of Heinrich Wilhelm Stiegel, founder of the Stiegel glass industry in Pennsylvania). New York: Alfred A. Knopf, 1941.

Kahn, Lisa. *Klopfet an, so wird euch nicht aufgetan.* Darmstadt: Bläschke, 1975.

Münsterberg, Margarete, trans. *A Harvest of German Verse.* New York: Appleton, 1916.

Pochmann, Henry A. *German Culture in America: Philosophical and Literary Influences, 1600-1900.* Madison: Univ. of Wisconsin Press, 1957.

Schurz, Carl. *Reminiscences.* 3 vols. New York: McClure, 1907.

_____. *Lebenserinnerungen.* Ed. Edward Manley. Boston: Allyn & Bacon, 1913.

Spuler, Linus. *Deutsches Schrifttum in den Vereinigten Staaten von Amerika.* Lucerne: Erziehungsdepartement, 1960.

Ward, Robert E., ed. *Deutsche Lyrik aus Amerika.* New York: Literary Soc. Foundation, 1969.

Zucker, A. E. *General De Kalb: Lafayette's Mentor.* Univ. of North Carolina Studies in Germanic Languages and Literatures, No. 57. Chapel Hill, 1966.

ITALIAN-AMERICAN LITERATURE

Valenti, Angelo. *Golden Gate.* New York: NYT Arno Press, 1975.

D'Agostino, Guido. *Olives on the Apple Tree.* New York: NYT Arno Press, 1975.

Forgione, Louis. *The River Between.* New York: NYT Arno Press, 1975.

Lapolla, Garibaldi M. *The Grand Gennaro.* New York: NYT Arno Press, 1975.

Pellegrini, Angelo M. *Americans by Choice.* New York: Macmillan Co., 1956.

DeVoto, Bernard. *Mountain Time.* Boston: Little, Brown and Co., 1947.

Mirabelli, Eugene. *The Way Inn.* New York: The Viking Press, 1968.

_____. *The Burning Air.* Boston: Houghton Mifflin, 1959.

Di Donato, Pietro. *Christ in Concrete.* Indianapolis: Bobbs-Merrill, 1937.

Ventura, Luigi D. *Peppino.* New York: William R. Jenkins, 1885.

Puzo Mario. *The Fortunate Pilgrim.* New York: Atheneum, 1965.

Pollini, Francis. *Night.* New York: G. P. Putman's Sons, 1961.

Cuomo, George. *Among Thieves.* Garden City, N.J.: Doubleday, 1968.

Arleo, Joseph. *The Grand Street Collector.* New York: Walker, 1970.

Green, Rose Basile. *The Italian-American Novel.* Rutherford-Madison-Teaneck: Fairleigh Dickinson Univ. Press, 1974.

La Piana, Angelina. *Dante's American Pilgrimage.* New Haven: Yale Univ. Press, 1948.

Fucilla, Joseph. *The Teaching of Italian in the United States: A Documentary History.* New York: NYT Arno Press, 1975.

JAPANESE-AMERICAN LITERATURE

Chin, Frank, Jeffery Paul Chan, Lawson Fusao Inada, and Shawn Wong, eds. *Aiiieeeee!: An Anthology of Asian-American Writers.* Washington, D.C.: Howard Univ. Press, 1975.

Hosokawa, Bill. *Nisei: The Quiet Americans.* New York: Morrow, 1969.

Houston, Jeanne Wakatsuki, and James D. Houston. *Farewell to Manzanar.* Boston: Houghton Mifflin, 1973.

Hsu, Kai-yu, and Helen Palubinskas, eds. *Asian-American Authors*. Boston: Houghton Mifflin, 1972.

Inada, Lawson Fusao. *Before the War: Poems As They Happened*. New York: Morrow, 1971.

Mori, Toshio. *Yokohama, California*. Caldwell, Idaho: The Caxton Printers, Ltd., 1949.

Okada, John. *No-No Boy*. Rutland, Vermont: Charles E. Tuttle Co., 1957.

Okubo, Mine'. *Citizen 13660*. New York: Columbia Univ. Press, 1946.

Sone, Monica. *Nisei Daughter*. Boston: Little, Brown and Co., 1953.

Weglyn, Michi. *Years of Infamy*. New York: Morrow, 1976.

LITHUANIAN-AMERICAN LITERATURE

Rubulis, Aleksis. *Baltic Literature*. Notre Dame: The Univ. of Notre Dame Press, 1970.

Šilbajoris, Rimvydas. *Perfection of Exile: 14 Contemporary Lithuanian Writers*. Norman: The Univ. of Oklahoma Press, 1970.

Vaičiulaitis, Antanas. *Outline History of Lithuanian Literature*. Chicago: Lithuanian Cultural Institute, 1942.

Ziedonis, Arvíds, et al., ed. *Baltic Literature and Linguistics*. Columbus, Ohio: Association for the Advancement of Baltic Studies, 1973.

Zobarskas, Stepas. *The Lithuanian Short Story: Fifty Years*. New York: Manyland, 1975.

A number of articles on Lithuanian literature appear in two English-language journals: *Lituanus*, published in Chicago, Antanas Klimas, ed., and *Journal of Baltic Studies*, published in New York, Arvíds Ziedonis, ed.

Translations

Baranauskas, Antanas. *The Forest of Anykščiai*. Trans. Nadas Rastenis. Los Angeles: Lithuanian Days Publishers, 1956.

Baronas, Aloyzas. *Footbridges and Abysses*. Trans. J. Zemkalnis. New York: Manyland, 1965.

Donelaitis, Kristijonas. *The Seasons*. Trans. Nadas Rastenis. Los Angeles: Lithuanian Days Publishers, 1967.

Gliauda, Jurgis. *House Upon the Sand*. Trans. Raphael Sealey and Milton Stark. New York: Manyland, 1963.

Jurkūnas (Šeinius), Agnas. *Rejuvenation of Siegfried Immerselbe*. Trans. Albinas Baranauskas. New York: Manyland, 1965.

Krėvė, Vincas. *The Herdsman and the Linden Tree*. Trans. Albinas Baranauskas, Pranas Prenckus and Raphael Sealey. New York: Manyland, 1964.

Landsbergis, Algirdas, *Five Posts in a Market Place*. New York: Manyland, 1964.

Landsbergis, Algirdas and Mills, Clark, ed., *The Green Linden: Selected Lithuanian Folksongs*. New York: Voyages Press, 1964.

_____. *The Green Oak: Selected Lithuanian Poetry in English Translation*. New York: Voyages Press, 1962.

Ramonas, Vincas. *Crosses*. Trans. Milton Stark. Los Angeles: Lithuanian Days Publishers, 1954.

Vaičiulaitis, Antanas. *Noon at a Country Inn*. Trans. Albinas Baranauskas et al. New York: Manyland, 1965.

Zobarskas, Stepas, ed. *Lithuanian Quartet: Aloyzas Baronas, Marius Katiliškis, Algidas Landsbergis, Ignas Šeinius.* New York: Manyland, 1962.
Zobarskas, Stepas, ed. *Selected Lithuanian Short Stories.* New York: Voyages Press, 1959.

NATIVE AMERICAN LITERATURE

Brandon, William. *The American Heritage Book of Indians.* New York: Dell, 1964. [Brandon's work has been recently reprinted and revised to *The Last Americans— The Indian in American Culture.* Hightstown, N.J.: McGraw-Hill, 1974.]
Brown, Dee. *Bury My Heart at Wounded Knee.* New York: Holt, Rinehart & Winston, 1970.
Deloria, Vine, Jr. *Custer Died For Your Sins.* New York: Macmillan, 1969.
Fey, Harold, and D'Arcy McNickle. *Indians and Other Americans*, rev. ed. New York: Harper & Row, 1970.
Momaday, N. Scott. *House Made of Dawn.* New York: Harper & Row, 1969.
_____. *The Way to Rainy Mountain.* Albuquerque: Univ. of New Mexico, 1969.
Rosen, Kenneth, ed. *Man To Send Rain Clouds.* New York: Viking, 1974.
_____. *Voices of the Rainbow.* New York: Viking, 1975.
Rothenberg, Jerome. *Shaking the Pumpkin: Traditional Poetry of the Indian North Americans.* New York: Doubleday, 1972.
Sanders, Thomas, and Walter Peek, eds. *Literature of the American Indian*, Beverly Hills: Glencoe Press, 1973.
Welch, James. *Riding the Earthboy 40.* New York: Harper & Row, 1976.
_____. *Winter in the Blood.* New York: Harper & Row, 1974.

NORWEGIAN-AMERICAN LITERATURE

Ager, Waldemar. *Christ Before Pilate: An American Story.* Trans. anon. Minneapolis: Augsburg Publishing House, 1924.
_____. *I Sit Alone.* Trans. Charles Wharton Stork. New York: Harper & Brothers Publishers, 1931.
_____. *When You Are Tired of Playing.* Trans. J. J. Skørdalsvold. Eau Claire Wis.: Fremad Publishing Co., 1907.
Foss, Hans Anderson. *The Cotter's Son.* Trans. Joel G. Winkjer. Alexandria, Minn.: Park Region Publishing Co., 1963.
_____. *Tobias: A Story of the Northwest* 1899.
Johnson, Simon. *From Fjord to Prairie; Or, In the New Kingdom.* Trans. C. O. Solberg. Minneapolis: Augsburg Publishing House, 1916.
Rønning, N. N. *Lars Lee: The Boy from Norway.* Minneapolis: The Christian Literature Co., 1928.
Rølvaag, Ole Edvart. *The Boat of Longing.* Trans. Nora O. Solum. New York: Harper & Brothers Publishers, 1933.
_____. *Giants in the Earth.* Trans. Lincoln Colcord and the author. New York: Harper & Brothers Publishers, 1927.
_____. *Peder Victorious.* Trans. Nora O. Solum and the author. New York: Harper & Brothers Publishers, 1929.
_____. *Pure Gold.* Trans. Sivert Erdahl and the author. New York: Harper & Brothers Publishers, 1930.
_____. *Their Fathers' God.* Trans. Trygve M. Ager. New York: Harper & Brothers Publishers, 1931.

_____. *The Third Life of Per Smevik*. Trans. Ella Valborg Tweet and Solveig Zempel. Minneapolis: Dillon Press, Inc., 1971.

Strømme, Peer. *Halvor: A Story of Pioneer Youth*. Trans. Inga B. Norstog and David T. Nelson. Decorah, Iowa: Luther College Press, 1960.

POLISH-AMERICAN LITERATURE

Koscielska, Regina. "Portrait of a Polish American." *Immigrants and Migrants*. Ed. David W. Hartman. Detroit: New University Thought, 1974, pp. 114-18.

Lopata, Helena Znaniecki. *Polish Americans: Status Competition in An Ethnic Community*. Englewood Cliffs, New Jersey: Prentice-Hall, 1976.

_____. "The Polish American Family." *Ethnic Families in America: Patterns and Variations*. Eds. Charles H. Mindel and Robert W. Habenstein. New York: Elsevier, 1976, pp. 15-40.

Novak, Michael. "The Sting of Polish Jokes." *Newsweek*, 12 April 1976, p. 13.

Radzialowski, Thaddeus. "A View From the Polish Ghetto." *Ethnicity*, 1, No. 3 (1975), 125-50.

Sandberg, Neil C. *Ethnic Identity and Assimilation: The Polish American Community*. New York: Praeger, 1974.

Sanders, Irwin T. and Ewa Morawska. *Polish American Community Life: A Survey of Research*. New York: Polish Institute of Arts and Sciences in America, 1975.

Wytrwal, Joseph. *Poles in American History and Tradition*. Detroit: Endurance Press, 1969.

PORTUGUESE-AMERICAN LITERATURE

Andrade, Laurinda C. *The Open Door*. New Bedford, Mass.: Reynolds-DeWalt, 1968.

Carvalho, James A. *Haole, Come Back*, by James Oaktree [pseud.]. Chicago: Adams Press, 1975.

Dos Passos, John. *The Best Times: An Informal Memoir*. New York: The New American Library, 1966.

_____. *Century's Ebb: The Thirteenth Chronicle*. Boston: Gambit, 1975.

_____. *Chosen Country*. Boston: Houghton Mifflin, 1951.

_____. *Facing the Chair: Story of the Americanization of Two Foreignborn Workmen*. Boston: Sacco-Vanzetti Defense Committee, 1927.

_____. *The Fourteenth Chronicle: Letters and Diaries of John Dos Passos. Edited and with a biographical narrative by Townsend Ludington*. Boston: Gambit, 1973.

_____. *The Portugal Story: Three Centures of Exploration and Discovery*. Garden City, New York: Doubleday, 1969.

Lage, Fausto P. *Fantastic Dilemma*. Philadelphia, Dorrance, 1951.

Lewis, Alfred. *Home is an Island*. New York: Random House, 1951.

Oliver, Lawrence. *Never Backward: The Autobiography of Lawrence Oliver, A Portuguese-American*. Ed. Rita Larkin Wolin. San Diego: Neyenesch Printers, 1972.

Roll, Elvira Osorio. *Background: A Novel of Hawaii*. New York: Exposition Press, 1964.

_____. *Hawaii's Kohala Breezes*. New York: Exposition Press, 1964.

PUERTO RICAN LITERATURE
History and Criticism

Arriví, Francisco. *Areyto Mayor*. San Juan: Instituto de Cultura Puertorriqueña, 1966.

Babín, María Teresa. *Jornadas literarias: temas de Puerto Rico*. Barcelona: Ediciones Rumbos, 1967.

Borinquen: An Anthology of Puerto Rican Literature. Trans. Barry Luby. Ed. María Teresa Babín and Stan Steiner. New York: Alfred A. Knopf, 1974.

Canino Salgado, Marcelino. *La copia y el romance populares en la tradición oral de Puerto Rico*. San Juan: Instituto de Cultura Puertorriqueña, 1968.

Essays

Alonso, Manuel A. *El Jíbaro: cuadro de costumbres de la isla de Puerto Rico*. San Juan: Instituto de Cultura Puertorriqueña, 1970.

Meléndez, Concha. *Obras completas*. San Juan: Instituto de Cultura Puertorriqueña, 1970.

Muñoz Rivera, Luis. *Obras completas*. Introducción, notas, y recopilación de Lidio Cruz Monclava. San Juan: Instituto de Cultura Puertorriqueña, 1968.

Fiction

Días Alfaro, Abelardo. *Terrazo*. Prólogo de Mariano Picón Salas. San Juan: Instituto de Cultura Puertorriqueña, 1967.

González, José Luis. *La galería y otros cuentos*. México: Biblioteca Era, 1972.

Marqués, René. *Otro día nuestro*. Prólogo por Concha Meléndez. San Juan: Instituto de Cultura Puertorriqueña, 1955.

Zeno Gandía, Manuel. *Obras completas*. Río Piedras: Ediciones del Instituto de Literatura Puertorriqueña, Universidad de Puerto Rico, 1955-1958.

Poetry

Arce de Vázquez, Margot, Laura Gallego, and Luis de Arrigoitía. *Lecturas Puertorriqueñas: Poesía*. Sharon, Conn.: Troutman Press, 1968.

Diego, José de. *Obras completas* (poesía). Prólogo de Concha Meléndez. San Juan: Instituto de Cultura Puertorriqueña, 1966.

Hernández Aquino, Luis. *Entre la elegía y el requiem: poemas*. Río Piedras: Editorial Edil, 1968.

Lloréns Torres, Luis. *Obras completas*. San Juan: Instituto de Cultura Puertorriqueña, 1967-1969.

Palés Matos, Luis. *Poesía, 1915-1956*. Introducción por Federico de Onís. San Juan: Ediciones de la Universidad de Puerto Rico, 1968.

Poesía Puertorriqueña. Selección y prólogo de Luis Hernández Aquino. Río Piedras: Universidad de Puerto Rico, 1954.

Rivera Chevremont, Evaristo. *Antología poética (1929-1965)*. Introducción, selección, y notas por María Teresa Babín y Jaime Luis Rodríguez. San Juan: Editorial del Departamento de Instrucción Pública, Estado Libre Asociado de Puerto Rico, 1967.

Theatre

Arriví, Francisco. *Tres piezas de Teatro Puertorriqueño*. San Juan: Editorial del Departamento de Instrucción Pública, Estado Libre Associado de Puerto Rico, 1968.

Marqués, René. *The Oxcart*. Trans. Charles Pilditch. New York: Scribner, 1969.

Teatro Puertorriqueño: Primer festival de teatro. San Juan: Instituto de Cultura Puertorriqueña, 1959.

SERBIAN-AMERICAN LITERATURE

Brown, Francis J. and Roucek, Joseph S. *Our Racial and National Minorities: Their History, Contributions, and Present Problems*. New York: Prentice-Hall, Inc., 1939.

Central Committee of Serbian National Defense. *Spomenica: Fortieth Anniversary of Serbian National Defense*. Chicago: Serbian National Defense, 1950.

Dragutinovich, Dragoslav. *From Travelled Roads: Short Stories*. Melbourne, Australia: Unification Printers and Publishers, 1970.

Editorial Committee. *Almanac American Srbobran* (English and Serbian). Pittsburgh, Pennsylvania: American Srbobran, 1951; 1960; 1961; 1962; 1963.

Editorial Committee. *Spomenica: Thirtieth Anniversary of Serbian Orthodox Monastery St. Sava and Sixtieth Anniversary of Serbian Orthodox Church in America*. Libertyville, Illinois: St. Sava Monastery, 1953.

Govorchin, Gerald G. *Americans from Yugoslavia: A Survey of Yugoslav Immigrants in the United States*. Gainesville: Univ. of Florida Press, 1961.

Ibrovac, Miodrag. *Claude Fauriel et la fortune européene des poésies populaires grecque et serbe*. Paris: Didier, 1966.

————. *Anthologie de la Poésie Yougoslave: des XIXe et XXe siècles*. Paris: Librairie Delagrave, 1935.

Pupin, Michael. *From Immigrant to Inventor*. New York: Scribner's, 1960.

Simic, Charles. *What the Grass Knows*. San Francisco: Kayak Press, 1967.

————. *Somewhere Among Us a Stone is Taking Notes*. San Francisco: Kayak Press, 1969.

————. *The Young American Poets*. Ed. Paul Carroll. Chicago: Fallett Publishing Co., 1968. pp. 338-94.

Velimirovich, Nicholai D. *The Life of St. Sava*. Libertyville, Illinois: Serbian Eastern Orthodox Diocese, The Serbian Orthodox Monastery of St. Sava, 1951.

SLOVENIAN-AMERICAN LITERATURE

Barac, Antun. *A History of Yugoslav Literature*. Trans. Petar Mijušković. Ann Arbor: Department of Slavic Languages and Literatures, University of Michigan, n.d.

Christian, Henry A. *Louis Adamic: A Checklist*. Kent: Kent State University Press, 1971.

Clissold, Joseph. *The Slovenes Want to Live*. New York: The Yugoslav Information Center, 1943.

De Bray, R. G. A. *Guide to the Slavonic Languages*. London: J. M. Dent and Sons, 1951.

Filipič, Lojze. *Linhartovo izročilo*. Ljubljana: Drama Slovenskega narodnega gledališča, 1957.

Gobetz, Giles Edward, and Adele Donchenko, eds. *Anthology of Slovenian American Literature*. Willoughby Hills and Kent: Slovenian Research Center of America, 1976.

Janez, Stanko. *Zgodovina Slovenske književnosti.* Maribor: Obzorja, 1957.
Kmecl, Matjaž, Tine Logar, and Jože Toporišic. *Slovenski jezik, literatura in kultura.* Ljubljana: Seminar slovenskega jezika, literature in kulture, 1974.
Lavrin, Janko, and Anton Slodnjak, eds. *The Parnassus of a Small Nation.* Ljubljana: Državna Založba Slovenije, 1965.
Slodnjak, Anton. *Geschichte der slowenischen Literatur.* Berlin: Walter de Gruyter, 1958.
Slodnjak, Anton. *Slovensko slovstvo.* Ljublijana: Mladinska Knjiga, 1968.
Tischler, Joseph. *Die Schprachenfrage in Kärten vor 100 Jahren und Heute.* Celovec: Rat der Kärnter Slowenen, 1957.

UKRAINIAN-AMERICAN LITERATURE

Čyževs'kyj, Dmytro. *A History of Ukrainian Literature (From the 11th to the end of the 19th Century).* Trans. Dolly Ferguson, Doreen Gorsline, and Ulana Petyk. Edited and with a Foreword by George S. N. Luckyj. Littleton, Colo.: Ukrainian Academic Press, 1975.
Halych, Vasyl. *Ukrainians in the United States.* San Francisco: R. & E. Research Associates, 1969.
Kuropas, Myron B. *Ukrainians in America.* Minneapolis: Lerner Publ., 1972.
Luciw, Theodore. *Father Agapius Honcharenko, First Ukrainian Priest in America.* New York: Ukrainian Congress Committee of America, 1970.
Luckyj, George S. N., ed. *Modern Ukrainian Short Stories.* Littleton, Colo.: Ukrainian Academic Press, 1973.
Luzhnyts'kyi, Hryhor Merriam. *Ukrainian Literature Within the Framework of World Literature: A Short Outline of Ukrainian Literature from Renaissance to Romanticism.* Philadelphia: "America," 1961.
Manning, Clarence Augustus. *Ukrainian Literature: Studies of the Leading Authors.* Foreword by Watson Kirkconnell. Jersey City, N.J.: Ukrainian National Association, 1944.
Mirchuk, Ivan, ed. *Ukraine and Its People: A Handbook With Maps, Statistical Tables and Diagrams.* Munich: Ukrainian Free University, 1949.
Shtohryn, Dmytro M., ed. *Ukrainians in North America: A Biographical Directory of Noteworthy Men and Women of Ukrainian Origin in the United States and Canada.* Champaign, Ill.: Association for the Advancement of Ukrainian Studies, 1975.
Sokolyszyn, Aleksander. *Ukrainian Selected and Classified Bibliography in English.* New York: Ukrainian Information Bureau, 1972.
Their Land: An Anthology of Ukrainian Short Stories. Ed. Michael Luchkovich. Jersey City, N.J.: Svoboda Press, 1964.
Ukraine: A Concise Encyclopaedia. 2 vols. Prepared by Shevchenko Scientific Society. Ed. Volodymyr Kubijovyč. Toronto: Univ. of Toronto Press, 1963-1971.
The Ukrainian Poets, 1189-1962. Selected and translated into English verse by C. H. Andrusyshen and Watson Kirkconnell. Toronto: Univ. of Toronto Press, 1963.
Weres, Roman. *Ukraine: Selected References in the English Language.* 2nd ed., enlarged and up-to-date. Chicago: Ukrainian Research and Information Institute, 1974.
Weresh, Wasyl, ed. *Guide to Ukrainian-American Institutions, Professionals and Business.* New York: Carpathian Star Pub. Co., 1955.
Zyla, Wolodymyr T. "Manifestations of Ukrainian Poetry and Prose in Exile." *Books Abroad,* 50, No. 2 (1976), 318-25.

632

YIDDISH-AMERICAN LITERATURE

Hapgood, Hutchins. *The Spirit of the Ghetto*. New York: Funk and Wagnall, 1902.

Howe, Irving and Greenberg, Eliezer, eds. *A Treasury of Yiddish Poetry*. New York: Holt, Rinehart and Winston, 1969.

—————, eds. *A Treasury of Yiddish Stories*. New York: Viking, 1954.

—————, eds. *Voices from the Yiddish*. Ann Arbor: Univ. of Michigan, 1972.

Howe, Irving and Libo, Kenneth. *The World of Our Fathers*. New York: Harcourt, Brace, Jovanovich, 1976.

Lifson, David. *The Yiddish Theatre in America*. New York: Thomas Yoseloff, 1965.

Liptzin, Sol. *History of Yiddish Literature in America*. New York: Jonathan David, 1972.

Madison, Charles. *Yiddish Literature*. New York: Frederick Ungar, 1968.

Mark, Yudel. "Yiddish Literature," in Louis Finkelstein, ed. *The Jews: Their History, Culture and Religion*, 4 volumes. Philadelphia: Jewish Publication Society, 1949.

Rischin, Moses. *The Promised City: New York's Jews 1970-1914*. Cambridge: Harvard Univ., 1962.

Sanders, Ronald. *The Downtown Jews*. New York: Harcourt, Brace and World, Inc., 1969.

NOTES ON THE AUTHORS

Branimir Anzulovic, a native of Zabreb, Yugoslavia, is Visiting Assistant Professor in the Comparative Literature Program at Indiana University. He earned a Diploma from the Department of Philosophy, University of Zagreb, and the Ph.D. degree in Comparative Literature from Indiana University. Dr. Anzulovic has taught Serbo-Croatian at the University of Chicago and Indiana University, and he has taught Comparative Literature at Prescott College. He has been awarded both a Fulbright travel grant and a University of Chicago scholarship. Among his publications are numerous film and theater reviews and articles such as "Estilo y civilización," "Tolstoi and the Novel," and "Literary Mannerism: A Review of Research." Currently he is preparing a study on the problem of periodization in literary history.

María Teresa Babín is Professor of Puerto Rican Studies at Herbert H. Lehman College of the City University of New York and Professor of Spanish at the Graduate Center of CUNY. A native of Puerto Rico, she received the degrees of A.B. and A.M. from the University of Puerto Rico, and the Ph.D. from Columbia University. Her books include *Introducción a la cultura hispánica* (1949), *El Mundo poético de García Lorca* (1954), *García Lorca. Vida y Obra* (1955), *La prosa mágica de García Lorca* (1962), *Fantasía Boricua* (1956), *Panorama de la cultura puertorriqueña* (1958), *La Hora Colmada* (1969), *Las Voces de tu Voz* (1962), *La Cultura de Puerto Rico* (1970), *The Puerto Ricans' Spirit* (1971), *Jornadas Literarias* (1967), *Siluetas Literarias* (1967), and *Borinquen: An Anthology of Puerto Rican Literature* (co-editor, with Stan Steiner, 1974). She has taught at the University of Puerto Rico, Hunter College, New York University, and the City University of New York; she has lectured on Puerto Rican and Spanish authors in different educational and cultural institutions in the United States and Central America. Professor Babín is a Corresponding Member of The Hispanic Society of America and a member of the Commission on Minority Groups and the Study of Language and Literature of the Modern Language Association. Recently she was named to the Commission for Cultural Affairs of New York City by the Mayor of the City, and is a member of the Region 2 Archives Advisory Council. She has been awarded literary prizes for her books by the Institute of Literature of Puerto Rico (1955) and the Institute of Puerto Rico in the City of New York (1970).

Nona Balakian is Associate Editor of *The New York Times Book Review*. Her book reviews and essays have appeared in *The New York Times* since 1944, as well as in *Kenyon Review, The New Leader, Books Abroad* and other literary publications. She is the co-editor (with Charles Simmons) of *The Creative Present: Notes on Contemporary American Fiction* (1963) and author of a pamphlet, *The Armenian-American Writer* (1957). Miss Balakian is presently at work on a critical study of William Saroyan.

Alwyn Barr, Professor of History, served as Director of Ethnic Studies at Texas Tech University from 1971 to 1975. He teaches Black history and is the author of *Black Texans: A History of Negroes in Texas, 1528-1971* (1974), as well as other books and articles on United States history.

Peter Boerner is Professor of Comparative Literature, Germanic Languages, and West European Studies at Indiana University. Born in Estonia, he grew up in Germany and received the Ph.D. from the University of Frankfurt am Main. He has taught at Stanford University, the State University of New York in Buffalo, and the University of Wisconsin. He has been a fellow of the Collège d'Europe in Bruges and of the Guggenheim Foundation. While his earlier publications dealt mostly with the work of Goethe (*Goethes Tagebücher*, 1963; *Goethe*, 1964, Goethe, *Sämtliche Werke* in 45 volumes, 1961-1963), in recent years he has written on the diary as a literary genre (*Tagebuch*, 1969), and on international literary relations. At present he is doing research on national images in European and American literature.

Peter D. Bubresko, native of Yugoslavia, is Associate Professor of French at Texas Tech University. He earned the B.A. in 1933 and the M.A. in 1935 from the University of Belgrade. He also studied at the University of Grenoble (1933-1934). Recipient of a scholarship from the French Goverment (1936-1939), he studied at Sorbonne. Under the guidance of Paul Van Thiegem, he prepared in Paris a doctoral thesis on Yovan Dutchich, a study interrupted by the war. Professor Bubresko taught seven years at the Junior College level in Yugoslavia and West Germany, and later in America in St. Olaf College (1960-1963). He has done graduate work in the Contemporary French Novel at Laval University (1963-1964) on a grant of the American Lutheran Church of America. Currently, Professor Bubresko is preparing for publication his critical study on "Yovan Dutchich and his Literary Heritage," written in French, and is working on a book to be entitled "America Seen from France of Today." Editor of the weekly *Liberty* in Chicago, he has published articles and essays in American-Serbian dailies and reviews, and, in 1951 published (with Yovan Djonovich) three posthumous works of Yovan Dutchich, which appeared in Yugoslavia in 1969 in the collected works of Yovan Dutchich.

Armand B. Chartier is Assistant Professor of French at the University of Rhode Island (Kingston). He received the A.B. from Assumption College, the M.A. and Ph.D. in French from the University of Massachusetts at Amherst. He has also studied Russian at the Army Language School in Monterey, California. Active in many ethnic organizations, he is currently a member of the American and Canadian French Cultural Exchange Commission (State of Rhode Island); he is First Vice President of the Comité de Vie Franco Américaine and Vice President of the Council for the Development of French in New England. He has also been instrumental in obtaining grants in the areas of Canadian Studies and Ethnic Heritage Studies. He is a Special Assistant to Governor Philip W. Noel. Dr. Chartier is a regular contributor to the *MLA International Bibliography*, an Editor of *Modern Language Studies*, an editorial consultant for the *Louisiana Review* and has published in the field of Québécois literature. He is the author of a thematic bibliography of "Franco-Americana" and is at present completing a book on Barbey d'Aurevilly.

Aldo Finco is Professor of Italian at Texas Tech University. A native of Italy, Professor Finco received the B.A. from Boston University, and the M.A. and D.M.L. (Doctor of Modern Languages) from Middlebury College. He did work at the University of Florence both before and after he earned the doctorate. Professor Finco is the author of *L'arte di Antonio Fogazzaro* (1970), *Letture italiane per conversazione* (1971), *Appunti* (1972), and *Profili di Grammatica italiana* (1975). His articles concerning topics from Dante to contemporary literature have appeared in various national journals. He has presented scholarly papers at several language conventions throughout the United States and Italy. Professor Finco is the recipient of a grant from the National Endowment for the Humanities. He was also awarded a Faculty Research Grant from Texas Tech University to be spent in Florence, Italy.

Edmundo García-Girón is Professor of Romance Languages at Texas Tech University. He received the B.A., M.A. and Ph.D. from the University of California, Berkeley. In addition to his own publications (translations of novels and stories by Eduardo Barrios, Benito Lynch, essays by Benjamín Subercaseaux, articles on Latin American literature and Spanish Modernismo and Modernistas), Dr. García-Girón has been instrumental, as a sometime language editor for D. C. Heath and Prentice-Hall, in the publication of numerous grammars, readers, workbooks, records and tape programs for college-level courses in French, German, Russian and Spanish. During World War II he also organized and directed a translation unit and stenographic pool for the Office of the Coordinator of Inter-American Affairs in Washington. His current research is mainly on ethnic studies, and he is now preparing for publication a local Chicano bibliography. Dr. García-Girón has taught at the University of California (Berkeley), the University of Oregon, Marquette University, and Western Reserve University.

Everett A. Gillis is Professor of English at Texas Tech University. He earned B.A. and M.A. degrees from Texas Christian University and Ph.D. degree from The University of Texas. Professor Gillis was Chairman of the Department of English at Texas Tech University, 1964-1969. His teaching interests include American literature, modern poetry, and literary criticism. He is a member of numerous professional organizations, including Texas Institute of Letters, Texas Poetry Society, Modern Language Association. Professor Gillis is the author of *A College Forum, The Waste Land as Grail Romance, Oliver La Farge* and four volumes of verse: *Who Can Retreat?* , *Hello the House!* , *Sunrise in Texas* and *Angles of the Wind.*

Giles Edward Gobetz or, in Slovenian, Edi Gobec, a native of Slovenia and now a naturalized American citizen, has studied languages, philosophy, and sociology at Slovenian, German, Italian, and American schools and was awarded a Ph.D. in Sociology and Anthropology by Ohio State University in 1962. After teaching at Ohio State University and the University of Maryland, he is currently Professor of Sociology and Anthropology and Director of the Slovenian Studies Program at Kent State University and Executive Director of *Slovenski Ameriski Institut*—The Slovenian Research Center of America, Inc. He is past editor of *Naš Cilj, Akademik, Slovenski Visokošolski Zbornik*, and the Cleveland Society for the Blind Research Series, and current editor of Slovenian Research Center of America Slovenian Heritage Series, Newsletter, and Bulletin, associate editor of *The International Journal of Contemporary Sociology*, and secretary of Euram Books. An author of seven books, with three additional volumes currently in print, and of over 200 articles and book reviews, Gobetz was selected an Outstanding Educator of America in 1971, and he received an Achievement Award "for special contributions to the field of Science and Inventions" in 1974. He is a vice president of DTK, the International Social Science Honor Society.

Carl Hammer, Jr. (born 1910 in North Carolina) is Horn Professor of German and Chairman of the Department of Germanic and Slavic Languages at Texas Tech University. He earned the B.A. at Catawba College, the M.A. at Vanderbilt, and the Ph.D. at the University of Illinois. He also studied at the Universities of North Carolina,

Jena, and, as post-doctoral Ford Fellow (1953-54), at Columbia, Princeton and Tübingen. In 1964 he toured the Federal Republic as guest of the German government. Before joining the Texas Tech faculty in 1964, he taught at Vanderbilt and Louisiana State University. He has held summer appointments at Montana State and Southern Illinois University (in 1966, at the latter's NDEA Institute in Germany). Dr. Hammer was formerly associate editor (for German) of the *South Central Bulletin*, president of the Texas Chapter, American Association of Teachers of German, and a national counselor of Delta Phi Alpha. He has published nine books and monographs and thirty-five articles and essays. His book *Goethe and Rousseau* won the 1972 Kentucky Foreign Language Conference Award.

Lawson Fusao Inada is Associate Professor of English at Southern Oregon State College. He received the B.A. from Fresno State University and the M.F.A. from the University of Oregon. He has taught at the University of New Hampshire and Lewis and Clark College. A third-generation Japanese American from the multi-ethnic West Side of Fresno, California, he spent his early years in American Concentrations Camps in California, Arkansas and Colorado. He is the author of *Before The War: Poems As They Happened* (William Morrow and Company, 1971), the first poetry volume by an Asian American to be published by a major firm. He is an editor of *Aiiieeeee! : Asian American Writing* (Howard University Press, 1974; Doubleday paperback, 1975), and his poetry has been anthologized in a number of works, including *Speaking For Ourselves* (Scott, Foresman, 1975), *Modern Poetry of The American West* (Brigham Young University, 1975), and *The American Poetry Anthology* (Avon, forthcoming). In 1972, he was awarded a Writing Fellowship from the National Endowment for The Arts. He is a founder and Director of C.A.R.P. (Combined Asian American Resources Project), and has conducted multi-ethnic literature seminars for MLA, CCCC, and NCTE. Visual Communications of Los Angeles has produced a documentary film entitled: *I Told You So: Lawson Fusao Inada.*

John T. Krumpelmann is Emeritus Professor of German at Louisiana State University. A native of New Orleans, he received the B.A. and M.A. degrees at Tulane before going to Harvard, where he earned the A.M. and Ph.D. degrees in German. Directly after completing the Ph.D., he was a travelling-fellow of Harvard at the Universities of Munich and Berlin. Professor Krumpelmann has taught at Tulane, Harvard, Lehigh, the University of North Carolina, St. Stephen's College of Columbia University, Clark University, the University of Berlin (Summer, 1933), and the University of Frankfurt. He is author of *Southern Scholars in Goethe's Germany* and of many articles in scholarly journals. Included among his awards are a Fulbright Professorship (to lecture at the University of Frankfurt), the Officers' Cross of Order of Merit of the Federal Republic of Germany, and Honorary Membership of the International Mark Twain Society. He is a charter member and past president of SCMLA.

Walter Lagerwey, a native of Grand Rapids, is Professor of Germanic Languages at Calvin College, where he occupies the Queen Juliana Chair for the Language, Literature, and Culture of the Netherlands. He graduated from a Dutch secondary school in Utrecht and received the M.A. at Columbia University and the Ph.D. at Michigan University. He also studied at the Free Reformed University of Amsterdam. His publications include *Guide to Dutch Studies, Bibliography of Textual Materials for the Study of the Dutch Language, Literature, and Civilization* and *Speak Dutch.* He is the author of "The History of Calvinism in the Netherlands" in *The Rise and Devel-*

opment of Calvinism, a Concise History and of "Dutch Language and Culture in America" in *Neglected Language Conference Report.* He is a member of Maatschappij der Nederlandsche Letterkunde (Leiden) and of Bilderdijk Vereniging.

William J. Lynch is Professor of English at the Montgomery County Community College. From 1958 to 1973, he was Chairman of the English Department at that college. He earned the A.B. at the St. Joseph's College, the M.A. at Boston College, and the Ph.D. at the University of Pennsylvania. He has taught at St. Joseph's College and has served there as a Chairman of the English Department. He is a book reviewer for *America, Best Sellers* and the recipient of a sabbatical from Montgomery County Community College for research on a book dealing with the literature emerging from the struggle in Northern Ireland. In 1970 he delivered a paper concerning this literature at the American Association for Advancement of Science. Professor Lynch is a member of the Pennsylvania Council of Teachers of English and a member of Alpha Sigma Nu (Jesuit honor society).

Paul R. Magocsi is a specialist in East-Central European history and in the history of nationalism. He received the B.A. and M.A. from Rutgers University and the M.A. and Ph.D. in history from Princeton University. He also studied at Charles University in Prague and at Lajos Kossuth University in Debrecen, Hungary. In 1969-1970 he participated in the United States Department of State exchange as a visiting member of the Historical Institute of the Czechoslovak Academy of Sciences in Prague. Dr. Magocsi came to Harvard University in 1971 as a research associate in the Center for Middle Eastern Studies, then in 1973 was appointed to a three-year term in the Society of Fellows. He is also an associate of the Russian Research Center, the Ukrainian Research Institute, managing editor of the Harvard Series in Ukrainian Studies, and an editor of the Harvard Ethnic Encyclopedia. Dr. Magocsi is the author of numerous articles that have appeared in the *Slavic Review, East European Quarterly, East-Central Europe, Austrian History Yearbook, Queens Slavic Papers,* as well as in scholarly journals in Great Britain, Luxembourg, Austria, Czechoslovakia, and Yugoslavia. He completed two Rusyn-English phrase books and a 600-page study entitled "The Shaping of a National Identity: Developments in Subcarpathian Rus', 1848-1948," to be published by Harvard University Press.

Valters Nollendorfs, a native of Latvia, received the B.A. and M.A. from the University of Nebraska and the Ph.D. from the University of Michigan. He is Professor of German and Chairman of the Department of German at the University of Wisconsin-Madison. He has published a book and several articles on Goethe; he is editor of the German scholarly journal *Monatshefte* and coeditor of a forthcoming volume, *German Studies in America.* In 1975, he served as Chairman of MLA German 3 Group. He is also author of several articles dealing with Latvian literature and has been chosen President-Elect of the Association for the Advancement of Baltic Studies. He is intimately acquainted with current Latvian literature; he founded the literary-cultural magazine *Juanā Gaita* (The New Way) in 1955 and organized the Latvian Writers' Association in 1972, and has served as its president since that time.

Nikolai P. Poltoratzky is Professor of Slavic Languages and Literatures at the University of Pittsburgh. Born in Istanbul, he was brought up in Bulgaria where he graduated from a Russian high school (gymnasium) in Sofia. He received his university education in Bulgaria, Germany, and France, where he obtained the Ph.D. degree from the University of Paris (Sorbonne) in 1954. The following year he immigrated to the United States, where he was a research associate in a Soviet area project at Brooklyn College and taught, before moving to the University of Pittsburgh, at the Summer Institute of Soviet Studies at Middlebury College, Michigan State University, and, during a summer session, at the University of California at Berkeley. He is active also in academic administration; he has served as Assistant to the Director of the Institute of Soviet Studies at Middlebury College (1958-1965), Director of the Department of Foreign Languages' Russian Program at Michigan State University (1962-1964), and Chairman of the Department of Slavic Languages and Literatures at the University of Pittsburgh (1967-1974). Author of numerous articles and reviews on Russian literature, thought and civilization, in Russian and English, and of a book in Russian, *Berdiaev and Russia* (*N. A. Berdiaev's Philosophy of the History of Russia*, 1967), he has also edited three collections of essays by American, Canadian, and European scholars (in Russian).

Tomás Rivera is Professor of Spanish in the College of Humanities and Social Sciences and Associate Dean of the College of Multidisciplinary Studies at the University of Texas at San Antonio. Born in Crystal City, Texas, he spent the first twenty years of his life in the migrant labor stream that went throughout the Midwest. He earned the Associate in Arts degree and the M.Ed. degree at Southwest Texas Jr. College, the M.A. and Ph.D. degrees from the University of Oklahoma. His publications include *La ideología del hombre en la obra poética de León Felipe* (literary criticism), "*. . . y no se lo tragó la tierra*" "*. . . and the earth did not part*" (fiction), *Always and other poems* (poetry), and a number of articles, short stories, and poems. Among the awards that Professor Rivera has received are the Danforth Foundation Associateship for Husband and Wife (for service provided by husband and wife to students) and the *Premio Quinto Sol*, a national literary award for the best work by a Mexican American. The latter award was granted in 1971 for a novel-collection of short stories entitled "*. . . y no se lo tragó la tierra*" "*. . . and the earth did not part*." This work has been reviewed favorably in Europe, Latin America, Mexico, and the United States.

Francis M. Rogers, a student of the development of the Romance languages and of medieval and Renaissance literature, especially of Portugal, is Professor of Romance Languages and Literatures at Harvard University. He earned the A.B. degree at Cornell University, and A.M. degree in Romance Languages and Literatures and the Ph.D. degree in Comparative Philology (Linguistics) at Harvard University. Then he was appointed to a three-year term as a Junior Fellow in the Society of Fellows at Harvard. Professor Rogers has a number of honorary degrees from various American colleges and universities, and a doctorate (hon.) from the University of Bahia, Brazil. He is also an Honorary Professor of the National University of San Marcos, Peru. At Harvard he was Dean of the Graduate School of Arts and Sciences and twice Chairman of Harvard's Department of Romance Languages and Literatures. Professor Rogers is the author of numerous articles on Portuguese dialects, phonetics, maritime history, and the overseas expansion of Portugal, including the migration to the United States. His book *Higher Education in the United States: A Summary View* has appeared in many translations in European and Asiatic languages. The author of many books, he is best known for *The Travel of the Infante Dom Pedro of Portugal* and *The Quest for Eastern Christians: Travels and Rumor in the Age of Discovery*. These two books jointly received the Camões Prize for 1961-1962.

Dmytro Shtohryn is Professor of Library Administration and member of the Faculty Senate at the University of Illinois at Urbana-Champaign. A native of Ukraine, Professor Shtohryn received the M.A. in Slavic Studies, and the Ph.D. in Slavic Studies-Ukrainian Literature at the University of Ottawa. There he also earned the B.L.S. degree in Library Science. He has taught Ukrainian literature as Visiting Professor at Indiana University and at the University of Ottawa. Professor Shtohryn is the editor of *Catalog of Publications of Ukrainian Academy of Sciences, 1918-1930* and of *Ukrainians in North America: Biographical Directory of Noteworthy Men and Women of Ukrainian Origin in the United States and Canada.* He is the author of a book *Switla i tini ukrajins'kykh studij u Harvardi* and of numerous articles on Ukrainian literature and culture. Dr. Shrohryn is a recipient of The Glorier Society of Canada Award and of the Silver Medal of Guy Sylvestre, Librarian of the Parliiament of Canada.

Frank R. Šilbajoris, Professor of Slavic Languages and Literatures at Ohio State University, was born in Kretings, Lithuania. Exiled from home by the war, he attended the University of Mainz, Germany, later received the B.A. in English from Antioch College, and the M.A. and the Ph.D. in Russian from Columbia University. He has taught at Oberlin College and, since 1963, at Ohio State University. He has published *Russian Versification: the Theories of Trediakovskij, Lomonosov and Kantemir* (1968) and *Perfection of Exile: Fourteen Contemporary Lithuanian Writers* (1970). He has also published numerous articles on Russian and Lithuanian literatures. He was president of the Association for the Advancement of Baltic Studies (1973-1974), and he is a member of PEN International and of several professional organizations.

Lester A. Standiford is Assistant Professor of English and Director of the Creative Writing Program at The University of Texas at El Paso. Born in Ohio, he graduated from Muskingum College and received the M.A. and Ph.D. degrees from the University of Utah. He has taught at Utah and has served as Visiting Professor at Baylor University. His publications in minorities literature, film studies, and creative literature have appeared in such journals as *Southern Humanities Review, Beloit Poetry Journal, Kansas Quarterly*, and *Western Humanities Review.* His stories have appeared in a number of anthologies, including the recent *Bicentennial Collection of Texas Short Stories.* He has lectured and read before professional groups and campus audiences in Ohio, Utah, New Mexico and Texas. Presently he is preparing a fiction anthology for use in creative writing curricular and completing work on a collection of poems.

Rudolf Sturm is Professor of Italian and Slavic Literatures at Skidmore College. A native of Doubravice, Czechoslovakia, Professor Sturm received an *absolutorium* in law and political science at Charles University, Prague, and the Ph.D. degree in Slavic languages and literatures at Harvard University. He has taught at Boston College, Yale University, Hershey Jr. College and CCNY. He is the author of *Czechoslovakia, a Bibliographic Guide*, co-author of *Czechoslovakia, An Area Manual* (two volumes), and editor of *Egon Hostovský*, a Festschrift. Dr. Sturm has written numerous articles and studies for *Books Abroad, Encyclopaedia of Literature in the 20th Century, Harvard Slavic Studies, Italica, Modern Language Journal, Slavonic Encyclopaedia* and *World Book of Education.* He has lectured at major universities in the United States and abroad. Professor Sturm was Vice President of the Czechoslovak Society of Arts and Sciences in America (1968-1974).

Victor Terras, a native of Estonia, is Professor of Slavic Languages and Literatures and Chairman of Slavic Studies at Brown University. He earned the M.A. degree at the University of Tartu, Estonia, and the Ph.D. degree in Slavic Languages and Literatures at the University of Chicago. He has taught at the University of Tartu, University of Illinois, University of Wisconsin, and Ohio State University. His teaching fields include the Russian and Polish Languages, Russian and Comparative Literature, and Slavic Civilization. Professor Terras is the author of numerous articles on Russian, German, and Estonian literature, the Classics, Slavic linguistics, and East European history. He has published two college texts concerning Pushkin, several translations of Dostoevsky (into English), and two major monographs *The Young Dostoevsky* and *Belinskij and Russian Literary Criticism: The Heritage of Organic Aesthetics*. Professor Terras has edited the volume *American Contributions to the Seventh International Congress of Slavists* (Warsaw, August 1973).

Gerald Thorson, Professor of English at St. Olaf College, is currently Chairman of its Language and Literature Division. He has also served as Chairman of the Department of English at Augsburg College, has taught at Wagner College, and has been a Visiting Professor of American literature at the University of Iceland and Konstanz University in Germany. A graduate of Augsburg College (B.A.), he pursued further study at Minnesota (M.A.), Columbia (Ph.D.), Oslo, Wisconsin, and Grenoble. He has published articles on Norwegian-American literature, the contemporary American novel, and the preparation of teachers of English, poetry, and reviews; he is the editor of *Ole Rølvaag: Artist and Cultural Leader*. He was associate editor of *Response* (1969-1970), president of the Minnesota Council of Teachers of English (1960-1961), and Chairman of the Minnesota Association of Department of English Chairmen (1964-1970). His awards include a Torger Thompson Fellowship from Wisconsin and a Fulbright Fellowship to lecture in Iceland. In 1974 his alma mater, Augsburg College, presented him with a Distinguished Alumnus Citation.

Darwin T. Turner is Professor of English and Chairman of Afro-American Studies at The University of Iowa. He earned the B.A. and the M.A. at the University of Cincinnati, and the Ph.D. in English, and in English and American Dramatic Literature at the University of Chicago. His books include *Katharsis* (1964), *Nathaniel Hawthorne's "The Scarlet Letter"* (1967), and *In a Minor Chord: Three Afro-American Writers and Their Search for Identity* (1971). He is also co-author of *The Teaching of Literature by Afro-American Writers: Theory and Practice* (1972), editor, co-editor, and compiler of many other books. He has taught at the University of Michigan, A and T College and was a Visiting Professor at the University of Wisconsin, and the University of Hawaii. He was the recipient of Grant-in-Aid from American Council of Learned Societies (1965) and of Rockefeller Foundation's Research Grant (1971). Professor Turner holds the Creative Scholarship Award of the College Language Association and the Professional Achievement Award of the University of Chicago Alumni Association. He has been State Chairman for Iowa (1973-1975) and Director, Midwest Regional Board (1973, 1975), for the Second World Festival of Black and African Arts and Culture.

Daniel Walden, who has taught at Pennsylvania State University since 1966, previously taught at Michigan State University and Queens College. Professor Walden has the B.A. from CCNY, the M.A. from Columbia University and the Ph.D. from New York University. His books are *American Reform: The Ambiguous Legacy* (1967), *On Being Black* (with Charles Davis, 1970), *Reading in American Nationalism* (with

Hans Kohn, 1970), *W. E. B. DuBois: The Crisis Writings* (1972), *The Contemporary New Communities Movement in the U.S.* (with Gideon Golany, 1974), and *On Being Jewish: American Jewish Writers from Cahan to Bellow* (1974). Walden teaches a course on "Jewish Literature: The Yiddish Root and the American Stem" at Penn State, and is editor of the new journal *Studies in American Jewish Literature.*

David Hsin-Fu Wand teaches comparative literature at The University of Texas at Dallas. Born in China, he came to the United States when he was seventeen (in 1949) and was naturalized as a citizen in 1964. Dartmouth Class Poet in 1955, he received the M.A. in Creative Writing from San Francisco State College and the M.A. and Ph.D. in Comparative Literature from the University of Southern California. Editor of *Asian-American Heritage*, an anthology of American authors of Asian origin, he was recently appointed as a Commissioner on Minority Groups and the Study of Language and Literature by the Modern Language Association. He has contributed articles to such journals as *The Chinese World*, *Trace Literature East & West*, *Language & Style*, and *Paideuma*, and he is currently at work on a book about the relationship between poetry and the martial arts in the Sino-Japanese (samurai) tradition.

Brom Weber, Professor of English at the University of California, Davis, received the Ph.D. in American Studies at Minnesota. He has taught at the New School for Social Research, Purdue, DePauw, Washington, Colorado, Wyoming, and Minnesota; he has also taught as a Fulbright-Hays Professor in France and Korea. He has lectured in India, Turkey, Italy, England, Germany, and China. A co-founder of the Early American Literature Group of the Modern Language Association, he has contributed to and been an advisory editor of *Early American Literature.* He is currently preparing a collection of eighteenth-century American Loyalist writings for the Program for Loyalist Studies and Publications. He has written books on Sherwood Anderson and Hart Crane, edited the latter's poetry and letters, and also edited other books in American and twentieth-century literature. He has served on the editorial boards of various literary and scholarly magazines and contributed to such journals as *American Literature*, *Saturday Review*, *Modern Philology*, and *Sewanee Review.* He delivered a paper on "Our Multi-Ethnic Origins and American Literary Studies" at the first annual meeting (1974) of the Society for the Study of the Multi-Ethnic Literature of the United States and served as chairman of the society's program at the Modern Language Association's convention in 1975.

Paul Wrobel is an Anthropologist on the faculty of Detroit's Merrill-Palmer Institute. Before earning his doctoral degree at Catholic University, Washington, D.C., Dr. Wrobel spent five years on Peace Corps assignments in West Africa and the West Indies. He has published manuals on training Peace Corps volunteers and planning agricultural programs in Africa. But Dr. Wrobel's more recent work deals with Polish Americans in an urban setting. His publications include "Becoming A Polish American: A Personal Point of View" and "Notes On Organizing A Polish American Community." Dr. Wrobel is an associate of the National Center for Urban Ethnic Affairs (Washington, D.C.) and an advisor to WNET-TV (New York) on a series dealing with the lives of working-class Americans.